KILNS (in Geographical Order)

Type of Ceramics

P = Porcelain
R = Raku
St = Low- and high-fired stoneware (tôki, sekki)
SAK = One of the "Six Ancient Kilns"
ENG = One of the Enshû nana gama

1–66 Kilns des...
A–Y Kilns mentioned in glossary

M000265778

KILNS IN OKINAWA

1   Tsuboya 壷屋 (St)

KILNS IN KYÛSHÛ

2   Satsuma 薩摩 (St)
3   Ryûmonji 龍門司 (St)
4   Isshôchi 一勝地 (St)
5   Kôda 高田 (St)
6   Shôdai 小代 (St)
7   Unzen 雲仙 (St)
8   Arita 有田 (P)
9   Imari 伊万里 (Ôkawachi 大川内) (P)
10   Hasami 波佐見 (P)
11   Mikawachi 三川内 (P)
12   Utsutsugawa 現川 (St)
13   Karatsu 唐津 (St)
14   Takeo 威雄 (St, P)
15   Agano 上野 (St, ENG)
16   Takatori 高取 (St, ENG)
17   Koishiwara 小石原 (St)
18   Onta 小鹿田 (St)
A   Amakusa 天草 (P, St)
E   Hizen Yoshida 肥前吉田 (P)
R   Shiraishi 白石 (St)
V   Tanegashima 種子島 (St)

KILNS IN SHIKOKU

19   Tobe 砥部 (P)
20   Odo 尾戸 (St)
21   Ôtani 大谷 (St)
W   Uchiharano 内原野 (St)

KILNS IN HONSHÛ

22   Hagi 萩 (St)
23   Miyajima 宮島 (St)
24   Iwami 石見 (St)
25   Fujina 布志名 (St)
26   Sodeshi 袖師 (St)
27   Kazuwa 上神 (St)
28   Inkyûzan 因久山 (St)
29   Bizen 備前 (St, SAK)
30   Izushi 出石 (P)
31   Tanba 丹波 (St, SAK)
32   Akahada 赤膚 (St, ENG)
33   Asahi 朝日 (St, ENG)
34   Kyôto 京都 with Kiyomizu 清水 (St, P, R)
35   Zeze 膳所 (St, ENG)
36   Shigaraki 信楽 (St, SAK)
37   Iga 伊賀 (St)
38   Yokkaichi Banko 四日市万古 (St)
39   Tokoname 常滑 (St, SAK)
40   Inuyama 犬山 (St)
41   Seto 瀬戸 (P, St, SAK) with Akazu 赤津 (St)
42   Mino 美濃 (St, P)
43   Shitoro 志戸呂 (St, ENG)
44   Echizen 越前 (St, SAK)
45   Kutani 九谷 (P)
46   Ôhi 大樋 (R)
47   Shibukusa 渋草 (P, St)
48   Koito 小糸 (St)
49   Yamada 山田 (St)
50   Suzu 珠洲 (St)
51   Mumyôi 無名異 (St)
52   Kasama 笠間 (St)
53   Mashiko 益子 (St)
54   Aizu-Hongô 会津本郷 (St, P)
55   Nihonmatsu Banko 二本松万古 (St)
56   Sôma Koma 相馬駒 (St)
57   Ôbori Sôma 大堀相馬 (St)
58   Hirashimizu 平清水 (St)
59   Tsutsumi 堤 (St)
60   Kirigome 切込 (P, St)
61   Tsugaru 津軽 (St)
B   Banshôzan 万祥山 (St)
C   Dai 台 (P)
D   Etchû-Seto 越中瀬戸 (St)
F   Horikoshi 堀越 (St)
G   Kajichô 鍛冶丁 (St)
H   Kokuji 小久慈 (St)
I   Kosobe 古曾部 (St, ENG)
J   Mori 母里 (St)
K   Mumyôi 無名異 (Ôda, Shimane-ken) (St)
L   Mushiake 虫明 (St)
M   Naraoka 楢岡 (St)
N   Obayashi 尾林 (St)
O   Rakuzan 楽山 (St)
P   Sakazu 酒津 (St)
Q   Shinjô-Higashiyama 新庄東山 (St)
S   Shiraiwa 白岩 (St)
T   Shussai 出西 (St)
U   Tajima Banko 田島万古 (St)
X   Ujô 烏城 (St)
Y   Ushinoto 牛ノ戸 (St)

KILNS IN HOKKAIDÔ

62   Otaru 小樽 (St)
63   Tôraku 北楽 (St)
64   Watasuge 綿スゲ (St)
65   Taisetsu 大雪 / Asahikawa 旭川 (St)
66   Bihoro 美幌 (St)

KILNS (In Alphabetical Order)

Agano (15)

Aizu-Hongô (54)

Akahada (32)

Amakusa (A)

Arita (8)

Asahi (33)

Banshôzan (B)

Bihoro (66)

Bizen (29)

Dai (C)

Echizen (44)

Etchû-Seto (D)

Fujina (25)

Hagi (22)

Hasami (10)

Hirashimizu (58)

Hizen Yoshida (E)

Horikoshi (F)

Iga (37)

Imari (Ôkawachi) (9)

Inkyûzan (28)

Inuyama (40)

Isshôchi (4)

Iwami (24)

Izushi (30)

Kajichô (G)

Karatsu (13)

Kasama (52)

Kazuwa (27)

Kirigome (60)

Kôda (5)

Koishiwara (17)

Koito (48)

Kokuji (H)

Kosobe (I)

Kutani (45)

Kyôto with Kiyomizu (34)

Mashiko (53)

Mikawachi (11)

Mino (42)

Miyajima (23)

Mori (J)

Mumyôi (51)

Mumyôi (Ôda, Shimane-ken) (K)

Mushiake (L)

Naraoka (M)

Nihonmatsu Banko (55)

Obayashi (N)

Ôbori Sôma (57)

Odo (20)

Ôhi (46)

Onta (18)

Ôtani (21)

Otaru (62)

Rakuzan (O)

Ryûmonji (3)

Sakazu (P)

Satsuma (2)

Seto with Akazu (41)

Shibukusa (47)

Shigaraki (36)

Shinjô-Higashiyama (Q)

Shiraishi (R)

Shiraiwa (S)

Shitoro (43)

Shôdai (6)

Shussai (T)

Sodeshi (26)

Sôma Koma (56)

Suzu (50)

Taisetsu / Asahikawa (65)

Tajima Banko (U)

Takatori (16)

Takeo (14)

Tanba (31)

Tanegashima (V)

Tobe (19)

Tokoname (39)

Tôraku (63)

Tsuboya (1)

Tsugaru (61)

Tsutsumi (59)

Uchiharano (W)

Ujô (X)

Unzen (7)

Ushinoto (Y)

Utsutsugawa (12)

Watasuge (64)

Yamada (49)

Yokkaichi Banko (38)

Zeze (35)

Modern
Japanese
Ceramics

Photo 1. Wooden boxes (*kibako*) for storing ceramics

Modern
Japanese
Ceramics

PATHWAYS OF INNOVATION & TRADITION

Anneliese Crueger ◊ Wulf Crueger ◊ Saeko Itô
Photography by Thomas Naethe

LARK BOOKS
A Division of Sterling Publishing Co., Inc.
New York

Editors: Kimberly J. Nagorski; Museum for East Asian Art, Berlin National Museum
Senior Editor: Suzanne J.E. Tourtillott
Art Director: Thom Gaines
Cover Designer: Cindy LaBreacht
Assistant Editor: Shannon P. Quinn-Tucker
Associate Art Director: Shannon Yokeley
Art Production Assistant: Jeff Hamilton
Editorial Assistance: Delores Gosnell
Photographer: Thomas Naethe
Translated from German by: David Erban

Library of Congress Cataloging-in-Publication Data
Crueger, Anneliese.
  [Wege zur japanischen Keramik. English]
  Modern Japanese ceramics : pathways of innovation & tradition / Anneliese
Crueger, Wulf Crueger, Saeko Ito ; photography by Thomas Naethe ; translated
by David Erban.
     p. cm.
  Includes bibliographical references and index.
  ISBN-13: 978-1-60059-119-8 (hc-plc with jacket : alk. paper)
  ISBN-10: 1-60059-119-1 (hc-plc with jacket : alk. paper)
  1. Pottery, Japanese. 2. Pottery--Technique. 3. Kilns--Japan. I.
Crueger, Wulf. II. Ito, Saeko, 1924- III. Naethe, Thomas, 1954- IV. Title.
  NK4167.C7813 2007
  738.0952--dc22

                              2006101871

10 9 8 7 6 5 4 3 2 1

First printing: 2004

English translation © Lark Books, 2006

Published by Lark Books, A Division of
Sterling Publishing Co., Inc.
387 Park Avenue South, New York, N.Y. 10016

Text © 2004, 2007, Anneliese Crueger, Wulf Crueger, Saeko Itô
Photography © 2004, Anneliese Crueger, Wulf Crueger
Photography © 2007, Thomas Naethe
Cover photo: Kobashikawa Kiyomasa, Hip Flask, 2002
Photo 27, page 32, Miyazaki-mura Industry and Tourism Section, 916-0254 Fukui-ken, Niu-gun, Miyazaki-mura, Ozowara 7-8
Map of Japan, inside front cover, with the kind permission of the Japanese Consulate General in Düsseldorf, Germany

Distributed in Canada by Sterling Publishing, c/o Canadian Manda Group,
165 Dufferin Street, Toronto, Ontario, Canada M6K 3H6

Distributed in the United Kingdom by GMC Distribution Services,
Castle Place, 166 High Street, Lewes, East Sussex, England BN7 1XU

Distributed in Australia by Capricorn Link (Australia) Pty Ltd., P.O. Box 704, Windsor, NSW 2756 Australia

If you have questions or comments about this book, please contact:
Lark Books, 67 Broadway, Asheville, NC 28801, (828) 253-0467

Manufactured in China

ISBN 13: 978-1-60059-119-8
ISBN 10: 1-60059-119-1

For information about custom editions, special sales, premium and corporate purchases, please
contact Sterling Special Sales Department at 800-805-5489 or specialsales@sterlingpub.com.

FOREWORD

Today, very few of us have the good fortune, while pursuing a full-time profession, to build up a successful collection that represents the entire spectrum of an artistic genre from one period. Many desire to become involved with art and the purchase of art, but very few dare to put this desire into practice. Is this perhaps because we do not even begin to think about it seriously? Collecting means contemplation and study; it takes time and requires stamina, and above all, a love of the objects involved—not really the conditions for achieving success overnight.

But those who are not afraid of taking these "pains" will be richly rewarded. What joy it is to connect with the creator of an artwork through the work itself—the joy of handling an object from antiquity and being "in touch" with the past, or, as with the work of a contemporary artist, the joy of feeling it, living with it, and thus experiencing beauty. Financial reasons often hinder someone's desire to collect, or serve as a pretext for not beginning. Collection always means renunciation, too; having the willpower to renounce other things and to restrict oneself is difficult. But for those who have chosen this path, a different world opens up.

The authors of this book, Dr. Anneliese and Dr. Wulf Crueger, together with Saeko Itô, lead the readers into such a world by allowing them to share in the joys of collecting and the rich fruits of their knowledge. For more than 30 years, collecting and studying contemporary Japanese ceramics has been the Cruegers' interest. With the publication of this book, they continue a fruitful tradition of sharing insights into the arts. Generously, they pass on their knowledge and allow others to share in it.

In the West, interest in Japanese art was awakened in particular by private collectors, who aroused the enthusiasm of artists and art historians alike. Few areas of non-European culture have influenced the development of modern art and fine craft as lastingly as Japanese eighteenth- and nineteenth-century graphic art and Japanese ceramics since the 1920s. The *mingei* movement, founded by Yanagi Sôetsu (1889–1961) and intimately linked with the names of Hamada Shôji (1894–1978), Kawai Kanjirô (1890–1966), and Bernard Leach (1887–1979), preserves a tradition that was threatening to disappear with the opening of Japan to the West and the related industrialization. Besides the tea ceremony, it has been the culinary heritage of Japan in particular that has had the largest share in the survival and further development of a flourishing ceramics culture, which is probably unique in the world.

With this book, and on the basis of their own comprehensive collection, the Cruegers make it easy for admirers of contemporary Japanese ceramics to approach this important and lively field of Japanese art—to discover its roots and to experience its incomparable variety. In addition, with the aid of the section titled Information on Individual Kilns and Travel Notes, readers can discover in Japan itself this exciting and interesting field, and meet the potters in person. Just as visitors to Japan find their way from museum to museum with the assistance of *Roberts' Guide to Japanese Museums*, admirers of ceramics will find their way from kiln to kiln with the aid of the "Crueger."

Japanese art is safely stored in carefully inscribed boxes and containers, and as a rule is thus not easily accessible. Ceramics enthusiasts will be particularly grateful that with this publication, the Crueger Collection has been thrown open for all to enjoy. This book will also serve as a guide to the many sales and exhibitions that are planned throughout Japan.

July 2004

Willibald Veit
Museum of East Asian Art, Berlin

CONTENTS

INTRODUCTION

As scientists, we had our first contact with Japan—at that time the mecca for biotechnology—in the 1970s. We were already collectors of European ceramics, and we were immediately fascinated by the huge diversity of Japanese stoneware and porcelain. There are very few cultures in which tradition and modernity exist side by side as they do in present-day Japan. In the more than 100 pottery centers still in existence, one style is never wholly given up when something new has been created.

We became increasingly interested in the development of Japanese pottery kilns through the centuries. (In Japanese usage, the term "kiln" can refer to a single workshop or to hundreds of workshops or manufactories in one region.) During our annual journeys to the kilns (from Okinawa in the south to Hokkaidô in the north), to museums and exhibitions in the big cities, and to the ceramics centers with their large kilns, we became acquainted with the characteristics and origins of the local ceramics. Purchasing typical items over the past 30 years, we built up a ceramics collection from the major kilns. An introduction and an orientation was provided for us by the book *Earth 'n' Fire* by Amaury Saint-Gilles (regrettably out of print for many years now), in which the author gives an overview of the Japanese kilns.

A deeper understanding and study of the material in greater depth (with historical data often unclear) were only possible because of the happy circumstance that our teacher of Japanese and personal friend, Saeko Itô, had also been studying literature on Japanese ceramics for years. We should note that the historical dates quoted in this book, as well as details on ceramists and ceramics techniques, are based on Campbell et al. (1993) and Yabe et al. (2002). Names follow the Japanese convention, with the family name being quoted first, followed by the given name.

With the high value placed on asymmetry and the modest use of space, the Japanese aesthetic contradicts Western artistic ideals in many respects. In ceramics, traces of the production process, including conscious distortion as a sign of skillfully achieved naturalness, are preferred to a symmetry that is held to be static. The ideal of "emptiness" adopted from Zen Buddhism is seen in the manner in which glaze and decoration are applied. The clay and the firing process are decisive in the making process, in which the potter functions only as a kind of "midwife" for the object being created. This ideal corresponds to Japanese aesthetics and the way in which potters see themselves.

The distribution channels for ceramics are evidence of their significance in the lives of even the modern Japanese. As well as the exhibition spaces in the pottery centers, there are specialty shops and galleries in every town; the major department stores display reasonably priced, attractive, mass-produced wares, functional domestic wares for refined tastes, the products of young artists, and even high-priced items in separate art exhibitions.

During the pottery markets at the ceramics centers, the masses of visitors are quite incredible; for example, the Arita spring market attracts about 700,000 visitors. Generally, higher quality ceramics are sold in a special wooden box (*kibako*, see photo 1), and the potter's inscription is a certificate of authenticity.

Almost all ceramic objects, even the most valuable, are intended for use. Especially smaller forms are offered for sale and collected. There are major collections consisting only of tea or sake cups, which is explained in part by the cramped dimensions of Japanese living accommodations. Only in recent years have increasing numbers of larger-scale items been made, especially for exhibitions in museums, usually with international participation.

During exhibitions of our collection and at lectures in recent years, we have repeatedly been asked about easily accessible literature and, in spite of language difficulties, about travel to the kilns, some of which are situated in remote rural areas. For this reason, then, after giving an introduction on the historical evolution of Japanese ceramics, this book traces the historical development of the 66 most important traditional pottery centers, from their origins to present-day tendencies. Traditional forms and glazes are documented using photographs of pieces from our own collection. Additionally, there are examples of the avant-garde in its position between a return to early Japanese ceramics on the one hand and the influence of Western art on the other.

This book also provides ceramics enthusiasts with assistance by means of an extensive glossary, and information on travel, exhibitions and sales, literature, pottery associations, and museums. To facilitate communication, Japanese characters are also included. In the travel information section, times may be subject to change, but they provide basic guidance in journey planning.

No addresses of individual potters at the pottery centers are given—only those of pottery associations, tourist information centers, and museums, where maps and plans illustrating the main workshops are available. Before traveling to visit individual potters, it is essential to call ahead to inquire whether a visit is possible. Do not forget that visits cut into the production potter's working hours.

This book project would not have been possible without help. We received financial assistance from the Japanese-German cultural society (Förderverein japanisch-deutscher Kulturbeziehungen e.V.) in Cologne and the Lotte Reimers Foundation in Deidesheim. Comprehensive, informative literature was provided by pottery associations and tourist offices in all Japanese prefectures. We wish to express our heartfelt thanks to everyone involved. We owe special thanks to the Japan Foundation in Cologne; Mrs. Angela Ziegenbein and the foundation's former director, Mr. Masaru Sakato; as well as the staff at the Office for Information and Culture at the Japanese Consulate General in Düsseldorf—in particular, Carrie Kraemer.

We owe the fact that the beauty of Japanese ceramics has been made accessible to the Western eye to Mr. Thomas Naethe. A ceramist himself, he has captured the essential character of the individual objects with extraordinary sensitivity in his photographs. It was due to his first-class cooperation that this book was possible at all. We wish to express our profound gratitude to him.

DEVELOPMENT OF JAPANESE CERAMICS

>> Ceramics from the Jômon to the Heian Periods

Early Ceramics: Jômon and Yayoi Earthenware

In Japan's hunter-gatherer culture of about 12,000 years ago, sedimentary clays began to be used to produce low-fired earthenware, which may be considered the earliest examples of pottery in human history. The Jômon period received its name from the cord-marked Jômon earthenware (jômon-doki), in which impressions of cords were used to create a distinctive decoration and which was found all over Japan, from the Kuril Archipelago in the north to present-day Okinawa. Jômon pottery was brown-yellow to reddish in color, and later brown-black; it was built of coils or rings and was pit fired in a partially reduced atmosphere of 1112°F–1472°F (600°C–800°C). Six phases of development, as well as more than 70 regional styles, have been distinguished by archaeologists.

In the Incipient or Proto-Jômon period (from ca. 10,000 B.C.), food was stored and prepared in pots that at first were undecorated. Later, simple linear patterns and the imprints of carved wooden tools were added. In the Initial Jômon period (from ca. 7500 B.C.), crude cord markings appeared for the first time, parallel to the first anthropomorphic representations, which indicate use for religious purposes. Impressions of seashells, incised patterns, and applied clay decoration were added in the Early Jômon period (from ca. 5000 B.C.). The Middle Jômon period (from ca. 3500 B.C.) is considered the zenith of the Jômon culture, with its cord markings and lavishly applied and incised decoration on figurines and vessels. These sometimes featured sculpted substructures that were twisted and knotted clay strands. In the Late Jômon period

(from ca. 2500 B.C. or 2000 B.C.), these forms of decoration were discontinued in favor of incised lines framing areas of cord markings. At the end of the period, reduction firing took over, so that brown-black bodies became dominant. In both figurines and vessels of the Latest or Final Jômon period (1000 B.C.–300 B.C.), considerable regional differences developed.

In the following Yayoi period (ca. 300 B.C.–A.D. 300), immigrants from continental Asia introduced cultivation of rice in the paddy fields of northern Kyûshû, where it spread to northeastern Honshû. The inhabitants had now settled down, mainly on river estuaries, where they found a fine, plastic clay. The ceramics of that time, Yayoi earthenware (yayoi-doki), received its name from the location of the first findings excavated in the Yayoi district of Tôkyô. The smooth, thin-walled yayoi-doki with its reddish body was sparsely decorated and showed a distinct formal resemblance to bronze pots from the mainland. The new style spread throughout Japan, supplanting Jômon ceramics in western Japan, whereas in eastern Japan a mixture of both styles evolved, which was correspondingly varied in appearance. The unglazed Yayoi ware, like Jômon ceramics, was coil built, but it was finished on a crude potter's wheel.

Earthenware in the Kofun Period: Hajiki and Haniwa

Haji earthenware (hajiki) from the succeeding Kofun period (ca. A.D. 300–A.D. 710) is a direct descendant of Yayoi ceramics. It is an unglazed, reddish, coil-built earthenware without surface decoration, produced from the fourth century on for domestic and ritual purposes. Production ceased in the tenth century with the increasing importance of glazed wares. Little is known of the kilns, but it is assumed that specialist workshops were in operation, where, besides the mass production of Haji ware, *haniwa* (clay rings) were also made. These *haniwa* were unglazed earthenware cylinders, approximately 3¼ feet (1 m) in height and 15¾–19¾ inches (40 cm–50 cm) in diameter. Later, they became hollow figures reaching nearly 5 feet (1.5 m) in height and represented humans or animals, houses, and household objects. *Haniwa* cylinders and figures were erected on the huge burial mounds (*kofun*) of the Japanese ruling class.

First High-Fired Stoneware: Sueki

In the Kofun period (ca. A.D. 300–A.D. 710), Japan was united as one state for the first time, from Kyûshû to the Kantô plain, with Yamato (now Nara Prefecture) in the center. The court in Yamato conducted regular exchanges with continental Asia, leading to the introduction of the Chinese system of writing in the fifth century and of Buddhism in the sixth century. In the mid-seventh century, under Emperor Tenji (A.D. 626–A.D. 672), a central administrative system on the Chinese model was introduced.

In the field of ceramics, production methods for high-fired stoneware imported by Korean immigrants spread from the Ôsaka region to the whole of Japan. These Sue ceramics (*sueki*) were a gray, unglazed stoneware (*sekki*), reduction fired in a single-chamber, climbing Korean kiln (*anagama*) to about 2192°F (1200°C). They strongly resembled Korean ceramics from the Silla period. Pots were first built up from coils, then beat into shape with wooden paddles. In time, the increasingly complex forms of pots—initially created exclusively for ritual purposes—made the use of the wheel essential. As a product for the ruling class, Sue stoneware was superseded in the early seventh century by *sansai* (three-color) ware imported from China, but Sue ware continued to be produced in large areas of Japan for domestic purposes until the twelfth century, and in some kilns even as late as the sixteenth century.

First Glazed Ceramics: Shiki (Nara and Sanage Ware)

Whereas Sue ceramics only revealed randomly produced natural-ash glazes, in the Nara and Heian periods (A.D. 710–A.D. 794 and A.D. 794–A.D. 1185, respectively), the first genuinely glazed wares in Japanese ceramics history originated through the introduction of Chinese glaze technology.

Nara ware, which was made in the Nara region, first appeared with colored lead glazes on low-fired stoneware as three-colored ware (*sansai-tôki* or *Nara-sansai*) in green, white, and yellow-brown; as two-colored ware (*nisai-tôki*) in green and white; and as green-glazed ware (*ryoku-yû tôki*). From the ninth century until the disappearance of Nara ware in the twelfth century, only green-glazed ceramics replicating Chinese celadons were produced, initially for ritual purposes, but later as domestic ware.

In the late eighth century, *sueki* kilns at the western foot of the Sanage mountains (near present-day Nagoya) began reproducing the highly prized Chinese celadons by using a gray-green, wood-ash feldspar glaze on a white or gray body. The high-fired stoneware from these Sanage kilns, with its incised floral designs in the style of Chinese Song ceramics, was the most important ceramic product of the Heian period. Sanage kilns covered almost all of the needs of the upper class for wares such as jugs, storage jars, tableware, and writing utensils, and the ensuing mass production led to a decline in quality.

>> Medieval Ceramics

Two developments were characteristic of the Middle Ages (twelfth through sixteenth centuries) in Japan: the move from glazed to unglazed stoneware in the twelfth century and the emergence of tea ware in the fourteenth century. Both events had a decisive influence on the appearance of present-day ceramics.

Six Ancient Kilns

At the end of the twelfth century, the power that had previously been formally invested in the emperor was handed over to the Kamakura shogunate. The Kamakura period (1185–1333) was a phase of cultural decline during which the aesthetically refined courtly aristocracy of the Heian period lost its influence on styles. In ceramics, the demand for Nara and Sanage ware consequently fell away, too. At the same time, improved agricultural technology, with two harvests a year, led to an increased demand for storage vessels. Large unglazed jars (*tsubo* and *kame*) were particularly suitable. To satisfy this demand, most kilns changed what they produced, and many new kilns were constructed by the fourteenth century. Storage jars were made, as were mortars and the popular *yamachawan*—simple eating bowls in unglazed stoneware. On the other hand, some Sanage kilns founded a new center for the production of glazed wares after the discovery of white, kaolin-rich clay deposits in Seto.

For the best-known ceramics centers— Tokoname, Bizen, Echizen, Tanba, Shigaraki, and Seto—the expression "Six Ancient Kilns" (*roku koyô*) was coined around 1950. (The term "kiln" in Japanese usage may refer to the individual kiln itself or to centers with hundreds of kilns.) The outstanding characteristic of these Six Ancient Kilns is their continuity right up to the present day. More than 70 such medieval centers are now known. The archeologist Narasaki Shôichi classifies the most important centers according to their development as follows:

Seto (41) and Mino (42) evolved from the Sanage kilns, and with the continued production of glazed stoneware, they followed the tradition of Nara and Sanage ware. Up to the mid-fifteenth century, Seto was considered the center for glazed wares with yellow-green ash glazes, amber *ame-yû* glazes, and iron-brown *tenmoku* glazes. As a consequence of civil wars from 1467 to 1568 (*sengoku-jidai* or "Century of the Warring States," beginning with the Ônin Civil War from 1467 to 1477), production moved to Mino in the mid-fifteenth century, where new vessel forms and glazes were developed.

Tokoname (39), Atsumi, and other centers converted their production of Sanage ware to unglazed storage vessels. The firing process was optimized by building the *anagama* kilns on inclines that were 20 to 30 percent steeper and by adding a column between the fire box and the firing chamber to split the flame. These technical improvements, which took place between the late tenth and the twelfth centuries, made temperatures over 2372°F (1300°C) possible.

Echizen (44), a Sue kiln, adopted the Tokoname technology.

Bizen (29), Tanba (31), Shigaraki (36), and Iga (37), originally Sue kilns, converted from reduction to oxidation in the improved *anagama*.

Suzu (50), a Sue kiln, continued to produce gray-black, reduction-fired ware.

The unglazed ware is stoneware with a natural-ash glaze (*yakishime*). During the firing, the wood ash on the pots melts at above 2264°F (1240°C) and forms a natural glaze. At above 2372°F (1300°C) in reduction, the glaze vitrifies (*bîdoro*). The appearance of the ware from the various kilns depends on the quality of the clay and the firing technique. So-called *mitsu no keshiki* ("three landscapes") are especially highly valued. These are *hi-iro*, the "fire color" of the clay in various shades of red to red-brown; *koge*, the scorch marks; and finally *bîdoro*, vitrified glass in green to blue-green.

Tea Ceramics: Early and Classic Periods

As in other cultures, the development of ceramics in Japan would have proceeded along the lines of storage vessels and simple domestic wares if the emergence of the tea ceremony in the fourteenth century had not led to tea ceramics. The term tea ceremony (*chanoyu*) refers to the preparation and drinking of powdered green tea (*matcha*) with guests. *Chanoyu* was originally based on fundamental aesthetic and spiritual principals of Zen Buddhism and is also termed "The Way of Tea" (*chadô* or *sadô*).

Green tea has been known in Japan since the eighth century. In 1191, the monk Eisai (1141–1215) brought the ritual of drinking *matcha*, in which powdered green tea is whisked with hot water, back to Japan from China. For more than 100 years, drinking tea in Buddhist monasteries had been practiced to aid the Zen monks in their concentration during meditation and prayer.

From the mid-fourteenth century, tea was also being drunk socially outside monasteries. The Muromachi period (1333–1568) was characterized by wars and domestic instability, ruled by the Ashikaga shogunate (1338–1573) of the Ashikaga family. The Ashikaga shogunate, which had assumed power after the Kamakura shogunate had been driven out, demonstrated its aristocratic status by sponsoring the arts. The seat of the shogunate had been moved to the Muromachi district of the imperial city Kyôto. Under the protection of the Ashikaga family, Zen Buddhism spread: the Zen-inspired arts such as garden architecture, the tea ceremony, and *ikebana* (flower arrangement), spread to society from the monasteries. A new elite of the courtly and warrior aristocracy formed, demonstrating wealth and power in sumptuous tea gatherings, where large numbers assembled in luxurious rooms, using precious Chinese tea utensils in lacquer, porcelain, or celadon. Tea masters were responsible for purchasing these Chinese items (*karamono*) and for organizing the tea "parties." Members of the lower warrior classes, who could not afford the expensive *karamono* articles, had access to Seto ware, which was very much in demand, with its ash glazes that resembled celadons.

The loss of central power by the Ashikaga shogunate to the ambitious local feudal rulers (*daimyo*) after the Ônin Civil War (1467–1477) and the "Century of the Warring States" (*sengoku-jidai*) led to the merchant classes achieving increased social importance; many of them were devotees of the tea ceremony or served their feudal lords as tea masters. Under the influence of Zen Buddhism, the tea masters changed the tea ceremony to one with a simple and restrained aesthetic. Among the most influential in this respect were Murata Shukô (1423–1502), Takeno Jôô (1502–1555), and

his pupil Sen no Rikyû (1522–1591). The tea room was reduced in size; utensils and decoration were restricted to the bare necessities.

Sen no Rikyû added the concept of *sabi* (the appreciation of used, worn, and even visibly repaired objects) to this *wabi* aesthetic. In developing a specific aesthetic for tea utensils, there was a shift in values away from the perfect Chinese ceramics toward unglazed, irregular pots with evidence of the making process. The *wabi-sabi* aesthetic was most perfectly embodied in Ido tea bowls—the simple, rough rice bowls of Korean peasants. Parallel to this, the tea masters discovered the unglazed wares from the Six Ancient Kilns, and from Iga, where initially smaller storage vessels as *objets trouvés* became tea storage jars (*chatsubo*) or jars for fresh water (*mizusashi*). Under instruction from the tea masters, potters soon began to produce unglazed pottery solely for the tea ceremony.

It was Sen no Rikyû, a wealthy merchant, who had the greatest influence on the development of the tea ceremony. He had served the great warlords Oda Nabunaga (1534–1582) and Toyotomi Hideyoshi (1537–1598) as a tea master. He summarized the essence of *chadô* in the four concepts, "harmony, respect, purity, and tranquility," and established firm rules for the setting and procedure of the tea ceremony, which even today are the basis of the great tea schools: Ura Senke, Omote Senke, and Mushanokôji Senke.

A number of innovations in ceramics were initiated as a result of the tea ceremony. In Kyôto, the first raku tea bowls were made on instruction from Sen no Rikyû around 1579. The first independently developed Japanese glazes, including *kiseto* (yellow Seto) from the fifteenth century, and in the sixteenth century, *setoguro* (black Seto) and white *shino* glaze with its variations in color, were produced in Mino, where many potters from the neighboring Seto had taken refuge during the Ônin Civil War. The development of the tea ceremony led to the development of new types of vessels, such as tea bowls, freshwater jars, tea caddies, *ikebana* vessels, as well as a great number of pieces for the *kaiseki* meal during the tea ceremony. With the spread of the *ôgama*—large *anagama* kilns—to the Seto and

Mino areas in the early sixteenth century, these innovations were accessible to broad sections of the population.

>> Ceramics of the Edo Period

During the Azuchi-Momoyama period (1568–1600), the political unification of Japan was overseen by Oda Nobunaga (1534–1582) and completed by Toyotomi Hideyoshi (1537–1598). Hideyoshi, who served the emperor as Lord Chancellor without ever being appointed a *shô-gun*, was a devotee and patron of the tea cere-mony. His two unsuccessful campaigns to invade Korea in 1592 and 1597—the so-called ceram-ics campaigns—were of great significance to the development of Japanese ceramics in the Edo period (1600–1868). During the retreat, hun-dreds of Korean potters were brought to Japan, mainly as prisoners of war. Their settlement in the domains of the feudal lords of Kyûshû and in Hagi in western Honshû meant that new tech-nologies had arrived in Japan, including the kick wheel, new glazing and decorative tech-niques, and the multichamber climbing kiln (*noborigama*), which increased the possibility of reproducible firings through its improved flame path. It soon spread throughout Japan.

After Hideyoshi's death, his follower Tokugawa Ieyasu (1543–1616) fought his way to power after the military victory of Sekigahara in 1600 and was appointed a *shôgun* by the emperor in 1603. Ieyasu chose Edo, a small provincial town in the east of Japan, as the seat of the Tokugawa shogunate, which remained in power until 1867. Within a few years, Edo had blossomed to become the splendid capital of the *bafuku*. Reforms in the administrative system and the economy that accompanied the introduction of the Bakuhan political system led to great social, economic, and cultural change.

With the introduction of the closed-door policy (*sakoku*, or National Seclusion) in 1639, whereby the Tokugawa shogunate wanted to put an end to Western expansionism and to increasing Christianization, no foreigner was allowed to set foot on Japanese soil. Trade with the Dutch and the Chinese was done exclusively from the small, artificial island of Dejima, off the coast of Nagasaki. The next 200 years of Japanese history were a period of inner and outer peace. The Edo period as a transition from the Middle Ages to the early modern era was a cultural high point, which was not dominated by the courtly aristocracy and the warrior class but rather by the urban population of the great cities: Edo (now Tôkyô), Naniwa (now Ôsaka), and Kyôto. Although they were of the lowest rank in the Confucian social order, behind warriors, peasants, and tradespeople, wealthy merchants had become the trendsetters.

Tea Ceramics: Late Period

As it had been in the sixteenth century, the devel-opment of numerous local pottery styles was fur-thered by the political system. Many of the local rulers appointed by the shogunate were devo-tees of the tea ceremony. The appreciation of *chadô* meant that local kilns were set up and sponsored by the *daimyô* as feudal kilns (*hanyô* or *goyôgama*). The best pieces of these special ceramics from the provinces, known as *kuniyaki*, were presented to the shogunate and the impe-rial family for official functions, while the remain-der was usually sold for considerable gains. The *han* administration thus furthered the develop-ment of individual local styles and endeavored to ensure that production methods were kept secret.

The tea masters of the early Edo period were more heavily involved in the design of new tea utensils. Potters, who had now made the transition from anonymous craftspeople to renowned art-ists, cooperated. The two tea masters, Furuta Oribe (1544–1615) and Kobori Enshû (1579–1647), are par-ticularly noteworthy in this context. With the so-called Oribe-*yaki*, Oribe created a completely new style of ceramics. On the unusually formed vessels, there are asymmetrical decorative surfaces con-sisting of green copper glazes and areas with iron oxide underglaze brushwork (see Mino, 42). Enshû gave his support to seven kilns in particular (the *Enshû nana gama*): Agano (15), Akahada (32), Asahi (33), Kosobe, Shitoro (43), Takatori (16), and Zeze (35), which he declared particularly suitable for the production of the elegant tea ceramics he preferred.

At the same time, the tea masters ensured the preservation and further refinement of traditional styles, such as unglazed stoneware from Bizen and Tokoname; stoneware with natural-ash glazes, from Shigaraki and Iga; raku ware or stoneware with classic Mino glazes (*shino, kiseto*, and *setoguro*); and the *oribe* style. New centers for tea ceramics also appeared, such as Karatsu and Hagi, which were strongly influenced by the Korean potters from the Hideyoshi campaigns. In the view of devotees of *chadô* at that time, raku ware (Kyôto, 34; Ôhi, 46) was most highly appreciated, followed by ceramics from Hagi (22) and Karatsu (13). This viewpoint—*ichiraku nihagi sangaratsu*—is still held today.

By the mid-sixteenth century, tea was often brewed, using unfermented green tea leaves (*sencha*). The various methods of preparing the different teas led to the development of specific types of ceramics in porcelain and stoneware, which were adopted in the product ranges of many kilns and enjoyed a lively demand, especially in the nineteenth century. Banko ware, in particular, is well known in this context (Yokkaichi Banko-*yaki*, 38; Nihonmatsu Banko-*yaki*, 55).

Porcelain and Decorated Stoneware

In the early seventeenth century—probably 1605–1610—Korean potters succeeded in firing the first soft-paste porcelain after the discovery of suitable raw materials in Arita (8) on Kyûshû. Within just 30 years, the production of blue-and-white porcelain (i.e., with cobalt blue underglaze brushwork, *sometsuke*) was flourishing. Between 1643 and 1647, Sakaida Kakiemon I developed the technique of polychrome overglaze enamel for porcelain. The technique originated in China. Soon, porcelain with polychrome painting was appearing in various styles, such as *ko*-Imari porcelain, with its sumptuous brocade style. Porcelain from Arita and the surrounding Hizen region, initially blue-and-white ware and later Kakiemon and *ko*-Imari ware, was exported to the rest of Japan via the port of Imari.

After the collapse of China's porcelain industry resulting from civil war, porcelain was exported from 1650 on by the Dutch East India Company (VOC) to Southeast Asia and Europe. In the second half of the seventeenth century, porcelain manufacturing had reached a high point in the Hizen region with Arita (8), Mikawachi (11), and Hasami (10). It is generally agreed that the best Japanese porcelain was produced in the utmost secrecy in Ôkawachi (9), in the official kiln (*hanyô*) of the Nabeshima clan. It was not commercially traded, however. Besides this, there was also Kutani porcelain (45), which on the evidence of excavations, is assumed not to have been produced in Ishikawa Prefecture during the first phase of production, but in Arita.

In accordance with the changing wishes of the aristocracy to have an elaborately equipped tea ceremony, as well as the requirements of the urban elites for high-quality domestic wares, an innovation followed in Kyôto in the mid-seventeenth century in the form of overglaze-decorated stoneware by Nonomura Ninsei (ca. 1627–ca. 1695) and Ogata Kenzan (1663–1743). With their decorative styles, both artists and their pupils influenced the development of ceramics far beyond the bounds of Kyôto. Many potters from the provinces were sent by their feudal lords or by rich merchants to be trained in Kyôto, or the Kyôto masters were invited to the provinces. Today, *shiro*-Satsuma (2) and Inuyama-*yaki* (40) still follow the tradition of these Kyôto wares.

With the exception of a few kilns still producing utensils for the tea ceremony, the production of ceramics was dominated by domestic wares at the end of the eighteenth and in the early nineteenth century. In spite of a small number of newly established kilns, such as Kasama (52) at the end of the eighteenth century and Mashiko (53) in 1853, which produced domestic wares in glazed stoneware, there was a decline in commercial demand for glazed and especially unglazed stoneware. All over Japan, including the old ceramics centers, a large number of kilns were built for the production of the highly esteemed porcelain, including Tobe (19) from 1777; Kiyomizu in Kyôto (34) from 1781; Izushi (30) at the end of the eighteenth century; Aizu-Hongô (54) from 1800; Seto (41) from

1807; Inuyama (40) from 1826; Kirigome (60) from 1834; Hirashimizu (58) from 1847; and Shibukusa (47) from 1878. Domestic wares and high-quality tableware were produced, as were utensils for the tea ceremony.

>> Meiji Restoration and Industrialization

The first indications that the Tokugawa shogunate might collapse appeared as early as the Tempô era (1831–1844), with peasants' revolts, famine, and economic crises. In 1854, the American fleet under Commodore Matthew C. Perry forced the opening of Japan under the Convention of Kanagawa. Because of its military inferiority, the shogunate felt compelled to sign more treaties with Western powers. The general political dissatisfaction, as well as these treaties, which were very unfavorable to Japan, provoked a wave of resistance, especially from a group of *samurai* from Kyûshû, causing the abdication of the Tokugawa *shôgun* in 1867 and the transfer of state power to Meiji Tennô Mutsuhito (1852–1912). The reinstatement of the emperor in 1868, termed the Meiji Restoration, was consolidated in the Boshin Civil War (1868–1869) by victory over the remaining Tokugawa troops.

After the Meiji Restoration, economic and social reforms, such as the free selection of profession and the freedom of establishment, followed. In 1871, the feudal system came to an end with the *haihan-chiken*; the domains, or *han*, awarded by the shogunate as fiefdoms were abolished and were replaced by the system of prefectures (*ken*) that is still in place today. Tôkyô, the former Edo, was proclaimed the seat of the emperor and the new capital.

Japan was opening up to the West, and a number of delegations formed, such as the famous Iwakura Mission, which traveled through Europe and America from 1871 to 1873. The appointment of specialists from abroad and the import of foreign technologies brought about a rapid improvement of the infrastructure, especially in the construction of roads and railways, as well as swift industrialization in a number of fields. In 1889, a constitution was proclaimed along Prussian-German lines. Within a brief period, Japan had developed into a modern state.

The potters of the many feudal kilns were robbed of their livelihoods by the abolition of the feudal system, and the consequences of industrialization added to the difficulties many traditional kilns found themselves in. The Japanese government had invited European and American engineers to set up ceramics plants along Western lines. So it was that the German chemist Gottfried Wagner (1831–1892) came to Japan and introduced Western production methods, from the preparation of clay to new firing and decorating techniques, first by setting up a factory in Nagasaki and then one in Arita beginning in 1870. Porcelain thus became a mass-produced item that could be distributed cheaply throughout Japan on the new transportation routes.

Many of the traditional local kilns, which had existed for many generations of potters, were superseded by factories. In his writings, Wagner appealed for the use of modern technologies to strengthen and preserve traditional crafts. After the first successes of Japanese ceramics at the World's Fairs in Paris (1867), San Francisco (1871), and Vienna (1873), the Meiji administration also adopted this viewpoint and encouraged the production of traditional Arita and Kutani porcelain, as well as Satsuma ware. Many potters profited from the export boom; ceramics from other kilns thus also made their way to the West. In many cases, this "export ware" had lost its original simplicity and was replaced by richly decorated objects with stylistic features from China and the West.

In the West, contact with the Japanese concept of form and decoration gave rise to Japonisme, a prelude to art nouveau. Around 1870, the customary Western distinction between art and craft appeared in Japan too. Whereas *bijutsu* refers exclusively to fine art (painting and sculpture), *gei-jutsu*, as a general term for visual and performing arts, includes painting and sculpture, theater, music, architecture, and *ikebana*, as well as the crafts. In contrast to the West, even today both fields of the arts are equally highly esteemed.

>> Twentieth-Century Developments

The decline of traditional crafts in Japan was a result of the abolition of the feudal system, along with industrialization and the economic recession at the end of the Taishô period (1912–1926), with the loss of export markets overseas. There were, however, three currents at the beginning of the twentieth century that were responsible for the long-term resurgence of ceramics in particular: first, the folk art (*mingei*) movement; second, the renaissance of tea ceramics with the revival of Karatsu, *shino*, Hagi, and Bizen wares, through masters from the old potter families such as Nakazato Muan (1895–1985), Arakawa Toyozô (1894–1985), Miwa Kyûsetsu X (1895–1981), and Kaneshige Tôyô (1896–1967); and third, the advent of studio potters. Additionally, state support in the mid-twentieth century provided a powerful impetus, so that by the 1970s, the growing purchasing power of the population brought about a boom in ceramics that still endures today, if in a somewhat diminished form.

Folk Art (*mingei*) Movement

The term *mingei* as an abbreviation of *minshû-teki kôgei* (folk art) was coined in 1925 by the philosopher Yanagi Sôetsu (Muneyoshi, 1889–1961). Yanagi was deeply impressed by the beauty of local crafts, such as ceramics, woodwork and bamboo, metal and leather, dyeing and weaving, papermaking, sculpture, painting, and calligraphy. Together with the potters Hamada Shôji (1894–1978), Kawai Kanjirô (1890–1966), and Tomimoto Kenkichi (1886–1963), who later left the *mingei* group, Yanagi founded the Japanese folk art movement. Its aim was to record and research the traditions of folk art, to collect folk art objects, to make them accessible to the public, and to further the production and sale of authentic folk art products. The objects were to be produced mainly by hand at an affordable price by artists who were to remain anonymous; they were not to be made as individual pieces

but in large numbers, and they were not to be signed.

The group traveled all over Japan, searching for local potters who were encountering great difficulties or had even given up their kilns. They encouraged craftspeople to make a new start, which in some cases made it necessary to rediscover techniques that had been lost. In 1931, Yanagi, Hamada, and Kawai founded the Japan Folk Art Association (*Nihon mingei kyôkai*) and started the magazine *Mingei*, which is still published today. The Japan Folk Crafts Museum (*Nihon Mingeikan*) was opened in 1936 for the collection of folk art objects, with Yanagi as its first director.

Yanagi's legacy was summarized posthumously in the book *The Unknown Craftsman: A Japanese Insight into Beauty* by the English potter Bernard Leach (1887–1979), who had joined Yanagi during his stays in Japan and is considered to be one of the founders of the *mingei* movement.

In contrast to the Arts and Crafts Movement initiated in the West by William Morris (1834–1896), which left no lasting traces, the *mingei* movement had a beneficial effect in Japan until well into the second half of the twentieth century. The diversity of local ceramics was preserved. Additionally, the revival of old traditions brought about a distinct improvement in quality, and the handmade objects in their simple beauty awakened the interest of a broad section of the population, so that many *mingei* kilns, such as Tsuboya (1), Koishiwara (17), Onta (18), Ôtani (21), Fujina (25), Aizu-Hongô (54), and Ôbori Sôma (57), to name only the largest, are economically secure. Famous folk art kilns such as Mashiko (53) still attract potters from all over the world.

State Support

For more than 100 years, the Japanese state has protected objects of historical and artistic interest. As early as 1897, a law was passed for the preservation of ancient temples and shrines (*koshaji hozon hô*), and in 1929, a law followed for the preservation of national treasures (*kokuhô hozon hô*).

From 1907 on, the education ministry officially supported annual art exhibitions. A group of experts appointed by the ministry decided who was to participate in the Bunten (*monbushô bijutsu tenrankai*, Ministry of Education Fine Arts Exhibition). In 1919, controversy developed within the ministry and the team of experts between a more traditional and a more Western orientation in Japanese art. After a number of organizational changes in 1958, the former imperial art exhibition was continued as the independent Nitten foundation (*Nihon bijutsu tenrankai*, Japan Fine Arts Exhibition).

After a fire in 1949 at the Hôryû-ji temple near Nara, the state passed a law in 1950 to protect cultural properties (*bunkazai hogo hô*), which was extended in 1954 and 1975. It protects monuments and historical sites, natural monuments, and landscapes of outstanding beauty; folk art; and tangible and intangible cultural properties. Among the tangible cultural properties are buildings, paintings, sculptures, books, and archaeological finds, and also objects from the applied arts, such as ceramics. They are either listed as Registered Tangible Cultural Properties, or they are proclaimed Important Tangible Cultural Properties (more than 12,000 exist), some of which are designated as National Treasures (there are more than 1000).

Among the Intangible Cultural Assets designated by the ministry of education are the performing arts—for example, Nô, Bungaku, Kabuki, dance, and music—and techniques, such as doll making, weaving and dyeing textiles, lacquer work, metal, paper and bamboo work, and ceramics. Examples of the ceramic techniques that are supported include firing and glazes; examples include *shino*, *oribe*, and *tenmoku*.

Masters of the respective disciplines may be honored with the highest state distinction as Bearers of Important Intangible Cultural Assets (*jûyô mukei bunkazai hojisha*), generally better known as Living National Treasures (*ningen kokuhô*). They are obliged to care for, develop, and document their specific techniques, as well as train young craftspeople. Since 1955, 32 ceramists have been designated Living National Treasures (see Living National Treasures on page 21). The list with the newly appointed *ningen kokuhô* is published annually.

Since 1974, there has been a law to further the traditional crafts industry; it supports crafts companies and groups of companies that produce traditional products adapted for the present day, mainly by hand and largely from traditional materials. For example, 17 projects have been supported in ceramics, in Mashiko, Tokoname, and Shigaraki, and in the Seto and Mino regions.

Along with state-organized programs, similar ones, under which potters, workshops, and special techniques are honored and protected, are run by the prefectures and the municipalities. In addition, local, regional, and national pottery centers and museums are supported. Thus, the Shigaraki Ceramic Cultural Park was established in Shigaraki in 1990. It covers about 988 acres (400 hectares), includes a museum and studios for guest artists, and has served as an example, even for smaller pottery centers.

Living National Treasures (Ceramics)

Name	Dates of Birth and Death	Year Designated	Place of Work/Kiln; Reason for Designation
Hamada Shôji	1894–1978	1955	Mashiko; folk art (mingei)
Ishiguro Munemaru	1893–1968	1955	Kyôto; temmoku glaze
Tomimoto Kenkichi	1886–1963	1955	Tôkyô, Kyôto; overglaze painting, porcelain (iro-e jiki)
Arakawa Toyozô	1894–1985	1955	Mino; shino and setoguro
Kaneshige Tôyô	1896–1967	1956	Bizen-yaki
Katô Hajime	1900–1968	1961	Seto/Yokohama; overglaze painting, porcelain (iro-e jiki)
Fujiwara Kei	1899–1983	1970	Bizen-yaki
Miwa Kyûsetsu X	1895–1981	1970	Hagi; tea ceramics
Nakazato Muan (Tarôemon XII)	1895–1985	1976	Karatsu-yaki
Kondô Yûzô	1902–1985	1977	Kyôto; porcelain, cobalt underglaze painting (sometsuke)
Miwa Kyûsetsu XI (Jusetsu)	b. 1910	1983	Hagi; white glaze (shiro hagi-gusuri)
Tsukamoto Kaiji	1912–1990	1983	Gifu Prefecture; white, and blue-and-white porcelain (hakuji and seihakuji)
Kinjô Jirô	1912–2004	1985	Okinawa; Tsuboya-yaki with sgraffito (kakiotoshi)
Shimizu Uichi	1926–2004	1985	Kyôto; iron glazes (tetsu-yû)
Fujimoto Yoshimichi	1919–1992	1986	Tôkyô; overglaze painting, porcelain (iro-e jiki)
Tamura Kôichi	1918–1987	1986	Sano; iron brushwork (tetsu-e)

Name	Dates of Birth and Death	Year Designated	Place of Work/Kiln; Reason for Designation
Yamamoto Tôshû	1906–1994	1987	Bizen-*yaki*
Imaizumi Imaemon XIII	1926–2001	1989	Arita; overglaze painting, porcelain (*iro-e jiki*)
Matsui Kôsei	1927–2003	1993	Kasama; marbled ware (*neriage*)
Suzuki Osamu	b. 1934	1994	Mino; *shino*
Inoue Manji	b. 1929	1995	Arita; white porcelain (*hakuji*)
Katô Takuo	1917–2005	1995	Mino; three-colored ware (*sansai*)
Fujiwara Yû	1932–2001	1996	Bizen-*yaki*
Shimaoka Tatsuzô	b. 1919	1996	Mashiko; cord-marked ceramics with slip inlay (*jômon zôgan*)
Miura Koheiji	1933–2006	1997	Sado Island; celadon (*seiji*)
Tokuda Yasokichi III	b. 1933	1997	Kutani; colored porcelain (*sai-yû jiki*)
Yamada Jôzan III	1924–2006	1998	Tokoname; small teapots (*kyûsu*)
Sakaida Kakiemon XIV	b. 1934	2001	Arita; overglaze painting, porcelain (*iro-e jiki*)
Yoshida Minori III	b. 1932	2001	Kutani; underglaze gold decoration (*yûri-kinsai*)
Itô Sekisui V	b. 1941	2003	Sado Island; *Mumyôi-yaki*
Isezaki Jun	b. 1936	2004	Bizen-*yaki*
Hara Kiyoshi	b. 1936	2005	Yorii, Saitama Prefecture; iron glazes (*tetsu-yû*)

Modern Developments

In the development of ceramics during the twentieth century and to the present day, three trends can be observed. A few ceramists—very few—remain within the tradition or follow it without any change. Most further develop traditional forms and glazes. And some artists, after extensive training, depart entirely from tradition and turn to unrestricted creative activities. One thing that made this possible was the freedom of profession after the Meiji Restoration. Potters who did not come from the traditional potter families have increasingly made use of this opportunity. Around 1910, the first potters ceased producing typical local wares and followed their artistic inclinations to the full. Tomimoto Kenkichi (1886–1963), for example, repeatedly developed new, innovative decorations for his overglaze paintings, which, as mass-produced wares, were intended to add aesthetic quality to everyday life. The Akatsuchi Group was founded in 1919 by Kusube Yaichi (1897–1984) and Yagi Isshô (1894–1963) as an association for individual artists. Even before the Second World War, some potters had fully developed their individuality and originality. Ishiguro Munemaro (1893–1968) and Arakawa Toyozô (1894–1985) can be regarded as examples of this.

As a result of the opening of the country, new techniques from the West were developed. Some potters traveled the countries of origin of the highly prized Korean and Chinese ceramics and became acquainted with these ancient pottery traditions. Shards of shino ware from the Momoyama period were discovered in Japan, and many potters who were fascinated by the tea wares of this era took up the old techniques and developed them further.

After the war, there were more radical changes in the ceramics scene. Art schools, colleges of ceramics, and new training institutions in many traditional pottery towns opened to young people. Architects, designers, and sculptors also turned to ceramics. Many aimed to study abroad or to have prolonged placements with renowned Western artists, mainly in the United States or the United Kingdom. Thus, the training of the postwar potters' generation has been thorough in both technical and artistic fields. Conception and technical execution still form a single unit in contemporary Japan.

In the late Shôwa period, the exhibition system was modernized. A number of traditionally oriented ceramists left Nitten, where creative artists exhibited who felt indebted both to Japanese and Western classicism, or to the mingei movement with its annual Japanese Traditional Crafts Exhibition (Nihon dentô kôgeiten). These artists joined new organizations, either dedicated to traditional functional ceramics or to the avant-garde. Thus the Shikôkei group founded by porcelain artists in the Kyôto district of Gojô-zaka was associated with a school of ikebana and created very modern ikebana vessels. As early as 1950, the group showed ceramic sculptures by Noguchi Isamu (1904–1988) in its exhibition. Sôdeisha (1948–1998), in which the avant-garde was represented, was also a group founded in Kyôto, by Yagi Kazuo (1918–1979), Yamada Hikaru (1924–2001), and Suzuki Osamu (1926–2001). The Sôdeisha artists, who first exhibited in the Takashimaya department store in Ôsaka, rejected any functionality for their obujê-yaki (from the French objet) and tôchô (ceramic sculpture). Clay and technique were what mattered; the objects were intended to be expressive in themselves.

Two styles have governed the avant-garde from the second half of the last century up to today: the influence of the West (Europe and the United States) and the return to the styles of Jômon, Yayoi, and Sue ceramics, which was furthered by intensive excavations by the state. Traditional forms and techniques continue to be developed, but abstract, formally extreme sculptures are equally a part of the ceramics scene.

PRODUCTION TECHNIQUES

Many traditional potters and studio ceramists still perform all working operations themselves (see photos 2–7), although others buy commercially available clays and materials. As extensive overviews of specifically Japanese techniques are already available, only a few typical aspects will be outlined here.

Besides porcelain and raku, the preferred ceramics genre is high- and low-fired stoneware. Clay extraction is described in the next section (see photos 2–4). The next step is the forming of the pot. While industrial mass production uses modern methods such as slip casting porcelain or press molding stoneware, the potter's wheel is still in use for serial production, even in medium-sized studios. Wheels (see photo 5), which almost always turn clockwise in Japan, are often of the kick wheel (ke-rokuro) or electric varieties, and are more rarely hand driven (te-rokuro). For throwing larger vessels, isolated examples of wheels driven by a second person can still be found. Power wheels are mainly in use for mass production of bowls, vases, and tea bowls thrown off the hump, for example. When removing the pot from the wheel head with twisted wires or cords, the highly esteemed shell patterns are created on the foot.

Besides throwing on the wheel, other forming techniques are used. The oldest technique for medium and large pots is to build them up from coils of clay, which are rolled out by the potters between their hands as clay coils or spirals. These are built up from a firmly compressed base to form the walls of the vessel. The piece is then formed on the wheel (himozukuri) or shaped with a wooden paddle from outside and with a corresponding "anvil" from the inside [tataki (zukuri)]. Box forms are assembled from clay slabs that have been cut to size [tatara (zukuri)]. Bowls may be press molded (uchigata) into plaster or bisqued clay molds. Smaller ceramic objects, such as raku bowls, are hand built (tebineri). A small number of studio potters carve their objects from a clay block as they would sculptures (kurinuki).

The pots receive their final form—for example, adding a spout on a bowl, assembling the components of a teapot, trimming, burnishing (see photo 8), faceting, forming rims, and intentionally deforming objects (see photo 9)—immediately after throwing, while still wet, or after drying to a leather-hard state. The shaping of the foot of a pot (i.e., the footring, kôdai) receives much attention in accordance with Japanese aesthetics. Further methods are described in Decorating and Glazing Techniques (see pages 27–31).

The finished pot is dried completely, usually in the open air—a process that depends on the weather conditions and may take several days or even weeks (see photo 6).

Pots that are to remain unglazed are then fired without further treatment. Pots to be glazed are, with few exceptions, bisque fired to 1202°F–1742°F (650°C–950°C). The glaze is applied more easily to bisqued ware, and underglazes adhere better to the pot's surface during the glaze firing. Finally, the glaze or main firing to 2012°F–2372°F (1100°C–1300°C) follows (see Decorating and Glazing Techniques on page 29); this may take hours, days, or even weeks, depending on the type of clay and kiln (see Kilns and Firing on page 31, and photo 7). The cooling period of sometimes more than a week also influences the appearance of the pots.

Onta, Japan

Photo 2. Water-driven crusher (*karause*)
Photo 3. Levigation (*suihi*); settling tank
Photo 4. Stiffening the clay in bowls and on a
drying oven
Photo 5. Throwing teacups on a kick wheel
Photo 6. Drying the unfired (green) ware in the
open air
Photo 7. Multichamber climbing kiln (*noborigama*)

Photo 8. Burnishing *shudei* teapots (Mumyôi-*yaki*, Watanabe Tôzô; Sado Island, 51)
Photo 9. Distortion as a design feature; Inagaki Mitsunori, stoneware *sake* cup, wood-ash glaze (*kai-yû*); Seto (41)

>> Clay Preparation

The Japanese potter has the following priorities: first the clay, then the firing process, and finally—only in third place—is the potter, who merely provides assistance in the production process. Japan is a country rich in clay, with many deposits of various clays found in close proximity to each other. Potters still frequently dig their own clay, or at least a part of the clay mixture, for unglazed stoneware (*yakishime*). The clay (*tsuchi*) determines the appearance of the ceramic object (*tsuchi no aji*, clay flavor); wares typical of Bizen,

Iga, and Shigaraki, for instance. Mingei potters often have clay deposits near their potteries and prepare the clay themselves in all phases. In Mashiko, while the standard variety is supplied from a clay pit, some potters still exploit their own clay deposits.

Primary clays are often used. These consist of large particles, are not very plastic, and are formed directly from rocky minerals (*tôseki*, ceramic stone, was created from the heat and gases of volcanic material, as well as kaolin, a by-product of the acidic degradation of granite, for example). Secondary clays formed from primary clays by erosion, displacement, and mixing with other minerals and organic constituents, are also used. Secondary clays often contain substantial mineral fragments of the original rock, such as quartz or feldspar (for example, *gairome-*, *kibushi-nendo*), and consist of very fine, complex, broken clay-mineral particles mixed with organic material. They are consequently highly plastic and are often dug from beneath rice fields (*tatsuchi*) and from river valleys.

Clay is prepared in several phases. If the clay is found in a dry state or in the form of hard lumps, it must first be broken up, either industrially in power crushers, or in ball mills or water-driven crushers (*karause*, see photo 2) in traditional potteries. Some potters prefer clay cleaned only by hand, in which the many embedded pegmatite particles, which explode and melt during firing (*ishihaze*), are preserved.

Usually, crushing is followed by screening to remove coarse impurities. The fine clay, during the process of levigation (*suihi*), is washed several times (see photo 3), screened, thickened, and aged, first in the open air (see photo 4), then under cover. The aging process can take weeks or, in extreme cases, even decades (see Asahi and Kyôto, 33, 34, on pages 129 and 132 respectively). Aging alters the appearance of the clay and of the fired pot. Before use, the clay is homogenized in mechanical pug mills, or it is sometimes wedged with the feet (*ashimomi*), then wedged again after being left for several days, this time by hand using the spiral or "chrysanthemum" method (*kikumomi*) to remove trapped air bubbles.

To improve plasticity, reduce shrinkage, and improve refractoriness, clay bodies are frequently standardized industrially or produced individually by blending. Fine Seto stoneware clay is added (10 to 30 percent) to Mashiko clay, which is sandy, iron rich, and not very plastic. With the addition of 20 percent kaolin to Shigaraki clay, *kurodani* clay, which used to be available in Kyôto, is re-created for the production of white stoneware.

>> Decorating and Glazing Techniques

Many glazing and decorating techniques in Japanese ceramics are of Korean origin and are still in use today, nearly unchanged. New techniques, especially in the application of coloring agents, are also now being used.

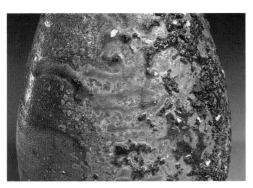

Photo 10. *Neriage* (or *nerikomi*, clay marbling); stoneware *sake* cup; Kasama (52)

Photo 11. *Nunome* (cloth texturing); stoneware bowl; Mino (42)

Photo 12. *Kushime* (combed decoration); porcelain mortar; Tobe (19)

Photo 13. *Haritsuke-mon* (or *chôka*, clay applications); stoneware teapot; Nihonmatsu Banko (55)

Photo 14. *Enokihada* (partially melted natural-ash glaze); stoneware wall-hanging vase; Bizen (29)

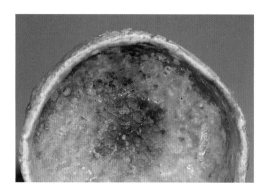

Decorating Techniques

Homogeneous bodies are not always used. Inhomogeneity may be a design feature; large quartz inclusions in Shigaraki clay, for example, produce the typical surface of the fired ware. Traces of iron in Mashiko clay can be seen as dark brown to black speckles in the pale clay. In the *neriage* technique, clays of different colors are combined (see photo 10).

Surfaces of still-moist pots can be enhanced by the use of colored slips (*kohiki*, slip dipping, see photo 58; *hakeme*, slip brushing, see photo 59); by cloth texturing (*nunome*, see photo 11); by paddling with carved bats; by impressing with stamps, shells or cords; or by using roller stamps. Lines can be incised into the clay with knives or combs (*kushime*, see photo 12). The pots are then fired as they are, or the incised areas are filled with slips or clays of a different color (*mishima* technique, see photo 60; *zôgan*, see photo 161). Works with celadon glaze often have large areas of relief patterns (*ukibori*). In its varying thickness, the glaze reveals nuances of color.

Another decorative technique is the application of preformed embellishments (*haritsuke-mon*, see photo 13). Some patterns are cut out in their entirety; for a specific type of porcelain, the "rice grain" pattern (*hotaru-de*) is produced by closing holes with a transparent glaze after the bisque firing.

Especially with unglazed *yakishime* ware, the firing conditions are consciously used to create decorative elements; examples include unmelted fly ash (*enokihada*, see photo 14), vitrified glass flows from the accumulation of flying ash (*bîdoro*, see photo 15), and red markings (*hidasuki*, see photo 16) created by wrapping rice straw ropes soaked in salt water around the pot before firing. Salt glazing (*shio-gusuri*) was introduced from Germany and England.

Glazing Techniques

Glazes, which are still prepared by many potters themselves, determine the appearance of ceramics. The pots are dipped wholly or partially in the glaze (*hitashigake*), where fingerprints frequently remain as unglazed areas (*yubi-ato*, see

Photo 15. *Bîdoro* (vitrified glass from fly ash); stoneware tea bowl; Iga (37)
Photo 16. *Hidasuki* ("fire cord"); stoneware freshwater jar; Bizen (29)

Photo 17. *Itchin* (slip trailing); stoneware plate; Fujina (25)

photo 95). Glazes are also poured (*hishakugake*) or splashed onto the pots (*uchigake*, see photo 65), dripped with various tools (*nagashigake*, see photo 67), or applied with a bamboo tube (*itchin*, see photo 17). Light-colored slip can be applied to a dark body with a stiff brush (*hakeme*, see photo 59) or wiped off with the fingers (*yubi-kaki*). Patterns are cut into pots completely covered with slip, as sgraffito (*kakiotoshi*, see photo 62) or as chatter marks (*tobigan'na*, see photo 65). If a pattern is brushed on using liquid latex, the covered area of the surface remains unglazed after glazing and removing the latex layer. Similar resist procedures are used with wax (*rônuki*, see photo 190), which burns out in firing, or paper stencils (*katagami*). If a leaf pattern is placed on a *tenmoku*-glazed surface and covered with a transparent glaze, the leaf silhouette remains (see photo 18).

Photo 18. Konoha-tenmoku (leaf skeleton on ten-moku glaze); Okada Yasumasa, stoneware tea bowl; Kawaguchi (Saitama Prefecture)
Photo 19. *Shita-etsuke* (underglaze painting) with iron oxide, *e-garatsu*; stoneware teacup; Karatsu (13)

Underglaze Painting

For underglaze painting (*shita-etsuke*), cobalt and iron compounds are used almost exclusively. Copper is used more rarely. For iron underglaze brushwork on stoneware (see photo 19), an iron ore with a 40-percent iron content (*oni-ita*) from deposits in the Mino region, or a 50-percent iron precipitate that collects in clay strata under rice fields, is used.

In Japan, underglaze painting on porcelain means cobalt brushwork (*sometsuke*) or painting with natural *gosu*, a 5-percent cobalt mineral with iron, aluminum, and manganese components. To prevent the color from running, a suspension of concentrated green tea is used. A somewhat indistinct purple or grayish shade of blue is produced by firing in reduction. Using an industrially produced mixture of pure cobalt, manganese, iron oxide, and nickel fritted at about 2192°F (1200°C) creates a brighter blue.

Glazes

The most important transparent standard glazes are ash glazes (*hai-gusuri*), feldspar glazes (*chôseki-yû*), and limestone glazes (*sekkai-yû*). By adding metallic oxides, various colored glazes are produced. These are mainly iron (*tetsu-yû*) or copper (*dô-yû*) glazes. Apart from the natural-ash glaze (*shizen-yû*) produced in a wood-burning kiln, glazes are usually made from various raw materials (ash, feldspar, and clay). Local materials and application techniques produce the color shading typical of individual kilns (see photo 20). Wood ash (*dobai*), rice-straw ash (*warabai*), but also domestic and industrial ash, are used. The lack of homogeneity of the ash causes variations in color (*madara-garatsu*, see photo 21). Shino (see photo 22) is an almost pure feldspar glaze with a low ash content that fires at a relatively low temperature of about 2192°F (1200°C). The varying proportions of feldspar and wood or straw ash and an increasing iron content are used to make the other classic Japanese glazes: celadon (*seiji*, see photo 47); *ame-yû* (amber, see photo 146); *kaki-yû* (persimmon, see photo 164b); and *ten-moku-yû*. By altering the application method of a *tenmoku* glaze, hare's fur glaze is created (see photo 104), and when oversaturated with iron, an oil-spot glaze (*yuteki-tenmoku*, see photo 37) is produced. Among the copper glazes, there are the green *oribe* glaze (see photo 189) and the red *shinsha* (oxblood, see photo 80). Special glaze variations include crystalline (see photo 23) and crackle glazes (see photo 24).

For a colorless porcelain glaze, the common forms of wood ash contain too much iron. These special glazes are now only rarely produced in small quantities from 30 percent ash of the *isu* tree (*distylium racemosum*) and 70 percent *tôseki*; most porcelain glazes now contain feldspar, silicates, limestone, kaolin, and magnesium oxide.

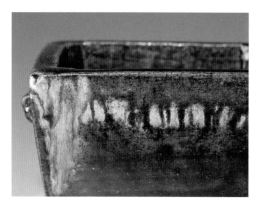

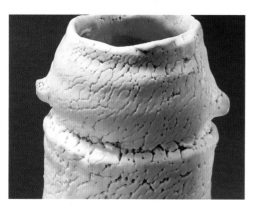

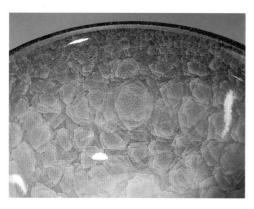

Photo 20. *Namako-yû* (rice-straw ash feldspar glaze); stoneware herring pot; Aizu-Hongô (54)

Photo 21. *Madara-garatsu* (mottled rice-straw ash feldspar glaze); stoneware *sake* bottle; Karatsu (13)

Photo 22. *Aka-shino* (feldspar glaze); stoneware vase; Mino (42)

Photo 23. *Kesshô-yû* (crystalline glaze); stoneware teacup; Taisetsu (65)

Photo 24. *Kan'nyu* (crackle glaze); Minegishi Seikô, stoneware tea bowl; Nasu (Tochigi Prefecture)

Photo 25. *Uwa-etsuke* (overglaze painting); stoneware plate; Mashiko (53)
Photo 26. *Uwa-etsuke* (overglaze painting); porcelain box; Arita (8)

Overglaze Enamels

Overglaze painting using enamels (*uwa-etsuke*) has been practiced in Japan since the mid-seventeenth century (see Sakaida Kakiemon I in Arita (8), on page 47). Today, enamels in red, green, blue, purple, black, white, and yellow, with and without underglaze painting, are used for overglaze decoration on Arita (8), Nabeshima (9), Kutani (45), and Seto (41) porcelain, as well as shiro-Satsuma (2), Kyôto (34), and Mashiko (53) stoneware (see photos 25 and 26). Additionally, gold and silver may be used as a powder or in leaf form. Overglaze enamels usually are fired in small muffle kilns (*nishiki-gama*) in oxidation to 1292°F–1562°F (700°C–850°C), but gold and silver are fired to 1112°F–1562°F (600°C–850°C), usually to about 1112°F (600°C). To achieve greater brilliance, they may need to be applied and fired several times.

Whereas rolling, printing, and spraying are common in mass production, many individual potteries still paint their work by hand, although in a kind of production line—each worker only executes certain brushstrokes.

>> Kilns and Firing

Along with cheaper and cleaner industrially produced kilns fired with oil, electricity, and especially gas, Japanese potters very frequently use traditional wood-burning, individually constructed kilns. These kilns originated in China and Korea but were developed further over the centuries in Japan. For the most part, Japanese red pine has been used as fuel because of its long flame, but cedar, cypress, larch, oak, and chestnut are also used.

The *anagama* (a single-vaulted, single-chamber climbing kiln) was first built in the fifth century on a natural slope and had only one opening for packing and stoking. Because of its form and the slope, it required no chimney and reached a firing temperature of about 2192°F (1200°C). From the tenth century on, a column behind the firebox improved the flame path, and the combustion area was enlarged. With this improved type of kiln, in which temperatures of over 2372°F (1300°C) could be achieved, fly ash could be melted to form a natural glaze. Since the Second World War, *anagama* kilns have been in frequent use again because of their relatively low construction costs and the natural-ash glaze effects.

The *ôgama* (a large single-vaulted, single-chamber climbing kiln), with lateral apertures for stacking, was built around 1400 in the Tokoname (39) region. Behind the firebox was a step, in front of which saggars stood on columns. These directed the flames vertically, then horizontally, through the stacked ware in the kiln. In Echizen (44), a 98½-foot-long (30 m), 20-foot-wide (6 m), pear-shaped *ôgama* was built, and in Inbe (Bizen, 29), the outlines of three *ôgama* can be seen on the outskirts of town.

In the late sixteenth century, the first *waridake-shiki-noborigama* (a split bamboo, single-vaulted, multichamber climbing kiln) was built in Karatsu (13). The chambers are separated by partitions with openings at the bottom, or by columns. This

Photo 27. Etsunan-*noborigama* in Miyazaki (Echizen-*yaki*, 44)

type of kiln is fired from the firemouth and from the lateral stoking ports. There is no chimney; kiln gases escape through a honeycomb-like back wall. In Tachikui (Tanba, 31), there are still approximately 20 such kilns today, measuring nearly 44 to 56 yards (40 to 50 m) in length, 2¼ yards (2 m) in width, and 4 feet (1.2 m) in height.

In the early seventeenth century, the first *renbôshiki-noborigama* (stepped, multivaulted, multichamber climbing kilns with chimneys) made their appearance. The individual chambers are arranged in steps up a hillside or on artificial ramps (see photos 7 and 27). The pots to be fired are stacked in the chambers from the sides and in saggars, either on the floor or on refractory kiln shelves. The advantage of multiple

chambers is that various firing conditions (oxidizing, reducing, and salt glazing) can be achieved at one time. There are examples of *noborigama* with three to twenty chambers, although not all chambers are always used. To reduce costs, oil or gas is often used to fire to bisque temperatures. Today, there are numerous local forms of kilns in existence, as well as combined forms constructed by individual potters.

In the ceramics industry, various downdraft kilns with designs of Western origin are in use. These kilns, which were first fired with coal and later with oil or gas, have various types of flame paths, depending on their designs. For instance, the *tokkuri-gama* used to fire sake bottles applies heat to the ware from below, while in the *tôen-shiki-gama*, the heat rises along the walls and is then directed downward from the ceiling of the kiln through the stacked ware.

Modern tunnel kilns for porcelain, which are mainly fired with gas for economic and environmental reasons, can reduce firing times to as little as three hours. Saggar firings for overglaze enamels are usually conducted in electric kilns.

Firing in a Five-Chamber *Noborigama*

Shimaoka Tatsuzô (Living National Treasure) works in Mashiko (53) with two *noborigama*, in addition to gas kilns for bisque firings and overglaze enamels. The five-chamber kiln he has perfected is fired with red pine two to three times a year for various types of ceramics.

In the first chamber—the combustion area (*takiguchi*)—large objects are put in through the firemouth (*ôguchi*). The work is raised from the kiln bat on the floor by seashells. The first of the four firing chambers (*shôsei-shitsu*) is packed by Shimaoka Tatsuzô with pieces that are to be exposed directly to the ash and that are to be fired in reduction. In the second reduction chamber, glazed pots are protected from direct contact with the flames by walls. The third chamber holds pots with colored glazes and is fired in oxidation, and the fourth chamber holds pots to be salt glazed.

To drive off residual moisture (*aburidaki*), the kiln is slowly heated for 24 hours from the combustion area, then the temperature is quickly raised to 1492°F (800°C) from the lateral stoking ports. In the next phase (*semedaki*), the temperature is raised to 2372°F (1300°C), with thick logs in the firebox and with wood of medium thickness from the lateral stoking ports (approximately 60 hours after firing has begun).

After examining samples drawn from the combustion area, all the apertures are closed in that chamber and further stoking with wood takes place in the second firing chamber to start reduction in this area. Large quantities of pine wood charcoal are then introduced to the first firing chamber to begin the carbon reduction process. At the same time, the third (oxidizing) chamber is brought up to its final temperature with thin pieces of wood. As soon as the last chamber has reached the final temperature of 2372°F (1300°C), salt is added two to three times. After four days of continuous stoking, firing is complete. All apertures are closed and a five-day cooling period (*reikyaku*) follows before the kiln is opened (*kamadashi*).

CERAMIC KILNS

>> Kilns in Okinawa

During the twelfth century, the chain of islands south of Kyûshû was formally independent as the kingdom of Ryûkyû but was under the influence of the Chinese imperial court. In 1609, after being conquered by the *daimyô* of Satsuma (South Kyûshû), Ryûkyû owed tribute both to China and Satsuma. It continued to exist as a kingdom, however, until the Meiji Restoration, when it was integrated into the structure of the Japanese state in 1879, under the name of Okinawa Prefecture.

Because of its geographical position, Okinawa had always been a center for trade with China, Korea, Japan, and Southeast Asia, especially for Chinese celadons in the fourteenth and fifteenth centuries. There was a lively cultural and economic interchange with neighboring Kyûshû.

Tsuboya 壺屋 (1)

On the Ryûkyû Islands, the local ceramics style was *arayaki*, an unglazed stoneware. In 1616, to improve the local ceramics industry, the Ryûkyû administration brought Korean potters to the Wakuta kilns from Satsuma (2), where they had produced glazed ware (*jôyaki*). Further product improvements followed, through the gain of the *aka-e* technique of overglaze decoration from China and through the amalgamation of the kilns in Wakuta, Chibana, and Takaraguchi to form a pottery center in Tsuboya, a district of the capital Naha. The term Tsuboya-*yaki* was derived from this, for Okinawan ceramics covers both *arayaki* and *jôyaki*. After the end of the Ryûkyû kingdom, Tsuboya-*yaki* was able to maintain its position in the market in spite of the import of cheap Japanese porcelain, and it gained further impetus throughout the *mingei* movement. Until the Second World War, unglazed *arayaki* was the main product, but today, glazed *jôyaki* predominates.

Because of atmospheric pollution caused by wood-firing *noborigama*, only gas- or oil-fired kilns have been licensed in Naha since 1970. Yachimun Street in the Tsuboya district is still the pottery center, with 15 studios, the ceramics museum, and two kilns that are under a preservation order: Fê-nu-*gama*, an *anagama* for firing *arayaki*; and Agari-nu-*gama*, a *renbôshiki-noborigama* for *jôyaki*. Potters who wished to continue firing in the traditional manner with wood moved to the potters' village of Yomitan, about 19 miles (30 km) north of Naha. Currently, there are approximately 100 pottery workshops in Okinawa Prefecture.

Arayaki (see photo 28), also known as *nanban-yaki*, is made from iron-rich clay coils using the *tatakizukuri* technique; for decorative effect, clay applications (*haritsuke-mon*) may be used. Storage jars and bottles for *awamori*, a local *shôchû* specialty, are the main products. *Arayaki* is fired in an *anagama* to 2012°F–2120°F (1100°C–1160°C) in oxidation.

Jôyaki is thrown on the wheel or pressed in molds. The objects are frequently covered with a white slip. Rice-straw and sugar-cane ash glazes, with the addition of iron, manganese, cobalt, or copper, are used. After glazing and with no bisque firing, the ware is fired for 10 to 30 hours in oxidation in a *noborigama*, or alternatively in a gas or oil kiln. Objects with *aka-e* overglaze in red, green, or yellow are fired a second time to 1472°F (800°C). In addition to inlay with white clay (*zôgan*); slip application with a slip trailer (*itchin*); and chatter marks (*tobigan´na*); *kakiotoshi*—a sgraffito technique—is a typical form of decoration. For this, the incised outline of the design (for example, plants, aquatic designs, or geometric patterns) is accentuated by iron or cobalt oxide underglaze painting. In 1985, Kinjô Jirô (1912–2004) was declared a *ningen kokuhô*—a Living National Treasure—for his *kakiotoshi* work (see photo 29). Typical *jôyaki* products include domestic tableware and curved hip flasks (*dachibin*, see photo

**Photo 28.   Tsuboya-*yaki*. Arakaki Eiyô, vase (*kaki*), 2001. 10¼ x 4 inches (26.3 x 10 cm).
Unglazed stoneware (*arayaki*).**

Photo 29. Tsuboya-*yaki*. Kinjô Jirô (Living National Treasure), hip flask with prawn design (*ebi-mon dachibin*), ca. 1985. 6 x 9½ x 3¼ inches (15.2 x 24.1 x 8.5 cm). Glazed stoneware (*jôyaki*), sgraffito technique (*kakiotoshi*); outlines accentuated by cobalt underglaze painting.

29) for water or *awamori*, as well as richly deco-rated urns (*zushi-game*) and the ubiquitous *shîsâ*—mythical lions that serve as sentinels against evil spirits—which are also produced in *arayaki*.

>> Kilns in Kyûshû

In the course of its history, the island of Kyûshû has absorbed many Chinese and Korean influ-ences because of its relative proximity to the mainland. The port of Karatsu, in the north of Kyûshû, is only approximately 125 miles (200 km) by sea from Korea. This is how the cultiva-tion of rice in paddy fields came to Japan via Kyûshû during the Yayoi period (ca. 300 B.C.–A.D. 300). In many migratory waves, especially in the late third and fourth centuries, Korean potters brought to Kyûshû technical improvements such as the hand-driven wheel, the *tatakizukuri* tech-nique for hand building vessels, and the single-chamber climbing kiln (*anagama*).

Ceramics in Kyûshû were deeply influenced by the many hundreds of Korean potters who had been brought to Kyûshû after the campaigns of Toyotomi Hideyoshi (1592 and 1597) and who were settled on their lands by the local feudal lords. Within a few decades, local ceramic styles had evolved, ranging from the strongly Korean-flavored glazed stoneware to the first Japanese porcelain. Thanks to the tenacity of Japanese potters, this rich ceramics tradition, which devel-oped over a period of centuries, was nurtured and kept alive even in difficult times so that today, porcelain and stoneware are produced in Kyûshû side by side and in the most varied forms.

Satsuma 薩摩 (2)

Satsuma-*yaki* is the term used to describe the ceramics produced in south Kyûshû, in the former domain of Satsuma (now Kagoshima Prefecture and parts of Miyazaki Prefecture). It is a collective term for the products made by 80 Korean potters who had been relocated in the

late sixteenth century to the area around the bay of Kagoshima in the extensive lands of Shimazu Yoshihiro, lord of Satsuma, after Toyotomi Hideyoshi's Korean campaigns. Satsuma-*yaki* is correspondingly varied in appearance, ranging from tea wares to domestic wares.

Present-day Satsuma-*yaki* comprises two groups of products: *kuro*-Satsuma and *shiro*-Satsuma. *Kuro*-Satsuma (black Satsuma, *kuromon*), a stoneware with black or brown ash glazes, has been produced since the early Edo period (1600–1868) from a dark, iron-rich clay. The main prod-ucts were tea wares and domestic tableware. After the discovery of deposits of white clay (*hakudo*) in 1623, *shiro*-Satsuma (white Satsuma, *shiromon*) was developed. Initially, it was a low-fired stoneware or semiporcelain with a yellowish white, porous, fired body and a transparent, fine crackle glaze. The first example of *shiro*-Satsuma is considered to be a tea bowl from 1673. The originally undecorated ware was reserved exclusively for the aristocracy. *Kuromon* and *shiromon* from this first phase of production are called *ko*-Satsuma.

After the Tateno kiln had adopted the tech-nique of overglaze enamels from Kyôto at the end of the eighteenth century, colored brocade ware with gold (*iro-e kinran-de*) was produced in Ninsei style. The mainly floral design was applied sparingly so that *shiromon* could be used as tea ware. By the end of the Edo period, *iro-e kinran-de* designs that covered the entire piece had developed, with landscapes and genre scenes in medallions on richly decorated backgrounds with a large amount of gold. These provoked enthusiastic admiration in the West at the World's Fairs at the end of the nineteenth century.

The five most important centers where Satsuma-*yaki* was fired during the Edo period were Tateno, Naeshirogawa, Genryûin, and Hirasa, along with the Ryûmonji-*gama*—a folk kiln (*minyô*) set up around 1598 that developed an individual style and that is discussed sepa-rately (see Ryûmonji, 3, on page 38).

The Tateno kiln, set up as a feudal kiln (*goyôgama*) in 1602 in Chôsa, near Aira, was moved to Kagoshima in Tateno (now Kagoshima) after the relocation of the feudal seat, and it was in use until 1871. Tea utensils were produced, first in *kuromon* style and later *shiromon*; by the end of the Edo period, *iro-e kinran-de* Satsuma was the principal product.

The Naeshirogawa kiln, set up in 1599 as a *minyô* by 40 Korean potters in Kushikino, was moved to Naeshirogawa (present-day Higashi-Ichiki Miyama) five years later. Initially, *kuromon* was made as domestic tableware, but after the discovery of *hakudo*, *shiromon* was also produced. In 1764, the Naeshirogawa potteries came under *han* administration, which arranged for the construction of more kilns in 1846 for the production of *hakuji* and *sometsuke* porcelain. At the end of the Edo period, the production methods for *iro-e kinran-de*-Satsuma were taken over from the Tateno kiln.

The Genryûin kiln, set up in Chôsa in 1663, was in existence until 1746 as a folk kiln. A typical glaze was the now-rare *jakatsu-yû* ("lizard" glaze)—a white, pastelike, rice-straw ash glaze covered with a black glaze that cracked during firing to resemble the scales of a reptile.

The Hirasa kiln dates back to 1766, when it was privately founded in Hirasa *sarayama*. With the assistance of Arita potters, first *hakuji* then *sometsuke* porcelain was produced; after 1786, *iro-e* ware with overglaze enamels was added. Developed in 1865, the so-called tortoise-shell glaze, *betsuko-yû*, with its yellow and brown glaze spots on a black glaze, is renowned. After several new kilns were set up during the Meiji period, the last Hirasa kiln closed down in 1941.

The zenith of the richly decorated *shiromon* in the Meiji period was stimulated by the export boom following the World's Fairs. By the end of the nineteenth century, *shiro*-Satsuma was so popular that clay from Kyûshû was made into Satsuma-style pots in Awata, near Kyôto, in manufactories such as Kinkôzan Sôbei VII, which employed more than 1000 people. Export ware produced around the turn of the century in Satsuma was generally considered to be of high quality, but the onset of mass production with forms and brushwork of inferior quality, together with the worldwide economic crisis, led to the collapse of the markets. In the twentieth century, some leading personalities from the old families in the world of ceramics, such as the ceramists

Chin Jukan XII–XIV in Miyama, successfully revived the old traditions. The successors of the Shimazu clan in Kagoshima set up production in 1983 to reproduce *shiromon* from the Edo period using traditional craft techniques.

Kuro and *shiro*-Satsuma are now produced in 28 workshops within the city limits of Kagoshima; the traditions of the old pottery town of Naeshirogawa have been preserved in 13 kilns in Higashi-Ichiki Miyama. On the Satsuma peninsula, another 67 potters are also still working, although stoneware in various styles can be found alongside the traditional Satsuma ware.

Kuromon ware is either thrown or press molded; larger objects are often hand built using the *himozukuri* technique; small vessels such as sake cups are pinched with the thumb from a ball of clay. The black glaze consists of powdered stone with an iron oxide content of up to 20 percent, mixed with domestic ash. The glaze firing takes place at 2192°F–2282°F (1200°C–1250°C). A typical product is the *kuro-choka* used to warm diluted *shôchû* (see photo 30).

Shiro-Satsuma is either thrown or slip cast. Vases and especially incense burners (*kôro*) have precisely executed perforations (*sukashibori*), which are incised into the leather-hard clay after the pattern of the openwork decoration is drawn on the surface. The ware is fired in oxidation for more than 12 hours to 2246°F–2300°F (1230°–1260°C). During cooling, the fine crackle characteristic of *shiro*-Satsuma develops. Whereas in mass production the design is applied with stamps and stencils, the overglaze decoration is carefully applied by hand on individually produced vessels (see photo 31). The overglaze firing takes six hours at temperatures of 1328°F–1472°F (720°C–800°C). Gold pigments are then fired to 1112°F–1256°F (600°C–680°C).

Ryûmonji 龍門司 (3)

The present-day Ryûmonji kiln, located north of Kajiki in Koyamada (Kagoshima Prefecture), dates back to a Satsuma kiln founded around 1598 by Korean potters in Chôsa, near Aira (see Satsuma, 2, on page 37).

Photo 30. **Satsuma-*yaki*. Shimazu Hisayoshi, pourer for warming *shôchû* (*kuro-choka*), with *sake* cups (*choko*), 1985. Pourer: 3 x 5¾ x 5¼ inches (7.4 x 14.5 x 13.3 cm). Sake cup: 1 x 2¼ inches (2.8 x 5.4 cm). *Kuro*-Satsuma, stoneware, iron glaze.**

Photo 31.   Satsuma-*yaki*. Katsuragi Takeshi, incense burner (*shiro-satsuma kôro*), 2002. 6 x 6½ inches
(15 x 16.4 cm). *Shiro*-Satsuma, stoneware, overglaze enamels, gold embellishment (*iro-e kinran-de*).

After the kiln had been relocated several times, in 1688 Yamamoto Wan'emon built the Yamamoto-*gama* in Koyamada, which is considered to be the origin of Ryûmonji-*yaki*, as the glazed stone-ware produced there was then termed. After being moved one more time within the town in 1718, the kiln remained in the same place until its reconstruction in 1955 in the same location. The development of an individual ceramics style began with Kawahara Hôko, who had become acquainted with several different production methods during his travels to Arita, Kyôto, and Seto, which he had undertaken after his apprenticeship at the Tateno-gama (see Satsuma, 2). He further developed these methods for the production of domestic tableware after taking over the Ryûmonji kiln around 1780. The Ryûmonji-*gama* remained in the hands of the Kawahara family until it was transformed into a cooperative (*Ryûmonji-yaki kogyô-kumiai*) after the Second World War. Since 1975, this cooperative has been run by Kawahara Shirô (born in 1949) and two partners.

In the workshop, which was set up close to the ruins of the *renbôshiki-noborigama* that was abandoned in 1955, all phases of the production process are undertaken. Clay and glaze materials come from the immediate vicinity and are generally prepared by hand. The main products are vases, tea bowls, teacups, *sake* sets, and shallow bowls in various sizes. Three distinct types of glaze that date back to Kawahara Hôko are in use: first, as a standard glaze, a black glaze (*kuro-mono*, black ware) made from iron oxide and domestic ash, with a blue-green, running copper glaze (*sei-yû tamanagashi*, see photo 32).

Second, *sansai* glaze in white, green, and brown, with dripped patterns in *ame* and *ryoku* glaze are applied over a white slip that covers the dark clay body of the pot. Many *sansai* objects are additionally decorated with chatter marks (*tobigan'na*). Third, *samehada* glaze, which is termed "shark-skin" glaze in accordance with its appearance, is used on tea bowls or vases. This glaze, which is rare in Japan, develops during firing when the glaze cracks open; the surface of the pot is covered with beige-brown bumps (see photo 33). The pots are fired in oxidation to approximately 2246°F (1230°C) in a five-chamber *noborigama* or in a gas kiln.

Isshôchi 一勝地 (4)

In the mountains south of Kumamoto, in Isshôchi, near Kuma (Kumamoto Prefecture), sits the pottery of Narita Katsuto. As a forerunner of the present-day workshop, the Shiromoto-*gama* was constructed in 1772 by Migita Denpachi as a feudal kiln (*goyôgama*) of the Sagara clan, in the castle district of Hitoyoshi. Besides running the pottery, Denpachi was also a *samurai* who served as a border guard—a dual function that the family fulfilled through seven generations up to the end of the feudal period. After finding a suitable deposit of *tôseki* in Isshôchi, Denpachi developed a fine semi-porcelain (*hanjiki*), with the assistance of potters from the Hizen, Ryûmonji, and Satsuma kilns. The glazes were predominantly a black iron glaze, and a wood ash and green copper glaze; slip brushing (*hakeme*) and dripping (*nagashigake*) were also used as decoration.

The kiln flourished until Migita Chûgo in the eighth generation, as a direct descendent of Denpachi, remained without offspring in the years after the Meiji Restoration. It was only in 1937 that the kiln was reopened by Chûgo's nephew, with the purpose of preserving the traditional Isshôchi-*yaki*. In 1957, Narita Katsuto, who had worked for more than 20 years in the Shôdai and Iwami workshops, took over the kiln in the tenth generation. The wares produced by the master of that period—tea ware, *sake* sets, bowls, vases, and tableware—are characteristically thin walled. The clay body, which is mixed from equal parts clay and *tôseki*, fires reddish in color. Additional characteristics of Isshôchi ware are white to blue-white spots and flowing rice-straw ash glaze over a brown-black glaze with a hint of green. This brown-black glaze consists of iron-rich powdered stone, feldspar, and wood ash (see photo 34). Individual pieces are fired with pine in the *noborigama*; serially produced ware is fired in an electric kiln. The extreme firing temperature of 2642°F (1450°C) is worth mentioning, as this is otherwise used only for Iga-*yaki* (37) or by studio potters to achieve special effects.

Photo 32. Ryûmonji-*yaki*. Kawahara Shirô, large *kuromono* bowl (*kuromono sei-yû tamanagashi ôbachi*),
2002. 3 x 12 inches (8 x 30.2 cm). Stoneware, flowing green copper glaze on black iron glaze.

Photo 33. Ryûmonji-*yaki*. Kawahara Shirô, tea bowl (*chawan*), 1985. 3¼ x 4½ inches (8.1 x 11.7 cm). Stoneware, *samehada-gusuri* (shark-skin glaze).

Photo 34. Isshôchi-*yaki*. Narita Katsuto, pourer (*kanbin*) for warming *shôchû*, with five small cups (*hai*),
1999. Pourer: 5 x 4¾ x 4½ inches (12.7 x 12.4 x 12 cm). Cup: 1¼ x 1½ inches (3 x 3.8 cm).
Semiporcelain (*hanjiki*), iron glaze and rice-straw ash glaze.

Kôda 高田 (5)

Kôda ware—a glazed stoneware produced in the area around the town of Yatsushiro, in the south of Kumamoto Prefecture—is also referred to as Yatsushiro- or Hirayama-*yaki*. When Tadatoshi, the son of Lord Hosokawa Tadaoki from Buzen (now a part of Oita Prefecture), was designated successor to the feudal lord of Higo (now Kumamoto Prefecture) in 1632, Korean potters from Agano (15) accompanied him. Two of the potters are said to have set up the Shôdai kiln (6), while Chon Hae (or Sonkai), who later bore the Japanese name of Agano Kizô, produced *chadôgu* (tea utensils) with two of his sons, first in the Naraki-*gama*, then from 1658 in the Hirayama-*gama* near Yatsushiro. Because the latter kiln was designated a *goyôgama* (feudal kiln) in 1669, the members of the Agano family were paid by the *han* administration, received the family name, and were entitled to bear swords—privileges the Shôdai potters also enjoyed.

Of the three lines of the Agano family, only the main line was able to maintain its workshop after the Meiji Restoration; the current master of the Agano Saisuke-*gama* is Agano Saisuke, in the eleventh generation. In addition, there are four other workshops in the Yatsushiro region, including the kiln of Sakai Masae and the Denshichi-*gama* of Aoki Osamu.

Kôda-*yaki*, which bears a great similarity to Korean Kôrai ware, was made for court. The tea ware from the time of the Naraki-*gama*, with iron and wood-ash glazes on a gray-brown firing clay, bears slip brushing (*hakeme*) and slip inlay designs (*zôgan*). The so-called *hakudo-zôgan* work with white clay predominates. During the later phase of production of the Hirayama-*gama*, domestic tableware, as well as *chadôgu*, was produced. There were also *zôgan* items with celadon glazes (*seiji-zôgan*), and increasingly reddish or dark-colored clays were used for the *zôgan* inlay. The main products of the Kôda kilns today are tea ware, *sake* sets, and vases with delicate *hakudo-zôgan* celadons. In contrast to the more intense greens of the Kôrai wares, the white of the clay inlay in Kôda-*yaki* contrasts clearly with the blue-gray of the celadon glazes (see photo 35).

Shôdai 小代 (6)

There is no reliable evidence about the origins of Shôdai-*yaki*, at the foot of Mount Shôdai, near Arao (Kumamoto Prefecture). When Hosokawa Tadatoshi was designated feudal lord of Higo (now in Kumamoto Prefecture) in 1632, he is said to have brought with him Korean potters from the pottery village of Agano (15) in Buzen, who had been settled there after Toyotomi Hideyoshi's Korean campaigns. Two of these potters, who were later permitted to bear the family names of Hin'nokôji and Katsuragi, fired glazed stoneware—Higo-*yaki*, as Shôdai ware was known until the middle of the eighteenth century—in their shared kiln. In 1769, the Kameyaki kiln was enlarged into a six-chamber *noborigama*. Tea utensils for court use and domestic tableware were both produced using red-brown firing clay with an iron glaze (*tetsu-yû*), and milky-white rice-straw and bamboo-ash glazes (*hakudaku-yû*); these wares at first resembled early Agano-*yaki*. To cover the increasing demand for pots among the rural populace, the *han* administration ordered the construction of three more kilns between 1831 and 1848, but the upheavals at the end of the nineteenth century led to the closure of all the Shôdai workshops until 1917.

Inspired by the *mingei* movement, Fukuda Hôsui (1928–1998), a distant relative of the Kameyaki-*gama* families and an enthusiastic collector of Shôdai ware, endeavored to initiate production. After much effort, especially with regard to authentic glazes, he set up his Mizuho-*gama* on the old site in 1973. Today, eight workshops near Mount Shôdai, between Arao and Nankan, and one workshop in Kumamoto are now producing Shôdai-*yaki* in the old style. The coarse, iron-rich clay is used to make domestic tableware and ceramics for the tea ceremony and *ikebana*; electric or kick wheels are used for throwing. For larger objects, the Korean *tataki* technique is often used. The pots are mainly dipped in rice-straw or rice-husk glazes, although other application techniques, such as *uchigake* (splashed glaze) or *nagashigake* (dripped glaze) are used as well. When reduction fired to about 2372°F (1300°C), the minerals in the ash react with

Photo 35. Kôda-*yaki*. Aoki Osamu, tea caddy (*seiji hakudo-zôgan chaire*) with bone lid and brocade pouch
(*shifuku*), 1985. 3 x 2 inches (7.5 x 5.2 cm). Stoneware, white clay inlay, celadon glaze (*seiji-zôgan*).

the iron in the clay to produce the soft shades of blue, white, and yellow typical of Shôdai-*yaki* (see photo 36).

Unzen 雲仙 (7)

Twelve hundred and fifty years ago, Nihonsan, a religious center in Unzen, in the Unzen Mountains (Shimabara Peninsula, Nagasaki Prefecture), disseminated Buddhism in Kyûshû. Nihonsan, the significance of which at that time was comparable to that of Kôyasan near Ôsaka today, developed into a cultural center for the production of its own ceramics, initially exclusively for ritual purposes but later for everyday use. Unzen-*yaki* remained a local product, however, and few pieces became commercially available.

In the twentieth century, interest in Unzen-*yaki* revived. In the Obama-*gama*, which was constructed by Honda Shinki in the Taishô period (1912–1926) and was initially used for the production of roofing tiles, Shigeta Hyakkansai from Tôkyô fired tea bowls and vessels for flowers between 1926 and 1953. The founder of modern Unzen-*yaki* is considered to be Ishikawa Heiji (known by the name of Seihô)—a photographer who built his first kiln in Unzen in 1960, then constructed a *noborigama* in 1977. In 1993, after Seihô's death, his daughter Hami and her husband Akira took over the kiln.

The products of the Ishikawa family are tea utensils and vases. Along with celadons and expressive *yakishime* work, their *tenmoku* tea bowls are noteworthy for their classic forms and their perfect *yuteki*- (oil-spot) *tenmoku* glaze (see photo 37).

Arita 有田 (8)

The porcelain produced in Arita (Saga Prefecture), in northwest Kyûshû, is referred to as Arita-*yaki*. Under the patronage of the Nabeshima clan, Arita developed into the largest center for porcelain in Japan until it was overtaken by Seto (41) in the mid-nineteenth century. In the Edo period, it was Imari, about 8 miles (13 km) north of Arita, that was the shipping port for porcelain from Arita and the rest of the Hizen region; Hizen ceramics from the Edo period are known as Imari ware elsewhere in Japan and especially in Europe. After the construction of a railway, Arita ware was shipped directly from Arita itself beginning in 1897, so that in the twentieth century, Arita-*yaki* gradually became the term established in Japan for porcelain made in Arita, whereas Imari-*yaki* (9) was reserved for ceramics made in Imari itself, and especially in neighboring Ôkawachi.

Legend has it that the production of porcelain in Arita dates back to the Korean potter Ri Sanpei, who, along with approximately 800 other potters, had been brought to the domain of Saga, in Hizen, by Lord Nabeshima Naoshige, after Toyotomi Hideyoshi's Korean campaigns. These potters initially produced Korean-style glazed stoneware around Karatsu and Takeo, and in the Arita region, until Ri Sanpei found *tôseki* rich in kaolin and feldspar in Izumiyama near Arita. In 1616, he began producing porcelain in Tengudani in Shirawaka. According to archaeological studies in the Tengudani region and newly discovered documents in the archives of the Nabeshima clan, the commencement of porcelain production can be dated as early as 1605–1610.

The Arita potters' village, Arita *sarayama*, consisted of two districts under Nabeshima administration: Sotoyama, with the stoneware kilns; and, situated to the east, Uchiyama with the Tengudani kilns and the Izumiyama *tôseki* quarry for the production of porcelain. From the outset, porcelain was made with cobalt underglaze brushwork (*sometsuke*). The first, relatively simple products reveal a similarity to Korean wares from the middle Yi dynasty (1392–1910); from 1630 on, Arita porcelain achieved the quality of Chinese blue-and-white ware and was strongly influenced by stylistic elements from the Chinese Ming dynasty (1368–1644). During this first phase of Arita-*yaki*, which is known as *shoki*-Imari (early Imari) and which lasted until 1643, the Uchiyama porcelain kilns mainly produced domestic tableware, as well as *sometsuke* ware, celadons (*seiji*), and celadons with blue brushwork. They also made porcelain with *sabi-yû*, a brownish iron glaze, and *ruri-yû*, a cobalt glaze the color of lapis lazuli.

**Photo 36.   Shôdai-*yaki*. Fukuda Hôsui, large plate (*warabai-yû uchigake ôzara*), 1998. 1¾ x 12¾ inches
(4.5 x 32.5 cm). Stoneware, rice-straw ash glaze, dipped, with splashed glaze.**

Photo 37. Unzen-*yaki*. Ishikawa Seihô, *tenmoku* tea bowl (*yuteki-tenmoku chawan*), 1992. 2½ x 4¾ inches (6.7 x 12 cm). Stoneware, *yuteki-* (oilspot) *tenmoku* glaze.

Typical techniques from the Ming dynasty (and still in use in Arita today), such as sprayed cobalt (*fukizumi*) and the so-called white celadon (*seihakuji*), were already found in *shoki*-Imari. Demand for *shoki*-Imari grew as its quality improved, so the Sotoyama kilns switched production from stoneware to porcelain. The Nabeshima feudal lords were not devotees of the tea ceremony—an exception among the aristocrats of this period. They fostered the production of porcelain for economic reasons and established regulations to improve quality and maintain the secrecy of production methods. The Nabeshima administration also supervised the distribution channels of the goods: the Japanese domestic market was supplied via Imari, and trade with China and Southeast Asia was first carried out via the port of Hirado. After Japan's seclusion from the outside world in 1639, it continued from Imari exclusively via Dejima, in Nagasaki harbor.

An important development in the history of Japanese porcelain was the adoption of polychrome overglaze painting from China, which Sakaida Kizaemon, later known as Kakiemon I, mastered between 1643 and 1647. This technique involved the painting of polychrome enamels on the high-fired glazed pot, which was fired again at a lower temperature. This technique of overglaze painting (*uwa-e* or *uwa-etsuke*), generally referred to as *iro-e* (colored painting), was referred to in Arita as *aka-e* (red painting), which is the origin of the widespread Western designation for this technique. Because of its similarity to the sumptuous textiles of the period, the term *nishiki-de* (brocade) was also in use. Three separate styles of *aka-e* can be distinguished: *ko*-Imari, Kakiemon, and *iro*-Nabeshima.

Ko-Imari ware was decorated in either three colors (*sansai*) or five colors (*gosai*)—red, green, yellow, blue, and manganese purple. Around 1658, the method of applying gold and silver was developed, from which Imari *kinran-de* (brocade ware with gold design) evolved. The outlines of *aka-e* designs were frequently drawn in cobalt underglaze (*some-nishiki-de*). The rich style of decoration covering the body of the pot was initially strongly influenced by the Chinese *fuyô-de* style of the late Ming dynasty (late sixteenth to

early seventeenth centuries). The central medallions surrounded by symmetrically arranged areas of pattern are typical of plates. Later, the *aka-e* painters increasingly adopted Japanese decorative elements. Production of *ko*-Imari was strictly controlled by the Nabeshima administration: in 1672, 150 workshops were licensed for production in and around Arita, with specialists responsible for the individual phases of production. Cobalt underglaze painting was executed in the immediate vicinity of the kiln, whereas overglaze painting was restricted to 11 families collected together in Uchiyama, in *aka-e machi* (town of red painting). The use of pattern books for designs was compulsory.

Kakiemon ware was fired in Nangawara-yama, in southern Sotoyama, by Sakaida Kakiemon I and his family. Restrained, elegant brushwork in the predominant iron red (*kaki*, persimmon) on a milky white background (*nigoshi-de*) was characteristic, with possible additions of a light blue, various greens and yellows, brown, and grayish purple. The designs, including flowers and birds, and clouds and dragons, were arranged asymmetrically around areas that were left white. The specialists employed for this painted decoration are said to have been trained *yamato-e* painters. Kakiemon ware was a model for the European Meissen porcelain of the early eighteenth century.

Iro-Nabeshima ware was produced in feudal kilns (*hanyô*) for the exclusive use of the Nabeshima clan and as presentation ware, under the strictest of security measures and the highest-quality standards. It is unclear whether the first two kilns set up in Arita—in Iwayagawachi, Uchiyama, in 1628, and in Nangawara-yama in the immediate vicinity of the Kakiemon workshop around 1660—already had the official status of *hanyô* of the Nabeshima clan. They finally settled in Ôkawachi, near Imari, and were recognized as feudal kilns in 1675. Whereas blue-and-white porcelain was made in Arita, the focus in Ôkawachi was on polychrome *iro*-Nabeshima and celadons (see Imari, 9, on page 60).

There were two reasons for the huge success of Arita porcelain in the second half of the seventeenth century: one was the growing demand of the newly affluent urban populace for porcelain eating and drinking utensils; but the decisive reason was the demand for exports to Southeast Asia and Europe. In China, the production of porcelain came to an almost complete standstill for almost 40 years beginning in 1644, because of the turmoil verging on civil war during the transition from the Ming to the Qing dynasty. The Dutch East India Company (Vereenigde Oostindische Compagnie, or VOC), which had exported large quantities of Chinese porcelain, filled this gap with Japanese ware. After two relatively small shipments in 1650 and 1651, the VOC officially decided in 1656 to order Imari porcelain for export to Southeast Asia and Europe. In 1659, as many as 33,910 pieces of blue-and-white porcelain were exported. *Ko-Imari* ware followed in the early 1660s, Kakiemon ware was preferred from 1670 to 1690, and in 1697, exports of large objects in superb Imari *kinran-de* also began.

In the range of goods being produced in Arita, there was a clear distinction between those for export—large articles and sumptuous decorations following the VOC's design collection—and the more restrained objects for the domestic market and for select-quality presentation ware for the family of the feudal lord, *kenjô*-Imari. Exports reached their zenith at the turn of the century; a marked decline began in 1730, and the last VOC order was executed in 1759. The reasons for this were the resumption of production in the Jingdezhen kilns in China, with lower prices and new designs (famille rose and famille verte), as well as the restrictive trade policy of the Tokugawa shogunate and the start of porcelain production in a number of European manufactories.

The loss of export markets had no consequences for the Japanese porcelain industry, because domestic demand for Arita tableware was so heavy that the Nabeshima administration had to permit an expansion of production in 1770. The consequence of this mass production at the end of the eighteenth and in the early nineteenth centuries was a deterioration of quality, although demand continued to rise. The forced opening of Japan in 1854 weakened the monopoly of the Nabeshima *han*, and wholesalers forged their own links for trade in Japan and overseas. Exports to the West picked up

again after 1867, when Arita ware was presented at the World's Fair. Large plates with diameters of 19¾ to 31½ inches (50 to 80 cm), which were increasingly popular as serving platters from the mid-nineteenth century on, appeared ever more frequently in the West as export ware (see photo 38). At the same time, the Meiji administration was promoting the modernization of porcelain production by Western experts, such as the German chemist Gottfried Wagner (1831–1892), who introduced modern firing techniques and new overglaze colors in Arita in 1870.

From the Meiji period to the present, many technical innovations have been introduced in porcelain production. Since the early eighteenth century, the basic raw material for Arita-*yaki* has been Amakusa-*tôseki* from Kumamoto Prefecture. It is preferred to Izumiyama-*tôseki* from Arita because of its greater purity. Crushing the porcelain stone, slaking with water, filtering, and pressing are now done by machines; forming is executed on the wheel or in molds, or is fully automatic. The ware is smoothed and dried before the bisque firing of 1562°F–1742°F (850°C–950°C). In the succeeding underglaze decoration, the fine outlines of the designs, as well as areas of blue, are applied with a brush, using *gosu* or, today, industrially prepared cobalt oxide; printing techniques are used in industrial mass production. The transparent glaze traditionally made with the ash of the *isu* tree (*distylium racemosum*) now contains limestone and is applied by dipping, pouring, or spraying. Among traditional potters, the main firing of 2336°F–2372°F (1280°C–1300°C) takes place in a wood-fired *noborigama* using saggars or in a gas kiln, whereas industrial mass-produced ware is fired in gas tunnel kilns. For white porcelain, celadons, *sometsuke*, and *ruri* porcelain, the glaze firing is the last phase of production. Overglaze enamels are applied as further decoration to *aka-e* ware, which is fired to lower temperatures of 1400°F–1562°F (760°C–850°C) in muffle kilns. If gold is applied, an additional firing to 1112°F–1292°F (600°C–700°C) is necessary.

About one-third of contemporary porcelain production in the more than 150 workshops in Arita is industrial porcelain, and two-thirds is tableware and high-grade decorative wares.

Photo 38. Arita-*yaki*. Large plate (*ôzara*), ca. 1880. 3½ x 24 inches (9 x 61 cm). Porcelain, Imari-*kinran-de*, *sometsuke* medallion with "Three Friends of the Winter" design (pine, bamboo, plum, *shô chiku bai*). Export ware.

Blue-and-white porcelain for everyday use is usually mass produced, but is of consistently high quality and attractive design. A number of porcelain painters have specialized in cobalt underglaze painting, with Chinese landscapes as the preferred design. A typical example is the *sometsuke* fresh-water jar (see photo 39) shaped by Hirosawa Masujirô (born in 1943) and painted by Iwanaga Shikô (born in 1944). Alongside blue-and-white ware, *ko*-Imari, Kakiemon ware, *iro*-Nabeshima, celadons, and white porcelain (*hakuji*) are produced, either in traditional workshops or long-established manufactories. Potters are increasingly turning their attention to handcrafted and hand-painted wares, and the number of studio potters in the Arita region is on the increase.

The award-winning companies of Kôransha and Fukagawa should be mentioned in a discussion of production tableware. Kôransha was set up 350 years ago by Fukagawa Eizaemon and privatized in 1870 after the Meiji Restoration. Elements of *ko*-Imari, Kakiemon, and *iro*-Nabeshima have been combined to form an unmistakable style. The Fukagawa Seiji manufactory, set up in 1894 by a descendant of Fukagawa Eizaemon, initially for the production of export ware, also produces tableware of high quality. Another manufactory worthy of mention is the 250-year-old Gen'emon kiln, with its high-quality tableware in the tradition of *shoki*-Imari.

The Kakiemon and Nabeshima traditions are being continued by the descendants of the old families. The Kakiemon workshop continues the tradition of polychrome overglaze painting in Kakiemon style (see photo 40). For his own work,

which he does not sign, Sakaida Kakiemon XIV (born in 1934) uses the milky white *nigoshi-de* glaze rediscovered by his grandfather and father. In 2001, Kakiemon XIV was designated *ningen kokuhô* (Living National Treasure).

The work of the Imaizumi family, who are descended from the porcelain painters of the *iro*-Nabeshima, exemplifies the classic elements of Nabeshima porcelain. The individual masters, however, have their own styles of decoration in their personal work based on *iro*-Nabeshima. Imaizumi Imaemon XIII (1926–2001), *ningen kokuhô* since 1989, transferred the *fukizumi* cobalt spraying technique to uranium compounds: on this background, which is termed *usuzumi* and is reminiscent of sprayed ink, stylized floral designs are painted (see photo 41). His younger son, Masato (born in 1962), has run the workshop since 2002 as Imaizumi Imaemon XIV. He fuses traditional *iro*-Nabeshima porcelain techniques with modern patterns in his trademark snowflake technique (*sekka sumihajiki*)—an ink technique on underglaze blue-and-white slip (see photo 42).

Artists of the younger generation, such as Obata Yûji (born in 1961; see photo 43), have succeeded in developing their own *aka-e* styles, which integrate traditional elements. Individual pieces in white or a light, bluish green porcelain (*hakuji* and *seihakuji*), which come to life through the play of light on the skillfully executed forms (see photo 198), have become increasingly important in recent years. Inoue Manji (born in 1929) is the master of this style; he was designated *ningen kokuhô* in 1995 for his flawlessly thrown *hakuji* work (see photo 44).

Photo 39.   Arita-*yaki*. Hirosawa Masujirô, painting by Iwanaga Shikô, fresh-water jar (*sometsuke-sansui mizusashi*), 2003. 8¾ x 6½ inches (22.3 x 16.4 cm). Porcelain, cobalt blue underglaze painting.

Photo 40. Arita-*yaki*. Workshop of Sakaida Kakiemon XIV (Living National Treasure), bottle vase (*hanabin*), 2001. 9¼ x 4¼ inches (23.3 x 11 cm). *Aka-e*-porcelain, flower and bird designs.

Photo 41.   **Arita-*yaki*. Imaizumi Imaemon XIII (Living National Treasure), spherical vase (*iro-e usuzumi sôka-mon kabin*), ca. 2000. 5½ x 5 inches (14 x 12.7 cm). Porcelain, *iro*-Nabeshima, blossom design on "sprayed ink" background.**

Photo 42. Arita-*yaki*. Imaizumi Imaemon XIV, lidded bowl (*sekka sumihajiki futamono*), 2005. 3 x 3¾ inches (7.4 x 9.4 cm). Porcelain, chintz flower design in snowflake technique, *iro*-Nabeshima.

Photo 43. Arita-*yaki*. Obata Yûji, square serving dish with cherry blossom design (*shôenji shidare sakura-mon kakemorizara*), 2002. 1 x 8¼ x 8¼ inches (2.4 x 22 x 22 cm). *Aka-e* porcelain.

Photo 44.   Arita-*yaki*. Inoue Manji (Living National Treasure), one-flower, gourd-shaped vase (*hakuji ichirinza*), pre-2000. 9¼ x 3¾ inches (23.5 x 9.5 cm). White porcelain (*hakuji*).

Imari 伊万里 (Ôkawachi 大川内) (9)

Imari porcelain is the customary term for wares from the Hizen region that were traded via the port of Imari (Saga Prefecture) during the Edo period (see Arita, 8, on page 47). In the town of Imari itself, the feudal lords of Nabeshima, who ruled a great part of Hizen province, were not prepared to give permission for the construction of a porcelain kiln, as they feared losing the secrets of the production process in the lively seaport. But Ôkawachi—a steep, easily overlooked valley near Imari—was considered an ideal location for the construction of the new Nabeshima *hanyô* when in 1675 it had to be moved for the third time for security reasons (see Arita, 8).

The Nabeshima ware, produced in the potters' district of Ôkawachi (Ôkawachi-yama), is still considered the best porcelain in Japan, with its fine, smooth body and its slightly greenish, pore-free glaze. It was intended as presentation ware and for the exclusive use of the ruling family. It was not permitted to be bought or sold; consequently, it was unknown in the West until the end of the nineteenth century.

After the introduction of polychrome overglaze painting by Soeda Kichizaemon on Ôkiwachi-yama, around 1675, *iro*-Nabeshima was produced with overglaze enamels in a bright iron red, a pale translucent yellow, a soft green, and a lilac purple. A few pieces are turquoise blue or black—without gold or silver—with the colors applied, for the most part, over outlines executed in underglaze blue (*some-nishiki-de*). Painting of Nabeshima ware, at least in part, is said to have been carried out in Arita by the Imaizumi family in *aka-e machi*. Most of the items are shallow bowls, measuring 4, 6, 7¾, or 11¾ inches (10, 15, 20, or 30 cm) in diameter, with forms and decoration clearly stipulated. In their choice of subject matter, the distinctly asymmetrical compositions, often in combination with textile patterns, frequently refer symbolically to the occasion of the presentation. On the undersides of the bowls, stylized representations of blossoms, twigs, and picture scrolls, for instance, are often found. On the characteristic raised footring (*kôdai*), there is often the typical "comb" design (see photo 46a).

Besides *iro*-Nabeshima, large quantities of celadons (Nabeshima-*seiji*) were produced, as were celadons with cobalt underglaze painting, known as *ruri*-Nabeshima (lapis-lazuli Nabeshima) and *ai*-Nabeshima (indigo Nabeshima), corresponding to the tonal value of the color. Annual production was limited to approximately 5000 pieces; less than 10 percent of any given firing was considered of suitably high quality. The remainder had to be destroyed.

The collapse of the feudal system as a result of the Meiji Restoration led to the creation of private enterprises in Ôkawachi. There are now 30 workshops, in which mainly *iro*-Nabeshima and celadons are produced. Even mass-produced goods such as the porcelain from the Hataman manufactory (founded in 1926), with its thin walls and high-quality painting, meet a very high standard (see photo 45). From the early days of Nabeshima-*yaki*, two families have descended to today: the Imaizumi family in Arita (see Arita, 8, on page 47) and the Ichikawa family in Ôkawachi. Ichikawa Kôzan XVIII (1907–1982) played a leading role in reviving and preserving the old Nabeshima tradition after the Second World War. His son Kôjo (born in 1956 and appointed as Kôzan XIX in 1993) makes *iro*-Nabeshima (see photo 46) and the typical, intense green Nabeshima celadons (see photo 47) in the old *hanyô*. Kôzan does not, however, see it as his task to develop the Nabeshima tradition any further, but rather to reproduce historical models as faithfully as possible in order to make the former beauty of this porcelain accessible to present-day users.

Hasami 波佐見 (10)

The porcelain made in the area of the former Ômura domain (now part of Nagasaki Prefecture), around the town of Hasami, especially blue-and-white ware and celadon, is termed Hasami-*yaki*. Together with Arita, Mikawachi, and Ôkawachi, Hasami was part of the greatest porcelain center of the Edo period.

As early as 1580, there had been a kiln for glazed stoneware, and in 1599, the Korean potter

Photo 45. Imari-*yaki*. Hataishi Shinji, the Hataman company, tea set with *tachibana* (type of orange) fruits (*some-nishiki tachibana-mon chaki*), 2001. Side-handled small teapot (*kyûsu*): 3 x 5½ x 4 inches (7.7 x 14.2 x 9.9 cm). Water cooler (*yuzamashi*): 2 x 3¾ inches (5.1 x 9.7 cm). Teacups (*sencha chawan*): 1½ x 2½ inches (4 x 6.5 cm). Porcelain, *iro*-Nabeshima, *some-nishiki-de* technique.

Photo 46. Imari-*yaki*. Ichikawa Kôzan XIX, shallow bowl with Kerria Rose design (*iro-e iwa ni yamabuki zu gosunzara*), 2000. 1¾ x 6½ inches (4.3 x 16.2 cm). Porcelain, *iro*-Nabeshima.

Photo 46a. Back view of bowl, with "comb" design on the typical footring (*kôdai*)

**Photo 47.   Imari-*yaki*. Ichikawa Kôzan XIX, bowl for sweets (Nabeshima-*seiji kashibachi*) with orchid relief
design, 2001. 2¼ x 8½ inches (5.8 x 21.9 cm). Porcelain with celadon glaze, Nabeshima-*seiji*.**

Ri Yûkei was instructed by Lord Yoshiaki from Ômura *han* to construct the 180-foot (55 m) Hatanohara-*yô*, a 24-chamber *noborigama*. Around 1630, the kiln was converted from stoneware to porcelain, with cobalt underglaze painting (*sometsuke*), as well as celadon (*seiji*). Over the next 20 years, the emphasis was on the production of *seiji*. The celadons from Hasami were considered to be the best at that time. Making export ware in the Hizen region for the VOC (see Arita, 8, on page 47), starting in 1650, led to the construction of new kilns; in Hasami, the *han* administration had three *sarayama* set up. Of the porcelains made there, by far the best known are the so-called Compura bottles for sake and soy sauce, which are widespread in Europe and Southeast Asia. These bottles come from the company COMPURA (from the Portuguese word for trader) and are simple, thick-walled vessels with inscriptions in Latin characters, such as "JAPANSCH ZOYA," in cobalt blue underglaze.

After the end of the export boom for simple blue-and-white ware around 1690, Hasami increasingly supplied the domestic market with relatively low-priced *sometsuke* domestic wares. The popular *kurawanka* tableware, with its simple flower or lattice pattern, was sold all over Japan. Its name came from the dialect of traveling tradespeople from Ôsaka, who sold food in this ware; *kurawan-ka* means "eat up." In time, the porcelain made from Amakusa-*tôseki* became whiter and thinner walled, and the brushwork more skillful. For the mass production of this ware, the *han* administration built two of the largest *noborigama* in Nakaoyama, a district of Hasami, at the end of the Edo period; the ruins of the 525-foot (160 m) Nakao-Uwa-*gama* are still in existence.

Since the Meiji Restoration, Hasami has managed to consolidate its position in the market by continual modernization of production methods. In mass production, the pots are formed mechanically or by slip casting; for *sometsuke* decoration with asbolite, various printing techniques have been developed. During the early twentieth century, coal—and later crude oil—was used for firing; today, gas-fired tunnel kilns are in operation. Just as in neighboring Arita, there are many small- to medium-sized enterprises, which, along with the large manufactories, have often specialized in individual stages of production. In addition, a number of small workshops maintain the old craft traditions with handmade and hand-painted pieces.

There are currently 130 workshops in the town, mainly involved in the production of blue-and-white ware for households and restaurants. Additionally, Hasami is known for its celadons with cobalt underglaze painting and delicate mesh-design ware (*âmime*) with cobalt decoration (see photo 48). Along with traditional forms, modern design can also be found, an achievement especially of Mori Masahiro (born in 1927), one of the major representatives of modern Japanese porcelain design. While he was head of the design office of Hakusan Tôki Co., Ltd. (1956–1978), and later working on his own, Mori combined contemporary serial production with traditional manual arts and crafts (see photo 49). Mori has received many national and international honors. More than 100 of his products have been distinguished in Japan for their outstanding design, and many, such as his famous soy sauce cruet that has been in production since 1958 (see photo 50), for their timeless design.

Photo 48. Hasami-*yaki*. Incense burner (*kôro*), 1999. 2¼ x 3 inches (5.6 x 8 cm). Porcelain, mesh design
(*âmime*), cobalt underglaze painting (*sometsuke*), fired in the Kinpô-*gama*.

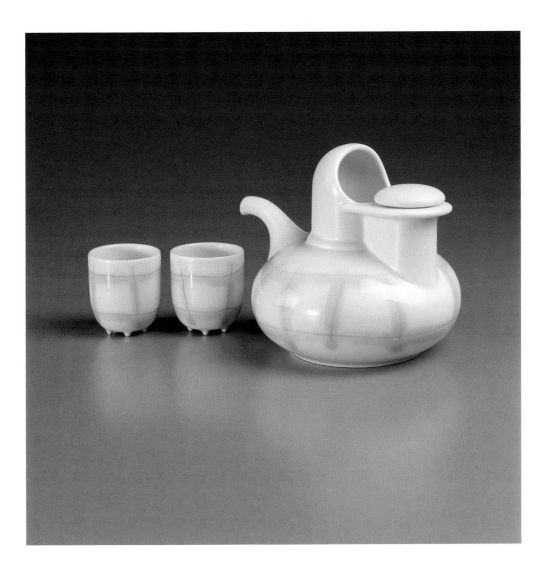

Photo 49.   Hasami-yaki. Mori Masahiro design, the Hakusan company, *sake* cooler set (*hiyazake shuki*), 1999. Pourer (*chûki*): 4½ x 6¼ x 5¼ inches (11.6 x 15.8 x 13.3 cm). *Sake* cup: 2 x 1 ¾ inches (5 x 4.5 cm). Slip-cast porcelain, *hori tôkusa* (engraved grass) underglaze design.

Photo 50. Hasami-*yaki*. Mori Masahiro design, the Hakusan company, soy-sauce cruet "G-type" 1958 (*shôyusashi*), 1999. 2¾ x 3 x 2¼ inches (7.2 x 7.7 x 5.6 cm). Slip-cast porcelain, *tenmoku* glaze.

Mikawachi 三川内 (11)

During the Edo period, the ceramics fostered by the Hirado clan were named after the family residence, the island of Hirado, to the northwest of Kyûshû. They are thus termed Hirado-*yaki*, the name under which they are best known in the West. The term Mikawachi-*yaki*, which only became widespread after the Meiji Restoration, refers to the later *hanyô* in Mikawachi, near Arita (Nagasaki Prefecture).

As in all of Hizen province, Hirado ware dates back to the settlement of Korean potters after Toyotomi Hideyoshi's Korean campaigns in 1592 and 1597. On the instruction of *daimyô* Matsuura Shigenobu, the potter Koseki produced *hakeme* and *kohiki* stoneware in the style of the Korean Yi dynasty. He was located in Nakano, on Hirado. After the discovery of more suitable clay deposits, the Korean potter Kosei and his son Imamura San'nojô constructed a kiln in Mikawachi, which, under the direction of San'nojô, was designated the official porcelain *hanyô* of the Hirado clan in 1637. To expand porcelain production, the *han* administration had the three *sarayama* built: Kihara, Enaga, and Mikawachi. High-quality Amakusa-*tôseki* mixed with Ajiro clay from Mitsudake made it possible to develop the characteristic milky white Hirado porcelain of the early eighteenth century.

Sometsuke porcelain with cobalt underglaze painting, as well as white ware (*hakuji*) and, more rarely, objects with a dark iron glaze, were first produced. In the heyday of Hirado ware (1751–1843), under the particular protection of the Hirado clan, methods and designs were increasingly refined. Mesh-design wares (*âmime*), *sukashibori* objects (perforated ware), and paper-thin Hirado-*etsuzan* (an eggshell porcelain), required the highest degree of skill. Many objects were decorated with complex applications of molded figures. The design typical of Mikawachi-*yaki* in its *sometsuke* porcelain was *karako-e*—the representation of children in Chinese clothing at play, in the style of the Kanô school of painting. These wares, which were known as *kenjô-karako-e*, were produced exclusively as presentation ware.

While some kilns in the Enaga *sarayama* mass produced *kurawanka* rice bowls (see Hasami, 10, on page 60), the porcelain produced in the feudal kilns of the three *sarayama* was not allowed to be sold on the Japanese market. Under financial pressure, however, the *han* administration tried to gain access to the export markets in Europe and Southeast Asia. From 1830 on, trade was carried out via the VOC, and a range of products, especially coffee cups, was adapted to the Western market. After the collapse of the feudal system in 1868, the Mikawachi kilns entered private hands. The presentation of Mikawachi porcelain at the World's Fairs around the turn of the century caused a sensation; much of the Hirado porcelain in Western collections is from the Meiji period.

In 1899, the founding of a school of design in Mikawachi guaranteed that a high standard of craft skills would be preserved, right up to the present day. Even today, only objects produced in large numbers are created with mechanical assistance. There are currently 36 workshops; many make traditional tea sets, *sake* sets, plates, bowls, vases, incense burners, and *saikumono* (ornamental objects). Masters in the fourteenth generation produce *sukashibori* items or Hirado-*etsuzan*. *Karako-e* blue-and-white ware is made by Nakazato Ichirô in the 17th generation (see photo 51). Young artists make use of traditional stylistic elements (see photo 52), or they execute new design ideas in porcelain or stoneware.

Photo 51. Mikawachi-*yaki*. Nakazato Ichirô, shallow bowl in style of presentation ware (*kenjô-karako-e moribachizara*), 2000. 2 x 10¼ inches (5.2 x 26 cm). *Sometsuke* porcelain, *karako-e* design.

Photo 52. Mikawachi-*yaki*. Mukae Sunako, painting by Fujimoto Eriko, drinking cup (*hakutai san'nin karako-e koppu*), 2000. 3¾ x 2¼ inches (9.3 x 5.9 cm). Hirado-*etsuzan* porcelain (eggshell porcelain), *karako-e design* in cobalt underglaze blue.

Utsutsugawa 現川 (12)

The stoneware that used to be produced in Utsutsugawa in the region of the Isahaya clan (today a part of Nagasaki Prefecture), bears the name of the place of its production—Yagami or Utsutsugawa-*yaki*. According to the records of the Isahaya clan, the first kiln was founded in 1691 by Tanake Keibuzaemon, in the village of Yagami (present-day Utsutsugawa). Tanake had been transferred there by the Nabeshima *han*. The kiln had an eventful history. Its heyday was in the early eighteenth century; there are reports of attempted reopenings in 1784 and 1807 after its closure in 1749. Utsutsugawa-*yaki*, a thin-walled, red-brown ware made from iron-rich clay, was famed for its delicate slip brushing (*hakeme*) decoration, combined with painted designs; Utsutsugawa-*yaki* was referred to as the Ninsei ware of Kyûshû and was traded as far away as Kyôto.

After the closure of the kilns at the end of the Edo period, there were unsuccessful attempts to resume production from 1895 on. It was only in the early Shôwa period that there was a renaissance of Utsutsugawa-*yaki*, with Yokoishi Gagyû, who was fascinated by the delicacy of this ware. Yokoishi Gagyû was a master in the twelfth generation of the Gagyû-*gama*, situated between Arita and Sasebo, in the Kihara *sayarama* of Mikawachi. The kiln that is run today by Yokoishi Gagyû (born in 1925), in the thirteenth generation, is the only one to produce Utsutsugawa-yaki in Japan. The relatively coarse *hakeme* technique that originated in Korea has been developed to a state of some refinement. For this Kihara *hakeme*, as it is called, a light-colored slip is applied with a broad brush (*hake*) to the earth-brown background of thinly thrown objects, such as tea ware, vases, and bowls. The slip is then thinned or marbled with a wet brush to create the impression of waves on the sea or grass waving in the wind. Painted designs complete the work. The most common designs are white cranes (see photo 53) and floral designs, which transform the simply formed vessels into delicate landscape pictures.

Karatsu 唐津 (13)

The port of Karatsu, in Saga Prefecture, northern Kyûshû, was strongly influenced by Korean and Chinese sources because of its relative proximity to Korea. There is evidence of Korean stylistic elements in ceramics produced as early as the sixth century. There are reports of the immigration of Korean potters to Kyûshû over the centuries. From the mid-sixteenth century on, Korean tea wares, in contrast to Chinese wares, were held in increasingly high regard. This caused Lord Hata from the Matsuura clan to have high-fired, glazed stoneware made by potters from the north of Korea in the seven Kishidake kilns near Karatsu. These kilns are the first examples of a new type of kiln in Japan—the *waridakeshiki-noborigama* ("split bamboo kiln"), which permitted firings at high temperatures under controlled conditions. Domestic wares were produced, from which tea masters such as Sen no Rikyû and Furuta Oribe selected suitable objects for the tea ceremony.

After Toyotomi Hideyoshi's Korean campaigns, further impetus was provided by the settlement of Korean potters under the patronage of Lord Terasawa from Karatsu, who was himself a tea master and a pupil of Sen no Rikyû. Along with a smoother-running kick wheel, new decorative techniques were adopted, such as iron underglaze painting and slip inlay (*mishima*), slip brushing (*hakeme*), and slip dipping (*kohiki*) in the style of Korean ceramics from the Yi dynasty. The new wheel, which permitted throwing in series "off the hump," and the kilns with up to 20 firing chambers, led to a huge expansion of production capacity. In more than 200 kilns, large quantities of household goods for distribution all over Japan and export to Southeast Asia were made. Tea ceramics for the exclusive use of the ruling family were either fired in special smaller kilns (*oniwa-gama*) or fired once a year in specially reserved chambers of the larger kilns. The triumphal progress of Hizen porcelain put an end to the demand for these wares, known as *ko*-Karatsu (old Karatsu), around 1630. Most kilns began producing porcelain; a few so-called folk kilns (*minyô*) continued to produce stoneware

Photo 53.   Utsutsugawa-*yaki*. Yokoishi Gagyû, bowl for sweets with two white cranes (*shirasagi niwa kashibachi*), 2001. 2¼ x 6½ inches (6 x 16.5 cm). Stoneware, Kihara *hakeme* design.

for domestic purposes until they began the production of *okimono* (ornamental objects) during the nineteenth century.

In the mid-nineteenth century, there was only one official feudal kiln (*hanyô*) left for the production of tea ceramics—a kiln that dated back to the Tashiro-*gama* and that was set up in 1596 by a number of potter families in Imari. In 1707, after repeated relocations, two of these families (Nakazato and Ôshima) set up the Ochawan-*gama* in Karatsu. It was in operation without interruption until the Meiji Restoration. The wares produced in this kiln between 1734 and 1871, made with a carefully prepared body, and cloud and crane designs in the *mishima* technique, are referred to as kenjô-Karatsu ("presentation Karatsu"). The famous *oku-gôrai* tea bowls, which were also made there using fine clay with feldspar glazes, adhered to the model of the Korean Ido tea bowls, which were highly esteemed by the tea masters.

After the end of the feudal system, only the Nakazato family continued the enterprise. Karatsu regained importance under Nakazato Shigeo (1895–1985), who took over the workshop as Tarôemon XII in 1927. He rebuilt the Ochawan-*gama* along the lines of the old Kishidake kilns and revived the techniques of *ko*-Karatsu after extensive research and excavations. For his services in reviving the Karatsu tradition, Tarôemon XII was designated *ningen kokuhô* (Living National Treasure) in 1976. Of his five sons, the eldest, Tadao (born in 1923), took over the family business as Tarôemon XIII in 1969. His *tataki* vessels, with their special *mishima* surfaces and sgraffito decoration, are highly prized. The third son, Shigetoshi (born in 1930), followed the Karatsu tradition with his Sangen-*gama*, built in 1973. After extensive studies abroad, the fifth son, Takashi (born in 1937), began working with the unglazed wares traditionally produced on the island of Tanegashima, south of Kyûshû. After his return to Karatsu, he constructed the Ryûta-*gama*, in which, besides the traditional Karatsu-*yaki*, he has further developed this unglazed ware—known as *karatsu-nanban*—with his son Taki (born in 1965). Since 2002, the successor to Tarôemon XIII (now Houan) has been his son Tadahiro (born in 1957), now Tarôemon XIV.

Because of the achievements of the Nakazato family, Karatsu attracted potters and aficionados of Karatsu-*yaki* in the second half of the twentieth century. Today, it is possible to find high-fired Karatsu stoneware in all its traditional diversity in more than 60 workshops in Karatsu and the immediate vicinity.

Karatsu-*yaki* is made from a local clay, which is used without any preparation apart from thorough wedging, to produce a brown or brown-gray fired body. The pots are thrown on the wheel, and because of the limited plasticity of the clay, their interiors are formed with a special bamboo tool (*hera*). Larger objects are built up from coils of clay and either thrown to shape on the wheel or paddled using the *tataki-zukuri* technique. With the exception of the tea caddies, the thrown objects have footrings, and the coiled pots have flat bases. Simple forms are preferred. Three feldspar glazes are used: a milky, transparent, wood-ash feldspar glaze; a white wood-ash glaze with the addition of rice-straw ash; and an amber to dark brown wood-ash feldspar glaze with iron oxide. Glazes are poured, or the pots are dipped in the glaze, but the footring and frequently the lower portion of the object remain unglazed. Firings are in various types of *noborigama*, without a bisque firing, over a period of 30 to 40 hours in light reduction to a temperature of 2282°F to over 2372°F (1250°C to over 1300°C).

There are various types of Karatsu-*yaki*, the most important of which are distinguished as follows according to glaze and decoration:

muji-garatsu – undecorated ware with a wood-ash feldspar glaze

madara-garatsu – "mottled Karatsu," characterized by a spotted surface (*madara*) with traces of blue, caused in reduction firing by the silicic acid present in the grayish-white rice-straw ash running in uneven layers over a transparent, dark brown glaze (see photos 21 and 54)

e-garatsu – "picture Karatsu," with iron oxide underglaze painting, covered with a transparent grayish feldspar glaze (see photo 55) or, more rarely, with a thick, cream-colored covering glaze (*shino-e garatsu*; see photo 56). The plant or geometrical designs are applied by the potters, not by specialist painters.

Photo 54. Karatsu-*yaki*. Kojima Yoshiaki, fresh-water jar (*mizusashi*), 1997. 8 x 7 inches (20.4 x 17.5 cm). Stoneware, *madara-garatsu*.

Photo 55. Karatsu-*yaki*. Workshop of Nakazato Tarôemon XIII, large plate (*ôzara*), 2001. 2½ x 12 inches (6.4 x 30.3 cm). Stoneware, iron oxide underglaze painting, *e-garatsu*.

chôsen-garatsu – "Korean Karatsu," a dark brown or black iron glaze, with an opaque white rice-straw ash glaze (see photo 57)

hori-garatsu – engraved ware with a bold pattern (*hori*) cut into its light clay body, covered by a transparent feldspar glaze. (If the pattern is traced in iron oxide, it is termed *hori e-garatsu*.)

kohiki-garatsu – slip-dipped ware, in which the entire body of the object is covered with a white slip and clear glaze (see photo 58)

hakeme-garatsu – slip-brushed ware, with a brushed-on design in white slip (see photo 59)

mishima-garatsu – ware with slip inlay (*mishima* technique) in the style of Korean ceramics from the Yi dynasty: the pot is decorated with incised lines or impressed designs that are filled with a white or reddish slip. The pot is then covered with a transparent glaze (see photo 60).

ao-garatsu or *ki-garatsu* – "blue" or "yellow Karatsu"; iron glaze that is blue-green when fired in reduction, and yellow in oxidation

karatsu-nanban – unglazed ware modeled after *nanban-yaki* from Tanegashima (see photo 61)

The range of products includes tea bowls in typical Korean forms, additional vessels for the tea ceremony, *sake* sets, and domestic wares. Remarkable continuity and diversity are characteristic of Karatsu-*yaki*. It is, however, by no means a mere copy of *ko*-Karatsu, but a further development, with independent designs based on a centuries-old tradition. Among admirers of tea ceramics, Karatsu-*yaki* still comes in third in popularity behind raku-*yaki* and Hagi-*yaki*.

Photo 56. Karatsu-*yaki*. Nakazato Shigetoshi, *sake* cup (*choko*), 1995. 1½ x 2¾ inches (3.8 x 7 cm). Stoneware, iron oxide underglaze painting, *shino e-garatsu*.

Photo 57. Karatsu-*yaki*. Workshop of Nakazato Tarôemon XIII, bottle vase (*hanaike*), 2001. 7½ x 4½ inches
(19 x 11.5 cm). Stoneware, *chôsen-garatsu*.

Photo 58. Karatsu-*yaki*. Ôhashi Yutaka, "husband and wife" teacups (*meoto yunomi*), 2001.
Heights: 3 x 3 inches (7.6 x 7.7 cm) and 2¾ x 2¾ inches (7.2 x 7.2 cm). Stoneware, *kohiki-garatsu*, iron oxide underglaze painting.

Photo 59. Karatsu-*yaki*. Workshop of Nakazato Tarôemon XIII, bowl (*hachi*), 2001. 3½ x 7¾ inches (8.7 x 19.6 cm). Stoneware, *hakeme-garatsu* with iron oxide underglaze painting.

Photo 60.   Karatsu-*yaki*. Nishikawa Kazumitsu, tea bowl (*mishima chawan*), 1997. 2¾ x 5½ inches (7 x 14 cm). Stoneware, *mishima-garatsu*.

Photo 61. Karatsu-*yaki*. Nakazato Taki, wide-mouthed vase (*tsubo hanaire*), 2001. 4½ x 6 inches (11.7 x 15 cm). Unglazed stoneware, *karatsu-nanban*.

Takeo 威雄 (14)

The area around Takeo-Onsen east of Arita (Saga Prefecture) owes its ceramics tradition to Korean potters who were moved to the Kofuku-ji temple in Takeo by Gotô Ienobu, the Lord of Takeo, after Toyotomi Hideyoshi's Korean campaigns. By the mid-seventeenth century, there were more than 200 kilns in the region around Takeo. The items produced, which were heavily influenced by Korean styles and differed only slightly in form and decoration from Karatsu ware, were known as Takeo-Karatsu-*yaki*. The predominant decorative methods were combing patterns (*kushime*) or forming marks by wiping with the fingers (*yubikaki*), sgraffito (*kakiotoshi*), slip inlay (*mishima*), and slip brushing (*hakeme*), along with iron underglaze painting in combination with splashed brown and green glazes (*uchigake*). With the triumphal progress of porcelain in neighboring Arita, domestic wares produced in Takeo lost much of their importance.

Today, there are 18 workshops in the area of Takeo, some of which produce domestic ware or studio ceramics in stoneware and porcelain. More than half the potteries still dedicate themselves to the production of stoneware in Takeo-Karatsu style, endeavoring to maintain and further develop the Korean tradition today. One of these kilns is the Tadashi-*gama*, set up in 1973 by the industrial designer Inoue Tadashi (born in 1919). He gained the inspiration for the production of his *zôgan*, *hakeme*, and *kakiotoshi* work from ceramics made 500 years ago during the Korean Yi dynasty. Now his workshop is run by his son, Inoue Kôichi (born in 1953). His vases, *mizusashi*, plates, and bowls are fired in electric or gas kilns, or in the *maki-gama*, to 2228°F (1220°C). His objects in a *totsubori* style are remarkable: the body of the pot is covered in a light-colored slip, through which traditional designs, such as peonies, birds, or fish are carved to reveal a pale brown clay body (see photo 62).

Agano 上野 (15)

The kiln in Agano (near Akaike, Fukuoka Prefecture), which is one of the seven famous *Enshû nana gama* of the tea master Kobori Enshû, was founded by Lord Hosokawa Tadaoki in 1602. Tadaoki, a pupil of the tea master Sen no Rikyû, brought the Korean potter Sonkai from Karatsu to Agano, where intially three *noborigama*—Kamanokuchi-*gama*, Iwayakôrai-*gama*, and Sarayamahon-*gama*—were built. Sonkai and two of his sons later moved to Yatsushiro and began producing Kôda or Yatsushiro-*yaki* (see Kôda, 5, on page 45). The remainder of the family continued to run the Agano kilns. Initially, the glazed stoneware produced in Agano strongly resembled Karatsu (13) and Takatori (16) ware; tea wares and domestic objects were produced. For the production of tea ceramics for the clan, the Saenba-*gama*, an *oniwa-gama* set up in the early Edo period (1600–1868) near the present-day city of Kitakyûshû, is now in use. Because of the support of Kobori Enshû, Agano-*yaki* became famous for its tea utensils and was able to preserve this reputation throughout the upheavals of the Meiji Restoration.

Today, Agano is one of the folk art kilns; tea utensils and domestic tableware are made. Although the objects are compact in form, they are strikingly delicate and lightweight. In the small town, there are 28 workshops, whose works are exhibited in the individual studios as well as in the ceramics center (established in 2002) and the affiliated gallery. There is no mass production in Agano. The clay comes from the surrounding hills, and requires lengthy and intensive preparation.

The wares, which are mainly thrown, are bisque fired for 5 to 6 hours to 1472°F–1562°F (800°C–850°C), glazed, and fired in the wood-burning *noborigama*, or fired for approximately 10 hours in a gas kiln. There is a wide range of decorations, including combed, sgraffito, *mishima*, and freely painted ones. In addition to the earlier iron, wood-ash, and rice-straw ash glazes, the three-colored glaze (*sansai-yû*), and the opaque or semitransparent beige ash glaze with a flowing green copper glaze (*ryoku-yû nagashi*; see photo 63) characteristic of Agano-*yaki*, are found.

Photo 62. Takeo-*yaki*. Inoue Kôichi, fresh-water jar (*kakiotoshi botan-mon mizusashi*), 2002. 5¼ x 6¾ inches (13.3 x 17.3 cm). Slip-coated stoneware with peony design in a sgraffito technique (*totsubori*).

Photo 63. Agano-*yaki*. Jôno Toyozô, incense burner (*ryoku-yû nagashi kôro*), 2001. 4¾ x 5¼ inches (12 x 13.2 cm). Stoneware, semitransparent ash glaze with flowing green copper glaze.

Takatori 高取 (16)

Takatori stoneware is now produced in several kilns in northeast Kyûshû—Koishiwara and Fukuoka (both in Fukuoka Prefecture), for example. The first Takatori kiln, Eimanji-takuma-yô, was constructed by the Korean potter Pal-san at the foot of Mt. Takatori, near the present-day town of Nôgata, on instruction of the *daimyô* Kuroda Nagamasa around 1601. Pal-san came to Japan with Toyotomi Hideyoshi during the Korean campaigns, adopted the Japanese name Takatori Hachizô, and fired simple tea wares and domestic ceramics in his *waridakeshiki-noborigama*. In 1614, after discovering deposits of suitable clay, he constructed the Uchigaso-yô, a 14-chamber *noborigama* along the lines of those in Hizen and Karatsu. Quality tea wares with a wide range of designs were now produced here on a large scale, but in the Yamada-*gama* dating from 1625, only the most basic domestic tableware was produced. The products from the first three Takatori kilns are termed *ko*-Takatori and were usually glazed in white, black, or amber.

In Hachizô's fourth kiln, the Shirahatayama-*gama*, a seven-chamber *noborigama* built in Nakamura in 1630, only tea ceramics, known as Enshû Takatori-*yaki*, were made, under the guidance of the tea master, Kobori Enshû. Takatori is thus considered one of the *Enshû nana gama*. The elegant articles, especially the tea caddies (*chaire*), were thin walled with smooth surfaces. All together, seven different glazes were used—in particular, a transparent, celadon-like, light green glaze (*takamiya-yû*); an iron-rich brown glaze; and a golden yellow glaze, typical of Takatori (*takatori-yû*), that covered the pot's surface with flowing glaze to produce a regular pattern.

After additional kilns were founded to the south of the present-day pottery village of Koishiwara (17), where excavations have provided evidence of experiments in the production of *sometsuke* porcelain, some of the Takatori potters remained in Koishiwara, but two families were settled near the castle of the Kurado clan in Fukuoka at the end of the seventeenth century. The Higashi-Sarayama kiln only produced tea wares and *okimono* (ornamental objects) as presentation ware under the strict supervision of the Kurado clan, whereas the Nishi-Sarayama kiln produced domestic tableware from 1718 on.

With the end of the feudal era in 1868, the production of Takatori tea wares came to a temporary standstill but was resumed in 1880 by the potters from the Nishi-Sarayama kiln who made domestic wares. In the mid-twentieth century, a final closure of the kiln threatened until the ceramist Takatori Seizan (1907–1983) succeeded in reviving the Enshû-Takatori techniques when she set up her new kiln near Koishiwara in 1957. She was the eleventh representative of the Takatori family in direct descent. This tradition, now in the twelfth generation, is still being maintained by Takatori Hassan, with brown iron glazes prevalent on the thin-walled bodies of the pots. Because of the reawakened interest in the tea ceremony since the Second World War, more Takatori kilns have been set up at the old locations, including Fukuoka, and are producing small quantities of tea utensils in the style of Uchigaso and Shirahatayama ware (see photo 64).

Koishiwara 小石原 (17)

Koishiwara and Onta (18)—the two *sarayama*, as potters' villages are known in northern Kyûshû—are located in neighboring valleys near the town of Hita, in the former domain of Fukuoka, but they now belong to different prefectures (Fukuoka and Oita). In both *sarayama*, folk art wares with a strong Korean influence are still produced. Clay preparation, forming, and decorative techniques differ only slightly.

Koishiwara dates back to the family of the Korean potter Takatori Hachizô, who was brought to the domain of Fukuoka during Toyotomi Hideyoshi's Korean campaigns in 1592 and 1597. The family set up Takatori kilns in various locations for the production of high-quality tea wares (*chadôgu*), on instruction from the *daimyô*, Kuroda Nagamasa (see Takatori, 16). One example is the Tsuzumi-*gama*, built by Hachizô's second son Hachizô-sada'aki in Koishiwara in 1665. In 1682, Lord Kuroda Mitsuyuki invited potters from Hizen to the *sarayama* of Koishiwara, where about 10

Photo 64.   Takatori-*yaki*. Onimaru Hekizan, tea bowl (*chawan*), 2000. 2¾ x 4¾ inches (7 x 12.2 cm). Stoneware, iron glaze.

kilns were soon in operation. Excavations provide evidence that at least one of the kilns (Nakano-kami-no-hara-*gama*) was producing white porcelain (*hakuji*) and *sometsuke* porcelain with cobalt underglaze brushwork up to the early eighteenth century, while the other kilns produced domestic wares such as storage jars, mortars, plates, or bottles for storing alcoholic *shôchû* in heavy unglazed or ash-glazed stoneware.

By the mid-eighteenth century, the typical decorative methods for Koishiwara had evolved, and the term Koishiwara-*yaki* became established for the wares previously termed Nakano-*yaki*. From the crisis of the Meiji Restoration to the present day, this type of folk art has retained its character nearly unchanged. The ceramics made in Koishiwara in 52 potteries are mainly domestic tableware, ranging from large plates and lidded jars to teacups and small plates and bowls.

The local dark-firing clay is obtained from a soft, yellowish rock that is crushed mechanically after drying. The further preparation of the clay and the forming process correspond to the methods described in Onta (18).

The decorative techniques practiced in Koishiwara include *hakeme*, a slip-brushing technique in which a white slip is applied to a dark body with a broad, flat brush (*hake*). The *hake* is also used for *uchi-hakeme*, a method in which a plate is covered in slip while it is leather-hard, then decorated with a radial pattern created through rhythmical applications of the *hake* while the plate is turning (see Onta, 18, and photo 66). On large plates, an *uchi-hakeme* pattern is often combined with finger-combed patterns (*yubikaki* or *shitômon*). Combed decoration (*kushime*) is also common, as are wax-resist patterns (*rônuki*) and slip painting with a bamboo tube (*itchin*). A frequently used decorative technique called *tobigan'na* or *kasurimon* (chatter marks) requires a great deal of experience: a partially dry coat of white slip on a leather-hard pot is scraped away with a flexible trimming tool (*kanna*) while the object is slowly rotated. This produces a regular pattern of chatter marks on the light surface (see photo 65).

The pots, which are either decorated in the *hakeme* style or slip coated, are covered with a transparent glaze (*furashi-yû*) before the final firing.

There are also glazes that completely cover the surface, such as a black glaze (*koku-yû*) and a brownish iron glaze (*katsu-yû*). White (*shiro-yû*), amber (*ame-yû*), and green glazes (*seiji-yû*) are often applied as a flowing overglaze (*nagashigake*) on a brown or black background (see Onta, 18, and photo 67), or as a splashed glaze (*uchigake*) on the light-colored *tobigan'na* ware (see photo 65).

The traditional main firing—40 hours to 2372°F (1300°C)—takes place in a wood-fired *noborigama*; however, gas and electric kilns are being used increasingly in Koishiwara.

Onta 小鹿田 (18)

The *sarayama* in which Onta-*yaki* is fired in present-day Oita Prefecture is only separated from neighboring Koishiwara (17) by a mountain ridge. In 1705, after discovering abundant clay deposits, the Koishiwara potter Yanase San'emon, together with his cousin Kuroki Jube and the local Sakamoto family, began to produce pottery in the *sarayama* on instructions from Lord Kuroda Norimasa. The production methods for domestic tableware in glazed stoneware, which were taken over from Koishiwara, were passed on virtually unchanged from generation to generation at the Onta kilns for more than 300 years. Only members of the three old families (Yanase, Kuroki, and Sakamoto) run the ten workshops in existence today. Since the 1920s, the wares produced there have been called Onta-*yaki*, after the neighboring hamlet of Onta, but were originally termed Hita or Sarayama-*yaki*. The public was not aware of the ware's existence, and it was only sold by traveling tradespeople in the immediate vicinity, as far as nearby Hita.

This only changed with the *mingei* movement. After several visits, Yanagi Sôetsu, founder of the *mingei* movement, expressed great appreciation of the place and its unspoiled tradition in his book *Hita no sarayama*, which popularized Onta-*yaki*. Because the economic recovery of the 1960s, together with improved distribution channels and increasing tourism, made ceramics a stable source of income, the ten families, who until then had farmed as well as made pottery,

Photo 65. Koishiwara-*yaki*. Kajiwara Fujinori, large plate (*tobigan'na ni uchigake ôzara*), 2000. 2¼ x 13½ inches (5.8 x 34.2 cm). White slip-coated stoneware, with chatter marks (*tobigan'na*), splashed glaze (*uchigake*).

were able to focus exclusively on the production of folk art wares from 1960 on.

The iron-rich Onta clay is almost identical to the material used in Koishiwara. After digging, the dried lumps must first be broken up in water-driven crushers (*karause*). This method permits only a limited quantity of clay to be processed. For the next step of levigation, the pulverized clay is immersed in water and, after filtration at each stage, passes through various settling tanks so that the heavy material sinks to the bottom while the finer particles remain in suspension. After the final stage of sedimentation, a thick, smooth slurry remains. This is dried in bisqued forms in the open air or in special ovens until the clay has reached its working consistency. Clay preparation requires more than a month from start to finish (see photos 2–7).

Because of limited quantities of clay, only two people are employed to throw in each workshop—usually father and son. Large objects are built up and shaped on a kick wheel, using the Korean *himozukuri* technique. For the production of small items, especially when throwing "off the hump," the only concession to modern times is the use of an electric wheel. The range of products, as well as decorative and glazing techniques, corresponds to Koishiwara-*yaki*. *Uchi-hakeme* plates in grayish white, amber, and light green shades (*shiro*, *ame*, or *seiji-yū*) are common (see photo 66), as are brown- or black-glazed lidded jars with flowing overglaze decoration (*nagashigake*, see photo 67).

The ware is usually fired just once, and the main firing is always in the wood-burning *noborigama*. Five families share one kiln with eight large chambers, and the remaining five families each has its own *noborigama*. The limited production today means that the pots are bought by dealers immediately after every firing, and only *omiyage* quality remains locally. A visit to the seemingly medieval village inhabited by only ten families is still well worthwhile. Because of its exclusively traditional production methods, Onta-*yaki* was included by the state in its list of Intangible Cultural Properties in 1970.

Photo 66. Onta-*yaki***. Kuroki Saito, large plate (***uchi-hakeme ôzara***), 1999. 2¼ x 12 inches (6 x 30.7 cm). Stoneware, celadon glaze (***seiji-yû***), ***uchi-hakeme*** design.**

Photo 67.   Onta-*yaki*. Yanase Asao, lidded jar (*nagashigake futatsuki-tsubo*), 1999. 5 x 4¾ inches
(12.6 x 12.5 cm). Stoneware, brown iron glaze (*katsu-yû*), glaze patterning by dripping (*nagashigake*).

>> Kilns in Shikoku

Over the centuries, Shikoku, the smallest of the four main islands in Japan, was largely separated and isolated by the Inland Sea from developments in Honshû and Kyûshû. There was no successor to Sue ware, which evidence shows was produced in the sixth and seventh centuries. It was only after potters from Kyûshû and Honshû settled in Shikoku at the end of the seventeenth century that typical local ceramics developed. After improvements in transportation that came with three bridges constructed and connected to the main island of Honshû at the end of the twentieth century, the potteries now benefit from increased tourism.

Tobe 砥部 (19)

The largest kiln in Shikoku is located in the village of Tobe, situated to the south of Matsuyama (Ehime Prefecture). The name Tobe is derived from the whetstones (to-ishi) produced there. Waste material from this production process was used to make stoneware, as numerous records from the period between 1736 and 1741 show. The pots, bowls, and sake bottles were decorated with iron underglaze painting and a grayish-white ash feldspar glaze.

The production of porcelain, for which Tobe is known today, began in 1777 on instructions from Lord Ôzu, with the construction of a kiln in Gohonmatsu-kanbara by Sugina Jôsuke. The technology came from Hizen with the support of Lord Ômura: at first, undecorated porcelain, a grayish white ware with a thickly applied, greenish glaze, was produced (hakuji). Later, the production technique for sometsuke porcelain with cobalt underglaze painting came from Hasami.

After the discovery of a high-grade porcelain stone (Kawanobori-tôseki, which is still in use today) near Tobe, it became possible to make sometsuke porcelain with an almost pure white body and delicate brushwork for tableware and tea-ceremony utensils. From 1825 on, high-quality ceramics in brocade style (nishiki-de) could be produced using techniques from Arita.

Porcelain with relief decoration and a light yellow color was a new development from the Tobe potter Mukai Wahei of the Aizan-gama, and it was awarded a prize at the World's Fair in Chicago in 1893. Increasing awareness of Tobe-yaki, then known as Iyo ware, set in motion an export boom to China, Southeast Asia, and the United States. Demand fell in the early twentieth century because of a drop in quality caused by the introduction of industrial mass production.

It was only at the end of the 1960s, with the modernization of methods and changes in the product range, that production was once again on an economically sound footing. During his visit to Tobe in 1953, Yanagi Sôetsu, the founder of the mingei movement, had recommended the production of thick-walled vessels with simple brushwork in mingei style. With the revival of folk art consciousness in the 1960s, these wares enjoyed great popularity as tableware, sake sets, teacups, and vases; new forms such as wine bottles and coffee sets were also introduced.

Eighty-nine workshops are now in operation in Tobe. Production is largely mechanized; the crushed porcelain stone is ground in ball mills and prepared by machine. The thick-walled pieces are usually created using molds; more rarely, they are thrown or slab built. Simple cobalt underglaze decoration is applied to bisque ware (fired to 1742°F [950°C] for one to two hours in electric kilns), either by printing or with a stencil; less frequently they are painted by hand. After coating the forms with a very thin layer of transparent glaze made of porcelain stone, lime, and wood ash, the ware is fired for 15 to 24 hours in a gas kiln to 2372°F (1300°C). Objects with overglaze decoration in red or red and green require an additional firing to 1472°F (800°C). Alongside the mechanized production of prevalent domestic ware in Tobe (see photo 68), a return to high-quality craft skills among some potters can be seen in their celadons, hakuji wares, and sometsuke work (see photo 69), as well as their tanôji objects, which frequently have delicate relief decoration.

Photo 68. Tobe-*yaki*. Ornamental plate (*kazarizara*), 2001. 1¾ x 12½ inches (4.3 x 31.5 cm). Porcelain, cobalt blue underglaze (*sometsuke*), fired in the Baizan-*gama*.

Photo 69. Tobe-*yaki*. Taizan Yoshiaki, vase (*hanaire*), 1997. 7¾ x 4¼ inches (19.8 x 10.5 cm). *Sometsuke*
porcelain, "Three Friends of the Winter" design (pine, bamboo, plum, *shô chiku bai*).

Odo 尾戸 (20)

A low-fired, glazed stoneware with cobalt under-glaze painting (*sometsuke-tôki*), known as Odo-*yaki* or Nôsayama-*yaki*, is now produced in Nôsayama, a suburb of the town of Kôchi (Kôchi Prefecture).

The first kiln was constructed in 1653 as an *oniwa-gama* (small feudal kiln) for the Yamanouchi clan in Odo by the potter Kuno Shôhaku, from Ôsaka. From white Odo clay, he made high-quality ceramics—thin-walled, wheel-thrown ware in Karatsu and Kyôto style, with overglaze painting, using *gohon-de* and celadon glazes. In 1669, the Tosa *han* administration ordered a *noborigama* to be built north of the castle of Kôchi for the production of blue-and-white porcelain. Unsuitable raw materials led to the failure of this project, however, so stoneware continued to be made. After the discovery of clay deposits in Nôsayama, the *han* administration ordered the Nôsayama-*gama* built in 1820 as a further attempt to produce porcelain, which had a strong resemblance to Tobe ware. After the markets were flooded with cheap porcelain at the end of the nineteenth century, the Nôsayama potters restricted themselves to the production of *sometsuke* stoneware.

Today, Odo-*yaki* is produced by two potter families in Kôchi. The old Nôsayama-*gama* is run by Doi Shôji (born in 1937) and his son Hiroyuki (born in 1968), although both of the family's *noborigama* have been replaced by gas kilns for environmental reasons. A very pale clay is used to make a light stoneware fired to 2192°F (1200°C). For the most part, they create tea ceramics and vases with elegant cobalt underglaze painting and a glaze resembling *gohon-de* (see photo 70). Tani Yasuo (born in 1941), the second potter, makes *sometsuke* stoneware from light clay, typical of Odo-*yaki*. He also uses an iron-rich clay to make vessels with strongly colored glazes, such as *sei-yû*, *koku-yû*, and *ame-yû* (blue, black, and amber glazes).

Ôtani 大谷 (21)

In Ôtani, situated in Tokushima Prefecture (formerly Awa), near the Naruto Straits, the ceramics tradition derives from Bun'emon, an itinerant potter from Kyûshû. Around 1770, he demonstrated the potter's wheel to the villagers and created so much enthusiasm with his skills that he was permitted to construct a kiln. The twelfth *daimyô* of Awa, Hachisuka Haruaki, supported these activities and in 1781 had a *hanyô* (official kiln) built by the potter Manshichi, from Hizen, for the production of blue-and-white porcelain. Subsequently, 27 potters and firing masters were recruited from Hizen to work in Ôtani, but faults in the construction of the kiln and the poor quality of the available clay caused the enterprise to fail in 1783, after only two years.

The present form of Ôtani-*yaki* goes back to the indigo merchant Kaya Bungoro, who brought the potter Chûzô from Shigaraki to Ôtani. Chûzô taught Bungoro's younger brother how to make stoneware jars as tall as a man (*kame* and *tsubo*), which were needed for water storage and for the production of indigo dye. Domestic tableware was produced in the *noborigama* constructed in 1784, especially *kame* and *tsubo*, which were traded as far as the Kansai region into the early twentieth century.

Alongside domestic tableware, the largest stoneware jars in western Japan—with a volume of up to approximately 320 gallons (1200 liters)—are now made as a specialty in eight potteries. Large bowls for the garden (*suirenbachi*), with diameters of up to 55 inches (1.4 m), are also made to contain water lilies. A technique has been developed for the production of these vessels: one potter builds up the vessel on the wheel from arm-thick coils of clay, while a second man lying on the ground turns the wheel (*ne-rokuro*). In the past few years, however, the *ne-rokuro* have been superseded by heavy-duty electric wheels. The iron-rich clay is local and easily workable. Smaller objects are thrown on the wheel or formed in molds.

After bisquing for 8 hours to 1472°F (800°C), the pots are glazed, for the most part, with an iron-rich, red-brown slip glaze (a mixture of clay from beneath local rice paddies and bamboo ash), but also, sometimes, with a black manganese glaze (see photo 71). Clay applications or impressed designs are used for decoration; or lightning, lotus,

Photo 70. Odo-*yaki*. Doi Shôji, fresh-water jar (*akikusa no e mizusashi*), 2003. 5¼ x 6¾ inches (13.3 x 17.3 cm). Stoneware, "Autumn Grass" design in cobalt blue underglaze painting, *gohon-de* glaze.

Photo 71. Ôtani-*yaki*. Mori Yukio, small bowl for aquatic plants (*suirenbachi*), 2000. 3 x 10½ inches (7.5 x 26.6 cm). Stoneware, black-brown manganese glaze.

Photo 72. Ôtani-*yaki*. Yano Kan'ichi, ornamental vessel (*ibushi kazaritsubo*), 2001. 7 x 9¼ inches (17.8 x 23.4 cm). Unglazed smoked stoneware, combing (*kushime*).

or chrysanthemum designs may be incised in the surfaces of the pots. The main firing is to 2246°F (1230°C). The large *noborigama* that used to be fired with wood over a period of five days and nights have recently been replaced by electric and gas kilns. Only the *noborigama* of Yano-tôen is still in operation. Besides functional ware, individual pieces are also made using the traditional techniques. The unglazed and smoke-fired wares of Yano Kan'ichi (born in 1942) are noteworthy (see photo 72).

>> Kilns in Honshû

Honshû is the largest of the Japanese islands, with West Honshû and Central Honshû situated between Kyôto and Tôkyô, along with the northeast region of Tôhoku. Japan's cultural heartland is situated in contemporary West Honshû, where Yamato is located. This is where the legendary Jimmu, a direct descendant of the sun goddess Amaterasu Ômikami, is said to have set up his empire and to have become the first emperor of Japan in the seventh century B.C. In historical times, the Yamato empire emerged in the fourth century A.D. as the first united Japanese state in the Yamato plain (now Nara Prefecture).

Kyôto has been considered the most important cultural center over the centuries; it became the imperial capital in 794, at which time it was called Heian-kyô. It remained the spiritual and religious center of Japan when Edo, contemporary Tôkyô, became the seat of government in the Tokugawa Shogunate during the Edo period (1600–1868). The Sanage kilns, which provided court society with prestigious ceramics during the Heian period, are situated in this central region of Japan, just like the medieval ceramics centers that evolved from them and which are represented by the Six Ancient Kilns.

In the course of the following centuries, many new kilns were set up, especially in western and central Japan with the support of the local daimyô. In the remote northeast of Honshû, this development was restricted to a small number of flourishing castle towns, such as Sendai and Aizu-Wakamatsu. Mashiko, to the north of Tôkyô, so famous in the West today, was only set up in the nineteenth century and developed as a result of the *mingei* movement into one of the major folk art kilns, with approximately 500 potters. Today, many studio potters who were trained in the ceramics centers feel more attracted to the rural areas in northern Honshû.

Hagi 萩 (22)

Hagi and its surroundings (Yamaguchi Prefecture) have been the home of Hagi-*yaki*, a high-fired glazed stoneware, for 400 years. During Toyotomi Hideyoshi's Korean campaigns (1592, 1597), Môri Terumoto, the *daimyô* of Chôshû (now Yamaguchi Prefecture), brought the Korean potter Ri Shakukô and his younger brother Ri Kei to Hagi. In 1604, the brothers, who were known by the name Saka, built the Matsumoto-*goyôgama* in the village of Matsumoto, near Hagi. Lord Môri Terumoto was a passionate devotee of the tea ceremony; he was a pupil of the tea master Sen no Rikyû and a friend of the tea master Furuta Oribe. For his own personal use and as presentation ware, he ordered tea ceramics from the Saka brothers in the style of the Korean Kôrai dynasty, with *mishima*, *hakeme*, and *kohiki* designs, as well as imitations of the highly regarded Korean Ido tea bowls from the Yi dynasty. Ri Kei, whom the *daimyô* honored by awarding the name of Saka Kôraizaemon, constructed the Fukagawa-*goyôgama* in Fukagawa, a district of the contemporary town of Nagato. More feudal kilns, such as the Matsumoto-*gama* built by the Miwa family in 1666, were constructed in Hagi itself. The style of the tea master Furuta Oribe gained increasing influence, so the production of *oribe* tea ceramics continued to grow well into the eighteenth century; among these tea ceramics, the *kutsugata chawan* (tea bowls in shoe form) are especially well known. Subsequently, the ceramics once again became simpler in form and decoration.

Under the protection of the Môri clan, the Hagi potters specialized in the production of tea ceramics (*chadôgu*) during the entire Edo period; Hagi has remained one of the few kilns that has produced tea ware almost exclusively right up to the modern era. With this limited range of products, the potters focused on the color and consistency of the clay bodies, and their interaction with glazes under various firing conditions. This led to the creation of mainly undecorated tea ceramics, corresponding in their simplicity to Sen no Rikyû's *wabi* aesthetic and highly regarded all over Japan. Tea experts rank Hagi-*yaki* second in popularity to raku ware from Kyôto, followed by Karatsu-*yaki*—a judgment that has not changed even today. The production of porcelain at the end of the Edo period was only a brief episode.

Hagi ceramics were referred to as *ko*-Hagi up to the time of Saka Kôraizaemon III (1648–1729), and in more recent literature, this term has extended to Hagi-*yaki*, to cover the entire Edo period. Production methods and the appearance of these wares have remained almost unchanged to the present day. Three basic types of clay are usually used in various mixtures: first, the light gray *daidô tsuchi*, a *gairome-nendo*, is formed by the decomposition of granite and is therefore rich in quartz particles. These particles are removed during the preparation of the clay, then added again in defined quantities for special purposes.

There are also the whitish yellow, kaolinlike *mitake* clay and the red-brown *mishima* clay, which is rich in iron. The standard body is called "Korean" clay, and consists of 7 to 8 parts *daidô* clay and 2 to 3 parts *mitake* clay. Cleaned and with quartz particles removed, the fine *hime* (princess)-*hagi-de* is made; through the addition of one part fine sand, the coarse *oni* (devil)-*hagi-de* is made; and through the addition of two parts *mishima* clay, a dark firing body is produced. The pots are thrown on a Korean kick wheel. Characteristic of Hagi-*yaki*, the pronounced footring (*kôdai*) may be split (*wari kôdai*) or notched one to three times (*kiri kôdai*).

Two types of glaze are in use. One is a transparent ash feldspar glaze (*dobai-yû*) with 30 to 70 percent hardwood ash, that turns light green in reduction. Oxidation produces a yellowish glaze, which, in combination with Korean clay, achieves a pinkish orange shade that is termed *biwa-iro* because of its resemblance to the edible fruit of the loquat (*biwa*) and that is typical of Hagi-*yaki*

(see photo 73). A second type of glaze—the white Hagi glaze (*shiro hagi-gusuri*)—is produced by adding straw ash (*warabai*) to *dobai-yû*. It resembles a layer of icing when it is applied thickly to the vessel (see photo 75).

Depending on the size of the kiln, the ware is fired with wood and without saggars in a *noborigama* for 14 to 40 hours. The temperatures reached in the first chamber are about 2444°F (1340°C) and 2156°F (1180°C) in the rear of the kiln. As the glazes react very sensitively to the clay and the firing conditions, color shades in the range of snow white, gray, *biwa-iro*, and lavender blue are achieved. On the iron-rich *mishima* clays, the colors range from gray to pink. Tea connoisseurs claim that the beauty of Hagi ceramics increases with use; fine cracks in the glaze, caused during firing by the grains of quartz, allow tea to penetrate the body, creating multiple changes of color, or the "Seven Changes of Hagi" (*Hagi no nana bake*).

To recover from the economic difficulties resulting from the Meiji Restoration in 1868, many Hagi potters began producing ornamental objects (*okimono*), which had come into fashion at that time. Nevertheless, many potteries were forced to close during the Taishô and early Shôwa periods. Some workshops survived, including the Fukagawa-*gama* of Saka Kôraizaemon X and the Matsumoto-*gama* of Miwa Kyûsetsu X. As a result of the renaissance of tea ceramics in the early twentieth century, the Saka family concentrated on their *biwa-iro* tea ceramics (see photo 73), whereas Miwa Kyûsetsu X (1895–1981) modeled his Hagi ceramics on the aesthetic of Shigaraki, Iga, and *shino* wares from the Momoyama period. His younger brother and successor, Miwa Kyûsetsu XI (born in 1910), perfected the characteristic white Hagi glaze. For these achievements, the Miwa brothers were designated *ningen kokuhô* (Living National Treasures) in 1970 and 1983 respectively. In 2003, Ryosaku (born in 1940), the first-born son of Miwa Kyûsetsu XI (now Jusetsu), assumed the title Kyûsetsu XII but left the line of noble Hagi traditions to make sculptural work and gold-covered *chawan*.

Today, about 100 potters work in Hagi, most of them in the traditional style; along with vases

Photo 73. Hagi-*yaki*. Saka Kôraizaemon XI, small teapot (*hôhin*), 1995. 2¼ x 4 x 3¼ inches (6 x 10.2 x 8 cm). Korean clay, *Biwa-iro* stoneware, ash feldspar glaze.

Photo 74. Hagi-*yaki*. Hadano Hideo, Ido-style tea bowl (*chawan*), 2005. 3¼ x 5½ inches (8 x 14.3 cm). Stoneware (*oni-hagi* clay), ash feldspar glaze.

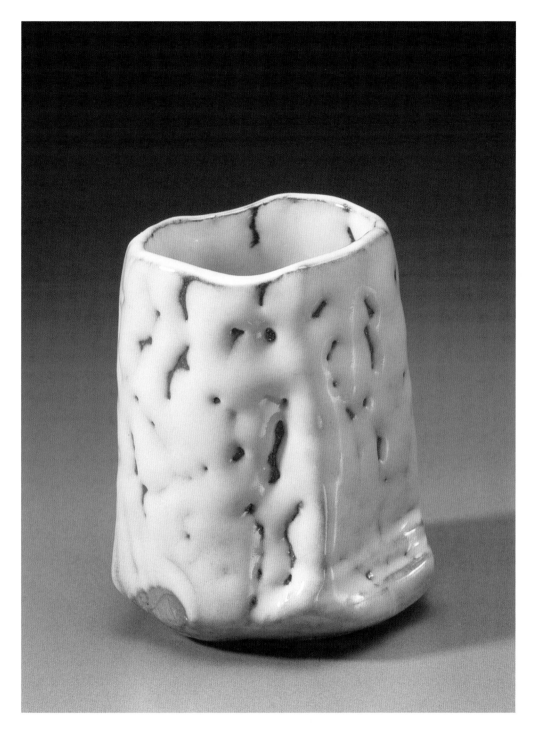

Photo 75. Hagi-*yaki*. Kaneta Masanao, teacup (*kurinuki yunomi*), 2000. 3¾ x 3¼ inches (9.4 x 8 cm). Carved stoneware in *kurinuki* technique, white Hagi glaze (*shiro hagi-gusuri*).

and *sake* sets, they mainly make tea ceramics. A typical example is the *chawan* made by Hadano Hideo (born in 1971) in the style of Ido tea bowls (see photo 74). Many younger artists have developed their individual styles based on traditional clay mixtures, glazes, and firing techniques. Two examples are Kaneta Masanao (eighth generation; born in 1953), who, since 1988 has carved tea ceramics, *sake* sets, and sculptures from blocks of clay using the *kurinuki* technique (see photo 75); and Miwa Kasuhiko (third son of Miwa Kyûsetsu XI; born in 1951), who studied in San Francisco in the late 1980s. His almost abstract-looking vessels and spatial objects are influenced by the West, although his work still has the typical white Hagi glaze. Saka Kôraizaemon XII (born in 1949) decorates the typical *biwa-iro* vessels his family makes with his boldly colored overglaze painting.

Miyajima 宮島 (23)

The Tôsai kiln belonging to the Kawahara family is situated in Miyajima-guchi, near Hiroshima, just before the point of departure for ferries to the holy island of Miyajima (Hiroshima Prefecture). Miyajima, one of the three most beautiful landscapes in Japan, is dominated by the Itsukushima Shrine, which is built out into the bay. Sand from the area of the shrine was considered by travelers to be a talisman that would guarantee a safe return; an offering to the shrine was made with earth from the traveler's destination. At the end of the eighteenth century, potters began to form vessels from sand found around the shrine as offerings to the three goddesses of the Itsukushima-*jinja*. Miyajima-*yaki* is thus termed Osuna-*yaki* (sand ceramics).

The commercial phase of the Tôsai kiln began during the Bunsei era (1818–1830). Lord Asano had special tea bowls made with a portion of the holy sand, and these were highly popular up to the end of the Edo period. The kiln discontinued production as a result of the Meiji Restoration in 1868. In 1909, after his training in Kyôto, Kawahara Tomijiro (Tôsai I) built the present Tôsai kiln, which has been fired with varying degrees of success. The Kawahara family reopened the kiln in 1939

as *jinja-goyôgama* under the patronage of the Itsukushima shrine. Clay from Miyajima was used until 1945, and from Minagata-guchi (Higashi-Hiroshima) thereafter. Today, tea ceramics are produced in the third generation by Kawahara Tôsai (see photo 76). In 1991, the ceramics of the Tôsai-*gama* were designated the Hiroshima Prefecture's Traditional Art Craft. In addition to the Kawahara kiln, there are two other workshops in Miyajima-guchi.

Iwami 石見 (24)

Iwami-*yaki* is the general term for the glazed stoneware that used to be fired mainly in the former Iwami region, now Shimane Prefecture, around the towns of Hamada, Ôda, Asahi, Masuda, and Gôtsu. Between 1704 and 1711, the production of ceramics is first mentioned in a permit to dig clay and sell pottery. Around 1763, a potter from the Yamaguchi region introduced the technique for the production of smaller vessels, such as bowls and *sake* bottles. Approximately 20 years later, the method of producing larger items came from Bizen. Jars for fresh water (*daihandô*) more than 3 feet (1 meter) in height were the specialty of Iwami-*yaki*. With the support of the *han* administration, the jars were taken by ship from Kyûshû as far as Hokkaidô.

Using the *himozukuri* method, three potters were necessary to produce a *daihandô* from more than 400 pounds (200 kg) of clay. One was responsible for building up the vessel from arm-thick coils of clay on a wheel that had to be driven by two other men using a rope. Firings were in a large *noborigama*. The heyday of the *daihandô* was from the early Shôwa period, with more than 100 kilns in operation, up to 1960, when the introduction of running water even in rural areas, as well as inexpensive plastic goods, made the ceramic water jars superfluous. The potters converted their production to domestic wares, tea sets, vases, lidded jars for pickles, umbrella stands, and patio furniture, all of which, under the influence of the *mingei* movement, found approval as typical folk art. Today, the red-brown glazed pickle jars are the trademark of Iwami-*yaki* (see photo 77).

Photo 76. Miyajima-*yaki*. Kawahara Tôsai III, teacup (*yunomi*), 1999. 3½ x 3¼ inches (8.8 x 7.8 cm). Stoneware, transparent ash feldspar glaze.

Photo 77. Iwami-*yaki*. Shimada Haruo, lidded jar for pickles (*tsukemono-game*), 2003. 9 x 8 inches (23 x 20.5 cm). Stoneware, red-brown *kimachi-yû*, dark glaze runs (*nagashigake*).

Fourteen workshops are now in operation in Gôtsu, Hamada, Ôda, and Asahi, with 15 more in the remainder of the Iwami region. Currently, high-quality clay containing kaolin from Gôtsu and Hamada is used. Small items are thrown on the wheel, but for larger pieces, the *himozukuri* method is still employed, as it was in the Sekishû Shimada-*gama* built in 1935, which the current master, Shimada Haruo (born in 1923) took over from his father. Typical glazes include the red-brown *kimachi-yû* from the local iron-rich Kimachi stone; *kôkado-yû*, a milky white, high-fired glaze from white clay and feldspar; and an alkaline glaze, which is ochre-colored in oxidation and green in reduction. Dripped patterns or underglaze painting with *tessha*, an iron-rich alluvial deposit, are used for decoration. The ware is fired to 2372°F (1300°C) in gas kilns; the big *noborigama* is still fired once a year (see Information on Individual Kilns and Travel Notes, page 308).

Fujina 布志名 (25)

In 1766, Funaki Yojibei set up a kiln to produce glazed stoneware in the village of Fujina, in the Tamayu region beside Lake Shinji, near Matsue in Shimane Prefecture. In subsequent years, the many branches of the Funaki family constructed more kilns for the production of tableware. In 1786, the Matsue clan designated the Tsuchiya-*gama* a feudal kiln (*hanyô*) and in the early nineteenth century, added the Nagahara-*gama*. In these kilns, elegant wares in the style of Kyô, Seto, and Arita-*yaki* were produced; the items enhanced with gold decoration were particularly popular. Along with white and black glazes (*haku-yû*, *koku-yû*) and a green copper glaze, a yellow glaze (*ô-yû*) was made for the reproduction of *kiseto* ware, but at first this was dark in color and dull. The Fujina potters developed *ô-yû* further as a high-fired lead glaze, similar to lead galena glazes in the West. Since the Meiji period, these glossy glazes with their brilliant yellow color have been characteristic of Fujina-*yaki*, which thus holds a special position within Japanese ceramics.

Five of the Fujina kilns survived the upheavals of the Meiji and the Taishô periods. The best known is the Funaki-*gama*, founded in 1845; its later master Funaki Michitada (1900–1963) was heavily influenced by the *mingei* movement. Under the influence of Hamada Shôji and particularly Bernard Leach, who visited the kiln in 1954, he adopted the technique of traditional English slipware. The current master, Funaki Kenji (born in 1927), studied slipware firsthand on his trip to England in 1967. Together with his son Shinji (born in 1960), he produces Western-inspired domestic tableware in the spirit of the *mingei* tradition.

Another well-known Fujina kiln is Fukuma Shûji's (born in 1941) Yumachi-*gama*, an offshoot of the Funaki-*gama* founded in 1923, with a similar product range (see photo 78). The production process is partly mechanized in this case; the slip decoration is applied directly onto the green ware with bamboo tubes or paintbrushes. Fujina-*yaki* is fired in a gas, electric, or oil kiln to 2282°F–2372°F (1250°C–1300°C); the large *noborigama* have been closed down due to environmental concerns.

Sodeshi 袖師 (26)

In 1877, Ono Tomoichi (1842–1918), who had been trained by a Fujina potter, found rich clay deposits in Sodeshiura, the present-day district of Matsue in Shimane Prefecture, and built his kiln there. The most important products were braziers (*hibachi*) in Fujina style, which were also made by Ono Iwaijirô (1875–1943) in the second generation. The glazed stoneware known as Matsue-*yaki* or Isode-*yaki* was brittle and not very durable. Only in 1921, after Iwaijirô had studied in Kyôto, Seto, and Arita, was it possible to remedy this fault, and five years later, the head of the Ohara *ikebana* school requested the production of bowls for flower arrangements. Under the name of Sodeshi-*yaki*, flower bowls and domestic wares were made until 1940.

Present-day Sodeshi-*yaki*—vases and domestic ware—is pure folk art; the current master of the kiln, Ono Shin'ya (fourth generation, born in 1940), has been influenced by the *mingei* movement, and traces of the work of Kawai Kanjirô are unmistakable. On heavy, robust vessels that are fired with gas or oil, a light gray glaze with iron oxide brushwork predominates (see photo 79); blue (*sei-yû*) and green (*ryoku-yû*) copper oxide glazes are also typical.

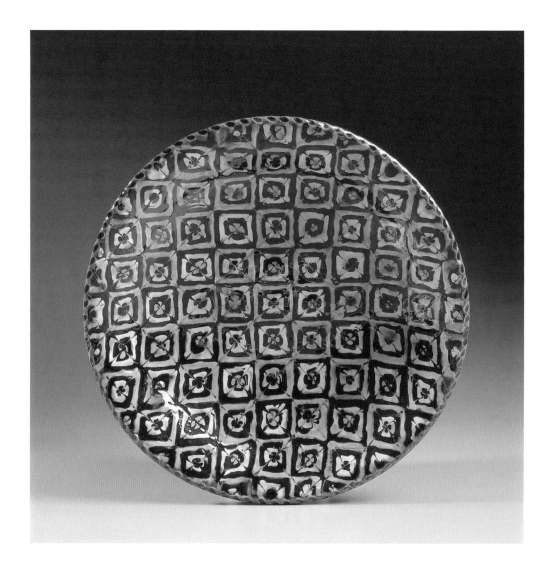

Photo 78. Fujina-*yaki*. Fukuma Shûji, large bowl (*surippu monyô ôbachi*), 2000. 3 x 14½ inches (7.4 x 36.8 cm). Stoneware, slip design, yellow lead glaze (*ô-yû*).

**Photo 79.   Sodeshi-*yaki*. Ono Shin'ya, container for spices (*yakumi-ire*), 1998. 3½ x 5¼ x 5¼ inches
(8.8 x 13.5 x 13.5 cm). Glazed stoneware, iron oxide design.**

Kazuwa 上神 (27)

The Kazuwazan-*gama* is located in the small village of Kazuwa, nearly 13 miles (20 km) outside the town of Kurayoshi (Tottori Prefecture). The turbulent history of the kiln began between 1751 and 1764 with the potter Wasaburo, from Hizen, who made glazed stoneware tableware in Kazuwa. This kind of ware was later termed Hakubizan-*yaki* and was produced until the Meiji Restoration. Around 1893, a doctor named Maeda Yôjin built the Kigyokazan-*gama* near the first kiln, and in this new kiln, two potters from Kyôto fired mainly tea bowls, *sake* bottles, plates, and lidded boxes. Around 1900 and at the end of the Taishô period (1912–1926), the kiln changed hands several times and was modernized. In 1934, Yamane Tôichi (1910–1995), a potter from the Iwami region, took over a kiln that was still in existence and continued to run it as the Kazuwazan-*gama*.

The ware, which has a reddish-yellow fired body and is made from a local clay, is wood-ash glazed in a light green-yellow that frequently shows areas of copper red. The oxblood tea bowls (*shinsha chawan*), which have been very famous since the end of the Second World War, are almost entirely covered with an elegant plum red (see photo 80). At present, the kiln is run by Yamane Tamiya (born in 1948), who continues his father's range of products. To keep costs low, the objects—tea bowls and tableware—are no longer fired in a *noborigama* but in an oil-fired kiln.

In 1948, Nakamori Otokichi, who worked at the Kazuwazan-*gama*, built his Kazuwa-*gama* in neighboring Fuirioka. The products of both kilns are called Kazuwa-*yaki*.

Inkyûzan 因久山 (28)

Records show that around the present-day town of Kôge (Tottori Prefecture), so-called Kunôji-*yaki* was already in existence around 1720, before Rokubei, a migrant potter from Kyôto, discovered high-quality clay deposits near Kôge 50 years later. Tottori clan leader Ikeda instructed him to teach two local potters, Osaki Chiryôemon and Ashizawa Kamegorô. In the following period,

the *han* administration arranged for additional kilns to be built, and it supervised production. The kiln of the Ashizawa family was designated an official kiln (*hanyô*) in 1795 and was given the name Inkyuzan-*gama*. At about the same time, the Shigaraki potter Kanzô settled in the Kôge region, and passed on his skills to the Kôge potters. At that time, four potter families—Osaki, Ashizawa, Kanzô, and Yamamoto—worked independently of each other until they lost their independence in 1855. At that time, the *han* administration amalgamated the workshops then in existence to form the Yoriai-*gama*, which until the end of the Edo period made glazed domestic ware and tea ceramics using stoneware.

With the Meiji Restoration, ceramics production initially came to a standstill. The Osaki family built another kiln in 1897; the Ashizawa family followed their example. Both kilns continued the production of traditional Inkyûzan-*yaki*, but the Kanzô family turned to the production of ornamental ceramics (*saikumono*). Of these three workshops, only the kiln of the Ashizawa family has survived. It was refurbished and modernized in 1939 and again in 1977. Today, Ashizawa Yoshinori (ninth generation, born in 1939) and his son, Yasunori (born in 1966), make tea ceramics, especially tea bowls, as well as fresh-water jars, vases, and domestic tableware. Local iron-rich clays are used in production, and ash as well as *namako* glazes are characteristic (see photo 81).

Cobalt underglaze painting in a limited number of designs can be found, especially bamboo motifs, as well as overglaze flower designs and impressed relief decoration. High-quality tea ceramics and vases are fired twice a year with red pine in a seven-chamber *noborigama*, but for the more frequent firings, the domestic wares are fired with oil in a four-chamber *noborigama*.

Bizen 備前 (29)

After Tokoname, Bizen is considered to be the oldest of the Six Ancient Kilns (*roku koyô*). In the Bizen region, centered around the town of Inbe (or Imbe) in present-day Okayama Prefecture, *yakishime*—an unglazed, dark, reddish brown

Photo 80. Kazuwa-*yaki*. Yamane Tôichi, oxblood tea bowl (*shinsha chawan*), 1982. 3¼ x 5½ inches (8.6 x 14.1 cm). Faceted stoneware, wood ash glaze, covered by copper glaze.

Photo 81. Inkyûzan-*yaki*. Ashizawa Yoshinori, vase (*namako-yû hanaire*), ca. 2001. 11¼ x 8½ inches (28.6 x 21.7 cm). Stoneware, *namako*-glaze.

stoneware—is produced in the tradition of Sue ceramics, which have been produced around present-day Ôsaka since the fifth century. In the second half of the Heian period (794–1185), Sue potters settled in the Bizen region because of the deposits of high-quality clay there and founded the potters' village of Inbe. This is why the term Inbe-*yaki* is sometimes applied to Bizen-*yaki*. The Bizen ware produced up to the end of the twelfth century has the characteristic gray-black coloring of *sueki* fired to 2192°F (1200°C) in reduction. With the technical improvements to the *ana-gama*, which enabled higher temperatures to be achieved, and the changeover to firing in oxidation, the typical appearance of *yakishime* developed toward the end of the twelfth century. Made of a sandy clay (*yamatsuchi*), thick-walled domestic ware, especially for large storage jars, was developed.

The reddish brown Bizen color, which is still typical today, emerged in the late sixteenth century with the introduction of iron-rich clay (*tatsuchi*). At the same time, the introduction of the wheel made it possible to produce in large quantities, after tea ceramics produced to the specifications of the tea masters had already begun in the late fourteenth century. The pots were fired in three huge kilns (*ôgama*)—Kita, Minami, and Nishi-*gama*—the foundations of which can still be seen in Inbe today. In the Azuchi-Momaya period (1568–1600), tea ceramics reached new heights with the development of various firing techniques. Bizen-*yaki* from the Kamakura (1185–1333), Muromachi (1333–1568) and Azuchi-Momoyama periods, is known as *ko*-Bizen.

In 1582, Toyotomi Hideyoshi, at that time military governor of Bizen province and a devotee of the tea ceremony, selected six of the best potter families from Inbe—the Kaneshige, Kimura, Mori, Hayami, Ohan, and Terami families—to produce tea utensils. Members of the first three families still work as potters today. During the Edo period (1600–1868), the local Ikeda clan supported the Bizen potters; the *han* administration oversaw supplies of raw materials such as wood and clay, as well as the distribution of the finished goods. Alongside tea ceramics and *saikumono* (ornamental objects) as presentation ware, large quantities of domestic items were produced, especially *sake* bottles and storage jars, which spread throughout Japan by land and sea.

By the middle of the Edo period, Bizen-*yaki* was experiencing fierce competition from the porcelain produced in Hizen and Kyôto. As a reaction to this, white Bizen (*gofun-bizen*), with a type of limestone coating, and colored Bizen (*iro-e bizen*) were produced, as were more refined, unglazed wares known as *inbe-de*. To create these, the thin-walled pots were covered with an iron-rich clay (*tatsuchi*) slip to produce a hard, glossy surface with shading from yellowish brown to deep purple. Falling sales and a shortage of wood as fuel led to the closure of the *ôgama*. Thus, the first *noborigama* was built in Inbe in 1830—the 52½-foot (16 m) Tenpô-*gama*. The products from this new type of kiln did not, however, achieve the aesthetic standard of earlier Bizen-*yaki*.

Through the loss of the patronage of the Ikeda clan and because the market was being flooded with industrially produced porcelain, the Meiji Restoration (1868) created a severe financial crisis for the potters from Bizen. Some workshops began producing drainpipes or beer and sake bottles, until inexpensive materials drove these ceramic products from the market, too. The only market niche left available for the Bizen potters was the mass production of ornamental objects (*saikumono*) for the emerging bourgeoise.

It was not until the twentieth century that Kaneshige Tôyô (1896–1967), a trained *saikumono* potter, revived the tradition of *ko*-Bizen from the Azuchi-Momoyama period. In 1932, he began redeveloping the lost techniques of clay preparation, throwing, and especially the firing typical of Bizen-*yaki*. For this he was designated *ningen kokuhô* (Living National Treasure) in 1956. Traditional Bizen-*yaki* flourished once again. Besides Kaneshige, other Living National Treasures were designated—in 1970, Fujiwara Kei (1899–1983), for the revival of *ko*-Bizen from the Kamakura and Muromachi periods; in 1987, Yamamoto Tôshû (1906–1994); in 1996, Fujiwara Kei's son Fujiwara Yû (1932–2001; see photo 82); and in 2004, Isezaki Jun (born in 1936).

Today, about 180 studios operate in Bizen and employ about 650 people. Although a number of workshops mass produce, there are nevertheless many famous artists. Some are motivated by tradition. Abe Anjin and Kaneshige Michiaki draw their inspiration from Zen and the aesthetic of the tea ceremony, and create classic items in Momoyama style. Mori Tôgaku continues the tradition of Bizen-*yaki* from the Edo period with his *ôgama*, which he built in 1972, whereas Yoshimoto Shûhô (born in 1938) works in Sue style (see photo 86). Other artists, such as Kakurezaki Ryuichi, Shimamura Hikaru, Imanari Kenji, and Kawabata Fumio (see photo 187) combine traditional firing techniques with contemporary sculptural forms.

The clay that is mainly used for Bizen-*yaki* is *tatsuchi*, a fine body that contains 3 percent iron and is dug many feet under rice fields. This clay is highly plastic due to the high proportion of organic matter it contains. As a rule, two parts *tatsuchi* and one part *yamatsuchi*, a sandy clay, are mixed together with *kurotsuchi*, a clay with a very high organic content.

Bizen ware is usually thrown and sometimes hand built or pinched for smaller objects. Sculptural work and *saikumono*, which are no longer common, are also hand built, and press molding may also occur. The most common objects are tea ceramics and vessels for flowers, as well as *sake* sets and tableware.

After careful drying in the open air to avoid cracking, the pots are fired with pine in the *anagama* or the *noborigama*; the kilns are constructed to take the special requirements of Bizen clays into consideration. The firing takes one to two weeks and is executed with extreme caution. Increasing the temperature up to 1832°F (1000°C) must be done slowly to avoid bloating caused by the organic material. To avoid warping, the final temperature of 2282°F (1250°C) must be precisely adhered to. This relatively low temperature does not permit the complete melting of the natural-ash particles, as is the case with Shigaraki and Iga-*yaki*. In spite of this limitation, the appearance of Bizen-*yaki* is highly varied due to the diverse effects of the flames on the pots, depending on their positions in the kiln. These originally random effects are now produced intentionally by the potters, a process that requires great skill and experience. Today, mass-produced items are sometimes fired in gas or electric kilns with the addition of wood ash in order to imitate the appearance of traditionally fired ware.

The main types of Bizen-*yaki* are as follows:

goma: "sesame," in which the wood ash adhering to the surface melts at 2264°F (1240°C) to form glaze spots resembling sesame seeds (see photo 82). Depending on the intensity and duration of the firing, yellowish beige to amber-colored patches of glaze form on the body of the pot (*nagashi goma*).

enokihada: the surface of the pot is covered with partially melted ash particles resembling the skin (*hada*) of the *enoki* fungus (see photo 83).

higawari: "fire change," also known as *yôhen*; shades between reddish violet and dark gray are caused by the alternation of reduction and oxidation firing using heavy or moderate stoking.

sangri: a metallic gray-blue color caused by chance in reduction (see photo 84), when objects are completely covered by ash and therefore are protected from fire and draft, or caused intentionally by covering with charcoal and closing the firing ports at 2192°F (1200°C).

fuseyaki: multicolored objects are created by covering parts of the exterior or interior surface to prevent deposits of ash.

botamochi: "rice cake"; round, reddish areas without deposits of ash are created by covering pots with balls of refractory clay, using rice chaff to prevent the clay from sticking to the pot.

hidasuki: "fire cord"; red markings on the pot caused by wrapping the pot with rice-straw ropes soaked in salt water, and firing in oxidation. Light-colored clay is used for this purpose because the iron in the clay reacts with soda in the firing. Today, *hidasuki* ware is often fired in saggars (see photo 85).

ao-bizen: "blue Bizen"; a deep blue-gray is produced in reduction firings on objects completely covered in rice straw (see photo 86), or by the addition of salt; salt-glazed blue Bizen is referred to as *shokuen-ao*.

Photo 82. Bizen-*yaki*. Fujiwara Yû (Living National Treasure), vase (*hanaire*), pre-1980. 8 x 3½ inches (20.5 x 9.2 cm). *Yakishime* stoneware, natural-ash glaze with *goma*.

Photo 83. Bizen-*yaki*. Wall-hanging vase (*kake-hanaire*) in calabash form, ca. 2000. 9 x 3½ inches
(23 x 9 cm). Unglazed stoneware, partially melted natural-ash glaze, *enokihada*, fired in the
Sanroku-*gama*.

Photo 84. **Bizen-*yaki*. Kimura Bifû, tea bowl (*chawan*), 1990. 3 x 4½ inches (7.6 x 11.8 cm). Unglazed stoneware, *sangiri*.**

Izushi 出石 (30)

The porcelain produced in seven workshops in the small castle town of Izushi (Hyôgo Prefecture) is a brilliant white and is highly esteemed among experts. The history of Izushi begins in 1764 with Izuya Yazaemon, who made glazed stoneware for everyday use. After the discovery of kaolin-rich Hitani-*tôseki* in 1789, the local Sengoku clan supported efforts to produce porcelain. With the assistance of Arita potters and using the *renbô-shiki-noborigama* in Hizen as a guide, the Maru-*gama* was built—a *hanyô*, which from 1801 on, fired porcelain tableware with cobalt underglaze painting (*sometsuke*). During the heyday of Izushi-*yaki* (1830–1844), several kilns were constructed and were run by tenant potters under the patronage of the local dynasty.

As a consequence of the Meiji Restoration, most of the workshops were initially forced to close. With the intention of providing a future for unemployed *samurai* by resuming the production of porcelain, an association of local potters set up a production co-operative in 1876. It was known as Eishin-*sha*. By the end of the nineteenth century, five kilns had already been reestablished in Izushi. To further improve quality, a research institute was set up under Tomoda Yasukiyo, from Kanazawa, which succeeded in developing the characteristic fired white porcelain body.

Aside from a negligible proportion of stoneware with overglaze brushwork, mainly porcelain is made in Izushi today. Hitani porcelain stone is no longer available in sufficient quantities in a suitable quality and therefore requires time-consuming preparation. The porcelain objects—tea wares and vases—are either wheel thrown or made in molds. A small part of the porcelain is decorated with cobalt underglaze brushwork or stamps; another specialty is the production of objects with a marbled surface of blue slip created by using the *suminagashi* technique. Typical Izushi porcelain is a pure white ware with *senbori* decoration, in which the lines of a (usually floral) design are incised in the surface of the leather-hard pot with a bamboo knife. After bisque firing for 12 to 20 hours to 1472°F–1652°F (800°C–900°C), two glaze variations are employed. In the first, the entire pot is covered with glaze so that the incised decoration can only be seen against the light. In the second technique, the incised decoration is covered with wax, and after the main firing of 20 hours to 2282°F–2372°F (1250°C–1300°C), the matte, unglazed areas contrast with the silky luster of the glaze (see photo 87). Pure white, *senbori*-decorated Izushi porcelain is unique in Japan.

Tanba 丹波 (31)

The production of Sue ceramics in the old province of Tanba was mentioned in *Nihon shoki*, a Japanese chronicle from 720. At the end of the twelfth century, there was a transition to medieval Tanba-*yaki*, a red-brown to gray-brown high-fired stoneware with natural-ash glaze that was first produced in Onohara and Tachikui, and later in Ôji, Inahata, Muramori, and Kamaya. Today, Tanba-*yaki* is only produced in Tachikui (Hyôgo Prefecture), and is therefore often called Tanba-Tachikui-*yaki*. Its long history makes Tanba one of the Six Ancient Kilns (*roku koyô*).

Tanba-*yaki* was a purely functional ware for the rural population: there was no patronage by a local feudal lord. For 250 years, production, using largely unchanged production methods, centered on mortars (*suribachi*) and, in particular, on storage jars (*tsubo* and *kame*). The base of the vessel, which reached up to about 23½ inches (60 cm) in height, was flattened onto a crude potter's wheel. The body of the pot was created from three to four coils of coarse, untreated clay on the slowly counterclockwise-turned wheel. Because of the long firing period of up to two weeks at temperatures of over 2282°F (1250°C) in the *anagama*, thick, yellow-brown layers of ash glaze settled on the pot (*haikaburi*), with flowing glazes in green to blue. Only from the beginning of the Azuchi-Momoyama period (1568–1600) was a part of the production, which had increased to 100,000 items per year, traded in central Japan.

Because of technical improvements beginning in 1600, the appearance and the product range of Tanba-*yaki* changed. The transition from *anagama* to *waridakeshiki-noborigama* allowed large numbers of pots of a consistent quality to be fired. By

Photo 85. Bizen-*yaki*. Kimura Sumio, fresh-water jar (*mizusashi*), 1990. 6½ x 6¾ inches (16.8 x 17.2 cm). Unglazed stoneware, *hidasuki*.

Photo 86. Bizen-*yaki*. Yoshimoto Shûhô, ceremonial bottle (*hiraka*) in *sueki* style, pre-2000. 6½ x 7¾ inches (16.5 x 19.8 cm). Unglazed stoneware, *ao-bizen*.

Photo 87. Izushi-*yaki*. Nagasawa Eishin, tea set (*kikubori senchaki*), 1995. Small teapot (*hôhin*):
3 x 4 x 3½ inches (7.4 x 10.4 x 8.8 cm). Water cooler (*yuzamashi*): 1¾ x 3¾ x 2¾ inches
(4.7 x 9.6 x 7 cm). Teacup (*sencha chawan*): ¾ x 2½ inches (4.8 x 6.4 cm). White porcelain
(*hakuji*), chrysanthemum design in *senbori* technique with wax resist (*rônuki*).

reducing firing times to about 50 hours, the quantity of ash flow fell, so that in a neutral kiln atmosphere, the character of the pot's surface was determined by the red-brown to deep purple of the iron-rich clay. To reproduce the effects of the natural-ash glazes, the potters added wood and bamboo ash at the end of the firing. Finally, glazes came into use: a brown-black glaze, amber-colored *ame* glaze, and the red-brown *akadobe* glaze typical of Tanba-*yaki*.

Using Korean kick wheels allowed the careful shaping of a wide range of forms. Braziers (*hibachi*), tea ceramics (*chatsubo, chaire, mizusashi*), and vases to the specifications of the tea master Kobori Enshû, as well as *sake* bottles, were made. From the late Edo period, *sake* flasks (*tokkuri*) in more than 50 forms are known, including the well-known lacquered umbrella and candle forms, and white-slip-coated flasks with a prawn design. Transport bottles for *sake* (*binbô tokkuri*) included the brewer's name or the brand written on a light brown body in white slip by using a bamboo tube (*itchin*). Other typical Tanba decorations were incised patterns, leaf-resist patterns, and *suminagashi*.

The fact that 57 workshops are now operating again in Tachikui after an economically difficult phase during the early twentieth century is a result of the revival in interest in ceramics. This is due in part to the *mingei* movement, but above all it is the result of the sponsorship by Hyôgo Prefecture since 1948. Many innovations, such as electric wheels, slip casting, and gas and electric kilns have enabled the production of relatively inexpensive mass-produced wares. Since 1968, the local potter's association has organized production of the local clay—a mixture of yellow clay rock and a plastic, dark, sedimentary clay—for all the workshops in the village. In spite of these innovations, Tanba-*yaki* has preserved its folk art character into the present. This is largely the achievement of Okuda Yasuhiro, who came to Tanba in 1949 and worked in the spirit of the *mingei* movement under the tutelage of Hamada Shôji. Some potters still follow the old traditions and maintain a high artistic standard.

In addition to throwing, coiling is common. Tanba-*yaki* owes its appearance mainly to the forms and decorative techniques of the late Edo period (see photos 88 and 89). The number of glazes is still limited: alongside black and white glazes, brown iron glazes, such as *kimachi* glaze (see photo 90), are most common. Before the glazes are applied, the pots are now bisqued to 1292°F–1652°F (700°C–900°C). The main firing is to 2372°F (1300°C); about 20 workshops still use *noborigama* of the *waridakeshiki* type. Some artists are fascinated by the interplay of modern forms and the color changes of unglazed wares during firing (see photo 91). Vases, *sake* sets, and tea ceramics are made as *yakishime*, but for domestic tableware, glazed items predominate.

In spite of the technical innovations, Tachikui is one of the few potters' villages to have retained its unspoiled rural atmosphere. The ceramics park opened in 1985: *Tachikui sue no sato*, with its museum, exhibition space, and shop for the local potters, is well worth a visit.

Photo 88. Tanba-*yaki*. Ôgami Masayuki, umbrella-shaped *sake* bottle (*yakishime kasa tokkuri*), ca. 1999. 9½ x 4½ inches (24 x 11.4 cm). Unglazed stoneware, with traces of natural-ash glaze.

**Photo 89. Tanba-*yaki*. Ôgami Noboru, *sake* flask (*ebi-e tokkuri*), ca. 1998. 5¾ x 3¾ inches (14.8 x 9.5 cm).
Stoneware, prawn design in *itchin* technique, black slip on white slip.**

Photo 90.   Tanba-*yaki*. Shimizu Toshihiko, hexagonal box (*rokkaku futamono*) with character *hô* (treasure), ca. 1995. 3½ x 9½ inches (8.7 x 24.1 cm). Stoneware, *kimachi*-glaze.

Photo 91. Tanba-*yaki*. Ichino Kiyoharu, incense burner (*yakishime kôro*), 2000. 5¼ x 3¾ inches (13.6 x 9.5 cm). Unglazed stoneware.

Akahada 赤膚 (32)

To the west of the old imperial city of Nara (Nara Prefecture) in the Akahada region, rich clay deposits exist; these were already in use during the Kofun period (ca. 300–710) for the production of earthenware and tiles for temple roofs. In the fifteenth century, braziers for the tea ceremony (*doburo*) were the main product. The history of contemporary Akahada-*yaki* began in 1575, when Toyotomi Hidenaga, the owner of Koriyama castle near Nara, instructed the potter Yokuro from Tokoname to build three kilns (Nishi-*gama*, Naka-*gama*, Higashi-*gama*). Ritual objects and tea ceramics in glazed stoneware were produced. After a period of decline, Akahada-*yaki* became very popular between 1615 and 1624 under instruction from the tea master Kobori Enshû; the Akahada kilns are among the seven *Enshû nana gama*.

Between 1644 and 1668, the famous Kyôto potter Nonomura Ninsei tried in vain to introduce the style and production methods of Kyôto ceramics to Akahada. It was only with Lord Yanagisawa Gyôzan, who brought the master potter Furuse Jihei from Kyôto to Koriyama castle in 1730, that Akahada-*yaki* really began to flourish. As a *hanyô*, the Akahada kilns were economically secure. Tea ceramics influenced by Hagi, Kyô, and Takatori-*yaki* were produced as luxury wares alongside domestic tableware. The Meiji Restoration (1868) led to the closure of kilns. Influenced by developments in the twentieth century, the old potter families returned to their traditions; at present, six Akahada kilns are in operation again, four in Nara and two in Koriyama. Among these, the Akahada-yamamoto-*gama*, originally the Naka-*gama*, is being run by Furuse Gyôzô (born in 1936), Jihei's direct descendant in the seventh generation; and the kiln that used to be known as Nishi-*gama*, now Masando-*gama*, is run by Ôshio Masayoshi (born in 1933) in the eighth generation.

The ceramics made in the Akahada region are referred to as Akahada-*yaki*, but the term does not specifically refer to a certain style. Since the time of Enshû, a fine yellowish clay has been in use along with the iron-rich, red-firing clay from Mt. Akahada. The pots are wheel thrown or press molded, then bisque fired to 1202°F–1292°F (650°C–700°C) and glazed. They are fired in reduction with pine in a *renbôshiki-noborigama* for 50 to 60 hours to 2372°F (1300°C). Three glazes, the *akahada san-shoku*, are considered typical of Akahada-*yaki*: a milky white, rice-straw ash glaze that is said to have been adopted from Hagi; a light-colored, opaque glaze; and a black iron glaze. The Akahada potters still go to great lengths to develop glazes with various kinds of plant ash, and they achieve soft shades of beige, salmon pink, and a light yellow. Besides the *akahada san-shoku* objects (see photo 92), ceramics with *nara-e etsuke* (see photo 93) are predominant among the *omiyage* items; an example is overglaze painting in red, green, and blue on a milky white Hagi glaze with designs from Nara (*nara-e yamato-e*).

Asahi 朝日 (33)

In the Uji region of Kyôto Prefecture, *sueki* finds show that pottery has been produced there since the sixth century. With its tea plantations established in the late twelfth century, Uji became a center for the tea ceremony (*chanoyu*) in succeeding centuries. In the late sixteenth century, the potter Tôsaku began to produce glazed stoneware to supply the tea master's needs. Products with the *asahi* (morning sun) stamp became known as Asahi-*yaki*. The great tea master, Kobori Enshû, gave his support to the kiln in 1640. It is one of the seven *Enshû nana gama*—kilns particularly suitable for the production of tea ceramics.

As a result of the increasing preference for porcelain, demand for Asahi-*yaki* fell off, so that the family of potters that had adopted the name of Matsubayashi was forced to supplement its income as tea planters from the mid-eighteenth to the mid-nineteenth century. Repeated patronage by the imperial family and adaptation to the fashion for drinking *sencha* led to a recovery in the second half of the nineteenth century.

In 1975, Matsubayashi Hôsai XIV (now Yukoan, born in 1921) was able to start firing the Genyo-*gama* he had developed. The kiln was a technical innovation; it combined the principles of the *anagama* and the *noborigama* with an electronic

Photo 92.   Akahada-*yaki*. Furuse Gyôzô, tea bowl (*chawan*), 1984. 3 x 5 inches (7.6 x 13 cm). Stoneware, milky-white rice-straw ash glaze.

Photo 93. Akahada-*yaki*. Ôshio Masayoshi, *sake* cup (*nara-e yamato-e guinomi*), 1995. 1½ x 2½ inches (3.7 x 6.6 cm). Stoneware, milky-white Hagi glaze, overglaze painting in the *nara-e* style.

control that permitted low-emission firings with pine. Since 1995, the eldest son Yoshikane (born in 1950) has continued the tradition of Asahi-*yaki* under the name of Matsubayashi Hôsai XV. Tea ceramics are still the main products.

The clay for Asahi-*yaki* is dug locally and matures for several years in the open air until the organic components have decomposed. Pots are wheel thrown. During firing, the interplay of various clay bodies with a thin, pine-ash feldspar glaze and alternating kiln atmospheres produces the milky white to transparent *gohon-de* glaze, with the light-colored spots on a reddish body that are typical of Asahi-*yaki*. The following types are classified by appearance (see photo 94):

benikase: shadings from deep red-brown to gray, with orange spots
kase: beige-gray glaze with pale spots. A clay mixture with clay prepared by the ninth generation (mid-nineteenth century) and the twelfth generation is used for this.
hanshi: color varying from gray-pink to light pink with cream-white spots.

Interesting surface effects are achieved (see photo 95) by adding other decorative techniques such as combing (*kushime*).

Neighboring the kiln is a museum that is worth seeing, with exhibits of every generation of Matsubayashi potters and documentation on the Asahi kiln.

Kyôto 京都 with Kiyomizu 清水 (34)

Kyô-*yaki* is the term that, since the nineteenth century, has become widely used for stoneware and porcelain produced in and around Kyôto. Before this time, the wares were known by the names of the kilns where they originated, such as Awata-, Mizoro-, and Kiyomizu-*yaki*. Ceramics made in kilns in Kyôto before 1800 are also known as *ko*-Kiyomizu, but after 1800, the expression Kiyomizu-*yaki* referred exclusively to porcelain produced in the district around the Kiyomizu temple. Today, Kiyomizu-*yaki* is often wrongly used for Kyô-*yaki*.

Kyôto, then called Heian-kyô, became the imperial capital in 794 and remained the seat of government for more than 800 years. When the Tokugawa Shogunate moved the capital to Edo (present-day Tôkyô) in 1603, Kyôto remained the seat of the imperial dynasty, and the intellectual and religious center of Japan.

The production of ceramics in the Kyôto region has been documented since the end of the fifth century. In the eighth century, lead-glazed Nara-*sansai* was being made, and from the ninth to the twelfth century, it was mainly a monochrome green ware. With the increasing influence of the tea ceremony, potters from Seto who had settled in Awata, a district in Kyôto, produced tea utensils.

Present-day Kyô-*yaki*—with its wide variety ranging from raku to stoneware and porcelain with underglaze and overglaze decoration—developed in the late sixteenth and the seventeenth centuries. Limited local clay deposits prevented Kyôto from developing any uniform kind of ceramics. Craftspeople made specialized wares in small series from the precious raw material that had to be shipped long distances. Furthermore, Kyôto attracted the most able artists and craftspeople from all parts of the country. In the long periods of peace during the Tokugawa Shogunate, the imperial family and the aristocracy sponsored the arts and maintained their own workshops, and also invited famous potters to Kyôto. Thus, the development of ceramics in Kyôto was determined by a number of outstanding artistic personalities who not only set the trends with regard to styles in Kyôto but also far beyond. Against this background, raku-*yaki*, with its restrained color, developed under the influence of tea master Sen no Rikyû's *wabi* aesthetic, while exquisitely colorful Kyô-*yaki* in stoneware and porcelain emerged in various forms to fulfill the demands of the tea masters in the early seventeenth century for more elegance in the tea ceremony (*kirei-sabi*, beautiful *sabi*).

Raku-*yaki*, which developed from Nara-*sansai*, is a quickly fired, lead-glazed earthenware, originally produced exclusively for the tea ceremony and only in the colors red (*aka-raku*) and black (*kuro-raku*), but later with amber, white, and more rarely, *oribe* green glazes as well. The first *aka-raku*

Photo 94. Asahi-*yaki*. Matsubayashi Hôsai XV, *sake* cups (*guinomi*). Left: *gohon-de* glaze, *benikase* type, 1999. 2 x 2¾ inches (5 x 7 cm). Center: *gohon-de* glaze, *kase* type, with finger marks (*yubi-ato*), 1999. 1¾ x 2¾ inches (4.4 x 7 cm). Right: *gohon-de* glaze, *hanshi* type, 1998. 1¾ x 2¾ inches (4.5 x 6.8 cm). All stoneware.

Photo 95. Asahi-*yaki*. Matsubayashi Hôsai XIV (now Yukoan), vase with combed design (*kushime kabin*), pre-1980. 7 x 7¼ inches (18 x 18.4 cm). Stoneware, *gohon-de* glaze, *hanshi* type, with finger marks (*yubi-ato*).

tea bowl is said to have been created in or around 1579, under instruction from the tea master Sen no Rikyû, by the tile maker Chôjirô, who was familiar with the *sansai* technique. The production of *kuro-raku* was successfully achieved around 1582. In recognition of his achievement, his successor Jôkai was awarded the *raku* seal (*raku*, joy) by Toyotomi Hideyoshi; from that time onward, Jôkai (Raku II) was entitled to take over the designation as the family name. The Raku family is still producing this special type of tea ceramics with Raku Kichizaemon XV (born in 1949). Alongside the Raku family, other workshops have also dedicated themselves to the production of traditional raku ware.

The production technique for raku wares is derived from *setoguro* tea bowls (see Mino, 42, on page 171), which Sen no Rikyû held in particularly high esteem and which has hardly changed even today. The clay body used for raku firings must be able to withstand rapid heating and sudden cooling. For *aka-raku*, Chôjirô used a fine, iron-rich clay, and for the higher-fired *kuro-raku*, a coarser, sandy body. The clay is dug and stored by the Raku family for succeeding generations; thus, the present fifteenth generation is using clay prepared by the twelfth generation. Today, a white stoneware body is used in the main; for *kuro-raku*, grog may be added.

Pots are usually shaped by hand or more rarely, as in the case of Kawasaki Waraku's tea bowls (see photo 96), on the wheel. The forming process itself then takes place by cutting (*hera ato*) and pinching. For *aka-raku*, the unfired pot is coated with an iron-rich ochre slip, then covered with a transparent lead raku glaze. Several coats of *kamogawa-ishi* glaze (made from iron- and manganese-rich stones from the bed of the Kamo river that flows through Kyôto) are applied to *kuro-raku* before the pot receives a transparent lead raku glaze. The firing of *aka-raku* objects to 1562°F–1832°F (850°C–1000°C) takes about 25 minutes after they are placed in a saggar in the small raku kiln. As soon as the glaze has matured, the pot is drawn from the kiln while it is still red hot and cools in the air. For black raku, the kiln is equipped with bellows because temperatures of 2192°F–2282°F (1200°C–1250°C) must be reached within a short period of time. The glaze matures within only 8 to 10 minutes. Since the body has not vitrified after this brief firing period, *kuro-raku* can be termed "high-fired earthenware."

When people began to turn to the *kirei-sabi* aesthetic in the early seventeenth century, a more elaborate tea ceremony became highly valued. In accordance with the taste of the aristocracy, this appreciation was propagated by the tea masters, Kobori Enshû, and to a greater extent, Kanamori Sôwa (1584–1656) with his tea style, the "tea of the palaces." With colorfully decorated stoneware and later, porcelain in unusual forms, a new stage in the development of ceramics began and continued into the nineteenth century. Nonomura Ninsei is inextricably linked with this development.

Nonomura Seiemon (ca. 1627–1695) named himself Nonomura after his birthplace in Tanba. In 1647, after training as a potter in Seto, he built his kiln in Omuro, Kyôto, immediately adjacent to Ninna-ji, a temple; he was permitted to incorporate *nin*, the first character of the temple's name, in his own artist's pseudonym. Ninsei is held to be the father of Kyô-*yaki* because he was the first potter in Japan to introduce overglaze enamel painting on stoneware (*iro-e*), which is still characteristic of Kyô-*yaki*. Ninsei was an excellent craftsman, and his vessels, such as tea storage jars (*chatsubo*), tea bowls, and incense boxes (*kôgô*) in figural forms were made with exquisite skill. The rich colors of his objects are never intrusive in their typical blue, green, red, brown red, ochre, and gold on a calm background of silver gray, black, or a creamy white that he developed himself. The composition of the decoration, in which he uses flowers or other ornaments, including *maki-e* lacquer work or kimono fabrics for his designs, always appears balanced. Ninsei is said to have founded no fewer than nine kilns in Kyôto, including the Mizoro-*gama* in Awata, with its refined *iro-e* decoration in blue, green, and gold on a creamy white crackled background. After the establishment of additional kilns, Kyôto became one of the leading ceramics centers of the Edo period, after the Hizen domain and the Seto-Mino region.

While Ninsei worked for his aristocratic clients, cooperating closely with the tea master Kanamori Sôwa, his pupil Ogata Kenzan (born Ogata Shinsei;

Photo 96. Kyô-*yaki*. Kawasaki Waraku, tea bowl (*chawan*), 2000. 3 x 4½ inches (7.5 x 11.6 cm). Black raku (*kuro-raku*).

1663–1743) worked for many years as a freelance potter—a studio potter in today's terms. Kenzan was erudite, but as a potter he was self-taught. His vessel forms (more side dishes and plates than tea ceramics) were simple and were used as supports for the decoration—often a combination of painting and calligraphy (an individual artistic genre in Japan) that was applied to a white slip background. On some of his works, his brother, the great Rimpa painter Ogata Kôrin (1658–1716), took over the painting while Kenzan was responsible for the calligraphy. Thus, the well-known square platters have a combination of calligraphy and painting in iron oxide underglaze (sabi-e) on a coating of white slip. Covering it all is a kind of transparent luster glaze. Other pieces combine sabi-e and sometsuke (cobalt underglaze painting) with overglaze enamels (iro-e). Ninsei had given Kenzan his secret glaze recipes (tô hô denshô), which the latter developed further. Ninsei and Kenzan were the first potters to sign their work. Until that time, a stamp from the individual kiln had been customary.

In addition to iro-e stoneware in Ninsei and Kenzan style, kûchû-Shigaraki—a yakishime stoneware made of clay mixed with sand in Shigaraki style—was made in the Awata kilns in the seventeenth century. Along with blue-and-white porcelain in the eighteenth and nineteenth centuries, these wares were also made by the famous Kyôto potters, Kiyomizu Rokubei I–III, and may still be found in Kyôto today. The work of the studio potter Hoshino Kayoko, who lives near Kyôto, is inspired by this style (see photo 185).

At the end of the eighteenth century, enthusiasm for the study of China resulted in Chinese wares being held in particularly high esteem, as they had been before the heyday of wabi tea ceramics. Because of Japan's seclusion, the demand had to be covered by domestic ceramics production. The first ceramist to dedicate himself to the reproduction of Chinese porcelain was Okuda Eisen (born Okuda Yôtoku; 1753–1811). He is said to have introduced the production of porcelain to Kyôto between 1781 and 1789. The newly constructed porcelain kilns, which appeared in rapid succession, were concentrated in the Kiyomizu Gojô-zaka district, immediately adjacent to the Kiyomizu temple. Much of Eisen's work, especially more refined domestic items in underglaze blue (sometsuke), alone or with overglaze decoration in green or red (gosu aka-e), were reproductions of Chinese ceramics of the late Ming (1368–1644) and early Qing (1644–1912) dynasties. Of Eisen's many pupils, the best known are Aoki Mokubei and Nin'ami Dôhachi II. Together with Eiraku Hozen, they are known as the "Three Famous Potters" of Kyôto from the nineteenth century.

Aoki Mokubei (born Aoki Sahei; 1767–1833), potter, poet, painter, and tea master, was very versatile in style and technique. Blue-and-white porcelain (sometsuke), white porcelain (hakuji), porcelain with overglaze enamels (iro-e) and in red and gold (akaji-kinran-de), celadons, Kôchi ware, stoneware with gohon-de glaze, and even small, unglazed (nanban style) teapots (kyûsu) were parts of his repertoire. He also painted figures in five colors on a red background, in the Chinese style—a decorative technique that he often used in his attempt to revive Kutani-yaki at the Kasugayama-gama in Kanazawa (1807–1808). Mokubei studied the Chinese models closely but used them as stimuli for his own individual creations.

Nin'ami Dôhachi II (born Takahashi Mitsutoki; 1783–1855) worked in Awata until he set up a kiln in Fushimi, near Kyôto, in 1842. Dôhachi specialized in tea ceramics and was famous for his recreations of other styles in stoneware and porcelain—his efforts to revive the Ninsei and Kenzan styles. Besides his decorated raku tea bowls, his unkin-de bowls are impressive, with the irregular, undulating rims integrated into the decoration of white cherry blossoms (sakura) and red maple leaves (momiji).

Nishimura Hozen (1795–1854) called himself Eiraku Hozen after Lord Tokugawa Naritsune had awarded him the eiraku seal (eiraku, eternal joy). Like the two other great masters of the nineteenth century, Hozen was familiar with all porcelain and stoneware techniques. For the most part, he produced tea ceramics: blue-and-white porcelain in the style of the shonzui ware from the Chinese Jingdezhen kilns in the late Ming dynasty; blue-and-white ware with overglaze decoration (gosu aka-e); celadons; stoneware with gohon-de glaze;

and Kôchi ware. However, Hozen's specialty was his *akaji-kinran-de*, with gold decoration on an iron red glaze as an imitation of lacquer work.

In spite of the Three Famous Potters, the development of ceramics in Kyôto stagnated during the nineteenth century. The introduction of technical innovations and the export boom in the latter part of the century encouraged bulk production and led to a decline in quality. The small studios, with their careful art-and-craft-based production, were forced out of the market. In the Meiji period, ceramics were among Kyôto's biggest export items, along with tea and raw silk. For instance, more than 1000 people were employed at the Kinkôzan Sôbei VII factory in Awata to make clay from Kyûshû into *shiro*-Satsuma. In the 1920s, there was a return to the values of Kyô-*yaki*, fostered by the Japanese state. Because of this development, four ceramists from the Kyôto region were designated *ningen kokuhô* (Living National Treasures). In 1955, the title was awarded to Ishiguro Munemaru (1893–1968) for his *tenmoku* glazes and to Tomimoto Kenkichi (1886–1963) for *iro-e jiki* (porcelain with overglaze painting); in 1977, Kenkichi's student Kondô Yûzô (1902–1985) was honored for *sometsuke* porcelain, as was Shimizu Uichi (1926–2004) in 1985 for his work with *tetsu-yû* (iron glaze).

The more than 200 workshops in Kyôto today are largely traditional in their production of high-quality ceramics: more than 90 percent is handmade, including objects ranging from domestic wares and tea ceramics, to incense boxes and burners and *ikebana* vessels. The production methods are as diverse as the highly varied styles of ceramics, but they are generally conventional. Tried and tested forms and decorations from the past 400 years are cultivated and developed, so that in present-day Kyôto, raku-*yaki* (see photo 96) can be found alongside classic Kiyomizu porcelain with cobalt underglaze painting in *shonzui* style (see photo 97) or with overglaze enamel decoration, and *sansai* ware that is frequently interpreted in a contemporary manner (see photo 98). Many tea bowls and *sencha* tea sets are covered with the *gohon-de* glaze alone, typical of Kyôto, or, as in the tea bowl of Yamamoto Yûji (born in 1945), with the glaze and the typical *unkin-de* decoration of the Dôhachi bowls (see photo 99). In contrast to this, the contemporary designs of Takiguchi Kazuo seem light in comparison; the cherry blossoms on his tea bowl appear to float (see photo 100). Takiguchi (born in 1953), whose individually made pieces with their black surfaces form a stark contrast to his tableware line, is considered one of the most renowned studio potters influenced by the Sôdeisha movement.

References to Kôchi ware, with its cloisonné-style surface treatment, are now only found on smaller objects (see photo 101), which is also true of figural representations such as mandarin ducks (see photo 102)—symbols of the bond of marriage—a design often chosen by Ninsei and the later masters for incense boxes (*kôgô*). Also typical of contemporary Kyô-*yaki* is a pale blue, heavily crazed celadon glaze on tea bowls and *sake* bowls in *tenmoku* form (see photo 103). A master of tenmoku glazes is Kamada Kôji (born in 1948), with his *yôhen-tenmoku* (hare's fur *tenmoku*, see photo 104) and the rare blue *yuteki-tenmoku* (oil-spot tenmoku, see photo 105). The traditional *mishima* and *hakeme* decorations are present in the work of the great Kyôto masters, but they also exert a fascination on the young generation, as the *hakeme* vessel of Yamamoto Tetsuya (born in 1969) demonstrates (see photo 106).

Among Kyôto's studio potters, there is a pronounced tendency toward individualism (for examples, see photos 186, 193, 194, 196, 200, and 205). The postwar avant-garde joined artists' associations such as Sôdeisha, but today's young art-school graduates tend to seek their individual artistic path free of any trends or movements.

Photo 97. Kyô-*yaki*. Heian Kitchô, "husband and wife" teacups (*meoto yunomi*), 2000. 3½ x 2¾ inches (8.8 x 7 cm) and 3¼ x 2½ inches (8.2 x 6.5 cm). Porcelain with cobalt underglaze painting (*sometsuke*) in the *shonzui* style.

Photo 98.   Kyô-*yaki*. Shimizu Yasutaka, lidded box (*futamono*), 1986. 3 x 3¾ inches (8 x 9.8 cm). Stoneware, *sansai* design.

Photo 99. Kyô-yaki. Yamamoto Yûji, tea bowl (*chawan*), 1988. 3¼ x 5 inches (8 x 12.6 cm). Stoneware, *gohon-de* glaze, overglaze painting in *unkin-de* design with cherry blossom (*sakura*) and autumn maple (*momiji*).

Photo 100. Kyô-*yaki*. Takiguchi Kazuo, tea bowl (*chawan*), 1998. 3¼ x 5 inches (8 x 13 cm). Stoneware, cherry blossom (*sakura*) overglaze design.

Photo 101. **Kyô-yaki.** *Sake* **cup (***guinomi***), 1992. 1¾ x 2 inches (4.3 x 5 cm). Porcelain in the Kôchi style, fired in the San-***gama***, Kiyomizu.**

Photo 102. Kyô-*yaki***. Chopstick rests (***hashioki***), 1998. 1¼ x 1¾ inches (3 x 4.7 cm) and 1 x 1¾ inches (2.7 x 4.2 cm). Porcelain, *iro-e kinran-de*, fired in the Shôhô-***gama***.**

Photo 103.   Kyô-*yaki*. Nishijima Hideki, *sake* cup (*guinomi*), 1984. 1¾ x 2½ inches (4.5 x 6.5 cm). Stoneware, celadon glaze with crackle (*kan'nyu*).

Photo 104.   Kyô-*yaki*. Kamada Kôji, *sake* cup (*choko*), 1988. 1½ x 3½ inches (3.5 x 9 cm). Stoneware, *yôhen-tenmoku* glaze (hare's fur *tenmoku*).

Photo 105.   Kyô-*yaki*. Kamada Kôji, *sake* cup (choko), 1998. 1¼ x 3½ inches (3.2 x 8.7 cm). Stoneware, blue *yuteki-tenmoku* glaze (oil-spot *tenmoku*).

Photo 106.   Kyô-yaki. Yamamoto Tetsuya, sake pourer (katakuchi), 1999. 2½ x 9¾ x 4¼ inches (6.5 x 25 x 11 cm). Stoneware with hakeme decoration.

Zeze 膳所 (35)

The only kiln that still makes Zeze ware is located in the town of Ôtsu, on Lake Biwa (Shiga Prefecture). The origins of production about 1600 are said to go back to the construction of a feudal kiln by Suganuma Sadayoshi, the *daimyô* of Zeze. According to other sources, all the kilns in Zeze domain in the Edo period are subsumed under the name of Zeze-*yaki* (such as Ôe, Kokubu, Bairin, and Suzumegatani). One of the first reliable descriptions of the Ôe and Kokubu kilns can be found in a 1678 travel journal, *Edo nikki*, by Morita Hisaemon. To achieve good results when throwing, local clay was often mixed with other clays. The characteristic iron and ash glazes were influenced by Seto ceramics from the fifteenth to seventeenth centuries. The potter and calligrapher Hon'ami Kôetsu (1558–1637) and the tea master Kobori Enshû (1579–1647) had a significant influence on the style of Zeze-*yaki*. Zeze is thus considered to be one of the seven *Enshû nana gama*. The only product was tea ceramics; freshwater jars (*mizusashi*) and tea caddies (*chaire*) from Zeze were especially highly esteemed and on an equal footing with Takatori and Seto ware.

Due to financial difficulties, Zeze kilns were forced to close down several times in the eighteenth and nineteenth centuries. With the support of local artists, Iwasaki Kenzô succeeded in reviving Zeze tea ceramics in the traditional style, beginning in 1919. Today, the kiln is run by his son, Iwasaki Shinjô (see photo 107). Situated adjacent to the kiln and founded in 1987 is a small museum for Zeze-*yaki* that showcases seventeenth-century tea ceramics.

Shigaraki 信楽 (36)

Shigaraki (Shiga Prefecture), located east of Lake Biwa, is one of the Six Ancient Kilns (*roku koyô*), and is still one of the great centers for the production of stoneware today. Since the fifth century, *sueki* and *hajiki* have been produced in the Shigaraki region, and in Shigaraki itself, some of the first kilns were built to produce roof tiles after the construction of an imperial palace in Shigaraki had begun on the orders of Emperor Shômu in 742. Due to a series of natural catastrophes, the capital had to be moved back to Nara three years later, and it is still not clear whether the *sueki* shards found among the temple ruins were in fact locally produced or if they came from one of the neighboring *sueki* centers such as Kagami, with its more than 50 kilns.

It was probably between 1268 and 1284 that Shigaraki, as the last of the Six Ancient Kilns, began the production of unglazed stoneware (*yakishime*); no data about the first kilns are available yet. The early Shigaraki vessels closely resemble wares from Tokoname, where by this time production was flourishing. It is therefore assumed that the optimized firing techniques from Tokoname had been adopted. Medieval Shigaraki-*yaki* was coil built; the white clay with its low iron content fired to colors ranging from salmon pink to red-brown, and the particles of pegmatite (grains of feldspar and quartz) rose to the surface as white stars (*hoshi*) during firing in the *anagama*. Natural-ash glazes ranging from gray-green to gray-blue are also formed. Besides mortars and other kitchen utensils, mainly storage jars (*tsubo*) were produced. Generally, the *tsubo* were undecorated, but a few had incised rope patterns on the shoulder.

In the second half of the fifteenth century, Shigaraki-*yaki* was discovered by the tea masters. Murata Jukô was the first to use Shigaraki-*yaki* for the tea ceremony; in the spirit of the *wabi-sabi* aesthetic, he selected small items such as flower vases, fresh-water jars, and storage jars for tea leaves from the range of simple domestic ware. Subsequent tea masters, such as Takeno Jôô, Sen no Rikyû, and Kobori Enshû asked Shigaraki potters to make *chadôgu* according to their specifications, and these ceramics were correspondingly known as Jôô, Rikyû, and Enshû-Shigaraki. In 1632, Shigaraki was licensed by the Tokugawa Shogunate as the sole supplier of storage jars for tea leaves (*chatsubo*) for the precious tea from Uji.

When Shigaraki lost its leading role in tea ceramics to Bizen and Iga in the second half of the seventeenth century, it once again made domestic wares, which until then had been produced parallel to its main product, tea ceramics. It was

Photo 107. Zeze-*yaki*. Iwasaki Shinjô, tea bowl (*chawan*), 1999. 2½ x 5 inches (6.4 x 13 cm). Stoneware, brown iron glaze, white cover glaze.

also during this period that production was largely converted to glazed wares: the introduction of the *noborigama* in the early seventeenth century made possible the mass production of this kind of glazed stoneware for storage jars, mortars, *sake* bottles, bowls, and plates. Production of *chatsubo* continued; the articles made during this period with white or brown glazes are particularly well known. In the mid-eighteenth century, Shigaraki was strongly influenced by nearby Kyôto; small vessels and candle holders for domestic altars (*tômyôzara*) were made in Kyô style, known as Kyô-Shigaraki. In Kyôto on the other hand, potters had been trying to reproduce the surface structure of *yakishime* from Shigaraki—the so-called *kûchû*-Shigaraki—since the seventeenth century. In the nineteenth century, Shigaraki-*yaki* glazes became more expressive, and the best-known items include the *chatsubo* with Hagi-*nagashi*, a green copper glaze flowing in streaks over a white Hagi glaze, and the *sansui dobin*, teapots with landscape scenes.

The dismantling of the feudal system that came about with the Meiji Restoration brought no profound changes for the Shigaraki kilns, which had always been municipally or privately owned. Industrialization led to the production of large bottles for sulphuric acid and *shôchû*, in addition to the mass production of domestic wares. Into the 1950s, 80 percent of charcoal braziers (*hibachi*) sold in Japan came from Shigaraki. Today, about 150 workshops produce tiles, planters, *bonsai* and *ikebana* vessels, garden furniture (*teienyôhin*), *hibachi*, umbrella stands, vases, domestic wares, and glazed reproductions of medieval *yakishime* ware, as well as *tanuki* (badgers) as lucky charms, ranging from key-ring pendants to man-sized figures.

Shigaraki clay is a *kibushi-nendo* from the sedimentary layers of Lake Biwa; due to its plasticity and refractory properties, it is industrially prepared and sold throughout Japan. For precision in the forming process, the pegmatite particles are removed, then added again in controlled quantities. The unmixed clay is unsuitable for throwing, so pots are coiled or more frequently press molded. Decorative techniques include impressed relief, incising and sgraffito techniques,

and underglaze painting with asbolite or *oni-ita*, as well as the use of colored glazes. Firing temperatures are about 2372°F (1300°C) in gas or electric kilns, which have been used in industrial production since 1960.

Besides mass production, there are a number of potters who continue the tradition of early *yakishime* in their work. The rediscovery of traditions through the *mingei* movement and the revival of ancient techniques in various other pottery centers in the years between the two world wars opened many potters' eyes to the beauty of the old Shigaraki-*yaki*. Around 1940, Takahashi Rakusai III and Ueda Naokata began production of *yakishime* in the style of early Shigaraki-*yaki*. Over the years, they developed their personal styles, which went beyond mere imitation. In 1958, Rakusai was honored at the World's Fair in Brussels. Together with the excavation of more than 200 medieval kilns in 1967, this led to a revival of enthusiasm for unglazed Shigaraki-*yaki*. A highly prized aspect of this type of ware is the so-called "three landscapes" effect (*mitsu no keshiki*), with "fire color" (*hi-iro*), scorch markings (*koge*), and vitrified glass (*bîdoro*), as well as the explosive bursts of pegmatite particles on the surface (*ishihaze*) at temperatures of over 2372°F (1300°C).

Firing, usually in a *noborigama* and more rarely in an *anagama*, lasts at least a week; red pine is used exclusively as the fuel. The first *anagama* in Shigaraki since the Middle Ages was reintroduced by Furutani Michio (1946–2000), who built about 30 different *anagama* to achieve various firing effects (see photo 108). The Shigaraki potters—masters of the interplay of various clays—work with 20 different blends, the position of the object in the kiln, and control of the kiln atmosphere between oxidation and reduction in order to retain the *hi-iro* reds and achieve a clear *bîdoro*. As a result, all stages, ranging from the unglazed body with pegmatite inclusions (see photo 108) to transparent natural-ash glazes (see photo 109) and heavy deposits of fly ash with *koge* and *bîdoro* (see photo 110) can be found on contemporary Shigaraki-*yakishime* vessels. This diversity in Shigaraki-*yaki* has inspired many studio potters to grapple with traditional techniques in their modern forms.

Photo 108. **Shigaraki-*yaki*.** Furutani Michio, bottle vase (*hanaire*), 1987. 10 x 5½ inches (25.2 x 13.8 cm). *Yakishime* stoneware, pegmatite inclusions and *ishihaze*.

Iga 伊賀 (37)

The area around Iga-Ueno (Mie Prefecture), in which Iga-*yaki* is produced, and the neighboring pottery center of Shigaraki are separated only by a range of hills; clay and production methods are largely identical. Like Shigaraki-*yaki*, Iga stoneware has its roots in Sue ceramics. The ceramics made for everyday use until the end of the sixteenth century were of coarse, unglazed stoneware. This changed during the reign of Tsutsui Sadatsugu (1584–1608), feudal lord of Iga province, tea master, and friend of Furuta Oribe. Tea ceramics made to his specifications—mainly fresh-water jars (*mizusashi*), vases, and tea bowls—came from at least three kilns in the castle town of Ueno. This rough, heavy type of ceramics, known as Tsutsui-Iga, reveals marks from the making process, and deformations of the body and the rim of the pot, as well as *mitsu no keshiki* and *ishihaze*. Changes during firing (*yôhen*) resulting in deep cracks were deliberately produced by the Iga potters as an expression of an "artificial" naturalness that was a feature of the Oribe style. The most famous *mizusashi* in Japan is one such Tsutsui-Iga pot with a cracked body; it is called *Yabure-bukoro* (Torn Pouch) in accordance with its appearance.

Tsutsui's successor, Lord Tôdô Takatora, a pupil of the tea masters Furuta Oribe and Kobori Enshû, had kilns built in Marubashira, near Ueno, for the production of his tea ceramics. The Tôdô-Iga made there was progressively refined, especially after Enshû had a relatively thin-walled type of ceramics with artificial glazes made between 1624 and 1644 (Enshû-Iga). Production came to a standstill around 1670.

There were many attempts to revive Iga-*yaki* during the Edo period. The ceramics, which were mainly glazed domestic wares, are referred to as *saikô*-Iga (revived Iga), as opposed to the *ko*-Iga of the Azuchi-Momoyama and early Edo periods. In the early eighteenth century, Marubashira became the center of domestic wares, with its tableware, teapots, and *donabe* (stoneware casseroles that could be placed directly on the open flame because of the thermal shock-resistance of the clay body). Around 1920, a mass-produced item, the *kisha dobin*, was added to the product range. These were small pots for hot tea sold at railway stations. Today, Marubashira is still the center of the production of *donabe* and glazed tableware, with more than 20 workshops in operation.

It is thanks to Tanimoto Kôsei (born in 1916) that Iga-*yaki* is now produced in the Momoyama style again—30 years ago, he was the only potter still working in the *ko*-Iga tradition. His traditional vessel forms, in combination with the *mitsu no keshiki* achieved during firing, make him the leading Iga potter. His eldest son Kei (born in 1948), who studied in Paris, as well as his third son Yô (born in 1958), and his student Fujioka Shûhei (born in 1947) now continue the classic Iga style in different forms. Yô, who studied in Kyôto, Paris, and Barcelona, uses the Iga techniques for his abstract objects, as well as for his traditional tea ceramics (see photos 15 and 111). Fujioka Shûhei creates vessels with powerful sculptural forms, emphasized by *mitsu no keshiki* effects (see photo 112).

The unique aspect of the Iga technique is the firing: In contrast to Shigaraki-*yaki*, the pots are fired more than 10 times in a *maki-gama* at temperatures of up to 2732°F (1500°C) until the potter has achieved the desired effect. In this manner, the moss green *bîdoro* that is typical of Iga-*yaki* can be produced; as a puddle of glaze on the interior of a tea bowl, it is highly esteemed by tea lovers as *tonbo no me* (dragonfly's eye; see photo 15).

Photo 109.   Shigaraki-*yaki*. Hashimoto Seibin, spherical vase (*tsubo*), 1998. 9¼ x 10½ inches (23.4 x 26.7 cm). *Yakishime* stoneware, transparent natural-ash glaze and *ishihaze*.

Photo 110.   Shigaraki-*yaki*. Tani Seiemon, vase with lugs (*mimi tsuki hanaire*), ca. 2001. 9 x 4¼ inches
(23 x 10.8 cm). Stoneware, heavy natural-ash glaze, scorch markings (*koge*), vitrified glass
(*bidoro*), and *ishihaze*.

Photo 111. **Iga-*yaki*. Tanimoto Yô, tea bowl (*chawan*), 1999. 3 x 4¾ inches (7.8 x 12.3 cm). Stoneware, natural-ash glaze, *ishihaze*.**

Photo 112. Iga-*yaki*. Fujioka Shûhei, *sake* flask (*tokkuri*), ca. 2001. 5¾ x 3¾ inches (14.4 x 9.8 cm).
Stoneware, natural-ash glaze, fire color (*hi-iro*), vitrified glass (*bidoro*), *ishihaze*.

Yokkaichi Banko 四日市万古 (38)

The name Banko-*yaki* goes back to the pottery merchant Nunami Rôzan, who set up a kiln near the Ise shrine between 1736 and 1741, and stamped his pots with the legend *banko fueki* (unchangeable eternity). Rôzan was well known, especially for his *aka-e* stoneware, a type of pottery with red overglaze painting on a beige-brown crackle glaze. He was summoned to Edo as the official potter by *shôgun* Tokugawa Ienari in 1785. In addition to his *aka-e* stoneware, he made copies of Chinese porcelain (mainly the famille rose and the famille verte), as well as Delft faience. His work as a whole is referred to as *ko-*Banko (old Banko), although his work from the Edo period is also known as Edo-Banko.

There was no successor to take over his workshop, and it was not until 1831 that Mori Yûsetsu purchased the Banko stamp from Rôzan's grandson and revived the *ko*-Banko style in his kiln in Asahi (Mie Prefecture). The colorful brushwork, with overglaze enamels in the Japanese style (*yamato-e*) on a cream glaze, which is termed Yûsetsu-Banko, was typical of his work. Using a brown clay body, Mori Yûsetsu also developed a thin-walled, unglazed, lightweight type of tea ware for drinking green tea (*sencha*), which came into fashion in the nineteenth century.

In 1829, a feudal kiln for the production of tea ceramics and domestic tableware in Shigaraki style was established in the town of Yokkaichi, in present-day Mie Prefecture. As a result of the Meiji Restoration, it was closed down. To create a source of income for the impoverished populace, Yamanaka Chûzaemon built a new kiln in Hamaisshiki, a district of Yokkaichi, in 1870. The main products were items in the Yûsetsu-Banko style, which were recognized in the West as export ware after they had been exhibited at the 1878 World's Fair in Paris. After suffering economic difficulties in the early twentieth century, Yokkaichi Banko-*yaki* resumed a successful phase after the Second World War.

Today, more than 10 workshops produce teapots, tea bowls, tea-ceremony utensils, vases, and *sake* jugs. The traditional styles are cultivated: alongside *aka-e* ware, Yûsetsu-Banko ceramics can be found, but it is the *sencha* tea sets made from a red, iron-rich clay, in unglazed red-brown to chestnut shades (*shudei*), that predominate. Some of the vessels are wheel thrown, but others, particularly the small teapots with side handles (*kyûsu*), are often pressed onto wooden forms (*kigata*) that can be dismantled, or are cast in plaster molds.

Decoration takes place at various stages of the making process: in the *herame* technique, a diamond pattern is cut into the surface of the moist clay with a bamboo knife, or *hera* (see photo 113). After further drying, the vessels are assembled and burnished, after which geometric or floral patterns or perforations (*sukashibori*) are incised. During the main firing in a gas or electric kiln, which takes 24 hours, final temperatures are 2156°F–2192°F (1180°C–1200°C). The typical brown color emerges in reduction, with the shade between red and brown determined by the residual oxygen content.

The production of the extremely light Yokkaichi Kata Banko-yaki is considered to be particularly difficult. Using a specially prepared clay, slabs are rolled out to paper-thinness and pressed on a form (*kata*) made of damp cloth stretched over wooden battens. Depending on the type of clay used, the color of the unburnished ware may vary between beige and brown (see photo 114).

Tokoname 常滑 (39)

The ceramics made south of Nagoya, on the Chita peninsula, around the town of Tokoname (Aichi Prefecture), are called Tokoname-*yaki*. Current research suggests that Tokoname is the oldest of the Six Ancient Kilns (*roku koyô*). The origins lie in unglazed Sue ceramics from the fifth century; from the eighth century on, gray-green glazed Sanage ware was made on the Chita peninsula. Potters from Tokoname made technical improvements to the single-chamber climbing kiln (*anagama*) so that firing temperatures of more than 2372°F (1300°C) could be achieved. Around 1100, Tokoname ceramics changed from the glazed *shiki* of Sanage ware to the unglazed, high-fired stoneware with natural-ash glazes (*yakishime*) of the Middle Ages.

Photo 113. **Yokkaichi Banko-***yaki***. Mori Iroku, tea set (***senchaki***), 1999. Side-handled small teapot (***kyûsu***):**
2¾ x 5½ x 3¼ inches (7 x 13.7 x 8.3 cm). Water cooler (*yuzamashi***): 1½ x 3¾ x 3½ inches**
(3.8 x 9.7 x 9.2 cm). Teacups (*sencha chawan***), with interior glaze: 2 x 2½ inches (5 x 6.5 cm).**
Shudei* ware, diamond facets (herame***).**

Photo 114.   Yokkaichi Kata Banko-*yaki*. Itô Jitsuzan, side-handled small teapot (*kyûsu*) with rotating knob (*maitsumami*), 1999. 3¼ x 4¾ x 2¾ inches (8.3 x 12 x 7.3 cm). Unglazed stoneware.

The first dated pot is from 1125. The main products were large storage jars, bowls, and urns that were used, beginning in 1150, for the storage of scrolls with Buddhist sutras. By around 1200, the Tokoname region had become the biggest ceramics center in Japan, with more than 3000 kilns in operation. The pots were traded all over Japan and were shipped from the port of Tokoname. The vessels from the twelfth to fourteenth centuries are termed ko-Tokoname (old Tokoname) and are made of a coarse, sandy body, the fired color of which ranges from red brown to shades of gray. The storage jars, which were up to 6 feet (1.8 m) tall, were coil built; the potter moved around the pot as he built up the walls. Shallow bowls were made on a primitive wheel. The forms were simple and powerful; the storage jars, with narrow bases and pronounced, rounded shoulders, remained undecorated apart from rare incised patterns, but were enhanced in appearance by the flowing of the gray-green natural-ash glazes from the wood-fired anagama.

With the ôgama—a large, technically improved anagama—the mass production of unglazed rice bowls (yamachawan) and other unglazed stoneware began around 1400. This was also called mayake ware. By 1694, twelve ôgama of this type were in use. Only from the seventeenth century on did the product range gradually shift toward utensils for the tea ceremony, flower vases, and smaller domestic items. Under the influence of the tea masters, the ceramics became more refined and were exclusively wheel thrown. In 1750, Watanabe Yahei became the first potter allowed to sign his work.

From the end of the Edo period and into the following Meiji period, Tokoname-yaki developed in various directions. Traditional mayake ware continued to be produced, but in 1830, Ina Chôza II developed a variation—the mogake technique, inspired by the hidasuki of Bizen ware. It is still in use today. Seaweed is wrapped around the pots to produce red markings on the light-colored body during firing. In 1834, the first renbôshiki-noborigama in Tokoname was built. The firing was easier to control in this type of kiln in comparison with the ôgama, making the development of red, unglazed shudei ware possible. This became an important area of ceramics production in Tokoname in the late nineteenth century. With the growing popularity of green tea (sencha), sencha tea sets were made from the early nineteenth century on, but red ware (akamono) from China remained the most sought after for tea drinking. For this reason, in 1878, Jin Shi Heng and other Chinese specialists were invited to establish the shudei method for the production of side-handled, small teapots (kyûsu) and teacups in Tokoname. Soon, a large number of workshops for the production of this type of pottery had been established. In 1887, in the export trade with the West, the so-called shudei-tatsu-maki—shudei vases with applications of dragons (haritsuke-mon) arranged around the body of the pot—briefly became a best-selling item.

For the shudei-kyûsu that are still made today on a large scale, only the finest-grained portion of a very iron-rich clay (tatsuchi) dug from under rice paddies is used. The components of the teapot are thrown and evenly dried before the surface is compacted by burnishing with a metal tool. This burnishing process is necessary to achieve the degree of sheen on the surface of the unglazed pots. After the strainer, spout, and handle are fitted, the pot is burnished again. Since 1878, incising Japanese characters and floral designs has been customary. Depending upon the quality of the clay, the oxidation firing takes place at 2012°F–2048°F (1100°C–1120°C) and must be kept under careful surveillance. Temperature fluctuations of as little as 50°F (10°C) produce variations in color in the red clay body, and the pots tend to crack very easily due to the heavy shrinkage of 20 percent to 30 percent. In mass production, these problems are now overcome by computer-controlled kilns. After firing, pots with incised decoration are rubbed with ink to bring out the designs.

The production of glazed stoneware began at the end of the nineteenth century, first with the brightly colored kinran-de-tôki for export, and second, with domestic wares with a wide variety of glazes; in 1901, salt glazing was introduced from Europe. Some workshops produced saikumono (ornamental objects).

Industrial ceramics became a major supplier of Tokoname-yaki. In the mid-nineteenth century, production of large bottles to hold industrial acids and the strong alcoholic drink, *shôchû*, as well as pipes, began. In the early Meiji period, the production of water pipes and drain pipes developed into an independent industry, which is still in existence. Sanitary wares, ceramics for the garden, and tiles are also produced. These mass-produced items were originally fired in more than 60 *noborigama*. The *kaku-gama*—a downdraft kiln introduced from Europe, originally fired with coal and later with fuel oil—was fired beginning in 1900. By 1929, 86 kilns of this type were in use; by this time, the kiln's flame path and fuel economy had been improved. For environmental reasons, these kilns were gradually replaced by electric and gas kilns during the second half of the twentieth century.

The disparate nature of Tokoname-*yaki* today is the result of developments over the past 200 years. There is the broad range of industrial ceramics (the most important economic factor in this large ceramics center), and more than 260 companies and 1000 employees. Functional wares also show a great deal of variety: the Ceramics Research Institute of the city of Tokoname, founded in 1961, encouraged young ceramists from all over Japan to settle in Tokoname. As a result, tea ceramics, vases, and tableware in glazed and unglazed stoneware, and in a wide range of styles, may be found. There is also the work of traditional artists/craftspeople (47 are state-recognized) who continue the Tokoname tradition with *mayake* ware, some in *mogake* technique (see photo 115), and *shudei* ware.

The best-known examples of Tokoname-*yaki* are the *kyûsu* made of red *tôki*, which are in use all over Japan. *Kyûsu* are also made in a wide range of forms and designs (see photos 116 and 117). In 1998, Yamada Jozan III (1924–2006), a traditional potter, was designated *ningen kokuhô* (Living National Treasure) for his *kyûsu* (see photo 117).

Some potters have returned to the tradition of unglazed stoneware. One of the outstanding representatives of this trend is Ôsako Mikio (1940–1995), whose natural-ash glazes in various shades of green enhance the simply formed bodies of his vessels (see photo 118).

Independent of local traditions, there are a number of studio potters in Tokoname who are successfully exploring new avenues. One is Koie Ryôji (born in 1938), who fires his powerfully expressive objects in a 65-foot (20 m) *anagama* in his native town of Tokoname; another is Yoshikawa Masamichi (born in 1946; see photo 199), who is also well known in the West for his celadons.

Photo 115.   Tokoname-*yaki*. Nakano Kôzô, side-handled small teapot (*kyûsu*) with water cooler (*yuzamashi*),
1997. Teapot: 3¼ x 5½ x 3¾ inches (8 x 14 x 9.4 cm). Water cooler: 1¾ x 4¾ inches (4.6 x 12 cm).
Unglazed pale stoneware, *mogake* technique.

Photo 116.   Tokoname-*yaki*. Side-handled small teapot (*kyûsu*), 2000. 3 x 4⅛ x 2¾ inches (7.5 x 10.4 x 7.1 cm). *Shudei* **ware, incised Japanese characters, fired in the Shôten-*gama*.**

Photo 117.   Tokoname-*yaki*. Yamada Jôzan III (Living National Treasure), side-handled small teapot (*kyûsu*), 2000. 2 x 5¾ x 4 inches (5.1 x 14.5 x 10.1 cm). *Shudei* ware.

Photo 118.   Tokoname-*yaki*. Ôsako Mikio, plate (*sara*), pre-1980. 1¾ x 9¼ inches (4.5 x 23.3 cm). *Yakishime* stoneware, natural-ash glaze.

Inuyama 犬山 (40)

Inuyama-*yaki*'s roots go back to Okumura Denzaburo, who between 1751 and 1764 constructed the Imai-*gama* near Inuyama in Aichi Prefecture. His domestic wares with ash, iron, and copper glazes, strongly influenced by the Seto-Mino style, are known as Kanzan-*yaki*. After the death of Denzaburo's son Gensuke, production was interrupted in 1781, and it was not until 1810 that Shimaya Sôkuro opened the Maruyama-*gama* in Inuyama. Besides the production of stoneware, the production methods for porcelain were adopted from Seto in 1826. In 1837, with the support of Lord Naruse, the head of the Inuyama *han*, Inuyama began to flourish with the production of tea ceramics. Porcelain in *gosu aka-e* style (in other words, with cobalt blue underglaze and overglaze painting) was made, as was *unkin-de* stoneware (cherry blossom and autumn maple decoration) with overglaze in the style of the Ninsei school in Kyôto. The remains of a *suyaki-gama*—a kiln for bisque firings of 1292°F–1652°F (700°C–900°C)—has survived from this period. Remains of two *honyaki-gama*—kilns for the main firing of the ware to 2372°F (1300°C)—and an *etsuke-gama*—a kiln for the firing of enamels to 1292°F–1562°F (700°C–850°C)—have also survived.

After the privatization of the kilns as a result of the Meiji Restoration, only roof tiles were produced, but soon after, Ozeki Sakujûrô made efforts to restore the kilns and revive the traditional techniques. Today, three potters in Inuyama—Takeyama Isao, Gotô Keiji, and Ôsawa Kyûji, along with Ozeki Sakujûrô IV (born in 1937) and his son—make Inuyama-*yaki* in the traditional manner. A light, fine-grained clay body with a colorless, transparent glaze is typical of Inuyama-*yaki*. Unkinde stoneware, enhanced with brilliant overglaze enamels and adopted from Kyô-*yaki* in the style of Nin'ami Dôhachi (see photo 119), is still characteristic; other works combine a floral design in red and green with gold and silver (see photo 120).

Seto 瀬戸 with Akazu 赤津 (41)

Seto-*yaki* is the term for ceramics made in and around the town of Seto, in the former province of Owari, now Aichi Prefecture. The Seto region, together with the neighboring region around Tajimi and Toki (Gifu Prefecture), where Mino-*yaki* (42) is produced, is the largest center for stoneware and porcelain in Japan today. In fact, Seto ware is so famous that most Japanese people use the colloquial term *setomono* (things from Seto) to describe ceramics.

Seto is one of the Six Ancient Kilns (*roku koyô*) and stems from the Sanage kilns of the Heian period. The potter Katô Tôshirô is traditionally said to have been the founder of Seto-*yaki*. According to legend, he returned to Seto from China in 1227 and began producing ceramics in the style of the Chinese Song dynasty. However, excavations have shown that during the twelfth century, after the discovery of white, kaolin-rich clay, Sanage potters had already started to migrate northward into the Seto area from the Nagoya region and had established the tradition of glazed Seto ceramics. With the yellow-green ash glazes of the early wares, the attempt was made to reproduce Chinese celadons. Not even through the resumption of trade with China one century later was it possible to cover the demand for ceramics from the upper classes, so the minor aristocracy continued to fall back on the copies from Seto. Thus Seto was the only one of the Six Ancient Kilns to continue the Sanage tradition with glazed ceramics.

The coil-built vessels were initially undecorated apart from occasional simple linear patterns, but by the end of the Kamakura period, objects with impressed, incised, combed, or applied decoration predominated. In addition to the yellow-green ash glaze (*kai-yû*), an early *kiseto* (yellow Seto), an amber iron glaze (*ame-yû*) was also used. To meet the requirements of the upper classes and to serve as ceremonial vessels, mainly *tsubo* with four lugs were produced, as were *sake* bottles in the Chinese Meiping form (*heishi*) and vases. Production in Seto increased dramatically at the beginning of the Muromachi period: the newly introduced potter's wheel

Photo 119. Inuyama-*yaki*. Ozeki Sakujûrô IV, bowl for sweets (*kashibachi*), 2001. 3¼ x 7½ inches (8.3 x 18.8 cm).
***Unkin-de* stoneware (cherry blossom and autumn maple design), overglaze enamels.**

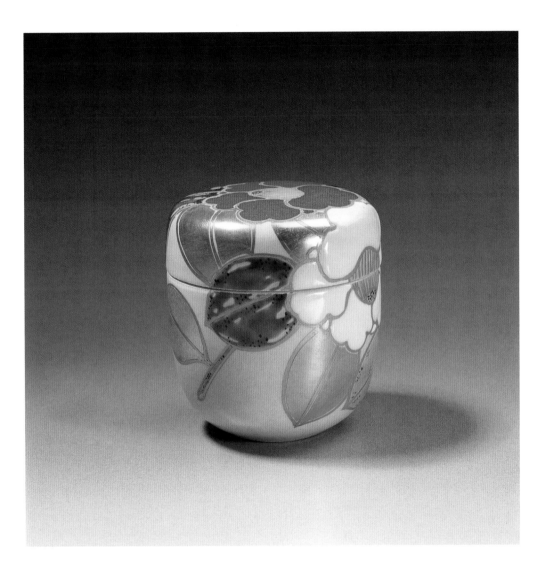

Photo 120. Inuyama-*yaki*. Ozeki Sakujûrô IV, tea caddy with camellia design (*tsubaki-e natsume*), 2001.
2¾ x 2½ inches (6.7 x 6.3 cm). Stoneware with overglaze enamels and gold and silver design.

permitted production in large numbers, including production of objects for everyday use. In the fourteenth century, the brown-black *tenmoku* glaze familiar from Chinese tea bowls came into use (*ko-seto*). As the tea ceremony spread, new vessel forms were required, and the tea caddies (*chaire*) that were made in large numbers enjoyed great popularity. The Seto ceramics from the first phase, which were fired in more than 300 kilns up to the end of the Muromachi period, are referred to as *ko*-Seto (old Seto), in contrast to the *tenmoku* glaze that is known as *ko-seto*.

In the mid-fifteenth century, there was a massive shift in production to Mino because Seto potters moved from Owari province to the neighboring Mino region during the Ônin Civil War and during the fighting in the following *sengoku-jidai* (Century of the Warring States). The consequence was a huge decline in Seto ceramics.

During the subsequent Azuchi-Momoyama period, Seto profited from the flourishing of tea ceramics and the development of glazes in Mino (*kiseto*, *setoguro*, *shino*, and later *oribe*; see Mino, 42). The workshops also produced tea wares under the patronage of Lord Oda Nobunaga and the tea master Furuta Oribe. These wares were fired in the *ôgama* that was introduced in the early sixteenth century. The fact that some of the glazes developed in Mino include Seto as the place of origin in their names—*kiseto* and *setoguro*—is due to the amalgamation of the Mino region with Owari province in 1567. From that point on, Mino was considered a part of neighboring Seto and was not deemed an individual pottery center until the end of the Edo period.

At the beginning of the Edo period, Tokugawa Yoshinago, Lord of Owari province, called the immigrant potter families back to the Seto region, where they settled in Shinano and Akazu. These kilns had to work for the clan, but they also had the freedom to make tea ceramics and domestic wares. The new developments in this period (around 1600) included a shift to the more efficient *renbôshiki-noborigama* kilns and the use of *ofuke* glaze, which, made of a white slip with the addition of feldspar, is a pale blue. In 1659, production of stoneware with cobalt underglaze painting began.

In the late eighteenth century, the Japanese ceramics market was dominated by Hizen porcelain. Sales possibilities for stoneware thus deteriorated, and the Seto potters experienced a commercial crisis. In 1801, the *han* administration tried to solve the problem by limiting production: the founding of new kilns was not permitted, and existing kilns, as *hongyô-gama*, could only be passed on to the eldest son. After these measures failed to produce the desired effect, it was decided that a local porcelain industry should be developed. With the support of the *han* administration, Katô Kichizaemon and his son Tamekichi constructed a kiln for blue-and-white porcelain. By 1804, there were as many as 28 porcelain kilns, although the quality of the products did not equal that of Arita ware. In 1804, Tamekichi went to Kyûshû and is said to have married into the workshop of Fukumoto Ninzaemon, near Mikawachi, and then returned to Seto in 1807 with the secret of porcelain production. As the limitations on the freedom of establishment did not apply to porcelain kilns, by 1822, 91 out of 157 workshops were already porcelain manufactories in which ceramics with cobalt underglaze painting, Seto-*sometsuke*, were made. Painting techniques improved under instruction from famous artists; preferred designs included landscapes, flowers and birds. In addition to large quantities of domestic tableware, large decorative vases and stacking boxes for food (*jûbako*) were made. The best Seto-*sometsuke* was made from 1830 until the opening of Japan and was shown in the West at the World's Fairs. By the mid-nineteenth century, Seto ware had displaced the more expensive Arita porcelain from its leading position in the Japanese market.

Besides Seto-*sometsuke*, *hongyô-yaki* continued to be produced in the nineteenth century, especially the saucers for oil lamps found in every household (*aburazara* and *andonzara*), as well as the heavy *ishizara* as dinner plates with cobalt or iron underglaze painting. A particularly popular design was the *umanome* (horse's eye) decoration, with concentric circles at the edge of the plate in iron-brown brushwork; this decoration is still in use today.

The turmoil of the Meiji Restoration was followed by a comprehensive modernization of the

Seto workshops. Porcelain production, which had adhered to Arita methods, was mechanized; more than two-thirds of the output was exported. Although *hongyô-yaki* continued to be made in artists' workshops, mass production became essential because the ware was distributed through large-scale wholesalers. During the early twentieth century, the changeover to coal-fired kilns occurred, so the traditional kilns previously used for porcelain production and the *hongyô* kilns used for stoneware largely disappeared. In addition, from 1965 on, oil, gas, and electric kilns were introduced.

Contemporary Seto-*yaki* has many faces: Seto is dominated by mass production, with more than 1000 companies. In addition, lower-priced domestic tableware predominates—mainly in porcelain, but also in stoneware. In nearby Nagoya, upmarket, Western-style, porcelain tableware—coffee, tea, and dinner sets—is made by the largest Japanese enterprise of this kind, Noritake, which was established in 1917. There has also been a return to high-quality Seto-*sometsuke* porcelain products from earlier times. A number of artists in the Seto region continue to make the traditional forms and designs in their *gosu* work, but others take a refreshingly modern approach to their painting style (see photo 121).

Stoneware is still produced in the traditional craft-based manner: the last *hongyô-gama*, a four-chamber *noborigama* from the late Edo period, is a good example. Belonging to the Mizuno family, it is now protected as a *bunkazai* (Cultural Asset). Mizuno Hanjirô (sixth generation; 1926–2002) worked in the *mingei* tradition; typical forms are the multicolored bowls, which are fired for more than 40 hours to 2282°F (1250°C). The *sansai* glaze with Oribe green, amber, and cream (see photo 122) is used. His son, Sôichiro (born in 1953), continues this ceramic style, known as *seto-hongyô*. Firings today are in a gas kiln or in a wood-fired *ôgama*.

Some potters have committed themselves to the traditional Seto glazes of the *ko*-Seto era during the Kamakura, Muromachi, and early Edo periods. Thus the original green-yellow ash glaze (*kai-yû*) is found mainly on tea bowls or sake bowls (see photo 9); the black-brown *tenmoku* glaze

known as *ko-seto* usually appears on vases (see photo 123). Momoyama-style tea ceramics with the *kiseto*, *setoguro*, and *shino* Mino glazes, as well as *oribe* ware, are now made equally in Seto and Mino, especially in the so-called Akazu-*yaki* (see photos 128 and 129) from the pottery center of Akazu, east of Seto, with its 41 workshops. Domestic wares were made here from early on, until Akazu became the site of a *goyôgama* for tea ceramics for the Tokugawa dynasty, during the Edo period. Stoneware with *ofuke* glaze, alongside cobalt underglaze painting, is also part of the repertoire of contemporary Seto potters. Similar to early *sometsuke* stoneware, the cobalt pigment is not bound in concentrated green tea, which prevents bleeding, as is usually the case with porcelain (see photo 124).

Along with the return to traditional ceramics, movements from the international art scene have been adopted. Seto and neighboring Mino have become focal points for studio potters, who develop their own personal, formal languages (see photos 189, 191, and 202).

Mino 美濃 (42)

Since the Meiji period, Mino-*yaki* has been the customary term for stoneware and porcelain produced in a large area around the cities of Tajimi and Toki, in the southeast of Gifu Prefecture. As in neighboring Seto (41; Aichi Prefecture), ash-glazed stoneware in Sanage style, known as *shirashi*, was produced from the eleventh century on, followed by unglazed *yamachawan*, which was made in huge quantities. More than 500 kiln sites are documented from this period. In the subsequent Kamakura period, ceramics production declined sharply in the Mino region, in contrast to the Seto kilns, which flourished. It was not until the Muromachi period that kilns were built again, initially around Toki, then around Tajimi. In these kilns, ceramics were surfaced with *tenmoku* or early *kiseto* glazes. The ware strongly resembled Seto ware, but as archaeological findings prove, it was produced in quantity even before the influx of Seto potters fleeing from the Ônin Civil War (see Seto, 41). Starting in the fifteenth

Photo 121. Seto-*yaki*. Kitajima Satoko, plate (*gosu sometsuke kaki sara*), ca. 2002. 1½ x 10½ inches (4 x 26.5 cm). *Sometsuke* porcelain, *kaki* (persimmon) design.

Photo 122. Seto-*yaki*. Mizuno Hanjirô, large bowl (*ôbachi*), 1998. 3¼ x 11¾ inches (8.5 x 30 cm).
Stoneware, *sansai*-glaze, *seto-hongyô*.

Photo 123. Seto-*yaki*. Tanahashi Jun, hexagonal vase (*kabin*), 1999. 7 x 3¼ inches (18 x 8.3 cm). Stoneware, *tenmoku* glaze, *ko-seto*.

Photo 124. Seto-*yaki*. "Husband and wife" teacups (*meoto yunomi*), produced in series, ca. 2000.
3½ x 2½ inches (9 x 6.3 cm) and 3½ x 2¼ inches (8.8 x 5.5 cm). Stoneware with cloth texturing (*nunome*) and cobalt underglaze painting (*sometsuke*).

century, through connections between the local ruling class and Kyôto, the center of the tea ceremony, tea ceramics began to flourish in the Mino region. *Kiseto* glazes, followed by *setoguro, shino,* and *oribe* glazes—regarded as the first independently developed glazes in the history of Japanese ceramics—were used.

The early *kiseto* glazes (yellow Seto) from the Muromachi period are considered to be attempts to reproduce Chinese celadons from the Song dynasty. The composition of the wood ash and feldspar glazes largely resembled that of the celadons; however, in oxidation instead of the reduction necessary for celadons, a dull yellow-green was formed. Beginning in the fifteenth century, this yellow was consciously developed further, probably to reproduce the then highly esteemed Chinese Ming wares. In the Momoyama period, two types of *kiseto* had emerged. One was *ayame-de kiseto* in a clear yellow, named after the incised iris design, over which were green spots of copper oxide (*tanpan*) that were typical of the period. Simple representations of plum blossoms, chrysanthemums, and radishes were popular patterns on thin-walled tea bowls, plates, and bowls. The second type of *kiseto, aburage-hada,* with its golden brown, matte, slightly grainy surface, owes its name to its resemblance to baked tofu. Information about its production is no longer available.

Setoguro (black Seto) was the first black glaze in the history of Japanese ceramics. An excavated *setoguro* bowl has been dated from between 1532 and 1555, and thus is older than the first black raku tea bowl from Kyôto, dated 1582. The glaze is made from ash and *oni-ita,* an iron ore mined near Mino. During firing, the vessel is removed glowing hot from the kiln after the glaze has matured, at temperatures above 2192°F (1200°C), and is immediately cooled. This type of glaze is therefore also known as *hikidashi-guro* (withdrawn black). Only tea bowls were fired using this technique. In addition, their characteristic cylindrical forms were an innovation: previously, *tenmoku* tea bowls with small feet and flared walls were customary.

Shino, an ash glaze with a high proportion of feldspar—the first high-fired white glaze in Japan—is said to have developed from an opaque white ash glaze used on *tenmoku* tea bowls to replicate porcelain surfaces. The origin of the name and the date of origin are subject to controversy, although the early Azuchi-Momoyama period seems likely. Plates and small side dishes (*mukô-zuke*) for the *kaiseki* meal during the tea ceremony were also made. In contrast to pots made in large numbers, from which the tea master randomly selected a well-executed vessel, careful production of individual pieces became the norm. Vessels were wheel thrown and often refinished by hand, or they were press molded. The deformations that are still typical of Japanese ceramics date back to *shino* wares. The surface of the thickly applied, milky *shino* glaze is referred to as *yuzuhada* (lemon peel) because of its appearance. A special clay (moxa clay, *mogusa,* from *gairome* type) and the damp, inefficient *anagama* were prerequisites for *shino* wares, with their long firings to relatively low temperatures of 2192°F (1200°C).

The best-known types of *shino* glaze are:

muji (no shiro) shino: an undecorated white *shino* covering the entire vessel in a thick coating of glaze.

e-shino: "picture *shino*," in which simple patterns were applied to the pot in *oni-ita* and covered with *shino* glaze. With *e-shino,* underglaze painting was employed for the first time in Japan.

nezumi-shino and *aka-shino:* gray *shino* and red *shino;* these depend on firing conditions. The vessel is covered with a layer of *oni-ita* slip, then *shino* glaze is applied. In a neutral atmosphere in the *anagama,* the slip fires gray; in oxidation, the slip-coated body shows through the otherwise thick, snowy white glaze in reddish to red "scorch" marks in areas where the glaze was applied more thinly (*hi-iro*).

Oribe ware has its origins in tea ceramics, which were made until 1624 in the style of the tea master Furuta Oribe. Technically, Oribe-*yaki* required the *noborigama,* which was introduced to Mino in 1597. The first kiln of this type—the Motoyashiki-*gama,* with 14 chambers and approximately 78 feet (24 m) in length—the ruins of which may still be seen today, was built by Katô Kagenobu to resemble the Kishidake kilns of Karatsu. *Shino* glaze fired in a *noborigama* produced a smooth, white, transparent glaze (*shino-oribe*) that is considered to have been a prototype for the production of *oribe* wares. Thereafter, green copper glaze on the unusual vessel forms, with their asymmetrical designs, was typical of *oribe*. The expressive *oribe* style was in total contrast to the *wabi* aesthetic practiced by the tea masters up to this time. The bowls and side dishes (*mukôzuke*), with their wide range of forms, are best known.

The main types of *oribe* are:

ao-oribe: green *oribe*, with areas of green glaze and *oni-ita* underglaze painting in the areas free of copper glaze.

narumi-oribe or *aka-oribe*: composed of white and red clay; the white clay is covered with green copper glaze, whereas the red clay body is layered with a white slip design.

sô-oribe: a uniformly green-glazed type of ware.

oribeguro and *kuro-oribe* (black *oribe*): on tea bowls, these were produced using the same methods as *setoguro*. Differences from the *setoguro* tea bowls are seen particularly in the high footrings and the sometimes bizarre distortions, such as in the well-known *kutsugata chawan* (tea bowls in shoe form). In contrast to *oribeguro,* with its completely black glazed surface, *kuro-oribe* has a glaze-free, light surface decorated with *oni-ita* brushwork.

Mino-*yaki* was distributed by the administration of Owari-*han*, along with items made in Seto under the name of *setomono*, so that up to the end of the Edo period, Mino was not perceived as an individual ceramic type in spite of its individual innovations in glaze and form (see Seto, 41).

As a result of changes in the *han* administration, beginning in 1624, ceramics production changed to simple domestic wares with *ame-yû* as the predominant glaze type, and tea ceramics were largely forgotten. In addition, the rise of porcelain production overwhelmed Mino stoneware, a development that could not be stopped by the introduction of stoneware decorated with overglaze enamels (*aka-e* Mino). With the beginnings of porcelain production in Seto during the early nineteenth century, many Mino kilns converted to the production of porcelain.

As in Seto, the Meiji period began with a phase of intense modernization. Large quantities of *aka-e* Mino and porcelain were produced as domestic ware, and specialties such as coffee sets for export were added to the product range. With advancing mechanization, Mino-*yaki* became a cheap mass product.

In the 1930s, however, a countermovement set in: the potter Arakawa Toyozô (1894–1985) discovered a *shino* shard near the ruins of the Mutabora-*gama* in Ôgaya. After further excavations, it was possible to prove that the famous glazes from the Momoyama period had been produced in Mino, and not—as had been assumed—in Seto. Consequently, many ceramists became interested in these techniques and tried to revive them. Arakawa himself set up his own workshop near the Mutabora-*gama* and dedicated his subsequent work to the *shino* glaze. In 1955, he was designated a *ningen kokuhô* (Living National Treasure) for the revival of *shino* and *setoguro* in the style of the Momoyama period. Promoted by Gifu Prefecture, a generation of well-trained potters, who dedicated themselves to ancient techniques, followed. Representatives of this direction are the two *ningen kokuhô*, Suzuki Osamu (born in 1934), honored in 1994 for *shino* ceramics; and Katô Takuo (1917–2005), honored in 1995 for three-colored (*sansai*) vessels in the style of Nara ware.

In the Seto and Mino regions today, mechanized mass production exists alongside work by ceramics artists and studio potters who are committed to the old traditions, and who make *kiseto* (see photo 125), *setoguro* (see photo 126), *oribe* (see photos 127–129, and 189), and *shino* ware. In particular, *shino* in all its variations (see photos 130 and 131) is a great attraction to many potters. It is thus no great surprise that at the end of the last century, an innovation arrived in the form of the indigo blue *shino* (*ai-iro-shino*; see photo 132) by Sakai Hiroshi (born in 1960). As in Seto, studio potters who have largely detached themselves from the old traditions (see photos 192 and 206) also work in the Mino region.

Shitoro 志戸呂 (43)

Current archaeological research indicates that
the production of Shitoro-*yaki* began in the mid-
fifteenth century with the construction of an
anagama by a potter from Mino, in the Shitoro
region, near Kanaya in Shizuoka Prefecture.
Stoneware with a brown iron glaze was produced in the style of *ko-seto*. In the sixteenth
century, the technique of firing an *ôgama* was
adopted from Seto. The main products were tea
ceramics and domestic wares with the typical
ash and iron glazes (*kai-yû* and *tetsu-yû* respectively) in Seto style. The body of Shitoro-*yaki* is
very hard and dense, and was thus highly suitable for the dry storage of tea leaves; tea storage
jars (*chatsubo*) for local tea merchants were the
main product from the kilns in Shitoro.

In 1588, the founder of the Tokugawa Shogunate,
Tokugawa Ieyasu, granted the Shitoro potters an
official trading license. He further aided the development of the region by appointing Kagenobu, a
potter from Mino, to adapt Seto-Mino technology
to local conditions. In the early seventeenth century, the construction of a number of *renbôshiki-
noborigama* in the village of Yoko'oka near Kanaya
provided optimized firings; the quality products
from the Shitoro kilns were esteemed even among
the ranks of the aristocracy. From 1624 to 1642, the
famous tea master Kobori Enshû lent his support
to the Shitoro kilns, which are therefore among the
seven so-called *Enshû nana gama*. In these years
of economic prosperity, 13 kilns were in operation.
However, when the market became flooded with
bargain-priced Seto and Hizen porcelain as a consequence of industrialization after 1868, more than
half of the Shitoro kilns were forced to close.

In the twentieth century, traditional ceramics
were again more widely appreciated by the general public, and this is also true of Shitoro-*yaki*
in its beauty and simple elegance. Currently, six
ceramists are working in the spirit of the Shitoro
tradition in the Kanaya region. The iron-rich clay
and the ingredients for the glazes are local; firings are in a wood-fired *noborigama* or in gas
kilns. The thrown objects have the customary
iron and ash glazes on a reddish body. If the two
glazes are applied on top of each other, the yellow-brown and black mottled surface typical of
Shitoro-*yaki* is produced during the firing (see
photo 133).

Echizen 越前 (44)

The historical pottery region of Echizen, centered around Miyazaki and Ota, is in contemporary Fukui Prefecture, by the Japan Sea. There
is evidence of the production of Sue ceramics from the fifth century on; the ruins of a *sueki*
kiln (*Shinmeigadani sueki kama-ato*) can be seen
in Miyazaki. In the twelfth century, the transition to high-fired unglazed stoneware with natural-ash glazes occurred, under the influence of
Tokoname. Excavations revealed approximately
200 *anagama* from this period, and Echizen is
consequently considered one of the Six Ancient
Kilns (*roku koyô*). For the most part, storage jars
and urns were produced.

The term Echizen-*yaki* as a collective term for
ceramics from Fukui Prefecture was only introduced in 1965; the wares from the Muromachi
period (1333–1568) are known as Kumadani-*yaki*,
and the later products from up to the middle of
the twentieth century are known as Ota-*yaki*.

In the heyday of Echizen-*yaki*, during the sixteenth and seventeenth centuries, the rural population's demand for storage jars and all kinds
of domestic wares grew. In Taira, near Ota, 12
groups of the so-called *Otamachi-taira-ôgamaya*
were in operation—42 large kilns in all (*ôgama*),
with a length of 82 feet (25 m) each. More than
40 types of vessels were offered, including local
specialties such as traps for octopus (*takotsubo*)
and markers for the burial sites of urns (*kame-
baka*). The goods were distributed by sea, along
the coast of the Sea of Japan from Shimane to
Hokkaidô. Because of a lack of support from the
local aristocracy and famous tea masters, tea
ceramics emerging in other areas of Japan were
of no importance in Echizen. In the second half of
the Edo period (1600–1868), a wide range of iron,
wood-ash, and straw-ash glazes developed with
the assistance of Mino potters, and wheels were
used for the mass production of smaller vessels
that had previously been produced by coiling.

Photo 125. Mino-*yaki*. Yamaguchi Jotetsu II, fresh-water jar (*mizusashi*), pre-1980. 5¾ x 6 inches (14.8 x 15.3 cm). Stoneware, *kiseto*, green spots of copper oxide (*tanpan*).

Photo 126.   Mino-*yaki*. Hori Ichirô, traveler's tea bowl (*hikidashi-guro tabi chawan*), ca. 2002. 3¼ x 4 inches (8 x 10.2 cm). Stoneware, *setoguro*.

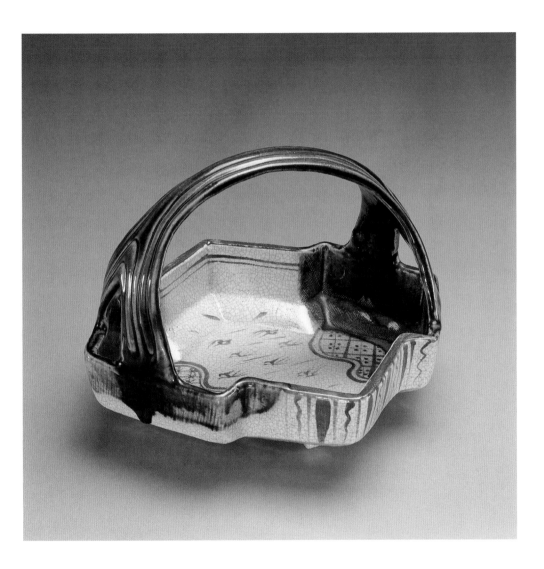

Photo 127. Mino-*yaki*. Kagesue Toroshi, Seto, dish with handle (*oribe matsukawabishi tebachi*), 2000.
6¾ x 9¼ inches (17 x 23.5 cm). Stoneware, *ao-oribe*.

Photo 128. Mino-*yaki*. Miyake Noriyasu, Akazu, set of plates for sweets (*meimeizara*), 2000. 4 x 3½ inches
(10.3 x 9.2 cm). Glazed stoneware, *ao-oribe* style.

Photo 129. Mino-*yaki*. Yamaguchi Masafumi, Akazu, tea bowl (*chawan*), 2000. 3 x 3½ inches (7.8 x 9.2 cm). Stoneware, *oribeguro* style.

Photo 130. Mino-*yaki*. Miura Shigehisa, vase in mallet form (*kinuta hanaire*), pre-2000. 8 x 5 inches (20.3 x 13 cm). Stoneware, *nezumi-shino*.

**Photo 131. Mino-*yaki*. Hori Ichirô, vase (*hanaire*), 2002. 9¼ x 5¼ inches (23.6 x 13.7 cm).
Stoneware, *aka-shino*.**

Photo 132. Mino-*yaki*. Sakai Hiroshi, indigo *shino* vase (*ai-iro-shino tsubo*), 2002. 7¾ x 6¾ inches (19.7 x 17 cm). Stoneware, *ai-iro-shino*.

Photo 133. Shitoro-*yaki*. Shirahata Hôetsu, storage jar for tea leaves (*chatsubo*), 1995. 6 x 5¾ inches (15.5 x 14.6 cm). Stoneware, iron and ash glazes applied on top of each other.

But in spite of efforts to the contrary, demand continued to fall; until after the Second World War, only six kilns were in use in the *Otamachi-taira-ôgamaya* district.

Extensive excavations after the Second World War brought the old traditions of Echizen-*yaki* back to mind. With the encouragement of the Society for the Promotion of Echizen in Fukui Prefecture, the first exhibition of contemporary ceramics took place in 1957. Since 1965, this event, known as *Echizen-yaki tôgeiten*, has taken place annually. The final breakthrough was achieved in 1970–1971 with the founding of the potters' village of *Echizen tôgei-mura* in Miyazaki, with its museum, exhibition space, a showroom, and galleries. Potters from all over Japan were attracted to *Echizen tôgei-mura* by settlement incentives. In Fukui Prefecture, there are now 72 workshops, 43 of which are in the Miyazaki region.

Echizen-*yaki* is correspondingly diverse in appearance. Traditional ware still predominates. It is fired to about 2372°F (1300°C) in an *anagama* or *noborigama*, with its body fired to dark gray and dark brown (see photo 134), and natural-ash glazes shading from brown-yellow or greenish to purple (see photo 135). *Botamochi* designs (see photo 136) can frequently be seen on bowls and plates. The refractory Echizen clay, which is rich in silicic acid, is frequently mixed with *tatsuchi* (clay dug from under rice paddies) to improve plasticity. Smaller objects are often wheel thrown or coil built. Without using a wheel, larger vessels up to 3¼ feet (1 m) in height are built up with coils as thick as a man's arm, as the potter moves around the pot. The master of this technique, who has been honored by MITI (Ministry of International Trade and Industry), is Fujita Jûrouemon VIII (born in 1922). He was the only Echizen potter who was still able to use this technique after the Second World War and who has played a decisive role in the revival of Echizen-*yaki*.

Among glazed wares, which are frequently fired in gas, oil, or electric kilns, *tenmoku* iron glazes, celadons, and slip decoration play an important part. Besides *sake* sets, tableware, and tea ceramics, Echizen potters mainly produce flower vases and bowls.

Kumano Kurôuemon (born in 1955), who is also very well known in the West, has a special position among the Echizen potters: a student of Fujita Jûrôemon VIII, he makes highly expressive pots with natural-ash glazes or *shino* glazes that he fires in a special *anagama* to an incredible 2768°F (1520°C). (See Studio Potters on pages 249–283 and photo 180).

Kutani 九谷 (45)

The exquisitely colorful Kutani porcelain comes from the region between Kanazawa and Kaga-Onsen, in Ishikawa Prefecture, the former domains of Kaga and Daishôji. In this region, a kiln near Daishôji produced tea ceramics in Seto style from the end of the sixteenth century. In 1655, after the discovery of kaolin and quartz in the Kutani region, Lord Maeda Toshiharu, from the Daishôji line of the Kaga dynasty, ordered the construction of two kilns in Kutani for the production of *iro-e* porcelain with overglaze painting for the tea ceremony. In 1661, when the products did not meet expectations, his successor sent a retainer, Gotô Saijirô, to Arita to learn the techniques of porcelain production practiced there. After Saijirô's return, both kilns are reported to have produced *sometsuke* porcelain with cobalt underglaze painting, as well as the characteristic *ko*-Kutani ware, a type of porcelain with overglaze enamels, for about 50 years. Two types were produced: *ao-de* (green) porcelain, in which the entire surface of the pot—usually a shallow bowl—was surfaced in green and yellow, or more rarely in aubergine; and the colorful *gosai* (five-colored) porcelain in the characteristic shades of Russian green, maize yellow, Prussian blue, red, and manganese purple. Around 1670 and 1710, production from the kilns came to a standstill, but the reasons for the closures are unknown. Archaeological evidence from the vicinity of the kilns also gives reason to doubt that this really was the production site for *ko*-Kutani. The latest research suggests that *ko*-Kutani was in fact produced in Arita on instructions from the Maeda family.

Photo 134. Echizen-*yaki*. Yamazaki Ryûichi, set of plates for sweets (*meimeizara*), 1999. 2½ x 8½ x 2¼ inches (6.3 x 21.6 x 6 cm). Yakishime stoneware.

Photo 135. Echizen-*yaki*. Miyoshi Kentarô, vase (*Echizen wazumi hanaire*), 2001. 9½ x 5 inches (24 x 12.6 cm). Stoneware, natural-ash glaze, and scorch markings (*koge*).

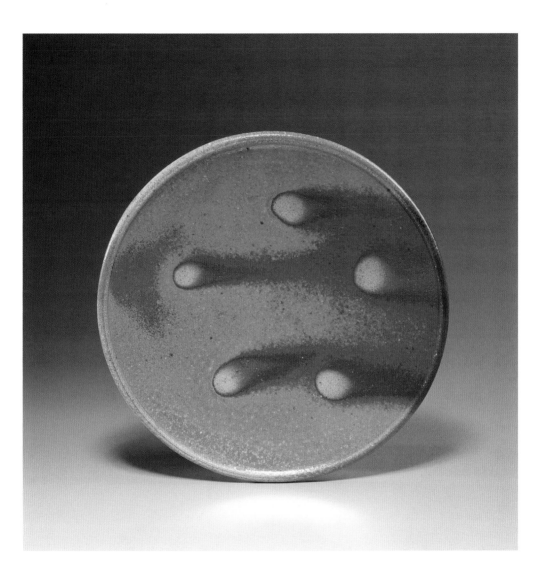

**Photo 136. Echizen-*yaki*. Fujita Jûrouemon VIII, plate (*sara*), 1999. 1 x 8½ inches (2.6 x 21.5 cm).
Stoneware, natural-ash glaze, *botamochi* resist.**

Over the next century, stoneware and raku were certainly produced in the domains of Kaga and Daishôji, but not porcelain. Only from 1807 on, when the Kaga clan attempted to revive ko-Kutani ware, was porcelain with overglaze enamels produced in a number of kilns. The term saikô-Kutani (revived Kutani) has been established for Kutani-yaki from this second phase of production. There were five main styles: Mokubei, Yoshidaya, Iidaya, Eiraku, and Shôza ware.

The earliest attempt to revive the production of porcelain goes back to the famous potter Aoki Mokubei from Kyôto (see Kyôto, 34, on page 132), who in 1807 started up the Kasugayama-gama, near Kanazawa, but by 1808 he had returned to Kyôto. Figures painted in five colors in the Chinese fashion on a red background were characteristic of Mokubei's porcelain.

The Yoshidaya-gama, built by the merchant Yoshidaya Denemon in 1824, produced ceramics known as Yoshidaya ware, initially in Kutani, then in Yamashiro. This was intended to replicate ko-Kutani in the four basic colors of green, yellow, blue, and aubergine, but without red; or, as in ao-de ware, replicated in yellow and green. In spite of the brief production period of only seven years, the Yoshidaya-gama inspired the opening of many other kilns, in Komatso and Terai in particular.

At the Miyamoto-gama (1832–1859)—the reopened Yoshidaya-gama in Yamashiro—the porcelain painter Iidaya Hachirouemon developed the Iidaya style named after him, with its decoration painted in very fine lines (aka-e saibyô) of red with touches of gold.

The so-called Eiraku style goes back to Eiraku Wazen, son of the famous Kyôto potter, Eiraku Hozen. For the five years before his return to Kyôto in 1870, Wazen ran the Kutanihon-gama, formerly the Miyamoto-gama. Similar to Hozen's, his work was completely covered with underglaze red, and rich gold ornamentation was applied over the glaze (akaji-kinran-de).

Shôza ware made by Kutani Shôza at the Terai-gama built in Terai in 1841 had elements of previous ko-Kutani, Yoshidaya, Iidaya, and Eiraku styles, melded into a rich aka-e kinran-de decoration in overglaze enamels and gold. The addition of Western pigments later made nuances of color possible that could not be achieved previously.

The kilns from the late Edo period were private enterprises, but they were supported by the han administration by, for instance, a ban on sales of ceramics from other regions. In 1811, the Wakasugi-gama set up in what is now Komatsu to produce large quantities of sometsuke domestic porcelain was directly under the control of the han administration.

After the Meiji Restoration, and with the advances in industrialization, many of the workshops became small porcelain manufactories. Shaping and painting increasingly became separated in these workshops. Shôza ware satisfied European tastes with its somewhat overladen style, and after being presented at the World's Fairs in Vienna and Paris (1873 and 1878), it provoked an export boom that lasted until 1916. Between the two world wars, there was a drastic decline in production, but in the second half of the twentieth century, Kutani porcelain was able to maintain its share of upmarket porcelain sales alongside Arita and Imari ware.

Today, there are 474 firms in the region, ranging from manufactories to small, traditional artists' workshops, which together employ more than 2000 workers. Terai, where 80 percent of Kutani-yaki is made, is the center. The product range of contemporary Kutani-yaki includes tableware of all kinds, tea and sake utensils, incense burners (kôro), vases, ornamental plates (kazarizara), ornamental ceramic figures (okimono), and weights for picture scrolls (fûchin). Besides sometsuke ware (see photo 137), porcelain in ko-Kutani Yoshida style (see photo 138) and Iidaya style (see photo 139), as well as the other described styles of saikô-Kutani, can be seen. Aka-e kinran-de appears in many variations; in shonzui style, for example. In addition, traditional designs, such as the "Hundred Persons Poem" that appeared in the early Meiji period (see photo 140) and the aochibu technique (see photo 141) that was popular in the Taishô period, are cultivated unchanged.

Studio potters such as Takayama Kazuo (born in 1947) and Akaji Ken (born in 1938) consciously draw inspiration from the Kutani tradition (see photos 142 and 143). In 1997, Tokuda Yasokichi III (born in 1933) was designated *ningen kokuhô* (Living National Treasure) for his enamels, high-fired to 1904°F (1040°C), with their brilliant color in the tradition of *ao-de ko*-Kutani. In 2001, Yoshida Minori III (born in 1932) was honored for his difficult-to-fire work in *yûri-kinsai* technique (see photo 144), for which gold leaf is used as underglaze decoration.

Modern Kutani porcelain varies from a coarse body similar to stoneware or a thick porcelain to an almost transparent eggshell porcelain. The glaze is matte and ranges from gray, blue, or greenish white to the typical milky white. Production follows the manufacturing process developed for porcelain in Arita. Even today, the greater part of Kutani porcelain is painted by hand with great artistry, and it is characteristic for the reverse of the object to also be carefully executed, often continuing the designs from the front.

Ôhi 大樋 (46)

In 1666, to develop his own tea ceremony style, Lord Maeda Toshitsuna invited the Grand Master of the Ura Senke tea school, Senso Sôshitsu, to his court at Kanazawa, today in Ishikawa Prefecture. In Kanazawa, the Maeda family already provided support for the production of Kutani porcelain. The tea master brought the potter Chôzaemon Hodoan (1630–1712) with him from Kyôto. Hodoan found suitable clay deposits in Ôhi, near Kanazawa. Ôhi Chôzaemon, as he was subsequently allowed to call himself, had received the recipe for the famous *ame* (amber) glaze from his raku master Ichinyû (Raku Kichizaemon IV) in Kyôto. Under Ôhi Chôzaemon IV (Doan Kanbei, 1758–1839) and Ôhi Chôzaemon V (Hodoan Kanbei, 1799–1856), the range of glazes was expanded to include black and white Ôhi glazes.

By the time of the Meiji Restoration in 1868, the raku ware made by the Ôhi family was exclusively tea ceramics for the use of the Maeda clan. Due to economic difficulties during the political upheavals, after an interruption in production from 1868 to 1884, domestic ware also had to be produced. It was only with Ôhi Chôzaemon

IX (Todosai, 1901–1986) and the support of the grand master of the Ura Senke tea school that a successful return to the traditions of Ôhi tea ceramics was possible.

As a typical type of raku ware (see Kyôto, 34), Ôhi-*yaki* is still produced without a wheel, formed by hand, and refinished with the assistance of a spatula (*hera ato*). After the glazed pots have been loaded, the kiln is heated rapidly, and firing takes place at temperatures of 1742°F to over 2192°F (950°C to over 1200°C), depending on the glaze. After the glaze has melted, the piece is withdrawn from the kiln while still red hot, then rapidly cooled.

Today, the workshop of Ôhi Chôzaemon (Toshirô, born in 1927) is now in the tenth generation. Ôhi Chôzaemon X is one of the best-known contemporary Japanese ceramists. He works in several areas: raku wares with *ame* glazes and the typical white and black Ôhi glazes (see photos 145 and 146) are in the Ôhi family tradition, while at the same time his studio ceramics have been awarded several prizes. With more than 40 ceramic wall murals, he is also active in the field of modern architecture. His deep roots in tradition are revealed by his studies of classical Chinese porcelain and the ensuing work, such as the use of *tenmoku* glazes. His son Toshio (born in 1958), who studied in Boston for five years, has successfully sought to find a path between tradition and modernity (see photos 147 and 148).

In Kanazawa, there are three additional kilns in which Ôhi-*yaki* is made, all founded in the twentieth century.

Shibukusa 渋草 (47)

Shibukusu-*yaki*, decorated stoneware and porcelain distinctly influenced by Kutani, and made in two workshops in Takayama (Gifu Prefecture), was named after the Shibukusa district. Alongside Koita and Yamada, Shibukusa is the most recent of the three kilns to be set up in Takayama. In 1840, the *han* administration, together with local merchants, launched a project to produce high-quality ceramics. The Seto potter Toda Ryuzô, along with an experienced porcelain painter from

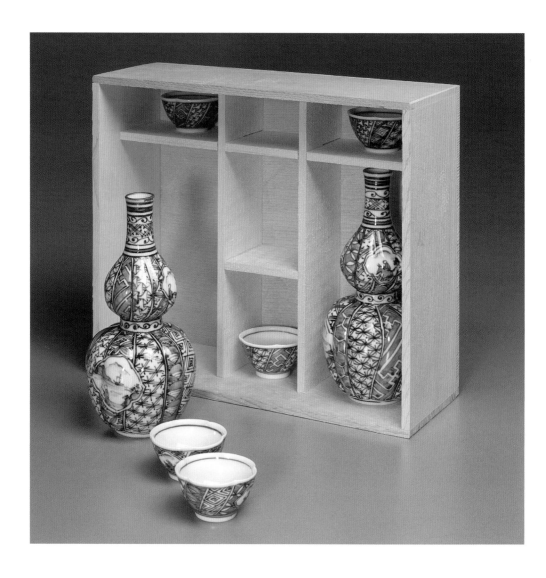

Photo 137. Kutani-*yaki*. Shimomichi Ryôhei, *sake* set (*shuki*) with two sake flasks (*tokkuri*) and five *sake* cups (*choko*), 2000. Flasks: 6¼ x 3 inches (16 x 7.8 cm). Cups: 1 x 2 inches (2.4 x 5 cm). *Sometsuke* porcelain.

Photo 138. Kutani-*yaki*. Nakamura Shigeto, incense burner (*ko-Kutani fû komon kachô-ga kôro*), ca. 2002. 4 x 3 inches (10 x 7.4 cm). Porcelain, *ko*-Kutani Yoshida style with flower and bird designs.

Photo 139. Kutani-*yaki*. Komekyû Kazuhiko, incense burner (*aka-e saibyô kôro*), 2000. 2¾ x 3½ inches (7.2 x 9.3 cm). Porcelain, Iidaya style.

Photo 140. Kutani-*yaki*. Sake goblet (*hyaku-nin isshu kôhai*), painting by Sumida Gakuyô, 1995.
2½ x 2¼ inches (6.4 x 5.5 cm). Porcelain, with "Hundred Persons Poem" decoration.

Photo 141. Kutani-*yaki*. Nakata Kingyoku, *sake* cup (*guinomi*), 1985. 1¾ x 2¼ inches (4.5 x 5.8 cm). Porcelain, *aochibu* (blue-green drops) technique.

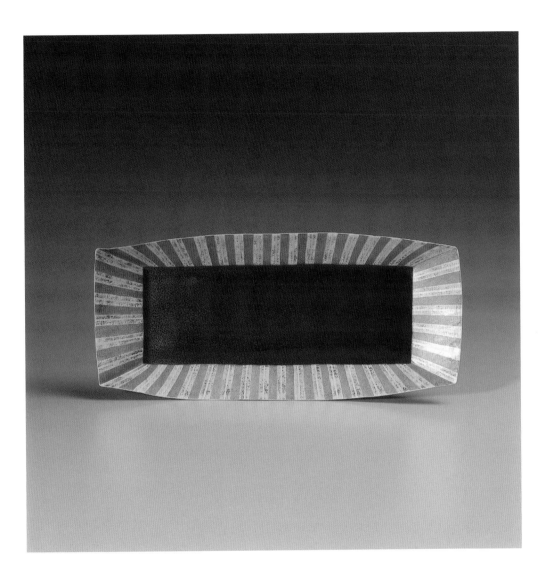

Photo 142. Kutani-*yaki*. Takayama Kazuo, rectangular plate (*sai-yû kinsai chôkakuzara*), 2000. 1¼ x 12½ x 5½ inches (2.9 x 32 x 14 cm). Porcelain, with colored stripes and gold.

Photo 143. Kutani-*yaki*. Akaji Ken, stacking box (*kasanebachi*), 2000. 6¾ x 9¾ x 8¾ inches (17.5 x 25 x 22 cm). Porcelain, *aka-e kinran-de* decoration.

Photo 144. Kutani-*yaki*. Yoshida Minori III (Living National Treasure), vase with evergreen magnolia decoration (*yûri-kinsai taisanboku mon kabin*), 2004. 11 x 4½ inches (27.7 x 11.8 cm). Porcelain, with gold leaf as underglaze decoration (*yûri-kinsai*).

**Photo 145. Ôhi-*yaki*. Ôhi Chôzaemon X, *sake* flask (*tokkuri*), 1986. 7½ x 3¾ inches (19 x 9.5 cm).
Raku, black Ôhi glaze.**

Photo 146. Ôhi-*yaki*. Ôhi Chôzaemon X, *sake* cup (*guinomi*), 2001. 2 x 2¾ inches (5 x 7 cm).
Raku, Ôhi *ame* glaze.

Kutani, made stoneware with red overglaze decoration, which became popular under the name of Hida-*aka-e* or Hida-Kutani. But in 1868, with the Meiji Restoration, the administration closed down this partially state-run operation. In 1878, a manufactory was set up by four local businessmen, headed by Miwa Genjirô. Later known as Hôkoku-*sha*, it was here that the techniques of the three great porcelain centers of Seto, Arita, and Kutani were adopted and developed for the production of independent products.

Besides pure white wares (*hakuji*) and celadons with *sometsuke* (cobalt underglaze painting), it is porcelain, exclusively decorated with *sometsuke* alone or in combination with overglaze painting, that has a characteristic appearance (see photo 149). Today, Shibukusa porcelain (Shibukusa-*jiki*) is exclusively handmade; throwing or forming in molds, as well as painting, is executed solely by specialists.

Shibukusa stoneware (Shibukusa-*tôki*) is also experiencing a renaissance in the tradition of Hida-Kutani ware. Under the current master, Toda Sôshirô, of the sixth generation, only working by hand is tolerated in the entire making process. The gray body of local clay with iron specks is covered with a transparent feldspar glaze; the overglaze painting, depicting red peonies or illustrations of Chinese children (*karako-e*, see photo 150), is characteristic.

Koito 小糸 (48)

In Takayama (Gifu Prefecture), three kilns have developed independently of each other. The oldest is Koito-*yaki*. At the invitation of the Lord of Takayama, the potter Takeya Genjurô came to Takayama from Kyôto, and in 1630, began to make his elegant tea bowls in high-fired stoneware, with iron and ash glazes. The subsequent history of the kiln is turbulent: after hard times, two potters attempted to produce porcelain in 1836, but the project failed only four years later. The kiln was not reestablished until 1946. From iron-rich clay, glazed stoneware is made for tea ceramics, vases, and restaurant tableware of a more select quality (*kappô shokki*). Iron glazes, such as *ame*, *kaki*, and *irabo*, are characteristic, as are tea and *sake* wares influenced by Seto, with bands of cobalt and iron underglaze painting (see photo 151). The cobalt blue *ao-irabo* glaze, which was only recently developed, is unique in Japan.

Yamada 山田 (49)

Little is known of the history of the Yamada kiln in Takayama (Gifu Prefecture), but it is said to have been built between 1764 and 1772 by a potter from Seto. From the raw, iron-rich local clay, ash-glazed stoneware was made for domestic purposes. At the end of the Edo period, a stoneware of gray-white clay, with a cobalt underglaze pattern known as *kasuri* textile design, was added. Both types of ceramics are still produced today. Yamada-*yaki* reached its peak in the Meiji (1868–1912) and Taishô (1912–1926) periods, with water jars and containers for food. Even today, it is purely a folk kiln, where alongside traditional domestic wares (see photo 152), westernized tableware catering to altered eating and drinking habits is produced.

Photo 147. Ôhi-*yaki*. Ôhi Toshio, *sake* cup (*guinomi*), 2001. 1¾ x 3 inches (4.6 x 7.5 cm). Raku, white Ôhi glaze.

Photo 148. *Ôhi-yaki*. Ôhi Toshio, ritual vessel (*Ôhi-yû kurokakebun saiki*), ca. 2001. 4¼ x 8¼ inches (10.7 x 21 cm). Raku, Ôhi *ame*-glaze, black Ôhi glaze.

Photo 149. **Shibukusa-*yaki*. Matsuyama Bunjirô, underglaze and overglaze painting by Soga Tokumaru and Ono Kasho, Hôkoku Company, bowl (*hachi*), 1999. 2½ x 6½ inches (6.5 x 16.5 cm). *Sometsuke* porcelain, overglaze brushwork.**

Photo 150. Shibukusa-*yaki*. Toda Sôshirô, square dish (*shihôzara*), 1999. 1½ x 10 x 9¾ inches (3.7 x 25.2 x 24.7 cm). Stoneware, transparent feldspar glaze, *aka-e* overglaze painting of Chinese children (*karako-e*).

Photo 151.   Koito-*yaki*. Nagakura Yasukuni, *sake* set (*shuki*) with *sake* flask (*tokkuri*) and two *sake* cups (*guinomi*), 1999. *Sake* flask: 5¾ x 2½ inches (14.8 x 6.3 cm). *Sake* cups: 1½ x 2¼ inches (4 x 5.7 cm). Stoneware, cobalt and iron underglaze painting.

Photo 152. Yamada-*yaki*. Kobayashi Hôzan, rice bowl (*gohan chawan*), 2000. 2½ x 5 inches (6.2 x 12.8 cm). Stoneware, iron and ash glazes.

Suzu 珠洲 (50)

During the fifth century, potters from Korea who made Sue ceramics (*sueki*) settled in the region surrounding the contemporary town of Suzu (Ishikawa Prefecture), at the tip of Noto Peninsula, by the Sea of Japan. Based on this tradition, a black-gray, unglazed stoneware known as Suzu-*yaki* was produced until the end of the sixteenth century. Excavations in and around Suzu revealed the remains of 40 kilns, and the oldest could be dated to 1143. In contrast to *sueki*, Suzu ware was produced in great quantities and fired in large *anagama*. The Suzu potters, who were also farmers, produced a wide range of domestic wares, including storage jars as tall as a man, as well as statues and vessels for religious purposes. Suzu-*yaki* spread as far as Hokkaidô through a flourishing sea-borne trade. In the sixteenth century, the popularity of this unglazed ware declined, but the precise reasons for the discontinuation of production are unknown.

Since 1976, the efforts of the municipality of Suzu and the local chamber of commerce have led to a revival of the Suzu-*yaki* tradition. Between 1979 and 1991, seven kilns were established; they produce tea and *sake* vessels, mugs for beer and coffee, smaller storage jars, and flower vases. In 1989, a ceramics center that is well worth a visit was set up in Takojima, north of Suzu; it documents the development of Suzu-*yaki* from Sue ware to the Middle Ages.

Suzu ware is made from coils on a wheel, in *himozukuri* technique. Alongside undecorated pots, simple incised or impressed designs can be found, similar to those on medieval items, such as the typical *ayasuki* (cedar) pattern. The unglazed wares are fired in an *anagama* over a number of days, first with oil, then with pine, at temperatures up to 2282°F (1250°C). During the process of carbonization in reduction, the iron-rich clay reacts with the carbon from the kiln atmosphere to form a surface with shades between pale gray and deep black (see photo 153), thus bearing the greatest resemblance of any unglazed wares to the original Sue ceramics.

Mumyôi 無名異 (51)

The largest island in the Sea of Japan is Sadogashima (Niigata Prefecture). In the Middle Ages, it was a penal colony, and its rich gold and silver deposits were exploited from 1601 into the twentieth century. By the end of the eighteenth century, Kurosawa Kintarô was producing large quantities of glazed domestic wares in Aikawa, on Sado. The *nanga* painting (which can still be seen today), with its freely executed designs in the Chinese style, is typical of this Kintarô-*yaki*. The red, iron-rich *mumyôi* clay comes from the gold and silver mines, and it is to this that the mainly unglazed ceramics from the island of Sado owe their name. In the early nineteenth century, Itô Jinbei first added *mumyôi* to a clay body for low-fired ceramics, which were similarly brittle to raku wares. Roof tiles and ventilation pipes for the mines were made. Finally, in 1831, Itô Tomisaburô, another potter from the Itô family, built the Sekisui-*gama* to make domestic wares, and is considered to be the first Mumyôi potter. After the Meiji Restoration, his son Tomitarô (Itô Sekisui I), along with Miura Jôzan, developed the high-fired, unglazed *shudei* ware known today as Mumyôi-*yaki*. For this, *mumyôi* is mixed one to one with another clay.

The pots are usually thrown; more rarely, they are hand built. After drying, the objects are burnished up to three times with cloths or a steel tool in order to compress the surface (see photo 8). The kiln must be heated slowly to 2192°F (1200°C), and in the traditional *noborigama*, the main firing takes five days. The characteristic red color of Mumyôi ware is a result of firing in oxidation; for some objects, the contrasting black areas are achieved by smoking without oxygen (see photo 154).

Today, on the island of Sado, there are 29 workshops, 14 of them in Aikawa. One of these kilns is the traditional Sekisui-*gama* overseen by Itô Sekisui V (born in 1941), who was designated *ningen kokuhû* (Living National Treasure) in 2003 for his typical unglazed Mumyôi-*yaki*, with its brilliant red-black contrast. His expressive *neriage* work has also been highly esteemed for more than 20 years (see photo 155). Watanabe Tôzô

Photo 153. Suzu-*yaki*. Nakayama Tatsuma, vase (*hanaire*), 2001. 10 x 5¾ inches (25.4 x 14.5 cm). Unglazed stoneware, smoked.

Photo 154. Mumyôi-*yaki*. Watanabe Tôzô, tea set (*chaki*), 2001. Side-handled small teapot (*kyûsu*): 3½ x 5¾ x 3¾ inches (8.7 x 14.7 x 9.8 cm). "Husband and wife" teacups (*meoto yunomi*): 3½ x 2¾ inches (8.7 x 6.7 cm) and 3¼ x 2½ inches (8.2 x 6.4 cm). *Shudei* ware, with "kiln change" marks (*yôhen*).

(born in 1939) also produces typical Mumyôi ware in his workshop, Tôgei-en, with the Kunizô-*gama* in Kanai, situated between Ryûtsu and Aikawa (see photo 156). Miura Koheiji (1933–2006), like some of the other Sado potters, used *mumyôi* clay for glazed stoneware in his Kohei-*gama* in Aikawa. In 1997, he was designated *ningen kokuhô* for his celadons.

Kasama 笠間 (52)

In the An'ei era (1772–1781), the farmer and potter Kuno Han'emon built a *noborigama* in Hakoda (present-day Kasama, in Ibaraki Prefecture), under the instruction of an itinerant potter from Shigaraki. With the help of Kichisaburô, a potter from Shigaraki, Han'emon's son-in-law Sehe'e finally managed to put the kiln into operation, under the name Kuno-*gama*. From the very beginning, the *daimyô* of Kasama lent their support to the production of ceramics, and in 1861 the Kuno-*gama* was placed under *han* administration along with six other kilns. In the following period, the production of stoneware was the most important area of trade in the Kasama region. The range of products mainly included large storage jars, mortars, and *hibachi* with a brown-black glaze; some objects resembled the Hagi-*nagashi* vessels from Shigaraki, with their green copper glaze striped over the white body.

After the end of the feudal system, the kilns were privatized. Traded from Tôkyô to Hokkaidô, the product range of storage jars, mortars, and storage jars for tea leaves remained virtually unchanged until the mid-twentieth century. However, the economic depression during the Taishô period and the change in lifestyles after the Second World War nearly caused Kasama-*yaki* to disappear. In contrast to neighboring Mashiko, Kasama did not benefit greatly from the *mingei* movement.

Beginning in 1957, Ibaraki Prefecture, which had become wealthy as a result of exporting electricity, provided intensive support. This took the form of recruiting designers and ceramists from farther afield, and building an institute for material development, a large ceramics center with exhibition and sales areas, and the Ibaraki Ceramic Art Museum, which opened in the spring of 2000. Today, there are about 400 potters working in and around Kasama, making domestic tableware, vases, and home accessories.

Three local clays very rich in iron, as well as a plastic clay from the north of Ibaraki Prefecture, are used in Kasama. Various shaping, decoration, and glazing techniques are used; firings are to 2282°F–2372°F (1250°C–1300°C) in wood-fired *anagama* and *noborigama*, or in gas, oil, or electric kilns.

In postwar Kasama-*yaki*, it is fairly typical that regional stylistic features are absent and that the potters follow their individual inclinations (see photos 157 and 158). Consequently, many studio potters and all stylistic variations ranging from *yakishime* to abstract overglaze decoration are to be found in Kasama (see photos 181 and 195). The *nunome* work, with its impressed textile designs, is well known. In particular, the *neriage* work of Matsui Kôsei (1927–2003; see photo 159) is famous. In recognition of this work, he was designated *ningen kokuhô* (Living National Treasure) in 1993. Matsui Kôyô (born in 1962) continues his father's work with slightly more restrained color.

Mashiko 益子 (53)

Since the construction of the first kiln in 1853 by Ôtsuka Keizaburô (he had learned his craft skills in neighboring Kasama), Mashiko, in Tochigi Prefecture, has been one of the folk kilns. Beginning in 1857, the Mashiko kilns came under the patronage of the lord of Kurobane, with the *han* administration taking responsibility for the distribution of the products. Simple domestic items in glazed stoneware, with *gosu* and iron decoration, were produced. After the privatization of the kilns in 1871, Mashiko style was influenced by potters who had moved there from Sôma, Aizu-Hongô, and Shigaraki. The increasing demand for domestic wares in the Tôkyô urban region was responsible for Mashiko becoming the largest pottery center in the Kantô region.

During the Meiji period, the main products were large teapots (*dobin*), with unglazed feet, for

Photo 155. Mumyôi-*yaki*. Itô Sekisui V (Living National Treasure), *sake* **bowl with floral design (***mumyôi neriage kamon choko***), 2003. 1½ x 4 inches (4.2 x 10 cm). Unglazed stoneware,** *neriage* **technique.**

Photo 156. Mumyôi-*yaki*. Watanabe Tôzô, spherical vase with "1000 dots" decoration (*senten-mon tsubo*), 2000. 8¼ x 7¼ inches (21.2 x 18.3 cm). *Shudei*-ware with chatter marks.

Photo 157. Kasama-*yaki*. Ôta Keizô, *sake* cup (*guinomi*), 1997. 2 x 3 inches (5.2 x 7.5 cm). Stoneware, light ash feldspar glaze, overglaze painting.

Photo 158. Kasama-*yaki*. Takano Toshiaki, water dropper (*suiteki*), 1999. 2¾ x 3 inches (7.3 x 8 cm). Unglazed stoneware, white and black slips, silver.

Photo 159. Kasama-*yaki*. Matsui Kôsei (Living National Treasure), *sake* cup (*guinomi*), 1998.
3 x 4½ inches (4.6 x 7.2 cm). Unglazed stoneware, *neriage* technique, burnished.

brewing tea or herbal infusions. The *sansui* dobin are renowned for their underglaze paintings of landscapes in iron brown and copper green on a white slip under a transparent glaze. In 1938, the ceramics painter Minagawa Masu (1875–1960) received first place for a *sansui dobin* at the First International Crafts Exhibition in Berlin. The *sansui dobin* are still made today by her granddaughter, Minagawa Hiro (see photo 160).

Mashiko's ongoing attraction to potters in Japan and the rest of the world began when Hamada Shôji (1894–1978), the co-founder of the *mingei* (folk art) movement, settled there in 1924 (for further details, see Development of Japanese Ceramics on pages 12–23). His successful experiments with local clays and with glazes he developed himself were rewarded in 1955 when he was designated *ningen kokuhô* (Living National Treasure). The ceramist Tamura Kôichi (1918–1987), who worked in Sano (Tochigi Prefecture), west of Mashiko, was also considered part of the Mashiko school and in 1986 was designated *ningen kokuhô* for his *mingei* work with iron oxide painting (*tetsu-e*).

Hamada's student Shimaoka Tatsuzô (born in 1919) is similarly rooted in the tradition of the *mingei* movement and was designated *ningen kokuhô* in 1996 for his *jômon zôgan* decorative technique (cord impressions with slip inlay; see photos 25 and 161). Shimaoka embodies the dilemma facing contemporary *mingei* potters: he says he carries the *mingei* idea in his heart, but as one of Japan's best-known studio potters and with his signed individual pieces, he is contradicting the *mingei* ideal of anonymity. Consequently, in 1991, Shimaoka resigned from the Japanese Art Association, an organization considered to be the most important representative of the *mingei* movement.

Although a small number of studio potters dig their own clay, the clay from the 100-year-old pit near Mashiko is commercially prepared. The sandy Mashiko clay is not very plastic and is thus frequently blended with other clays. The heavy, thick-walled pots are thrown, hand built, press molded, or slab built. The specific character of Mashiko ware is determined by the glazes made from natural red and ochre-colored earths; these include the typical red-brown *kaki* glaze favored by Hamada, a dark brown *tenmoku* glaze, and the black *koku* glaze. Straw ash, wood ash, or rice-husk ash, and a white clay are ingredients of the cream to gray-white *namihaku* glaze (see photo 162). With these and other glaze variations, a broad range of colors and surface textures can be achieved by pouring, dipping, applying in various thicknesses, using wax resist, brushing, and spraying (see photos 163 and 164 a–c). In the wood-firing *noborigama*, firings to 2192°F–2372°F (1200°C–1300°C) take 2 to 3 days, but in recent times, this type of kiln has been replaced by gas, oil, and electric kilns. Enamels fired to 1472°F (800°C) in green, yellow, and purple are especially reminiscent of Hamada and Shimaoka's works. There are also examples of salt glazing, which originated in Germany and England. (For details of Shimaoka's firing technique, refer to Firing in a Five-Chamber *Noborigama* on page 32).

Mashiko today is the largest folk-art pottery center in eastern Japan, with approximately 380 traditional workshops mainly producing domestic tableware. In addition, there are more than 100 studio potters. In the Kasama-Mashiko region, there are almost 1000 working potters, many of whom are studio potters (see photo 188).

Photo 160. Mashiko-*yaki*. Minagawa Hiro, teapot (*sansui dobin*), 2003. 5¼ x 10 x 5¾ inches (13.6 x 25.5 x 14.4 cm). Stoneware, white slip, underglaze landscape painting with iron and copper pigments.

Photo 161. Mashiko-*yaki*. Shimaoka Tatsuzô (Living National Treasure), diamond-shaped vase
(*ji-gusuri jômon zôgan daiya-gata hanaire*), 2002. 8 x 6 inches (20.4 x 15.4 cm).
Stoneware, *jômon zôgan* technique.

Photo 162. Mashiko-*yaki*. Tsuneo Narui, faceted *sake* bottle (*mentori tokkuri*), ca. 1980. 9¾ x 5¾ inches (24.5 x 15 cm). Stoneware, *namihaku* glaze.

Photo 163. Mashiko-*yaki*. Daiguchi Michiko, faceted cylindrical vase (*mentori tsutsukabin*), 1980. 12 x 4¾ inches (31 x 12.3 cm). Stoneware, gray-white glaze, unglazed areas (*hima*).

Photo 164a. Mashiko-*yaki*. Plate with pine tree design, from a set of ornamental plates (*kazarizara*), ca. 1975.
1¾ x 11 inches (4.4 x 28 cm). "Three Friends of the Winter" design (pine, bamboo, plum, *shô chiku bai*),
fired in the Satoyama *gama*.

**Photo 164b. Mashiko-*yaki*. Plate with bamboo design, from a set of ornamental plates (*kazarizara*), ca. 1975.
1¾ x 11 inches (4.4 x 28 cm). *Kaki*-glaze, "Three Friends of the Winter" design (pine, bamboo, plum, *shô chiku bai*), fired in the Satoyama *gama*.**

Photo 164c. Mashiko-*yaki*. Plate with plum blossom design, from a set of ornamental plates (*kazarizara*), ca. 1975. 1½ x 10¾ inches (4.2 x 27.8 cm). Blue oil-spot glaze, "Three Friends of the Winter" design (pine, bamboo, plum, *shô chiku bai*), fired in the Satoyama *gama*.

Aizu-Hongô 会津本郷 (54)

Stoneware and porcelain made in Aizu-Hongô and Aizu-Wakamatsu (Fukushima Prefecture, previously Aizu province) are known as Aizu-Hongô-yaki. After tile production for the construction of the castle complex in Aizu-Wakamatsu was started by Gamô Ujisato in 1590, the first lord of Aizu, Masayuki Hoshina, brought the Seto potter Mizuno Genzaemon to Aizu Hongô in 1645, where, from 1647 on, he made tea ceramics. After his early death, in 1648 the hanyô (official kiln) was taken over by his younger brother Chôbei, who made utensils for the tea ceremony in Seto style under the name of Setoemon, an honorary designation. To an increasing extent, he also made items for daily use, with the support of the han administration. At the beginning of the eighteenth century, the kiln became a minyô (folk kiln), at the same time increasing output.

First attempts to make porcelain in 1777 were unsuccessful, until Satô Ihee acquired the technology for porcelain production from Arita during a journey to the Japanese pottery centers in 1797. After his return, porcelain was made beginning in 1800, but it was only 20 years later that firing had been improved to the extent that the product was comparable to the white body of competing Seto ware. Under the direction of the han administration, an extensive ceramics industry developed, with exports to northern and central Japan. For the most part, blue-and-white porcelain with landscapes in the Chinese style was made, alongside glazed stoneware.

Because of the great popularity of the blue-and-white porcelain, the market share of stoneware steadily fell during the Meiji period (1868–1912). Additional hardships struck during the economic recession and a devastating fire in the Taishô period (1912–1926); out of 10 stoneware kilns in the Meiji period, only the Munakata kiln was in operation by 1926. Motivated by the mingei movement, the potters at the Munakata-gama adhered steadfastly to their tradition. The present master, Munakata Ryôichi (sixth generation; born in 1933), uses local clay from Mt. Hongô and fires domestic ware—including the well-known nishinbachi (slab-built square containers for salting herring)—in his noborigama. Munakata also throws large plates and vases, to which the deep brown namako glaze lends a wonderful vivacity, with its white accents and violet to indigo highlights (see photo 165).

By the mid-twentieth century, through a rigorous modernization of production and firing techniques, as well as the product range, other kilns were also able to participate in the revival. This is particularly true of the Nishida-gama founded in 1870 by the former samurai Nishida Sankuro. The wares, which are also known as Aizu-Suigetsu-yaki, are a gray-white hanjiki (semiporcelain) that the current master, Nishida Michito (fifth generation; born in 1964), produces by slip casting, using a mixture of clays from Hongô and Tajimi. The best known of the hand-painted cobalt underglaze designs are the medallions, with their representations of blooming apple branches or kaki trees (see photo 166).

Today, Aizu-Hongô-yaki is produced in 18 kilns in Aizu-Hongô and one in Aizu-Wakamatsu. Functional wares and vases are produced. In its diversity, this type of ceramics reflects its 350-year history: stoneware with a broad range of glazes can be found alongside hanjiki and porcelain decorated in a number of styles, from traditional cobalt underglaze painting in the Chinese style to contemporary designs.

Nihonmatsu Banko 二本松万古 (55)

Around 1700, at the invitation of the local lord in Nihonmatsu (Fukushima Prefecture), potters from Kyôto developed the tebineri kata kuzushi technique, which is very rare in Japan. For this, a thin slab of clay (tatara) is pressed with the fingers onto a wooden mold, which can be dismantled. After the object has dried, the individual mold pieces are extracted. In the mid-nineteenth century, Harukichi, the half-brother of the then proprietor of the kiln, Yamashita Sôsuke (fourth generation), and the potter Miuraya Bunsuke from Kyôto improved this method, which has survived to the present day. It is used especially for the production of side-handled, small teapots (kyûsu).

Photo 165. Aizu-Hongô-*yaki*. Munakata Ryôichi, ornamental plate (*kazarizara*), 1998. 2½ x 12 inches (6.7 x 30.7 cm). Stoneware, *namako* glaze.

Photo 166. **Aizu-Suigetsu-***yaki*. **Nishida Michito, shallow plate (***sara***), 2003. 1¼ x 10 inches (3 x 25.4 cm).**
***Hanjiki* (semiporcelain), kaki tree in cobalt underglaze painting.**

From the beginning of the twentieth century, the kiln had to struggle against financial difficulties and was forced to close at the beginning of the Shôwa period. In 1948, the ceramics firm Adachi Seitôjo attempted a revival, which failed after 12 years. After this, the operation was taken over by the potter Inoue Zenjiro, whose son Yoshio (born in 1949) now runs the workshop. In the traditional Nihonmatsu Banko style, *kyûsu*, sencha sets, and "husband-and-wife" teacups are now made as red or black-brown unglazed ware, with distinct finger marks and the typical application of plum blossoms (see photo 167). Since 1979, Inoue Yoshio has also restarted production of Nihonmatsu-*yaki*, a glazed stoneware that was developed as domestic ware for the mass market at the same time as Nihonmatsu Banko-*yaki*. Besides the usual pieces of tableware, items such as coffee cups and beer mugs were produced to target new markets. Along with Nihonmatsu Banko and Nihonmatsu-*yaki*, Inoue Yoshio also makes individual pieces, especially large *yakishime* flower containers.

An iron-rich clay from the nearby Abukuma River is used. After careful cleaning, it is mixed with a plastic clay. Objects are wheel thrown or produced using the *tebineri kata kuzushi* technique. The pots dry for a month and are then slowly fired in oxidation in a gas kiln to 2102°F–2192°F (1150°C–1200°C).

Sôma Koma 相馬駒 (56)

The ceramics tradition in the town of Sôma, located in Fukushima Prefecture in the northeast area of Honshû (Tôhoku), dates back to Lord Sôma Toshitane, who, as a devotee of the tea ceremony, was an admirer of the famous potter Nonomura Ninsei in Kyôto. At the instigation of the feudal lord, the Sôma potter Tashiro Gengouemon was trained under Ninsei. In 1626, Tashiro returned to Sôma and made stoneware for the tea ceremony under the name of Tashiro Seijiemon; he was permitted to use the character *sei* from Ninsei's name. The ruling family instructed Tashiro Seijiemon II to construct a *hanyô*, in which the products were made for their own exclusive use. This kiln, the Tashiro-*gama*, is

considered to be the oldest *noborigama* in Tôhoku still in use. After initial imitations of Ninsei's work, the stylistic features of Sôma Koma-*yaki* developed and are still in evidence today.

Materials for clay and glazes are found in the area. During firing, the high percentage of sand in the clay causes the typical crazing (*kan'nyû*), known as *aohibi*, in the celadon glazes. These glazes are only found on the inner surfaces of some pots. The outlines of one or more galloping horses (*hashiri goma*) executed in iron oxide underglaze brushwork are characteristic of Sôma Koma-*yaki*. The model for this design was a drawing by Kanô Naonobu commissioned in the mid-seventeenth century by the Sôma clan. It depicts the Sôma *nomaoi* festival, which still takes place today when wild horses are driven to pasture.

With the end of the feudal system as a result of the Meiji Restoration, Sôma Koma-*yaki* found its way onto the open market for the first time, became known in the West through the World's Fairs, and won several awards. The current master, Tashiro Seijiemon XV (born in 1947), who trained in Mino under Katô Takuo (1917–2005), Living National Treasure, mainly makes tea and *sake* utensils, as well as flower vases (see photo 168).

Ôbori Sôma 大堀相馬 (57)

In 1690, along with a potter from the Tashiro-*gama*, the official kiln of the Sôma clan in neighboring Sôma (see Sôma Koma, 56), Sama from Ôbori opened a folk kiln, near Namie, in present-day Fukushima Prefecture, to make objects for everyday use. The intensive support of the *han* administration (the ban on imports of Seto-Mino ceramics in 1733 and the opening of sales offices in Edo and Hakodate in 1804, for example) made the region around Namie, with more than 100 kilns, the largest ceramics center in Tôhoku up to the mid-nineteenth century. The Ôbori Sôma-*yaki* of that period was quite varied, with a wide range of glazes and decorative techniques. The drawings of galloping horses (*hashiri goma*), reminiscent of Sôma-Koma-*yaki*, were in evidence, as was the *aohibi* glaze (celadon glaze with crackle) that was developed around 1820.

Photo 167. Nihonmatsu Banko-*yaki*. Inoue Yoshio, sencha set (*tebineri chaki soroe*), 2002. Side-handled small
teapot (*kyûsu*): 3 x 5½ x 3¼ inches (7.6 x 13.7 x 8.5 cm). Teacups, glazed inside (*sencha chawan*):
1½ x 2¾ inches (4 x 7 cm). Saucer (*chataku*): ¼ x 3½ inches (0.9 x 9.2 cm). *Yakishime* stoneware,
tebineri kata kuzushi technique, with plum blossom applications.

Photo 168. **Sôma Koma-***yaki***. Tashiro Seijiemon XV, side-handled small teapot (***kyûsu***), 1999. 3 x 6 x 4 inches (8 x 15.6 x 10.5 cm). Stoneware, ***aohibi*** glaze (celadon glaze with crackle), horse design (***hashiri goma***) in iron oxide underglaze painting.**

After the Meiji Restoration, the number of kilns declined drastically. Exports to the United States—teapots with shark-skin (*samehada*) glaze in particular—secured the survival of a number of kilns. However, after improvements in transportation, the high-quality wares from Seto and Arita by and large drove the Tôhoku kilns out of the market. It was only with the support from MITI, which began in 1978, that a ceramics center in Ôbori Namie could become established. Today, 23 workshops are operating. Domestic wares and vases, as well as tea ceramics, usually covered with *aohibi* glaze, are the main products. Whereas the tea ceramics are strongly reminiscent of Sôma Koma-*yaki*, most of the other items are entirely covered with *aohibi* glaze. Along with the drawings of horses, a restrained decoration in gold is characteristic. For insulation, teapots, teacups, and *sake* sets are often double walled (*nijû-yaki*; see photo 169).

The objects are thrown using local clay and are painted with an iron oxide pigment after the bisque firing to 1652°F–1742°F (900°C–950°C). The celadon glaze, made from a special kind of feldspar from nearby Mt. Tôzan, is sometimes covered with an ash glaze after the main firing to 2282°F–2372°F (1250°C–1300°C) in a gas or electric kiln; gold is fired on at 1562°F (850°C). The cracks are emphasized by rubbing with black ink in the final phase.

Hirashimizu 平清水 (58)

The name Hirashimizu-*yaki* is derived from the small pottery village of Hirashimizu, which today belongs to the municipality of Yamagata (Yamagata Prefecture). It originated in the Bunka era (1804–1818), when Ono Tôjihei received permission to construct a kiln on the grounds of the Hira'izumi Temple. The glazed stoneware from this kiln bears a strong resemblance to Ôbori Sôma ware.

Around 1830, the Kyûshû potter Matsuura, together with Watanabe Gohei, a local man, and Itô Tôjûrô from Iwanami, undertook the first unsuccessful attempts to produce porcelain. It was only with the assistance of the potter Isuke

from Kirigome that Tôjûrô finally succeeded in producing high-quality porcelain in his Iwanami-*gama* in the year 1847. This Iwanami-*yaki* was nearly on a par with the quality of Arita ware. Inspired by the success of the Iwanami-*gama*, the first porcelain kiln was built in Hirashimizu in 1847.

By the beginning of the Meiji period, 20 porcelain workshops were distributing their products from northern Honshû to Hokkaidô. The local kaolin deposits were of such excellent quality that a bisque firing was unnecessary; the underglaze *gosu* painting was applied directly to the dried clay body. The products were typical functional forms, such as large bottles, pots, bowls, and platters. However, in 1901, the market collapsed when the opening of the railway gave the local market access to the favorably priced porcelain from Seto and the Arita area. The last porcelain was fired in Hirashimizu in 1934, leaving only three stoneware kilns.

After 1945, there were six kilns in the village of Hirashimizu, breaking new ground with their glazed stoneware. A previously unused fine body with iron inclusions, which melted through the typical blue-green glaze made of materials found on nearby Mt. Chitose, was used. Because of its similarity to the fruit, this type of ware is referred to as *riseiji* (pear celadon). The best-known glaze is *zansetsu-yû* (residual snow; see photo 170) from the Seiryû-*gama*, which is run by Niwa Ryôchi (fourth generation; born in 1931). His work is considered by experts to be among the best examples of Tôhoku ceramics.

Tsutsumi 堤 (59)

Ceramics production in Sendai (Miyagi Prefecture) began in the early seventeenth century with the production of roofing tiles for the erection of the castle and the castle town. In 1694, the potter Uemura Man'emon from the Imado-*gama* in Edo, commissioned by Date Tsunamura, the fourth Lord of Sendai, built the first officially licensed kiln, which was first used for tea ceramics known as Sugiyama ware. It was soon transformed into a folk kiln for domestic objects in glazed stoneware.

Photo 169. Ôbori Sôma-*yaki*. Sue Toshiaki, *sake* set (*shuki*), 1999. *Sake* flask (*tokkuri*): 5½ x 4¼ inches (14.3 x 10.7 cm). *Sake* cups (*choko*): 2⅛ x 2¼ inches (5.6 x 5.7 cm). Stoneware, double walled (*nijû-yaki*); *aohibi* glaze (celadon glaze with crackle), horse design (*hashiri goma*) in iron oxide underglaze painting, gold rim.

Photo 170. Hirashimizu-*yaki*. Niwa Ryôchi, tea bowl (*chawan*), 2000. 2¾ x 5 inches (7.3 x 12.5 cm). Stoneware, *zansetsu-yû* ("residual snow" glaze).

Some of the typical products were large storage jars, *sake* bottles, and kitchen utensils made of a rough, red-firing clay with black, red, or *namako* glazes, or *suiteki* (water droppers) in a finer type of clay. At the end of the eighteenth century, the kiln moved to Tsutsumi, situated to the north of Sendai (a location with good clay deposits), and experienced a boom lasting until 1830. After the Meiji Restoration, mass products from the Seto-Mino region (*kudarimono*) overwhelmed local production, for which the term Tsutsumi-*yaki* had become established. In the 1920s, water pipes and roofing tiles became the main products.

Today, traditional Tsutsumi ware is made in the Kanma-*gama* belonging to Haryû Kenba IV (born in 1927) and his two sons, Kyuma and Kazuma. In 1856, during a visit by Miura Kenya (Kenzan VI from Kyôto), Kenba I learned pottery making from him and was allowed to adopt the character *ken* from Kenya's name. The Kenba family moved its workshop from Tsutsumi to a suburb north of Sendai and now operates three gas kilns and a *noborigama*. The Tsutsumi tradition is continued with expressive vessels in reddish brown, sandy Tsutsumi clay. The rough surface of the body is coated with an iron glaze and overlaid by a thick white *namako* glaze (see photo 171); other glazes used are a newly developed vermillion, green, and gray made of paulownia wood ash, as well as a gritty, white-gray glaze. Storage jars and functional domestic wares are no longer made. The kiln now concentrates on vases and tea ceramics that are approved by the Ura Senke tea school.

Kirigome 切込 (60)

The origins of Kirigome-*yaki*, made in Kirigome, near Miyazaki (Miyagi Prefecture), are obscure, with dates varying between 1670 and 1830. Some sources date the founding of the kilns at the end of the seventeenth century and credit their founding to Date Tsunamura, the fourth Lord of Sendai, and his artistically minded father Tsunamune. Tsunamura is said to have invited potters to Kirigome from Arita to make high-quality porcelain as presentation ware. The Miyazaki-*yaki* mentioned in the eighteenth century in a chronicle of

the Date clan may well have been a precursor of Kirigome-*yaki*. The earliest documentary evidence of Kirigome-*yaki* was in 1834, and the earliest datable piece from 1835. Kirigome-*yaki* was at its peak between 1844 and 1860.

The few surviving pieces from this period and the shards from excavations prove that this was a carefully made *sometsuke* porcelain that was created from a fine white clay of Arita quality, painted with local *gosu* pigment, and fired in a *noborigama*. It was not placed in the kiln in the customary *kasane* way (in stacks), however, so it was probably intended for presentation ware for the Date clan. By the mid-nineteenth century, the percentage of mass-produced goods (*getemono*) in a coarser quality of clay was steadily on the increase. The typical products of Kirigome-*yaki* were plates in flower form with various shapes along the rim, and *sake* flasks like the *omiki tokkuri* (pair of *sake* flasks for the house altar) and the *koshibu tokkuri*, with their full-bellied form. Along with blue-and-white ware and pots with brown iron glazes, Kirigome-*sansai* was produced in the mid-nineteenth century and was known as "the flower of Tôhoku porcelain"; it was an elegant ware with white, aubergine, and turquoise glazes.

The Meiji Restoration led to the closure of the kilns. Attempts to revive them in 1918 as the so-called Kirigome Taishô-*gama*, with the support of Miyagi Prefecture, failed after only three years. Today, several kilns are working again in Miyazaki. Heavy and grayish in appearance, this porcelain, with its hard cobalt underglaze decoration (see photo 172), does not match the beauty of its predecessors from the nineteenth century, which are displayed at the museum at the ceramics center *Miyazaki tôgei no sato*. Apart from blue-and-white ware, *yakishime* and glazed stoneware comprise half of the output today.

Photo 171. Tsutsumi-*yaki*. Haryû Kenba IV, vase (*hanaire*), ca. 2002. 10¼ x 5 inches (26.2 x 12.5 cm). Stoneware, dark iron glaze, overlaid by white *namako* glaze.

Photo 172. Kirigome-*yaki*. Miura (Sugawara) Sanae, bottle vase (*hanabin*) in the form of *koshibu tokkuri*, 2003. 7¾ x 4½ inches (19.5 x 11.4 cm). Porcelain, cobalt underglaze painting.

Tsugaru 津軽 (61)

Like many other kilns set up in the early seventeenth century, Tsugaru-yaki has its origins in the production of tiles for the construction of fortifications—in this case, the castle in Hirosaki (Aomori Prefecture) built by Tsugaru Nobumaki, the second Lord of Hirosaki. His grandson Nobumasa boosted employment in his *han* by setting up several kilns that produced glazed stoneware for use as domestic tableware. Tsugaru-yaki was under the patronage of the Tsugaru clan until the abolition of the feudal system in 1871 as a consequence of the Meiji Restoration. After the extension of the railway system to the north, bargain-priced, mass-produced wares from the Seto-Mino region (*kudari-mono*) began to arrive in the prefecture, and local products were forced out of the market entirely by the early twentieth century. Because of the *mingei* movement, however, traditional Tsugaru ware has now found lasting appreciation.

There are now three workshops operating in Hirosaki, which make a simple but aesthetically pleasing ware decorated with thick, black *tenmoku* glaze and white rice-straw ash glazes from local raw materials. The main products are tea wares (*chaki*), *sake* sets (*shuki*), flower vessels (*kaki*), plates, and platters.

The approximately 50-year-old Sadayuki-*gama* run by Hayakawa Sadayuki for his *kakiotoshi* wares, which he only makes in small numbers, is well known (see photo 173). After bisque firing, a thick, white glaze is applied, then cherry blossom designs are carved out to reveal the gray clay body. The center of each blossom is painted in cobalt or iron. A transparent feldspar glaze is applied before the main firing in a gas kiln.

Photo 173. Tsugaru-*yaki*. Hayakawa Sadayuki, "husband and wife" teacups (*meoto yunomi*), 1984.
3½ x 2¾ inches (9 x 7 cm) and 3¼ x 2½ inches (8.2 x 6.7 cm). Stoneware, cherry blossom design in *kakiotoshi* technique with cobalt underglaze painting.

>> Kilns in Hokkaidô

Hokkaidô, in the north, is the second largest of the four main Japanese islands and is today a prefecture. The island was originally inhabited by the Ainu people; Japanese merchants only came to this remote region in the sixteenth century. Initially, only the southern parts of Hokkaidô closest to Honshû were settled by the Japanese, and in the Edo period, the Matsumae domain was established there. Neither the harsh climate nor the isolated location allowed a ceramics tradition to develop organically in Hokkaidô. In the late nineteenth century, the Meiji administration began a substantial campaign of development and settlement in Hokkaidô, as a result of which potters, too, came to settle there. However, the production of blue-and-white ware in particular soon had to be discontinued, as local clays were unsuitable.

With the support of the regional authorities, more than 300 ceramists have since settled in Hokkaidô. In 1968, the Hokkaidô Pottery Association (*Hokkaidô tôgeikai*) was founded, and it organizes annual exhibitions. In 1994, the Ebetsu Ceramic Art Center opened in Ebetsu, where bricks have been made on an industrial scale for more than 100 years. The center has developed into a showcase for Hokkaidô ceramics, with changing exhibitions and the permanent presentation of work by 70 local potters.

Hokkaidô ceramics differ widely in appearance due to the varied places of origin of the artists: along with *yakishime*, glazed stoneware is made, ranging from folk art to contemporary clay assemblages.

Otaru 小樽 (62)

The port of Otaru, located near Sapporo, is the site of the oldest kiln in Hokkaidô. The workshop, founded by Shirose Shinji in 1899, initially produced blue-and-white ware modeled after the products of Kyôto and Kutani, especially tableware and vases. Due to the nature of the available clays, production was soon restricted to glazed stoneware. Shirose Eisetsu (third generation)

refurbished the kiln in 1935 and established the reputation of the Shirose kilns with his work, for which he was awarded a number of prizes. Shirose Eisetsu's typical glazes include a white glaze known as *yuki-shino* (snow *shino*); a jade-green glaze (*ryoku gyoku oribe*); and a peach-red and green glaze (*tôkôryoku*), with shades ranging from pink and red to violet from one basic green glaze. Besides *yuteki-tenmoku* glazes and *zôgan* work with inlays of white and colored slips, influences from the original inhabitants of Hokkaidô, the Ainu, can be seen in the incised designs on plates.

Since the retirement of Shirose Shinji (fourth generation) in 2000, the kiln, Shirose-tôen, has been overseen by Yoshikawa Yukio, who has worked at the kiln since 1953. The clay is from neighboring Ebetsu. The most common glazes on wheel-thrown objects (vases and tableware) are white or jade green (see photo 174). The glazed work is fired in oxidation in an *anagama*.

Tôraku 北楽 (63)

The potter Sakaguchi Atsushi, who was born in Tôkyô in 1953, was trained in Tajimi, the center of Mino ceramics. In 1975, he began working with a gas kiln in Tajimi, but his goal was to work with a wood-fired *anagama*. Thus, he moved to Hokkaidô in 1980 after stays in Shikoku and Kyûshû. Working in Sapporo, he was firing an electric kiln in 1989. In 1990, he was able to build and fire an *anagama*, the Tôraku-*gama*, on an abandoned farmstead in Naganuma, near Sapporo. This is where he creates his expressive *yakishime* objects today, using the methods of the Momoyama period (1568–1600). Seashell impressions are characteristic of his work, as are ash incrustations and rivulets of ash glaze as evidence of wood firing with larch (*karamatsu*). Tôraku ware is thus also referred to as Karamatsu-*yaki* (see photo 175).

Photo 174. Otaru-*yaki*. Yoshikawa Yukio, vase (*ryoku gyoku oribe tsubo*), 2003. 7¼ x 4¾ inches (18.5 x 12.2 cm). Stoneware, jade green glaze.

Photo 175. *Tôraku-yaki*. Sakaguchi Atsushi, bottle vase (*hanabin*), ca. 2002. 8 x 4¼ inches (20.5 x 10.7 cm). Unglazed stoneware, shell impressions (*kaime*), natural-ash glaze.

Watasuge 綿スゲ (64)

Arazeki Yûsei (born in 1951) opened his workshop, which is named after cotton grass (Watasuge-tôbô), after training in Hokkaidô, first producing glazed stoneware and firing a gas kiln in Sapporo. Since 1986, he has fired an *anagama*, usually with larch. Named after the first kiln, the *anagama* is located in his native town of Kyôgoku. He blends local clay with those from Honshû. In addition to glazed ware (see photo 176), the main focus of his work is, increasingly, ceramics with a natural-ash glaze, in which he works to achieve characteristic *yôhen* effects.

Taisetsu 大雪 / Asahikawa 旭川 (65)

The Taisetsu-*gama* in Asahikawa was built in 1970 by Bandô Tôkô and his son Toyomitsu. While Bandô Tôkô's work was characterized by crystalline glazes (*kesshô-yû*, see photo 23), which are rare in Japan, his son first worked in *neriage*, which he had learned from Living National Treasure Matsui Kôsei (see Kasama, 52, on page 214) during his training. After taking over the kiln, Bandô Toyomitsu (born in 1947) has continued the work with crystalline glazes on a fine clay body. The thin-walled tea ware, vases, *sake* sets, and tableware are wheel thrown. Toyomitsu works to capture in his ceramics typical impressions of the four seasons in Hokkaidô, such as snow crystals (see photo 177), melting ice floes, lavender blossoms, and the morning mist in autumn. The elegant work of the Bandô family has won numerous awards.

In the past ten years, a small ceramics center has developed in Asahikawa, with a focus on the Taisetsu kiln and seven additional kilns, the *Arashiyama tôgei no sato*; there are more potters at work in and around Asahikawa. The glazed stoneware made in this region is called Asahikawa-*yaki*.

Bihoro 美幌 (66)

There are six kilns in the town of Bihoro, by the Sea of Okhotsk. The kiln of the ceramist Shiori Minoru (born in 1952, in Hokkaidô) has been in existence since 1981. He has reproduced the annual natural spectacle of the pack ice, with the flowing colors of the light blue sky, the white of the ice, and the deep blue of the sea, in his blue copper glazes with white overglaze (*sei-yû shiro-nagashi*, see photo 178). The glazed stoneware from the Bihoro-*gama*, mainly vases and tableware, is thus referred to as Ohôtsuku-*yaki*. Shiori Minoru has recently experimented with *yakishime* fired in the *anagama*, making the ceramics from a plastic, iron-rich clay mixed with sand from the local beaches.

Photo 176. Watasuge-*yaki*. Arazeki Yûsei, large plate (*ôzara*), ca. 2003. 3¼ x 13¾ inches (8.2 x 35.3 cm). Glazed stoneware.

Photo 177. Taisetsu-*yaki*. Bandô Toyomitsu, *sake* set with snow crystals (*ohôtsuku yuki-gesshô shuki*), 2003. *Sake* flask (*tokkuri*): 4¼ x 2¾ inches (10.6 x 7.2 cm). *Sake* cups (*choko*): 1½ x 2½ (4.1 x 6.2 cm). Stoneware, crystalline glaze.

Photo 178. Bihoro-*yaki*. Shiori Minoru, "husband and wife" teacups (*meoto yunomi*), 1992. 3½ x 2¾ inches
(9 x 6.8 cm) and 3 x 2½ inches (7.8 x 6.5 cm). Stoneware, blue copper glaze, white cover glaze
(*sei-yû shiro-nagashi*).

STUDIO POTTERS

Today, studio potters are influenced by Japanese traditions as well as by Western ideas of global reach, but connections to the other arts, such as the tea ceremony, *ikebana*, and the local culinary heritage have been retained. While ceramic sculpture, which has moved away from the vessel as a functional object and toward freely formed sculptures or installations, is created, it is nevertheless the study of the vessel, its forms, and its glazes that predominates. Studio potters experiment with unglazed and glazed stoneware, porcelain and other clay bodies, glazes, and the firing process. They frequently use several types of kilns and achieve results that have increasingly found international acclaim.

Artists no longer work alone in the traditional pottery centers, where—especially in the old potter families—the lines between traditional craft and studio ceramics are often fluid. Many have settled near centers of business activity and culture, with their art schools. Kyôto, especially, has come to be regarded as a center of avant-garde ceramics in Japan. A number of studio potters have also set up their studios in rural areas, such as Tôhoku (northern Honshû) and Hokkaidô, some with assistance from the state.

In this chapter, a small number of studio potters and their individual work (mainly vessels), which reveal the connection between tradition and modernity in the contemporary world of Japanese ceramics, will be introduced.

For many studio potters, unglazed stoneware still represents the greatest challenge. They experiment with various clays and study the effects of firing conditions on their results. In the interplay of the vessel form with the fired color of the unglazed clay, many artists have found their individual means of expression. Others see their personal challenge in the natural-ash glazes that are created by the unpredictable path of fly ash during the firing (see photos 179–183). Some artists have developed their individual approaches in experiments with the material (see photos 184–186), or they use traditional techniques to create modern forms (see photos 187 and 188).

Honma Shin'ichi, who was born in Kogota (Miyagi Prefecture) in 1948, is well known for his experiments with the firing process. He began producing ceramics at the age of 25 in Fujizawa (Iwate Prefecture), using a 32½-foot (10 m), half-underground, single-chamber kiln (*anagama*) that he constructed himself. In 1983, a 65½-foot (20 m) *anagama* of the same type followed. His thick-walled ceramics are hand built from an iron-rich, red-brown firing clay and formed with a paddle. The vessels owe their vibrant appearance to the contrast between unglazed clay and thick layers of partially melted ash from the wood firing (see photo 179).

An artist who is obsessed with the primeval force of fire is Kumano Kurôuemon, who was born in 1955 in Sabae, Echizen region, Fukui Prefecture. After a long apprenticeship with Fujita Jûrôemon VIII (see Echizen, 44, on page 178), Kumano has worked for almost 20 years to achieve firing temperatures of up to 2768°F (1520°C)—the temperature of molten lava inside an active volcano—in his 32½-foot (10 m), half-underground, split-bamboo-type *anagama*. He digs the most suitable clay for this in the mountains of his home. His voluminous pots and bowls are wheel thrown. The only glaze he uses is of *shino* type, but half of his production is unglazed. For the six-day firing, he uses oak, which he values highly because it is so rich in minerals. The failure rate of 80 percent per firing is enormous, but the results are correspondingly remarkable. His *shino* glaze, which is not fired in a saggar, has shades of red or blue, and because of its unique qualities, is known as *Kuma shino*. Along with shades of green or brown, the objects with a natural-ash glaze reveal the rivulets in blue and turquoise typical of his work. The pieces with natural glaze, which have gone through the firestorm in the kiln, are referred to by Kumano as "*oni* (devil) Echizen," and they resemble naturally occurring phenomena, such as mossy stones (see photo 180).

Born in 1952 in Iwate Prefecture, Kon'no Haruo trained mainly under Isezaki Mitsuru (born in 1934) in Bizen. He ran a workshop in Mashiko

Photo 179. Honma Shin'ichi, paddled jar, 1996. 10¾ x 5¾ x 5½ inches (27.5 x 14.7 x 14.6 cm). Unglazed stoneware, partially melted fly ash.

Photo 180. Kumano Kurôuemon, "Echizen devil" platter (*oni Echizen ôbachi*), 2004. 4 x 17¾ inches (10.3 x 45 cm). *Yakishime* stoneware, natural-ash glaze, shell impressions (*kaime*).

Photo 181. Kon'no Haruo, spherical vase (*yakishime tsubo*), 1997. 9¾ x 11 inches (24.4 x 28.3 cm).
** *Yakishime* stoneware with rivulets of ash glaze, *hi-iro* (fire color), *koge* (scorch markings).**

Photo 182. Kaneshige Moto'o, sculptural vase, 2004. 13¾ x 7 inches (34.8 x 18 cm). *Yakishime* **stoneware, natural-ash glaze.**

Photo 183.   Hatori Makoto, sculptural vase, 2002. 7¼ x 6½ inches (18.4 x 16.2 cm). Stoneware, natural-ash and salt glaze.

Photo 184. Mihara Ken, "*sekki*" flower vase (*sekki kaki*), ca. 2002. 11¼ x 12 x 6¾ inches (28.5 x 30.8 x 17.4 cm). Unglazed stoneware in the Sue ceramics tradition.

Photo 185. Hoshino Kayoko, bowl-shaped object, 2001. 5 x 10½ inches (12.6 x 26.4 cm). Unglazed stoneware, parallel incised linear design.

for 11 years before he moved to neighboring Kasama. His vessels, which he makes from a mixture of clays from the Kansai region and Lake Biwa, are fired for a week to 2336°F (1280°C) in his wood-fired *ana-noborigama*, a combination of *anagama* and *noborigama*. His powerful work shows to perfection the fire color (*hi-iro*), scorch markings (*koge*), and rivulets of ash glaze (see photo 181) that are highly esteemed in *yakishime* stoneware.

Kaneshige Moto'o was born in Bizen in 1945 as the fourth son of Living National Treasure Kaneshige Tôyô (1896–1967). After graduating from university in Tôkyô in 1968, he worked as an industrial designer for 30 years and switched to ceramics only at a later date. Since 2002, after the construction of his *anagama* in Misugi (Mie Prefecture), he has worked as a freelance ceramist. In his work, he uses the pale-firing Iga clay, which turns a shade of orange on unglazed areas during firing. The natural-ash glazes cover the light body as a transparent green, or they form a heavy incrustation with the scorch markings (*koge*). Kaneshige makes skillful use of these kiln effects to emphasize the form of his vessels (see photo 182).

Hatori Makoto, from Tamatsukuri, in Ibaraki Prefecture, was born in 1947 and has studied sculpture and has taught in Manchester and elsewhere. He uses Bizen stoneware and salt glazing (both traditional materials and techniques), but he has developed a contemporary, formal language in his sculptural vessels. They are thrown, distorted, carved, and treated with a salt solution. After firing with wood for eight days to 2102°F (1150°C) in reduction in an *anagama*, the objects acquire a grainy crystalline structure, along with the natural-ash glaze on the dark brown body (see photo 183).

The ceramist Mihara Ken, from Shimane Prefecture, was born in 1958, near Izumo, and trained under the *mingei* potter Funaki Kenji (see Fujina, 25, on page 109). Since setting up his own workshop in Kamiki, Shimane Prefecture, in 1983, Mihara Ken has pursued his own style. He refers to his work as *sekki*, the term for the gray, unglazed reduction-fired Sue ceramics, a stoneware produced in Japan, from the fifth to twelfth centuries. Mihara Ken digs the iron-rich clay on his own premises and coils his sculptural vessels using the Korean *himozukuri* technique. After bisquing, the pots are covered with a special refractory clay and gas fired for 40 hours in heavy reduction to 2318°F (1270°C). To retain the desired color, the kiln is then subjected to a very slow, controlled cooling period. Subsequently, the refractory layer of clay is brushed off to reveal the rough, matte surface of his sculptural vases, with colors shading from gray to gray-brown and blue-gray (see photo 184).

The trademark of ceramist Hoshino Kayoko, who was born in 1949 in Kyûshû and is now from Shiga (Shiga Prefecture), is her characteristic formal language, together with unglazed, earth-brown surfaces and delicate, parallel incised linear designs (see photo 185). Initially, she studied European history in Kyôto but then switched to training as a ceramist after being deeply impressed by Kyô-*yaki*. For her vessels and sculptures, she uses a mixture of several clays and Shigaraki clay, which, with its pegmatite inclusions, gives a lively texture to the surface of her work. She shapes her work by wedging and cutting with a wire, and creates the typical pattern of incisions with a file. She fires in an electric kiln to 2238°F (1226°C) in heavy reduction. On some objects, Hoshino emphasizes concave or cut surfaces with silver luster, applying silver powder and refiring to 1355°F (735°C).

Akiyama Yô, born in 1953 in Shimonoseki, Yamaguchi Prefecture, belongs to the most important group of present-day Japanese ceramics sculptors. In 1978, he graduated with a degree in ceramics from Kyôto City University of Art, where he now teaches. Akiyama was a student of Yagi Kazuo (1918–1979), co-founder of the avant-garde artists' group, Sôdeisha, in Kyôto. For the most part, Akiyama's nonfunctional sculptures and installations are of impressive scale. His black-carbonized ceramics are reminiscent of geological formations or lava eruptions; their fissured surfaces interact with the rusty brown of the iron particles that oxidize in the air. To achieve these effects, Akiyama developed a special technique at the end of the 1980s. From a mixture of light-colored Seto and other clays, he throws a cylinder on the wheel and dries the interior with a blowtorch so that cracks appear. He either turns the cylinder inside out so the distortions and fissures appear on the exterior, or he tears small pieces from it, which he then reassembles. He fires his work to 2282°F (1250°C). Until the mid 1990s, Akiyama smoke fired his sculptures to achieve a black finish. In his more recent work, he treats the surface with a mixture of vinegar and iron filings before firing. The illustrated object (photo 186), from the series *META-VOID 2004*, was made during Akiyama's workshop at the European Ceramic Work Center in Den Bosch, the Netherlands.

Itô Sekisui V (see Mumyôi, 51, on page 211) and Matsui Kôsei (see Kasama, 52, on page 214), who have already been discussed, are both Living National Treasures and masters of *neriage* (*nerikomi*), in which clays of different colors are layered to produce a marbled ware. This ancient Chinese technique is used by younger artists, too, such as Kawabata Fumio and Onuki Yoshiji.

Kawabata Fumio, born in Kanagawa Prefecture in 1948, was trained in Bizen (Inbe, Okayama Prefecture). He now has a studio there, where he produces delicate objects such as graceful bowls, vases, and fresh-water jars, with typical, apparently soft surfaces that are reminiscent of *washi* (Japanese hand-molded paper). For the body of the pot, he uses a clay that fires to a very light color and wedges in another clay that is rich in minerals. During the oxidation firing in an *anagama*, an orange pattern develops that is reminiscent of the classic *hidasuki* objects of Bizen-*yaki* (see photo 85), but Kawabata's are created using the *neriage* technique (see photo 187).

Onuki Yoshiji, born in 1953 in Tôkyô, was trained in the traditional Tsukamoto workshop in Mashiko. He assembles his *neriage* objects using layers of clay from Arita, Shigaraki, Seto, Tokoname, Bizen, and Mashiko (see photo 188)— six of the most important centers of traditional Japanese ceramics. Onuki feels that each of these clays represents the long history of these regions. In his studio in Motegi (Tochigi Prefecture) near Mashiko, the vessels are fired in reduction in a gas kiln to about 2354°F (1290°C), usually with a second or third firing to 2345°F (1285°C).

Many ceramists experiment with the surface treatment of colored stoneware, especially in the Seto-Mino region, with its glaze influences from the late Muromachi, Momoyama, and early Edo periods, and around Kyôto, with its school of polychrome overglaze painting on stoneware, which dates back to Nonomura Ninsei (ca. 1627–1695). The materials and methods used include glazes, slips (see photos 189–193), painting (see photos 194 and 195), and colored clays (see photo 196).

The work of Usui Kazunari, who was born in 1954, is characterized by *oribe* glazes on pieces with faceting (*mentori*, see photo 189); slip inlay (*zôgan*), and *kushime* techniques. Usui, who is from a family of ceramists in Seto, graduated in sculpture from the Nagoya University School of Art, apprenticed under Katô Shuntai II (1927–1995) in Seto, and since 1996, has worked in Nagasaka, Kita-Koma-gun (Yamanashi Prefecture).

Traditional decoration techniques, such as wax resist (*rônuki*, see photo 190), carved patterns, molded surfaces with ridges, and trailed iron and cobalt-oxide glaze patterns, are being used by the German potter, Gerd Knäpper, who was born in 1943. After his apprenticeship and work as a journeyman potter, he was recommended by Bernard Leach to study under Shimaoka Tatsuzô (born in 1919; Living National Treasure) in Mashiko, who also lent him support when he was setting up his own workshop in Mashiko in 1969. Knäpper caused a sensation in 1971 when as a foreigner he was awarded a first-place award in the traditional "Japan Ceramic Art Exhibition." He has worked in his studio, a refurbished country manor house in Daigo (Ibaraki Prefecture) since 1975. In his work, Knäpper uses the sandy clay from Mashiko, with additions of fine stoneware clay from Seto or Shigaraki to increase plasticity. He uses a mixture of various types of wood ash in his glazes and fires for 30 hours to 2372°F (1300°C) in a five-chamber *noborigama*.

Kawamoto Tarô, who was born in 1955 and is from Seto (Aichi Prefecture), has been influenced by his study of sculpture. For his abstract forms, Kawamoto normally uses a Seto clay from an *Ôshima* type that includes silica sand. For other clay bodies, however, he uses seven different clays. He coil builds his objects, starting with a clay slab

Photo 186.   Akiyama Yô, sculpture from the series *META-VOID 2004*. 8¾ x 11½ x 9½ inches (22 x 29 x 24 cm).
Black carbonized unglazed stoneware.

Photo 187.   Kawabata Fumio, sculptural vase, 2003. 8¾ x 7¼ inches (22.2 x 18.5 cm). Unglazed stoneware with colored clay inlay, *neriage* technique.

Photo 188. Onuki Yoshiji, sculptural vase, 2003. 17 x 12¾ x 5 inches (43.1 x 32.5 x 13 cm).
Unglazed stoneware, six colored clays.

Photo 189. Usui Kazunari, octagonal box (*oribe futamono*), 2001. 2½ x 6¼ inches (6.5 x 16 cm). Stoneware, *mentori* faceting, *sô-oribe* glaze.

Photo 190. Gerd Knäpper, vase, 1999. 11¾ x 8¾ inches (30 x 22 cm). Stoneware, ash glaze, wax-resist wave pattern (*rônuki*).

Photo 191. Kawamoto Tarô, vessel object, *Ring in the Exhibition*, 2002. 7¼ x 9¼ x 8 inches (18.3 x 23.5 x 20.2 cm). Stoneware, earth-colored slips, incised design.

Photo 192.   Kawakami Tomoko, spherical object, *Melancholy Dream*, 2002. 4¾ x 6¾ inches (12 x 17 cm). Stoneware, black glaze on interior.

Photo 193. Hayashi Koroku Plate, *shukôsai, Spring Dream* (*shukôsai haru no yume*), 2003. 1½ x 12½ inches
(4.2 x 31.7 cm). Stoneware, camellia design in inlaid slip technique.

Photo 194.   Maeda Masahiro, vase with cactus design (*iro-e kingin-sai hanaire*), pre-2000. 6¼ x 5¼ inches
(15.8 x 13.5 cm). Stoneware, overglaze painting, gold and silver decoration.

Photo 195.   Teramoto Mamoru, sculptural vase (*shikongin-sai kaki*), 2003. 9½ x 5 inches (24 x 12.8 cm).
Stoneware, blue-black glaze, silver and gold overglaze in *hakeme* technique.

Photo 196. Miyashita Zenji, sculptural vase, *Moeru Umi* (burning sea), 2003. 12½ x 7¾ x 3½ inches
(32 x 19.8 x 8.9 cm). Stoneware, applied clay strips colored with oxides (*saidei* technique).

Photo 197. Minegishi Seikô, jade-green tea bowl (*suiseiji shinogi-de chawan*), pre-2000. 2¾ x 5½ inches (7 x 13.9 cm). Stoneware, carved lines (*shinogi*), celadon glaze with crackle (*kan'nyu*).

Photo 198. Matsuo Shigetoshi, vase with flowing lines (*hakuji hô-ryû hanaire*), 1975. 9½ x 7¾ inches (24 x 19.4 cm). White porcelain (*hakuji*).

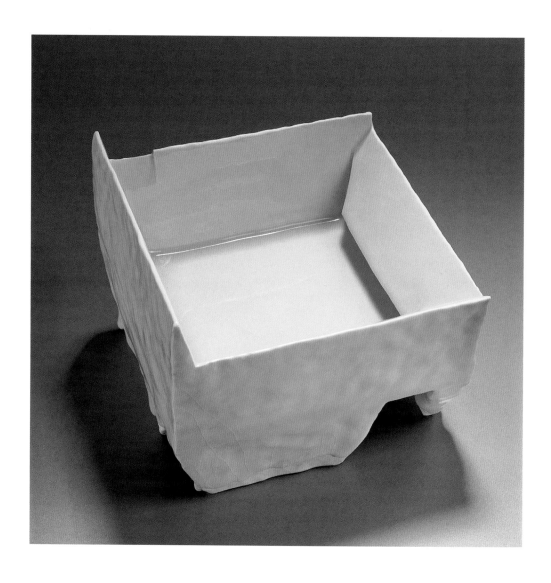

**Photo 199.   Yoshikawa Masamichi, flower container (*kayô*), 1998. 7 x 9¼ x 9 inches (18 x 23.6 x 22.7 cm).
Porcelain, celadon glaze (*seihakuji*), design in cobalt underglaze on the underside.**

Photo 200.   Fukami Sueharu, one-flower vase with three ridges (*sanryô ichirinza*), ca. 1986. 9¾ x 3¼ inches
(24.7 x 8.3 cm). Porcelain, celadon glaze (*seihakuji*).

on a support (*uma*). After forming, the surface is covered by clays of pasty consistency that are stained with metallic oxides. This clay coating is beaten by handmade ceramic tools to prevent peeling. Bisque firing up to 1436°F (780°C) in an electric kiln follows. To help create glaze patterns, he uses masking tape and applies thin glazes (transparent or ash glazes) with a sponge. After removing the masking tape, he fires the objects—still supported by the *uma*—in a gas kiln up to 2282°F (1250°C) in reduction (see photo 191).

The ceramist Kawakami Tomoko was born in 1957 in Takayama and trained in Tajimi (Gifu Prefecture). She creates thin-walled, cocoon-like objects, in which the earthy clay body with black inclusions remains visible, while the interiors are glazed a deep black. Her work derives its intensity from the contrast between seemingly archaic forms and the darkness of the interior (see photo 192). In 2005, Kawakami was awarded the prestigious Premio Faenza, Grand Prize at the 54th International Competition of Contemporary Ceramic Art in Italy.

After initial success in exhibitions, Hayashi Koroku, born in 1943 in Kyôto, a graduate of the Kyôto Municipal Institute of Industrial Research, and a student of Kusube Yaichi (1897–1984), increasingly turned to the study of clay and nature. Since 1990, he has developed his own style of decoration in his *shukôsai* series (*shukôsai* means the beauty of colored stone reflected from clear water). The basic color of his objects—mainly vases, plates, tea bowls, and other functional forms—is a deep brown or even a blue-green with shades of metallic blue to deep green. To this base, he applies his unique flower decorations, using an inlaid slip technique. His favorite design is the camellia blossom, which can be found on his pots in infinite variations (see photo 193).

Maeda Masahiro, born in 1948 in Kyôto, graduated from the Tôkyô National University of Fine Arts after studying under Fujimoto Yoshimichi (1919–1992) and Tamura Kôichi (1918–1987), both Living National Treasures. His classic overglaze enamel painting on stoneware seems simple at first but is actually modern in form and style (see photo 194). Colored slips are applied to the dried piece, and colored glazes are applied after the bisque firing; overglaze and gold decoration are added after the glaze firing.

Teramoto Mamoru, who was born in 1949 in Kanagawa, makes use of abstract overglaze painting. After training under Matsumoto Saichi (born in 1930; Kutani-*yaki*), he built his studio in Kasama, Ibaraki Prefecture. He makes ceramic wall murals for public buildings, and throws or hand builds pots to which he applies silver or gold dust suspensions in *hakeme* technique over blue-black or red slips (see photo 195).

Miyashita Zenji, born in 1939 in Kyôto, works in the tradition of colored Kyô-*yaki* and has a studio near the famous Katsura Villa in Kyôto. Miyashita studied at Kyôto City University of Arts, assisted his father Miyashita Zenjû (1901–1988), and apprenticed under Kusube Yaichi (1897–1984) and Kiyomizu Kyûbey (born in 1922). At a very early stage, he developed a unique technique for the surface treatment of his sculptural vessels—using layers of colored clays (*saidei* technique), a style that has brought him 18 Nitten prizes and worldwide recognition. He constructs his vessels with the aid of cardboard templates. After assembling and drying the pieces, successive wafer-thin layers of colored clay are applied in irregular strips. Miyashita has a palette of almost 100 clays of different colors, which he prepares with great care from mineral pigments and clay. To enhance the radiance of the colors, he sprays on a transparent glaze. He fires for 15 hours in a gas kiln to 2282°F (1250°C). The brilliant colors, ranging from pale ochre, yellow, and pink to greens, blues, and purple that Miyashita achieves using the *saidei* technique, lend a particular depth to his sculptural vessels and create associations with landscapes, drifting clouds, and rolling waves (see photo 196).

Celadon glaze on stoneware and porcelain, developed in China during the Song dynasty (960–1279), enjoyed great admiration in Japan, and the production of such glazes has presented a continuing challenge to potters through the centuries. Today, only a handful of studio potters who are fascinated by the depth and radiance of celadon glazes are prepared to face this challenge, with a success rate in the firing of less than 30 percent (see photo 197, celadon on stoneware; see photos 198–200, celadon on porcelain).

Photo 201. Ono Jiro, spherical vase (*tsubo*), 1998. 8¾ x 9½ inches (22.2 x 24 cm). Porcelain, *yûri-kinsai* (underglaze gold leaf) technique.

**Photo 202.   Nagae Shigekazu, vessel object, 1999. 7¾ x 12¾ x 11¾ inches (20 x 32.5 x 30 cm).
Colored porcelain bodies, *ikomi* technique.**

Minegishi Seikô, who was born in 1952 in Misato, Saitama Prefecture, is one of the few artists who have a command of celadon (seiji) and crackle glazes (kan'nyu) on stoneware. After pursuing studies in Kasama (52), Mashiko (53), and elsewhere, he constructed a kiln in Nasu (Tochigi Prefecture) at the end of the 1970s. For his broad repertoire of vessels, Minegishi uses the decorative technique of shinogi by carving deep relief ridges into the bisque-fired ware before applying the celadon glaze. During firing to over 2192°F (1200°C), kan'nyu with double and triple layers of crackle varying in size, color tones, and textures are formed. After 6000 trials, Minegishi is able to produce his kan'nyu celadons with a failure rate of only 40 percent; his success rate is due to his careful combination of clay blend with glaze composition and firing (see photo 197).

In the Arita region, the birthplace of Japanese porcelain, some ceramists in Saga Prefecture have concentrated on white porcelain (hakuji) or porcelain with a light, bluish green celadon glaze (seihakuji)—also known as white celadon. One of these artists is Matsuo Shigetoshi, born in 1934 in Arita, who lives and works in Takeo Onsen (see Takeo, 14, on page 84). Along with functional wares, Matsuo makes individual pieces. His vessels, with their flowing lines (hô-ryû) around the body, are fascinating, with the play of light on the subtle shades of color in the glaze, ranging from the pure white of hakuji to the light blue-green of seihakuji where the glaze has accumulated (see photo 198).

Some of the best-known ceramics in the West include the celadons of Yoshikawa Masamichi, who was born in 1946 in Chigasaki, Kanagawa Prefecture. He graduated in Tôkyô in 1968 as an industrial designer, then completed a potter's apprenticeship in the traditional location of Tokoname (39, Aichi Prefecture). He found a suitable workshop there in 1975. At first, he made porcelain with abstract cobalt underglaze decoration. Today, he specializes in producing thick-walled, cubed containers (see photo 199), vases, and platters with a celadon glaze in a pale blue-green (seihakuji) that sometimes runs to form droplets. The underside of his work is usually decorated with abstract designs in cobalt blue or more rarely with red copper lines. Yoshikawa's latest work, for which an old tunnel kiln in Tokoname

had to be reopened, is a mural relief at the entrance to the new airport opened to the south of Nagoya in 2005 for the World Exhibition in Aichi. This wall mural, which is 82 feet (25 m) long and 13 feet (14 m) tall, with three freestanding spherical forms, exemplifies Yoshikawa's typical celadon glaze and also fascinates with its austere geometric lines painted in cobalt underglaze.

Fukami Sueharu, who is known for his porcelain sculpture "blades" and "waves," was awarded the Premio Faenza, Grand Prize at the 43rd International Competition of Contemporary Ceramic Art in Italy in 1985, and since then has become one of the outstanding representatives of the younger generation of ceramists. He was born into a potter family in Kyôto in 1947 and studied ceramics at Kyôto Arts and Crafts Training Center. One of his porcelain pieces was accepted for the Nitten as early as 1967. In the following years, he concentrated on his trademark ice-blue seihakuji glaze. In 1980, he began to employ the high-pressure slip-casting technique usually used for the mass production of porcelain. In this method, porcelain slip is pumped under high pressure into molds made of semiporcelain. After drying the sharp contours are developed. After bisque firing, glazing with a spray gun, and the main firing to approximately 2282°F (1250°C), the pieces are carefully burnished. Neither in his sculptures nor in his thrown vases or bowls does Fukami tolerate any traces of the making process, which are otherwise so highly esteemed in Japanese ceramics. His work attains a high degree of perfection. It is not created from a dialogue with the material during the making process; with its clean lines and rational forms, it is carefully planned in advance, especially the interplay of form and color—a result of the various depths of the seihakuji glaze (see photo 200).

The work of studio potters who use porcelain covers a wide range. The development and mastery of specific techniques leads to the creation of new surfaces and forms (see photos 201 and 202). In addition to white porcelain and celadons, colored porcelain allows for a broad creative potential. Echoes of classic decorative techniques such as sometsuke and iro-e (see photos 203–205) sometimes produce surprising results, at times including work strongly influenced by Western trends (see photo 206).

The *yûri-kinsai* technique (underglaze gold decoration; see Yoshida Minori III, Kutani, 45, on page 188, and photo 144), which is rare in Japan, is practiced by Ono Jiro, who was born in 1953 in Tôkyô, and is from Ureshino, near Arita, in Saga Prefecture. Ono graduated in ceramic engineering from Arita Industrial Prefectural School. He learned the remarkably difficult technique of applying cut gold or platinum foil pieces under the glaze from his mother, ceramist Ono Hakuko (1925–1996). She had been inspired to use this decorative technique in the mid 1960s by the work of Katô Hajime (1900–1968; Living National Treasure). In this technique (see photo 201), the porcelain objects are first glazed and fired to 2372°F (1300°C), then gold leaf is fixed in a coat of lacquer at 1490°F (810°C). In all, six more steps follow, each with the application of glaze and a firing to 1472°F (800°C).

Nagae Shigekazu, born in 1953 in Seto, is considered to be one of the most innovative ceramists in the field of porcelain. He graduated from Seto Ceramics High School in 1972 and worked for several years in the family ceramics business, where he still maintains his studio. During this period, he discovered the *ikomi* method for his own work— a method of slip casting for mass production imported from Europe during the Meiji period. Nagae usually uses white or sometimes colored porcelain slip, which he pours or drips into plastic or plaster molds. During the firing in a gas kiln to 2336°F (1280°C), the plastic molds burn out, and the porcelain objects distort into curved forms, in a fashion predetermined by Nagae, to produce wonderful organic shapes, as do the dried objects from plaster molds (see photo 202).

Shômura Ken, born in 1949 in Arita (Saga Prefecture), oversees the Banko kiln, for the fifth generation, in his hometown. His work is a modern interpretation of *sometsuke* porcelain. The indigo underglaze decoration that Shômura uses to enhance classic forms such as platters, vases, and incense burners (see photo 203) is covered with a semitransparent, flowing glaze or a milky white glaze applied in varying thicknesses, reminiscent of glacier landscapes.

Japan has a long tradition of decorating porcelain with *iro-e* overglaze enamels in the style of *yamato-e* painting. One of the most important artists who worked in this style was Living National Treasure Fujimoto Yoshimichi (1919–1992). Fujimoto passed on this technique to a small number of students; one of them was Takahashi Makoto, who was born in 1948 in Ômiya (Saitama Prefecture) and who studied at Tôkyô University of Fine Arts and Music. In 1986, Takahashi set up his own workshop in Ogawara (Kanagawa Prefecture) and now continues this tradition. With its echoes of Kutani-*yaki* (45), the lidded container, in its delicate execution of a sparrow and pomegranate design (see photos 204 and 204a), is a typical example of this school of painting.

Kawaguchi Jun, born in 1951 in Yokohama, uses a completely different style of painting. His abstract mural objects—constructed from porcelain slabs with a wide range of small attachments in intense overglaze enamels—as well as his functional tableware in unconventional forms and decorations (see photo 205) are reminiscent of the pop art and comics that are omnipresent in Japanese advertising and *manga*. Kawaguchi, who studied under Yagi Kazuo (1918–1979) and graduated from Kyôto School of Arts in 1975, teaches in Tôkyô and Kyôto.

Shibata Masamitsu is another example of Japanese artists who create something new from an organic tradition. Born in 1961 in Toki (Gifu Prefecture) to a traditional family of Mino potters, he first studied economics, then graduated with a degree in ceramic design. Today, he works with the materials from his parents' pottery, to which he has added only Turkish blue as a new standard color. Fired in oxidation in a gas kiln, his semiporcelain objects, tea bowls, and plates in unusual combinations of form and color (see photo 206) could be classified as Mino-*yaki* with respect to the material. Their execution, however, is influenced by the West, leading to a synthesis of tradition and modernity.

Photo 203.   Shômura Ken, indigo-dye incense burner (*aizome kôro*), 2001. 4½ x 4¼ inches (11.5 x 10.7 cm).
Porcelain, indigo underglaze, semitransparent glaze.

Photo 204. Takahashi Makoto, lidded container, *Sparrow with Pomegranate* (*tôhako zakaro ni yamasuzume*), 2002. 4¼ x 6 inches (10.9 x 15.2 cm). Porcelain, polychrome overglaze painting.

Photo 204a.   Side view of the lidded container.

**Photo 205. Kawaguchi Jun, cup with side plate (from a ceramic puzzle setting), ca. 2002.
Cup: 3¾ x 3½ inches (9.9 x 8.8 cm). Plate: 4¾ x 4½ inches (12.3 x 11.5 cm).
Porcelain, overglaze enamel with gold decoration.**

Photo 206.   Shibata Masamitsu, bowl-shaped object, *Blue de Pop o Bowl*, 2002. 3 x 8¾ inches (7.4 x 22.2 cm). Semiporcelain, colored glazes.

GLOSSARY

aka-e 赤絵
"Red painting"; term mainly used in Arita for polychrome overglaze brushwork. See *iro-e.*

aka-e machi 赤絵町
"Town of red painting"; district of the town of Uchiyama, Arita, in which 11 families settled (by 1672, 16 families were in residence), with permission from the Nabeshima clan, to perform overglaze painting (*aka-e*). Besides *ko*-Imari, Nabeshima porcelain and *ko*-Kutani ware are said to have been painted in *aka-e machi.*

akaji-kinran-de 赤地金襴手
Gold brushwork on red ground, used by Eiraku Hozen on Kyôto (34) porcelain and by his son Eiraku Wazen on Kutani (45) porcelain.

akamono 赤物
Originally low-fired red earthenware; now also applied to unglazed stoneware with a red-brown fired body; *shudei*-ware is one example.

Amakusa-tôjiki 天草陶磁器
On Kyûshû (Kumamoto-ken, Amakusa-gun), the use of Amakusa-*tôseki* in making porcelain has been documented in the towns of Amakusa, Ôyano, Itsuwa, and Reihoku since 1676; in 1756, one kiln began with the production of stoneware. Today, there are 10 workshops; typical products include porcelain and double-glazed stoneware. See also *tôjiki.*

ame-yû 飴釉
Amber ash-feldspar glaze with 5 to 6 percent iron, sometimes with additions of manganese.

anagama 穴窯
Single-vaulted, single-chamber climbing kiln or sloping tunnel kiln; widespread in Japan since the fifth century.

aohibi-yû 青ひび釉
Celadon glaze with crackle (*kan'nyû*); typical of Sôma Koma- and Ôbori Sôma-*yaki* (56, 57).

Aoki Mokubei 青木木米
Potter from Kyôto (1767–1833), pupil of Okuda Eisen. One of the most famous Kyôto masters, along with Nonomura Ninsei and Ogata Kenzan. Particularly well known for *aka-e* and *sometsuke*, as well as celadon, which originated during the Chinese Ming dynasty (1368–1644). Was involved in the renaissance of Kutani-*yaki* (45).

arayaki 荒焼
Also referred to as *nanban-yaki;* high-fired unglazed stoneware. Along with *jôyaki*, a typical example of Tsuboya-*yaki* (1) made in Okinawa.

asbolite
See *gosu.*

Atsumi ceramics 渥美焼
Atsumi-*yaki;* unglazed stoneware with natural-ash glaze (*yakishime*). From the end of the twelfth through the end of the thirteenth century, a product made in multiples in approximately 100 kilns on the Atsumi Peninsula (now Aichi Prefecture).

bafuku 幕府
Shogunate; term used to refer to the governing of Japan by a *shogun* (warlord). The three shogunates were: the Kamakura shogunate (1192–1333); the Muromachi or Ashikaga shogunate (1338–1573); and the Tokugawa shogunate (1603–1867).

Bakuhan system, *bakuhan taisei* 幕藩体制
Government, economy, and administration of the Edo period (1600–1868).

Banshôzan-yaki 万祥山焼
Kiln founded in 1872 in Shimane Prefecture (Izumo-shi, Ôtsu-chô); produced *chadôgu* (tea ware), *sake* sets, and large *ikebana* (flower arrangement) vessels in stoneware with thick iron glazes.

bîdoro ビードロ
Vitrified glass. See also *mitsu no keshiki.*

bisque firing, bisque ware
See *suyaki.*

blue-and-white ware
See *sometsuke.*

Bunten 文展,
Monbushô bijutsu tenrankai 文部省美術展覧会
"Ministry of Education Fine Arts Exhibition"; annual exhibition under government sponsorship, 1907–1918. Growing disharmony between artists of traditional and Western styles led to the foundation of a number of successor organizations, including Teiten (abbr. for *Teikoku bijutsu tenrankai*, "Japan Fine Arts Exhibition"), started in 1919 and continued under the name of Nitten from 1958 on. See also *Nitten.*

burnishing
See *migaki.* See also *shudei.*

celadon
See *seiji; seiji-yû.*

ceramics
Japanese ceramics are classified in four main groups:

doki 土器 (earthenware), unglazed ware with a porous, colored body fired to 1472°F (800°C); Jômon and Yayoi-*doki* are examples.

tôki 陶器 (stoneware), porous and therefore usually glazed, colored clay, fired to 1832°F–2372°F (1000°C–1300°C); Karatsu- and Satsuma-*yaki* (13, 2) are examples.

sekki 炉器 (stoneware), unglazed or glazed ceramics impervious to water; vitrified, colored clay body, fired to 2192°F to over 2372°F (1200°C to over 1300°C); Shigaraki- and Iga-*yaki* (36, 37) are examples.

jiki 磁器 (porcelain), translucent, ceramics impervious to water with a white body consisting of quartz, feldspar, and kaolin, fired to 2282°F–2462°F (1250°C–1350°C); Arita- and Kutani-*yaki* (8, 45) are examples.

chabana 茶花
"Tea flower"; general term for an austere and simple form of flower arrangement used in the tea ceremony (*chanoyu*). See also *chanoyu; ikebana.*

chadôgu 茶道具
Also known as *sadô no mono;* tea ware for the tea ceremony.

chaire 茶入れ
Small tea caddy for *koicha* (powdered green tea used for the thick green tea in the tea ceremony); often kept in a silk brocade pouch (*shifuku*); see photo 35. See also **chanoyu.**

chanoyu 茶の湯
Literally "tea's hot water"; tea ceremony (also known as the Way of Tea, *chadô* or *sadô*). Preparation and consumption of *matcha* (powdered green tea) for guests according to a strict ritual. A simple tea ceremony takes approximately 40 minutes; the traditional form takes up to four hours. The procedure varies in the individual tea schools. As a rule, a simple meal (*chakaiseki* or *kaiseki*) is served first, followed by sweets, then *koicha*, a thick tea. As a symbol of harmony, all the guests drink from the same bowl. The thinner, frothy *usucha*, served in tea bowls appropriate for the occasion and for each guest, then follows with sweets. See also **matcha.**

chasen 茶筅
Brush cut from bamboo to whisk the *matcha* tea during the tea ceremony. See also **matcha.**

chataku 茶托
(Rare) saucer for *sencha* tea bowl. See also **sencha.**

chatsubo 茶壷
Storage jar for tea leaves.

chattering
Vibration of the trimming tool when held against the turning pot; often considered a fault, as this produces unwanted ridges on the surface of the pot. See also **tobigan'na.**

chatter marks
See **chattering;** *tobigan'na.*

chawan 茶碗
Tea bowl.

choka チョカ
Vessel in the shape of a teapot for warming *sake* or *shôchû*. See also **shôchû.**

chôka 彫花
Decorative technique: a linear (*senbori* 線彫り) or, more commonly, floral pattern incised in the leather-hard object with a wooden, bamboo, or metal knife (*ôbori* 凹彫り). In the case of *totsubori* 凸彫り, the pattern is left while the background is cut away.

chôka 貼花
See **haritsuke-(mon).**

choko 猪口
Also *choku;* small cup or bowl for serving *sake*.

chûsei 中性
Neutral kiln atmosphere.

cloth texturing
See **nunome.**

combing
See **kushime.**

copper glazes
See **dô-yû;** *ryoku-yû; sei-yû; shinsha-yû.*

crackle, crackled glaze
See **kan'nyu.**

dachibin 抱瓶
A hip flask for water or *shôchû* made in Okinawa, now mainly for ornamental purposes (see Tsuboya, 1, on page 34). See also **shôchû.**

daimyô 大名
"Great name"; local feudal lord during the shogunate in Japan. See also **bafuku.**

Dai-yaki 台焼
Kiln established in Tôhoku (Iwate-ken, Hanamaki-shi, Yumoto) during the mid-Meiji period, for porcelain and also for stoneware since the Shôwa period. Now one workshop; typical wares are *hakuji* (white porcelain) and *nuka-seiji*, a celadon from a thick, rice-husk glaze.

dobai-yû 土灰釉
Transparent ash-feldspar glaze made from 3 to 7 parts wood ash (*dobai*, ash of pine or cedar) and 7 to 3 parts feldspar as a flux. In oxidation, produces a pale yellow to yellow-brown glaze; in reduction, a light green glaze.

dobin 土瓶
Large teapot. See also **sencha.**

doburo 土風炉
Ceramic charcoal brazier for heating water during the tea ceremony.

doki 土器
See **ceramics**.

domestic tableware
Everyday objects for use with food *nichi-jô-katei-yôhin* 日常家庭用品.

donabe 土鍋
Stoneware casserole used for cooking directly over the flames.

dô-yû 銅釉
Ash glaze with copper; produces a red glaze in reduction (such as *shinsha* glaze, oxblood), and a green glaze in oxidation (such as an *oribe* glaze).

Dutch East India Company
See **VOC.**

engobe
See **keshôgake.**

Enshû nana gama 遠州七窯
Seven kilns (Agano, 15; Akahada, 32; Asahi, 33; Kosobe; Shitoro, 43; Takatori, 16; and Zeze, 35) that the tea master Kobori Enshû 小堀遠州 (1579–1647) proclaimed particularly suitable for the production of *sadô no mono* (tea ceramics for the tea ceremony) and that he particularly supported. Enshû—a *daimyô*, architect, garden designer, and tea master among the first three Tokugawa shoguns—was a student of the tea master Furuta Oribe and embraced *kirei sabi* aesthetics (*kirei*, beautiful) with thinly thrown, elegantly shaped, glazed tea ceramics. See also **Furuta Oribe.**

Etchû-Seto-*yaki* 越中瀬戸焼
Kiln established by Seto potters at the end of the sixteenth century in Toyama Prefecture (Naka-Niikawa-gun, Tateyama-chô); produced stoneware in Seto style (ash and iron glazes); closed down in 1916. The present-day kiln, with four workshops, was founded in 1947 and produces traditional domestic ware.

etsuke 絵付け
Underglaze and overglaze brushwork. Underglaze painting (*shita-etsuke*) with underglaze pigments (mainly cobalt, copper, and iron) is applied directly on the dried object or after the bisque firing, before the application of the transparent glaze and the glaze firing. In overglaze painting (*uwa-etsuke*), the overglaze enamels are applied after the glaze firing, and the pot is fired again, to 1292°F–1562°F (700°C–850°C).

famille rose, famille verte
Porcelain with overglaze enamels made in Jingdezhen during the Chinese Qing dynasty (1644–1911), from the second half of the seventeenth century; initially classified in France as "families," according to their predominant color; examples include the "famille rose" with an opaque pink to purple and the "famille verte" with decoration on an intense green background.

finger wipes
See ***yubikaki.***

five-part set
For cake plates, *sencha* tea bowls, etc., in contrast to six-piece sets in Europe. The number five is a lucky number in Japan.

footring
See ***kôdai.***

fukitsuke 吹き付け
Glazing by spraying.

fukizumi 吹墨
"Blown ink" technique of underglaze decoration; Chinese in origin. A paper stencil is placed on the object, and cobalt blue, for example, is sprayed on the piece, leaving the silhouette free of pigment.

Furuta Oribe 古田織部
(1544–1615), born as Furuta Shigenari, *samurai* (follower of Oda Nobunaga and Toyotomi Hideyoshi) and after the death of his teacher Sen no Rikyû, the most highly respected tea master of his time. For details of the ceramics style named after him, Oribe-*yaki*, see Mino, 42, on page 171.

futamono 蓋物
Lidded container.

futaoki 蓋置
In the tea ceremony, a rest for the lid of the iron kettle (*kama* 釜) used for hot water.

gairome-nendo 蛙目粘土
"Frog-eye" clay; low in plasticity, high in kaolinite content, with little iron; frequently with quartz and feldspar particles. Examples are the *daidô* clay of Hagi-*yaki* (22) and the moxa clay of *shino* ware (see Mino, 42, on page 171).

gama 窯
See ***kama.***

gendai dentô tôgei 現代伝統陶芸
Contemporary traditional ceramics.

getemono 下手物
Mass-produced domestic ceramics.

ginran-de 銀襴手
See ***kinran-de.***

gohan chawan 御飯茶碗
Rice bowl.

gohon-de 御本手
Milky white or transparent glaze on a light red clay body, with characteristic cream or pink halos around pinholes formed over larger grains in the clay. This is caused by the interplay of various clay blends with a thin pine-ash feldspar glaze, in alternating oxidizing and reducing kiln atmospheres during the latter part of the firing to about 2246°F (1230°C); typical of Asahi and Kyô-*yaki* (33, 34).

goma-yû 胡麻釉
Glaze spots resembling sesame seeds (*goma*) on unglazed stoneware, caused during firing by the melting of wood ash particles on the surface of the pot at approximately 2264°F (1240°C). If a yellow-beige glaze is formed on the entire surface, this is termed *nagashi goma* and is typical of Bizen-*yaki* (29).

gosu 呉須
Or asbolite; natural cobalt oxide (cobalt content approximately 5 percent) for blue underglaze painting on stoneware and porcelain. Iron, aluminium, and manganese impurities produce the characteristic blue-gray of old blue-and-white ware in reduction firing.

gosu aka-e 呉須赤絵
See ***some-nishiki-de.***

goyôgama 御用窯
Kiln under the patronage of the local *daimyô* during the Edo period (1600–1868). Used to produce ceramics for the imperial family, the nobility, *samurai*, and tea masters. This term covers both *hanyô* and *oniwa-gama*. See also ***hanyô; oniwa-yaki, oniwa-gama.***

grog
see ***shamotto.***

guinomi ぐい呑
Sake cup, larger than ***choko.***

hachi 鉢
Deep dish or bowl.

hai 杯
Also termed ***sakazuki;*** small cup or bowl for *sake*.

hai-gusuri 灰釉
Also termed *kai-yû*; gray-green plant-ash feldspar glaze used on high-fired stoneware.

haikaburi 灰被り
See ***shizen-yû.***

haiki 灰器
Ceramic brazier used in the tea ceremony for the transport of hot charcoal to the tea room.

Haji earthenware, *hajiki* 土師器
Unglazed, reddish earthenware produced from Kyûshû to the Kantô plain during the fourth to tenth centuries.

hakeme 刷毛目
Slip brushing; decoration technique of Korean origin; pale, usually white slip is applied to a darker body with a broad, flat brush (*hake*).

hakogaki 箱書
Inscription on a *kibako*. See also ***kibako.***

hakuji 白磁
White porcelain.

haku-yû 白釉
Collective name for opaque or semitransparent white glazes, such as *shino* glazes (feldspar glazes); straw-ash feldspar glazes (for example, *shiro hagi-gusuri*); the *nukajiro-yû* made of rice husks, which are rich in silicic acid; and glazes with added tin or titanium oxide (rare in Japan).

Hamada Shôji 浜田庄司
(1894–1978) co-founder of and leading potter in the *mingei* movement; born in Kawasaki (Kanagawa Prefecture), studied in Tôkyô, and worked with Kawai Kanjirô (1890–1966). In 1920–1924, assisted Bernard Leach (1887–1979) in setting up his pottery in England. Settled in Mashiko (53) after his return to Japan in 1924, where he utilized *mingei* ideas in his work. Designated *ningen kokuhô* (Living National Treasure) in 1955. See also *jûyô mukei bunkazai hojisha.*

han 藩
Fiefdom awarded directly from the *shôgun; daimyô* domain. In military, administrative, or fiscal matters, the smallest unit under the Bakuhan system during the Edo period (1600–1868). See also *bafuku; daimyô.*

hanaire 花入 or *hanaike* 花生
Flower vase.

haniwa 埴輪
"Clay ring"; term for cylinders or representations of animals or humans in reddish earthenware (*doki*) from the fourth to seventh centuries; placed on burial mounds during the Kofun period. See also **ceramics,** *doki.*

hanjiki 半磁器
Semiporcelain, midway between porcelain and stoneware in appearance, made of cleaned white clay (*seitôki*). The composition varies locally; the main ingredient is porcelain stone (*tôseki*), with the addition of whiting and feldspar. Fires to 2192°F–2282°F (1200°C–1250°C). Used for tableware, tiles, or domestic accessories. See also *tôseki.*

hanyô 藩窯
Official kiln of the *han;* during the Edo period (1600–1868), a kiln under the administration of the domain (*han*), or kilns that had to be licensed by the *han* administration and that were obliged to pay tribute to it. See also *han.*

haritsuke-(mon) 貼り付け(文)
Applied decoration; also called *chôka* 貼花 ("flower stuck on") when a flower decoration is used. Clay ornaments are pressed or luted onto the leather-hard surface. The applied clay can be modeled before attachment (for example, sprigged in molds) or after (for example, stamped additions, in which balls of clay are attached, then stamped).

hebigama 蛇窯
See *waridakeshiki-noborigama.*

hera 箆
Bamboo spatula used for trimming finished vessels such as raku bowls.

herame 箆目
Spatula cuts on wares, used for decoration.

hibachi 火鉢
Portable charcoal brazier used for heating.

hidasuki 火襷
"Fire cord"; decorative technique mainly used in Bizen-*yaki* (29), in which a rice-straw cord or rope soaked in salt water is wrapped around the body of the pot. In oxidation, the salt in the rope combines with the iron in the pale clay body used for this technique to produce red markings on the pot. In Tokoname-*yaki* (39), this effect is achieved by wrapping seaweed around the pot (*mogake* 藻掛け technique).

higawari 火変わり
"Fire change"; also known as *yôhen,* "kiln change." See also *yôhen.*

hi-iro 火色
"Fire color." See also *mitsu no keshiki.*

hikidashi-guro 引き出し黒
"Withdrawn black"; type of iron glaze achieved when tea bowls are withdrawn red hot from the kiln after the glaze has melted and are immediately cooled. This results in a dark black surface; see Kyôto (34), on page 132, and Mino (42), on page 171. See *setoguro;* also *koku-yû; raku* ware.

hima 火間
Areas of an object left unglazed to showcase the beauty of clay. See *tsuchi no aji.*

himozukuri 紐作り
Coiling and throwing; Korean technique for hand building vessels on the wheel. After beating the base of the vessel onto the wheel head, the body of the vessel is built up with coils, moistened with slip, and finished on a rotating wheel; typical of Koishiwara and Onta-*yaki* (17, 18).

hiraka 平瓶
Also *heihei,* ceremonial bottle; Sue ware from the Kofun period (ca. 300–710).

hishaku 柄杓
Water ladle; for example, made of bamboo, for the tea ceremony.

hishakugake 柄杓がけ
Glazing by pouring, for example, with a ladle (*hishaku*).

hitashigake 浸しがけ
Glazing by dipping.

Hizen-yaki 肥前焼
General term for *tôjiki* from the Hizen domain (now Saga Prefecture and part of Nagasaki Prefecture) in the northwest region of Kyûshû, during the Edo period (1600–1868) when the domain was under the control of the Nabeshima clan.

Hizen Yoshida-yaki 肥前吉田焼
Kiln on Kyûshû (Saga-ken, Fujitsu-gun, Ureshino-machi) in existence since the end of the sixteenth century, in which Korean potters reportedly made porcelain in 1577 after the discovery of *tôseki.* Production of *sometsuke* and *nishiki-de* porcelain until the present day; currently, 19 workshops for domestic porcelain. See also *nishiki-de; sometsuke; tôseki.*

hôhin 泡瓶
Small teapot for high-quality tea (see photo 73). See also *sencha.*

honyaki 本焼き
Glazed ware after the glaze or main firing.

Horikoshi-yaki 堀越焼
Kiln situated in Yamaguchi Prefecture (Hôfu-shi, Ôaza Edomari), established in 1788 by a Sano potter for the production of domestic objects made of iron-glazed stoneware. Peaked in the Taishô period through the *mingei* (folk art) movement; currently two workshops.

hoshi 星
See *ishihaze.*

hotaru-de 蛍手
Rice-grain pattern; decorative technique in which small holes pierced in the leather-hard pot are filled with transparent glaze after the bisque firing.

Ido bowl, ido chawan 井戸茶碗
Ido ware; simple stoneware with ash glaze made in the fifteenth century in Korea for daily use. Deep rice bowls with wide mouths (*ido*, well), used in Japan as tea bowls. The Kizaemon-Ido tea bowl, in which the *chadô* aesthetic of Zen Buddhism is seen to be embodied in its purest form, is the most famous.

ikebana 生け花
Literally "flowers kept alive"; flower arrangement, also called *kadô*, or the "Way of the flowers"; originated in Buddhist ritual flower offerings (*kuge*), introduced to Japan from China in the seventh century. From the fifteenth century, developed into a distinctive art form, with many styles and schools. See also **chabana.**

impressed patterns
Decorative method of texturing the surface of the unfired ware by rolling cords (cord-impressed patterns, *nawame* 縄目); using roller stamps (*kokuin rôrâ* 刻印ローラー) made of wood, bisqued clay, or plaster; or paddling (*tataki ita* 叩き板) using carved wooden paddles. See also **tataki** (**zukuri**).

Inbe-yaki 伊部焼
Rare term for Bizen-*yaki* (29).

irabo-yû 伊羅保釉
Wood-ash glaze; washed wood ash with equal parts feldspar produces a yellow-brown glaze in oxidation; in reduction, color ranges from olive to deep blue-green.

iro-e 色絵
Polychrome overglaze painting with enamels, fired to 1292°F–1562°F (700°C–850°C). On porcelain in China during the Ming dynasty (1368–1644); developed for Japanese porcelain by Sakaida Kakiemon I in Arita between 1643 and 1647. Usually termed *aka-e* (red painting) in the Arita region.

iro-e kinran-de 色絵金襴手
See **kinran-de.**

iro-e shonzui-de 色絵祥瑞手
Five-colored decoration in *shonzui* style. See also **shonzui.**

iron glazes
See **tetsu-yû.**

ishihaze 石はぜ
"Stone explosion"; in *yakishime* (high-fired, unglazed stoneware), pegmatite fragments (feldspar and quartz particles) migrate to the surface as white stars (*hoshi*), bursting open at temperatures over 2372°F (1300°C) to form small craters or cracks; typical of Shigaraki and Iga-*yaki* (36, 37).

itchin イツチン
Or *tsutsugaki*; slip trailing, decorative technique of applying slip with a bamboo tube to a different colored surface of the pot.

jiki 磁器
Porcelain; term derived from Italian *porcellana* (cowrie shell). Porcelaneous stoneware was produced in China during the Tang dynasty (618–907); true porcelain was produced beginning in the twelfth century during the Song dynasty (960–1279); in Japan, from early seventeenth century. Impervious ceramic product, usually translucent, low in iron content; usually consisting of 2 parts kaolin (refractory product of erosion, especially from granite), 1 part quartz, and feldspar as flux but proportions vary. Japanese porcelain (soft-paste porcelain)

contains more flux than European hard-paste porcelain and can thus be fired to 2282°F–2462°F (1250°C–1350°C), in contrast to hard paste, which is fired to 2516°F–2660°F (1380°C–1460°C).

Jômon ceramics, Jômon-doki 縄文土器
"Cord-marked" ware; coil- or slab-built earthenware with characteristic cord patterns, produced throughout Japan between 10,000 B.C. and 300 B.C.

jôyaki 上焼
Glazed stoneware produced in Okinawa, usually with *aka-e* overglaze painting; along with *arayaki*, typical example of Tsuboya-*yaki* (1) produced in Okinawa.

jûyô mukei bunkazai hojisha 重要無形文化財保持者
"Bearers of Important Intangible Cultural Assets"; since 1955, title awarded by the Japanese state to artists with a command of specialized techniques; better known by the popular term "Living National Treasure" (*ningen kokuhô*).

kabin 花瓶
Flower vase.

kaime 貝目
Impressions of sea shells on pots; occurs when pots are placed on shells as supports during the firing.

kaiseki (**ryôri**) 会席 (料理)
Also *chakaiseki*; meal during the tea ceremony. See also **chanoyu.**

kai-yû 灰釉
See **hai-gusuri.**

Kajichô-yaki 鍛冶丁焼
Goyôgama belonging to Nanbu-*han*, built in Tôhoku (Iwate-ken, Hanamaki-shi, Ishigami-chô) at the end of the Edo period. After closing down during the Second World War, reopened in 1947 as a *maki-gama* by a potter trained in Mashiko to make domestic stoneware with a *nukabai* (rice husk) glaze. See also **goyôgama; maki-gama.**

kake hanaire 掛花入
Wall-hanging vase.

kaki 花器
Vessel for flowers.

kakiotoshi 掻き落とし
Sgraffito; decorative technique of incising into a pale slip to reveal the clay beneath.

kaki-yû 柿釉
Persimmon-colored glaze; ash feldspar glaze consisting of 25 percent feldspar, 40 percent wood ash, 25 percent rice-straw ash, and additions of ground stone and limestone with 7 percent iron content; often used by Hamada Shôji; typical of Mashiko-*yaki* (53).

kaku-gama 角窯
Downdraft kiln introduced to Japan from Europe by Gottfried Wagner during the Meiji period. See also **Wagner, Gottfried.**

kama 窯
Also *yô*, kiln; *gama* as suffix on composite forms, such as names or technical terms. Used to distinguish types of kilns: Depending on fuel: *maki-gama* 薪窯, wood-fired kiln (see also *anagama; naborigama*); *sekitan-gama* 石炭窯, coal-fired kiln; *jûyu-gama* 重油窯, crude petroleum kiln; *haiyu-gama* 廃油窯, waste-oil kiln; *sekiyu-gama* 石油窯, kerosene kiln; *gasu-gama* ガス窯, gas kiln; *denki-gama* 電気窯, electric kiln. Depending on function: *suyaki-gama* 素焼き窯, kiln for bisque firing; *honyaki-gama* 本焼き窯, kiln for main firing; or *etsuke-gama* 絵付け窯 kiln for firing of enamels. See also **anagama; noborigama.**

kamajirushi 窯印
Stamp or signature on ceramic ware that identifies the kiln or potter. *Mingei* potters, such as Hamada Shôji, left their work unsigned.

kame 甕
Wide-necked storage jar.

kangen shôsei 還元焼成
Reduction firing; carbon-rich kiln atmosphere caused by incomplete combustion through lack of oxygen.

kan´nyu 貫入
Glaze crackle; when using clay and glaze with different rates of expansion, hairline cracks appear in the glaze upon cooling after firing.

Kanô school
School of painting founded by Kanô Morinobu, who assumed the name Tan´yû (1602–1674); *goyô-eshi* (official painter) of the Tokugawa shogunate in Edo. Most famous are the five scrolls painted in 1639–40 in the *yamato-e* style, depicting the life of *shôgun* Tokugawa Ieyasu. See also **yamato-e.**

karako-e 唐子絵
Decoration of stoneware or porcelain with representations of Chinese children (*karako*), typical of Mikawachi- or Shibukusa-yaki (11, 47).

karamono 唐物
Collective term for art from China, such as lacquer or metal work, ceramics, painting, and calligraphy.

kashibachi 菓子鉢 / **kashizara** 菓子皿
Dish or plate for serving sweets.

kasurimon 絣紋
See *tobigan'na.*

katagami 型紙
Slip decoration method; stencils (paper or thin cardboard) protect areas of a pot when slip is applied. A positive or negative pattern is revealed when the stencil is removed.

Kawai Kanjirô 河井寛次郎
(1890–1966), potter from Kyôto, leader in the *mingei* (folk art) movement along with Yanagi Sôetsu and Hamada Shôji.

kenjô 献上
"Presentation"; prefix for ceramics (for example, *kenjô*-Imari) of particularly high quality produced in feudal kilns (*hanyô*, *goyôgama*, *oniwa-gama*) and used for official clan gifts (*kenjôhin*, "presentation ware"). One example of this is *kenjô-karako-e* from Mikawachi (11), with representations of seven *karako* figures for the imperial court, five figures for the shogunate, and three figures for *daimyô* and *samurai.*

kensui 建水
Vessel for waste water in the tea ceremony.

Kenzan 乾山
See *Ogata Kenzan.*

keshôgake 化粧掛け
type of white slip used to cover the surface of a vessel, frequently as a background for brushwork.

kibako 木箱
Wooden box for packaging high-quality ceramics; frequently inscribed by the potter, usually with name, stamp, type of vessel and clay, and the name of the pot. The inscription (*hakogaki* 箱書) is proof of authenticity; the loss of the *kibako* usually means a distinct loss in the pot's value.

kibushi-nendo 木節粘土
"Wood knot clay"; fine, plastic, gray clay with a high kaolin content; fires white; usually contains particles of charcoal and quartz. Frequently used industrially, for example, Motoyama *kibushi* (Seto, 41).

kiku momi 菊揉み
"Chrysanthemum wedging"; wedging of clay that produces a flowerlike, spiral form.

kiln
See *kama.*

kinran-de 金襴手
"Gold brocade style"; overglaze decoration with gold or, more rarely, silver brushwork on stoneware and porcelain; highly ornamental style of decoration, usually in combination with overglaze enamels. The various categories are *iro muji kinran-de* (monochrome background; in gold on red, *akaji-kinran-de*); *iro-e kinran-de* or *aka-e kinran-de* (*nishiki-de*, polychrome painting in brocade style with gold); and *sometsuke kinran-de* (cobalt underglaze painting with overglaze gold). Silver decoration alone is referred to as *ginran-de* 銀襴手.

kinsai 金彩
See *yûri-kinsai.*

kiseto 黄瀬戸
Yellow Seto; in oxidation, yellow-firing wood-ash feldspar glaze (for details, see Mino, 42, page 171).

Kitaôji Rosanjin 北大路魯山人
Studio potter born in Kyôto as Kitaôji Fusajirô (1883–1959). After training in Kutani, he maintained his own studio in Kita-Kamakura. Because of his passion for Japanese cuisine, he created tableware suitable for serving, first *sometsuke* and *iro-e* porcelain in Imari and Kutani style, and later stoneware in Bizen, Mino, and Kyô (Kenzan) style; developed his own unmistakable style from these roots.

ko- 古
"Old"; as a prefix in connection with an early style of a specific type of pottery, usually during a precisely defined period.

Kobori Enshû 小堀遠州
(1579–1647), tea master. See also **Enshû nana gama.**

Kôchi ware, Kôchi-yaki 交恊焼
Polychrome glazed ware with relief decoration. Japanese reproduction of ceramics from the Chinese Ming dynasty (1368–1644). After firing the objects, which are only glazed on the interior, enamels are applied to the unglazed exterior, often in several layers, with a firing after each application (yellow, green, mauve; red does not adhere).

kôdai 高台
Footring, executed carefully by the potter, especially on tea bowls; regarded as a mark of quality, age, and origin of a pot. Various terms depending on the form: *wa kôdai* 輪高台 (ring); *mikazuki kôdai* 三日月高台 (half moon); *takenofushi kôdai* 竹ノ節高台 (bamboo node); *wari kôdai* 割高台 (split); or *kiri kôdai* 切高台 (notched).

kôgô 香合
Incense box.

kohiki 粉引
Slip dipping; decorative technique originating from Korean Yi dynasty. The leather-hard pot is dipped in or swabbed with white slip to cover the entire surface.

Kojiki 古事記
Oldest chronicle in Japan, dating from 712, beginning with the age of myths and gods up to the reign (593–628) of empress Suiko.

ko-Kiyomizu 古清水
Ceramics made in Kyôto before porcelain production began in 1800. Collective term for the products from the various kilns in Kyôto (34), such as Awata-*yaki* 粟田焼; Iwakura-*yaki* 岩倉焼; Kiyomizu-*yaki* 清水焼; Mizoro-*yaki* 御菩薩焼; Nogami-*yaki* 野神焼; Omuro-*yaki* おむろ焼; Otowa-*yaki* 音羽焼; Seikanji-*yaki* 清閑寺焼; and Shugakuin-*yaki* 修学院焼.

kokuin rôrâ 刻印ローラー
Roller stamps. See also **impressed patterns.**

Kokuji-yaki 小久慈焼
Kiln in Tôhoku (Iwate-ken, Kuji-shi, Kokuchi-chô), set up 200 years ago as the *goyôgama* of Hachinohe-*han*; existed until the Second World War; reopened in 1958 as a gas-fired kiln for the production of domestic and tea ware in stoneware surfaced with *koku-yû* and *ame-yû*.

koku-yû 黒釉
Along with *seiji* (celadon) and *haku-yû* (white glaze), one of the three best-known glaze types in eastern Asia. Collective term for black-brown, ash feldspar glazes with an iron content of 8 to 10 percent, high-fired at temperatures over 2282°F (1250°C). Traces of copper and magnesium oxide produce a blue-black glaze. Rapid cooling of red-hot pots produces a deep black. (See **hikidashi-guro,** "withdrawn black"; typical of **kuro-raku;** see Kyôto, 34, on page 132; **setoguro, oribeguro,** and **kuro-oribe,** see Mino, 42, on page 171.)

konoha-tenmoku 木の葉天目釉
Leaf skeleton embedded in brown-black *tenmoku* glaze before glaze firing; only possible with a few types of trees that are rich in minerals.

Kôrai-ware, kôrai-yaki 高麗焼
Ceramics produced during the Korean Koryo dynasty (Japanese: *kôrai*, 918–1392); unglazed ware in the Silla tradition, and glazed ware, such as celadons and white ware (all monochrome with an inlay decoration or painting) and iron-brown ware (celadons with iron oxide underglaze; stoneware with inlay decoration or brown-black glaze).

kôro 香炉
Incense burner.

Kosobe-yaki 古曾部焼
Ceramics produced in the Kosobe district of Takatsuki (Ôsaka-fu). The establishment date of the kiln is unknown; according to tea ceremony records, it belonged to the *Enshû nana gama.* Closed down at the end of the Meiji period; now produces tea bowls and domestic ware in glazed and unglazed stoneware.

kudarimono 下り物
Favorably priced, mass-produced ware from the Seto-Mino region; as a result of industrialization at the end of the nineteenth century, superseded typical local crafts.

kuniyaki 国焼
Original term for vernacular ceramics from the provinces, especially *chaire,* used by tea masters in the sixteenth and seventeenth centuries. Beginning in the mid-twentieth century, term for Japanese ceramics as distinct from Korean or Chinese wares. See also **chaire.**

kuromono 黒物
Collective term for ceramics with high-fired, black-iron glazes. See also **koku-yû.**

kushime 櫛目
Combed decoration, applied to the leather-hard pot with a comb. Frequently used on the inner surface of a mortar (*suribachi*).

kyûsu 急須
Side-handled small teapot for making *sencha* (see photos 115–117). See also **sencha.**

Leach, Bernard Howell
English potter (1887–1979), resided in Japan 1909–1920. Co-founder of the *mingei* (folk art) movement in Japan.

Levigation
See **suihi** 水簸.

Living National Treasure
See **ningen kokuhô.** See also **jûyô mukei bunkazai hojisha.**

maki-gama 薪窯
Kiln (*anagama, noborigama*) fired with wood (*maki*). Japanese red pine is preferred for this purpose because it is rich in resin and thus achieves a long flame in combustion.

marbling
Layering clays of different colors, see **neriage;** "ink flow" marbling, see **suminagashi.**

matcha 抹茶
Powdered green tea (*gyokuro* quality), for the tea ceremony; whisked to a frothy consistency with hot water in a tea bowl (*chawan*) with a bamboo whisk (*chasen*). See also **sencha.**

me 目
Small balls of unfired clay, used as wads to separate ceramic pieces during firing.

me ato 目跡
Wad marks on ceramic pieces after firing, left by fireclay wads used to separate stacked pots and prevent them from sticking together.

Meiji Restoration, Meiji ishin 明治維新
Strictly speaking, the revolution of January 3, 1868, when forces hostile to the Tokugawa shogunate forced it to relinquish power to the emperor. More broadly speaking, a series of political, social, and economic changes at the end of the nineteenth century as a consequence of the dissolution of the Bakuhan political system; led to the establishment of a modern state.

mentori 面取
Decorative technique of faceting the leather-hard surface of a pot with a wire or knife to form surfaces of equal size.

meoto yunomi 組湯呑み
Paired teacups; "husband and wife" tea bowls in different sizes (smaller for the wife) with identical decoration. Also corresponds to paired forms for rice bowls.

migaki 磨き
Burnishing. See also **shudei.**

Ming dynasty, Mindai 明代
Chinese dynasty, 1368–1644. In ceramics, the refinement of blue-and-white ware developed during the Yuan Dynasty (1279–1368), with cobalt underglaze painting on a very white body. After the emergence of overglaze painting with enamels (1426–1435), polychrome as well as monochrome porcelain, such as purple, turquoise, and imperial yellow, was produced. Between 1465 and 1487, polychrome brushwork with outlines in underglaze blue and with overglaze painting in five colors emerged.

mingei movement, *mingei undô* 民芸運動
Folk art movement in the early twentieth century; abbreviation for *minshû-teki kôgei* 民衆的工芸 (folk art).

minyô 民窯
Folk kiln; during the Edo period (1600–1868) produced everyday ware for the people.

mishima 三島
hakudo-zôgan; slip inlay. After dipping the pot in white slip (*hakudo*), an incised or impressed pattern is scraped clean to reveal a pattern. Term refers to the similarity to calendars printed in the Mishima shrine. See also ***zôgan.***

MITI, *tsûshô sangyô shô* 通商産業省
Abbreviated as Tsûsanshô; Ministry of International Trade and Industry.

mitsu no keshiki 三の景色
"Three landscapes"; in *yakishime*, highly prized effect with *hi-iro* 火色, "fire color" of the fired, unglazed body in various shades of red to red-brown; *koge* 焦げ, scorch markings, the burned or scorched areas on a piece; *bîdoro* ビードロ, vitrified glass, from the Portuguese term *vidoro* for glass, green to blue-green glaze flows from the natural accumulation of fly ash in reduction firing to temperatures of over 2372°F (1300°C).

mizusashi 水指
Fresh-water jar, usually lidded, for the tea ceremony.

mogake 藻掛け
See ***hidasuki.***

Mori-yaki 母里焼
Kiln in Shimane Prefecture (Nogi-gun, Hakuta-chô), established in 1844 as a *goyôgama* for the Mori clan. In the fifth generation, Inagaki Hiroshi now produces domestic ware using stoneware with blue copper glazes and iron glazes.

Mumyôi-yaki 無名異焼
Ceramics named after *mumyôi* (manganese and iron oxides found in silver and gold mines). Mumyôi-yaki is produced on the island of Sado in Niigata Prefecture (see Mumyôi, 51), and since the end of the nineteenth century, as domestic ware in Shimane Prefecture in the Minami-chô district of Ôda (see **Iwami**, 24, on page 106).

Mushiake-yaki 虫明焼
Kiln in Okayama Prefecture (Oku-gun, Oku-chô, Mushiake) set up in the mid-Edo period under the instruction of Kyôto potters as an *oniwa-gama* for the local Iki family for the production of tea ware. After a phase of producing *mingei* domestic ware, four workshops now exclusively produce stoneware tea ware, notable for its delicate green ash glazes with a hint of red.

nagashigake 流し掛け
Dripping; a pattern is produced on the leather-hard or bisqued pot by dripping glaze or slip with a bamboo tube, ladle, or brush.

nagashi goma 流し胡麻
See ***goma-yû.***

namagake 生がけ
Glaze application on unfired (green) ware.

namako-yû 海鼠釉
"Sea cucumber glaze"; common rice-straw ash glaze; color ranges from gray-green to deep brown with speckles or stripes of white through purple to indigo; examples are *madara-garatsu* (Karatsu-yaki, 13) and Aizu-Hongô-yaki (54).

nanban 南蛮
"Southern barbarians"; common term in the Edo period in relation to imported goods from Southeast Asia (Thailand, Indonesia, and the Philippines) and for Japanese painting in Western style. *Nanbanjin* is used to describe Europeans, especially the Dutch, Portuguese, and Spanish.

nanban-yaki 南蛮焼
Unglazed stoneware from Southeast Asia.

Naraoka-yaki 楢岡焼
Two-chamber kiln in Tôhoku (Akita-ken, Senboku-gun, Nangai-mura, Aza Nashikida) belonging to the Komatsu family. In existence since 1863 for domestic stoneware, typically with *namako-yû*. Gas kiln now also in use.

natsume 棗
Small tea caddy for *usucha* (powdered green tea of thin consistency used in the tea ceremony); usually lacquered, sometimes in clay (see photo 120). See also ***chanoyu.***

nawame 縄目
Cord-impressed patterns. See also ***impressed patterns.***

neriage 練り上げ
Or *nerikomi;* clay marbling, technique from the Chinese Song period (960–1279) for the production of marbled ware, using two or more clays stained in various colors or natural clays of different colors.

nerikomi 練り込み
See ***neriage.***

Nihon kôgei-kai 日本工芸会
Japan Craft Association.

Nihonmatsu-yaki 二本松焼
Stoneware produced in Nihonmatsu (Fukushima Prefecture) since ca. 1700; *minyô* for the production of domestic ware (see Nihonmatsu Banko, 55, on page 228).

Nihon shoki 日本書記
Or *Nihongi.* Along with the *Kojiki* (712), one of the oldest chronicles in Japan (720); begins with the age of myths and gods, continues up to the reign (686–697) of empress Jitô; consists of 30 volumes in Chinese.

nijû-yaki 二重焼
Double-walled ceramics; *nijû* (twice); typical of Ôbori Sôma-*yaki* (57).

ningen kokuhô 人間国宝
"Living National Treasure." See also ***jûyô mukei bunkazai hojisha.***

Ninsei 仁清
See **Nonomura Ninsei**.

nishiki-de 錦手
Brocade style of decoration, with overglaze painting on stoneware and porcelain, originally corresponding to brocade textiles in red, green, purple, yellow, and blue. With gold decoration *iro-e kinran-de.* See also ***kinran-de.***

nishiki-gama 錦窯
Muffle kiln for firing overglaze enamels on stoneware and porcelain to 1292°F–1562°F (700°C–850°C).

Nitten 日展, *Nihon bijutsu tenrankai* 日本美術展覧会
"Japan Fine Arts Exhibition"; oldest exhibition organization, successor of Bunten, the former imperial exhibition organization; first Nitten exhibition in 1946; since 1958, a public law foundation.

291

noborigama 登窯
Multivaulted, multichamber climbing kiln, introduced from Korea in Karatsu (13) as early as the end of the sixteenth century; present throughout Japan in early seventeenth century. Two types exist. See also **waridakeshiki-noborigama; renbôshiki-noborigama.**

Nonomura Ninsei 野々村仁清
Nonomura Seiemon; assumed the name Nonomura Ninsei (ca.1627–ca.1695). Introduced polychrome overglaze painting with silver and gold enamels on stoneware (*tôki*) in Kyôto (34).

nunome 布目
Cloth texturing; decoration method in which netting or textiles are impressed on damp clay.

Obayashi-yaki 尾林焼
Oldest kiln in Nagano Prefecture in Iida (Iida-shi, Tatsue), established by the Seto potter Mizuno Gizaburô in 1852; used for domestic ware. Of several kilns from the Meiji period, one workshop still produces ash-glazed stoneware.

ôbori 凹彫り
See **chôka** 彫花.

Oda Nobunaga 織田信長
(1534–1582), warlord and patron of the arts; united Japan along with Toyotomi Hideyoshi (1537–1598) and Tokugawa Ieyasu (1543–1616).

ôgama 大窯
"Large kiln"; single-vaulted, single-chamber *anagama* kiln of large dimensions for mass production; approximately 164 feet (50 m) long, 13 to 16½ feet (4 to 5 m) wide, and 6½ feet (2 m) high, with a capacity of up to 35,000 pots. Came into use around 1400 in the Tokoname (39) region and in the early sixteenth century in the Seto-Mino (41, 42) region.

Ogata Kenzan 尾形乾山
Ogata Shinsei; assumed the name Ogata Kenzan (1663–1743). Poet, painter, calligrapher, and potter, famous for his painted decoration in dark iron oxide on pale slip; along with his teacher Nonomura Ninsei, a leading exponent of overglaze painting on stoneware (*tôki*) in Kyôto (34).

okimono 置物
Ornamental ceramic objects placed in *tokonoma* (decorative alcove). See also **saikumono.**

(o)miyage お土産
Souvenir of a journey for those who remain at home, usually a local specialty, such as ceramics (mass produced) or culinary specialties.

oni-ita 鬼板
"Devil board" pigment; brown iron oxide ore with approximately 40 percent iron content, particularly common in deposits in the Mino region; frequently used for underglaze painting or as engobe under feldspar glaze of *nezumi* or *aka-shino* type.

oniwa-yaki お庭焼, **oniwa-gama** お庭窯
During the Edo period (1600–1868), tea ware produced in a small private kiln ("garden kiln," *oniwa-gama*) to the taste of the respective feudal lord or tea master, for his exclusive use and as presentation ware.

open work
See **sukashibori.**

Oribe 織部
See **Furuta Oribe.**

oribe 織部, **oribe-yaki** 織部焼
Ceramic style named after Furuta Oribe, with characteristic green copper glaze and unusual vessel forms (see Mino, 42, on page 171). See also **Furuta Oribe.**

oxblood
See **shinsha-yû.**

oxidation firing
See **sanka shôsei.**

ô-yû 黄釉
Characteristic high-fired yellow lead glaze for Fujina-*yaki* (25). Composition: feldspar (57 percent), whiting (28 percent), and lead (15 percent).

ôzara 大皿
Large plate.

porcelain
See **jiki.**

potter's wheel
See **rokuro.**

press molding
See **uchigata.**

raku ware, raku-yaki 楽焼
Usually hand-built stoneware items for the tea ceremony, which are fired quickly. Various glazes, such as the iron-rich *kamogawa-ishi* glaze for black raku (*kuro-raku*), are covered with a transparent lead raku glaze. When the glaze has melted after 5 to 40 minutes of firing to 1562°F–2282°F (850°C–1250°C), depending on the glaze, the pots are extracted red hot from the kiln for rapid cooling; see **Kyô-yaki** (34), **Ôhi-yaki** (46).

Rakuzan-yaki 楽山焼
Kiln set up near Matsue (Shimane-ken, Matsue-shi, Nishi-Kawazu) by a Hagi potter in the early Edo period; tea ware was produced with the support of the Matsudaira family. Contemporary Rakuzan stoneware with various iron glazes is mainly domestic ware.

reduction firing
See **kangen shôsei.**

relief carving
See **ukibori.**

renbôshiki-noborigama 連房式登窯
Multivaulted, multichamber climbing kiln, built on a slope with several rising chambers; lowest chamber used as the firing chamber. A chimney provides draft. See also **noborigama.**

rice-grain pattern
See **hotaru-de.**

Rimpa 琳派
Edo-period school of painting, founded ca. 1600; revived in the early eighteenth century by Ogata Kôrin (1658–1716), brother of the Kyôto potter Kenzan.

roku koyô 六古窯
Six Ancient Kilns; term coined around 1950 for the six most important medieval ceramics centers that date back to Sue and Sanage kilns and are still in use. Five of the centers—Bizen (29), Tanba (31), Shigaraki (36), Tokoname (39) and Echizen (44)—produce unglazed stoneware (*yakishime*), whereas in Seto (41), the tradition of Sanage ware (glazed stoneware) is continued.

rokuro 轆轤
Potter's wheel. Common wheels in Japan include hand wheels, *te-rokuro*; kick wheels, *ke-rokuro*; kick wheels for the production of large vessels (*ne-rokuro: ne*, sleep; see Ôtani-*yaki*, 21, on page 97); *ne-rokuro* (*ne*, sleep), in which the person driving the wheel lies on the ground and a second person shapes the vessel; electric wheels, *dendô-rokuro*; and jigger wheels, *kikai-rokuro*.

roller stamps
See **kokuin rôrâ**. See also **impressed patterns.**

rônuki 蝋抜き
Wax resist; decorative technique in which a wax pattern is painted on a leather-hard pot. The pattern remains free of slip when the slip is later applied; the wax burns off in the bisque firing.

ryoku-yû 緑釉
Light green to moss green copper oxide glaze (2 to 3 percent copper oxide), with lead compounds to lower the melting point; fired in oxidation to 1472°F–1652°F (800°C–900°C).

sabi 寂
Aesthetic ideal influenced by Zen Buddhism, with great significance for the development of the tea ceremony. *Sabi* (elegant simplicity) implies beauty in use (*yô no bi*), with an appreciation of patina and decay; *wabi* (taste of simplicity and calm) implies moderation and restraint, simplicity to the extent of poverty.

sadô no mono 茶道の物
Also *chadôgu*; tea ware for the tea ceremony.

saggar
See **saya.**

saikô- 再興
"Revived"; prefix for ceramics, for example, *saikô*-Kutani, revived Kutani (45); used to describe formerly abandoned styles that are reestablished.

saikumono 細工物
"Crafted thing"; ornamental ceramic figure often in the shape of an animal, god, or mythical creature. Used either as ornamentation on ceramic objects (the lids of incense burners and teapots, for instance) or, starting in the second half of the seventeenth century, placed in *tokonoma* (decorative alcoves); also referred to as **okimono.**

sakazuki 杯
Also *hai*; small cup or bowl for *sake*.

Sakazu-yaki 酒津焼
Kiln set up in Okayama Prefecture (Kurashiki-shi, Sakazu) in 1876. Supported by Hamada Shôji; now produces domestic stoneware with thick rice-straw and iron glazes.

sake 酒
Undistilled rice wine, fermented from rice since the eighth century; 15 to 16½ percent alcohol. Can be drunk hot or cold.

samehada-gusuri 鮫肌釉
Also called *same-gusuri* ("shark-skin" glaze); contraction and cracking of the glaze during firing caused by differing rates of expansion for glaze and clay body, so that, in Ryûmonji-*yaki* (3) for example, a granular surface is created.

Sanage kilns, sanage-yô 猿投窯
Sue kilns in Sanage, near contemporary Nagoya, which, in the eighth to twelfth centuries, produced stoneware with gray-green, wood-ash feldspar glazes ("Sanage ware") in the reproduction of celadons.

sanka shôsei 酸化焼成
Oxidation firing; firing with sufficient oxygen and an absence of carbon.

sansai (yû) 三彩 (釉)
Three-colored lead glaze originating in China in green, white, and yellow-brown. The production of low-fired, three-colored stoneware (*sansai tôki*), Nara-*sansai*, began in Japan during the Nara period (A.D. 710–A.D. 794).

sansui-mon 山水文
Landscape painting; frequent subject in Chinese art. In Japanese ceramics, mainly found as cobalt underglaze painting on porcelain. Found infrequently on stoneware in folk art; examples are *sansui dobin* (teapots) from Shigaraki (36), Seto (41), and Mashiko (53).

sara 皿
Plate.

sarayama 皿山
In northern Kyûshû, term for potters' village with several workshops in which typical ceramics are produced; in Arita (8), also *saraya*.

saya 匣鉢
Saggar; box made of refractory material to protect the pot from flames and ash during the firing.

seihakuji 青白磁
Also called "white celadon"; first produced in the Jingdezhen kilns during the Song dynasty in China, eleventh to thirteenth centuries. The wood-ash glaze used for this has a very low iron content and produces a light, bluish green glaze that appears almost white when applied thinly. Highly esteemed in Japan, especially in the early days of the tea ceremony; has experienced a comeback in the past 30 years, especially with Tsukamoto Kaiji (1912–1990; Living National Treasure).

seiji 青磁, **seiji-yû** 青磁釉
Celadon, celadon glaze; developed in China during the Song dynasty (960–1279). Ash feldspar glaze with little iron (maximum 3 percent), used on stoneware and porcelain, fired in reduction to approximately 2336°F (1280°C), producing shades from yellow to blue-green or gray-green. The Western term "celadon" refers to the blue-green clothing of Céladon, the protagonist in a pastoral play by Honoré d'Urfé.

sei-yû 青釉
Blue copper oxide glaze, fired in oxidation to approximately 1832°F (1000°C), with sodium or potassium to lower the melting point.

sekki 炻器
See **ceramics.**

senbori 線彫り
See **chôka** 彫花.

sencha 煎茶
Drink made of unfermented green tea leaves and hot water; known in Japan since the mid-sixteenth century, frequently used from nineteenth century on. *Sencha* (regular quality) is brewed in small teapots (often *kyûsu*) with hot water (158°F–194°F/70°C–90°C) and drunk in teacups (*yunomi*) or *sencha* tea bowls (*sencha chawan*). For *gyokuro*, the best quality, the water temperature is reduced in a water cooler (*yuzamashi*) to approximately 122°F (50°C); the tea is brewed in a *kyûsu* or a *hôhin* and is drunk from a small *sencha* teacup. *Bancha*, tea for everyday, is brewed in large teapots (*dobin*) with boiling water and served in teacups or large *sencha* tea bowls.

Sen no Rikyû 千利休
(1522–1591); one of the most important tea masters in Japan. He served Oda Nobunaga, then Toyotomi Hideyoshi, as a tea master and was largely responsible for the simplification of the tea ceremony (*wabi-sabi* aesthetic). The first raku tea bowls were produced in Kyôto at the end of the sixteenth century in accordance with his instructions. See also **sabi**.

setoguro 瀬戸黒
Black Seto; high-fired stoneware with an iron glaze; extracted from the kiln while red hot and immediately cooled (for details, see Mino, 42, on page 176). See also **hikidashi-guro**.

sgraffito
See **kakiotoshi**.

shamotto サァモット
Fired, ground clay added to unfired clay bodies to provide texture and strength, and to reduce the rate of shrinkage in drying.

shifuku 仕服
Brocade pouch for *chaire* (small tea caddy).

shiki 瓷器
Or *shirashi* 白瓷; the oldest glazed ware produced in Japan from the Nara and Heian periods (eighth to twelfth centuries). Refers to lead-glazed Nara ware and stoneware with wood-ash feldspar glazes from Sanage kilns.

Shinjô-Higashiyama-yaki 新庄東山焼
Set up in Tôhoku (Yamagata-ken, Shinjô-shi, Higashiyama-chô) in 1841 by a Shiraiwa potter as a *goyôgama*, later for the production of domestic tableware. Currently one workshop; stoneware with a clear green copper and *namako* glaze fired in a *noborigama* is typical.

shino 志野
White ash feldspar glaze with a high proportion of feldspar (for details, see Mino, 42, page 176).

shinsha-yû 辰砂釉
Or *dô-aka-yû*; copper glaze, fired red in reduction, termed "oxblood" (*sang-de-boeuf*) in Chinese ceramics.

shiragi
see **Silla**.

Shiraishi-yaki 白石焼
Goyôgama set up on Kyûshû (Saga-ken, Miyaki-gun, Kita-Shigeyasu-chô, Shiraishi) by the Shiraishi-Nabeshima family at the end of the eighteenth century, initially for the production of porcelain; transition to *Kyô-yaki*-style stoneware at the end of the Edo period. Today, six potter families produce folk art ceramics with *tobigan 'na* and *kakiotoshi* designs.

Shiraiwa-yaki 白岩焼
Kiln dating from 1771 built by a Sôma potter in Tôhoku (Akita-ken, Senboku-gun, Kakunodate-machi, Shiraiwa, Aza Moto-machi). After it was destroyed during an earthquake in 1900, it was rebuilt with the assistance of Hamada Shôji. Currently one workshop; domestic stoneware is produced, typically with *namako-yû*.

shirashi 白瓷
See **shiki**.

shîsâ シーサー
Mythical lions as guardians against evil spirits, made of glazed or unglazed stoneware; in Okinawa, frequently placed on roofs.

shita-etsuke 下絵付け
See **etsuke**.

shitômon 指頭文
See **yubikaki**.

shizen-yû 自然釉
Also *haikaburi*; natural-ash glaze produced during the firing of unglazed stoneware in a *maki-gama* (wood-burning kiln) by the melting and adhering of fly-ash particles to the pot at temperatures above 2264°F (1240°C).

shôchû 焼酎
Alcoholic distillation from the fermentation of molasses (*kô*), or rice, sweet potatoes, barley, rye, etc. (*otsu*), with an alcohol content of 40 to 90 percent; first produced in fifteenth century on the Ryûkyû islands (now Okinawa), termed *awamori*. Since the sixteenth century also produced on the main Japanese islands.

shôgun 将軍 / **shogunate**
See **bafuku**.

shokki 食器
Tableware.

shonzui 祥瑞
Type of *sometsuke* porcelain produced by the Jingdezhen kilns in China for export to Japan, mainly 1630–1640; the body of the pot is covered with a regular spiral pattern, often in combination with medallions (figures, landscapes, flowers and birds), that continues on the interior surfaces of the vessel and lid.

shudei 朱泥
Burnished, reddish brown, unglazed ware made of fine, iron-rich clay with a glossy surface produced by burnishing (*migaki*) when leather hard by using various materials such as camellia leaves or steel tools.

shuki 酒器
Sake vessels such as flasks (*tokkuri*) and cups of various sizes (*guinomi*, *choko*, and *sakazuki*, for example); frequently as a set with one or two *sake* flasks and two, three, or five *sake* cups.

Shussai-yaki 出西焼
Folk art kiln set up in Shimane Prefecture (Hikawa-gun, Hikawa-chô, Ôaza Shussai) by five potters in 1947, influenced by William Morris (Arts and Crafts Movement) and *mingei* (folk art) movement, and supported by Yanagi Sôetsu. Produced domestic glazed stoneware with *gosu*, *ame*, *kaki*, *koku*, and *ryoku* glazes.

Silla 新羅
In Japanese **shiragi**; Kingdom of Silla (57 B.C.–A.D. 935) during the "Three Kingdoms" period in Korea; Silla ceramics (*shiragi-yaki*) refers to a high-fired, unglazed stoneware, gray-black in color; precursor to Japanese Sue ceramics.

Six Ancient Kilns
See **roku koyô**.

slab building
See **tatara (zukuri)**.

slip
Liquid clay. See also **keshôgake**.

slip casting
Method of forming vessels by pouring a thin slip into a plaster mold that is drained after a certain amount of time, depending on the desired wall thickness of the object; common method in mass production of porcelain.

slip inlay
See **mishima; zôgan**.

slip trailing
See **itchin**.

Sôdeisha 走泥社
Literally "walking through mud company"; a group of avant-garde artists in Kyôto from 1948 to 1998, with members such as Yagi Kazuo (1918–1979), Yamada Hikaru (1924–2001), and Suzuki Osamu (1926–2001), who, as a counter-movement to folk art (*mingei*), had dedicated themselves to nonfunctional ceramics.

some-nishiki-de 染錦手
Also *gosu aka-e*; decorative technique for *iro-e* porcelain that combines overglaze and underglaze painting. The outline of the subject is drawn with cobalt blue underglaze, and the polychrome painting is executed with overglaze enamels.

sometsuke 染付
Underglaze painting in cobalt blue on stoneware and porcelain (blue-and-white ware). Before application, *gosu* is mixed with concentrated green tea, the tannic acid in which prevents the pigment from bleeding when the glaze is applied. See also **gosu.**

Song dynasty, Sôdai 宋代
Chinese dynasty, 960–1279 (also Sung dynasty); a high point in the history of ceramics, including porcelain beginning in the early twelfth century, and glazes, especially celadon crackle, and variations of *tenmoku* glazes such as hare's fur, tortoiseshell, oil spot, and inlaid leaf skeletons.

stamp
See *kamajirushi.*

stencil
see *katagami.*

Sue ceramics, sueki 須恵器
Derived from *sueru*, to sacrifice; also known as Iwaibe-*yaki*. Gray, unglazed stoneware (*sekki*) fired to 2192°F (1200°C) in reduction in an *anagama*; impervious to water through smoking at the end of the firing. *Sueki* is said to have come to the Ôsaka region in the fifth and sixth centuries with Korean immigrants; strong resemblance to Korean Silla ceramics. It spread throughout Japan and was made beyond the end of the twelfth century; strong resemblance to Korean Silla ceramics.

suihi 水簸
Wet processing; stage of clay processing during which the fine clay particles are separated from the coarse material by immersing the dried, pounded, and sieved clay in water. Fine particles remain in suspension and are transferred to the next settling tank. Depending on clay quality, this step may be repeated several times, resulting in a fine slurry, which is then dried.

suirenbachi 睡蓮鉢
Shallow bowl for growing water lilies (see Ôtani-*yaki*, 21, on page 97).

suiteki 水滴
Water dropper; used in calligraphy to drip water on an ink stone.

sukashibori 透かし彫り
Open work; perforation of leather-hard vessel wall to produce a pattern.

suminagashi 墨流し
"Ink flow"; marbling technique in which dark glaze runs are produced by shaking the pale-slip-covered pot while wet to produce a marbled pattern; first used in Tanba (31).

suribachi 摺鉢
Mortar; interior surface corrugated with *kushime* (combed pattern).

suyaki 素焼き
Bisque firing, also bisque ware. After drying and before glazing, the finished object is hardened at a low temperature of 1202°F–1742°F (650°C–950°C).

Tajima Banko-yaki 田島万古焼
Kiln built in Tôhoku (Fukushima-ken, Minami-Aizu-gun, Tajima-chô, Ôaza Tajima) around 1869 by a Nihonmatsu Banko potter, for the production of domestic ware and individual pieces resembling Nihonmatsu Banko-*yaki* (55). After closing down during the Second World War, it reopened in 1969, making mainly *sencha* sets highly esteemed by tea connoisseurs, and unglazed *tebineri* stoneware. Deocorative elements included fingerprint patterns and sprigged clay decorations (*chôka*), often with representations of figures (*saikumono*) as knobs for lids or as handles on the teapots.

Tanegashima-yaki 種子島焼
In the only town (Nishi-no-omote-shi, Nishi-no-omote) on the island of Tanegashima, south of Kyûshû, unglazed domestic stoneware comparable to *arayaki* (see Tsuboya, 1, page 34) is currently produced in seven workshops. Produced in this style since the beginning of the Edo period; influenced *karatsu-nanban* work of Nakazato Takashi (see Karatsu, 13, on page 72).

tataki (zukuri) 叩き (作り)
Coiling and paddling; originally a Korean technique of hand building a vessel with coils, then shaping it by paddling with wooden bats. Carved wooden paddles may also be used to texture the pot's surface.

tatara (zukuri) タタラ(作り)
Slab building; forming rectilinear objects by cutting and assembling clay slabs (*tatara*).

tatsuchi 田土
Clay dug from under rice fields; high iron content (3 to 6 percent) and very plastic due to high proportion of organic material; for example, Ôtani, Bizen-*yaki* (21, 29).

tea
See *matcha; sencha.*

tea caddy
See *chaire; natsume.*

tea ceremony
See *chanoyu.*

tebineri 手捻り
Hand built by pinching without the assistance of tools or wheel (for example, Nihonmatsu Banko-*yaki*, 55, on page 228).

Teiten 帝展, Teikoku bijutsu tenrankai 帝国美術展覧会
"Imperial Fine Arts Exhibition." See also **Bunten.**

tenmoku chawan 天目茶碗
Characteristically shaped tea bowl with a narrow foot, flared sides, a slight depression below the lip, and a thick roll of glaze where the glazed and unglazed surfaces meet; highly prized by tea masters; derived from Chinese Song ware (see photo 37).

tenmoku-yû 天目釉
Brown-black ash feldspar glaze with 5 to 15 percent iron content. In reduction firing, various effects are produced (*yôhen-tenmoku*): glaze flow produces paler stripes ("hare's-fur" *tenmoku*); excess iron causes crystal spots to appear on the surface (*yuteki-tenmoku*, oil-spot *tenmoku*).

tessha 鉄砂
Iron-rich alluvial deposit, used for underglaze painting or for glazes. See also **tessha-yû.**

tessha-yû 鉄砂釉
Black iron glaze with 20 percent iron content.

tetsu-yû 鉄釉
Iron glaze the colors of which darken as iron content rises: *seiji* (celadon), *kiseto* (yellow Seto), *ame-yû* (amber glaze), *kaki-yû* (persimmon glaze), *tenmoku-yû* (brown-black glaze), *koku-yû* (black-brown glaze), and *tessha-yû* (black glaze). Deep black glazes such as *kuro-raku, setoguro, oriboguro,* and *kuro-oribe* are produced by rapid cooling of red-hot pots. See also **hikidashi-guro; seiji.**

tobigan´na 飛び鉋
Or *kasurimon,* chatter marks; decorative technique developed in China during the Song dynasty (960–1279). Pale slip on the leather-hard pot is marked on a slowly revolving wheel by the "chattering" of a flexible trimming tool on the surface. In Japan, typical of Koishiwara and Onta-*yaki* (17, 18).

tôgei 陶芸
Art of ceramics.

Tôhoku 東北
Northeastern area of the main Japanese island of Honshû, includes the prefectures Fukushima, Yamagata, Miyagi, Iwate, Akita, and Aomori.

tôjiki 陶磁器
Ceramics, including porcelain.

tôki 陶器
See **ceramics.**

tokkuri 徳利
Sake bottle; larger bottles for transport and storage; smaller flasks, approximately 6 ounces (180 ml) for warming and serving *sake.*

Tokugawa Ieyasu 徳川家康
(1543–1616), warrior leader; after unification of Japan by Oda Nobunaga (1534–1582) and Toyotomi Hideyoshi (1537–1598), and after Hideyoshi´s death, Ieyasu assumed a great deal of Hideyoshi´s powers, establishing the Tokugawa shogunate (1603–1867). See also **bafuku.**

Tomimoto Kenkichi 富本憲吉
(1886–1963); studied ceramics from 1912 under Kenzan VI in Kyôto; worked in overglaze-decorated earthenware and stoneware, later specialized in porcelain; for a time, active in the *mingei* movement with Yanagi Sôetsu and Hamada Shôji. Designated Living National Treasure in 1955.

tôseki 陶石
Ceramic or porcelain stone, as a raw material to produce porcelain and stoneware, with quartz and mica or kaolinite as main constituents. Variants include Izumiyama, Amakusa, and Senzan-*tôseki* for Arita-*yaki* (8); Hasami-*tôseki* in Hasami (10); Kawanobori-*tôseki* in Tobe (19); Hitani-*tôseki* in Izushi (30); Shibukusa and Isai-*tôseki* in Gifu Prefecture; and Okubo-*tôseki* in Aizu-Hongô (54).

totsubori 凸彫り
See *chôka* 彫花.

Toyotomi Hideyoshi 豊臣秀吉
(1537–1598); warlord who in 1590 completed the unification of Japan, which had been started by Oda Nobunaga; also patron of the tea ceremony. His so-called ceramics campaigns in 1592 and 1597 were important for the development of ceramics in Japan: hundreds of Korean potters were taken especially to Kyûshû.

tsubo 壺
Narrow-necked storage jar.

tsuchi no aji 土の味
"Clay flavor"; beauty of unglazed fired clay in *yakishime*, or the unglazed areas of a pot (*hima*); for example, the footring (*kôdai*) of a tea bowl.

tsutsugaki 筒猫き
See *itchin.*

uchigake 打ち掛け
Splashed glaze; decorative technique used to create dripped patterns by splashing glaze on the pot with a ladle, hand, or thick brush (*dami-fude*).

uchigata 内型
Press molding; clay slabs (*tatara*) are pressed into molds to form an object. Molds previously made of wood or bisque-fired clay are now generally made of plaster.

uchi-hakeme 打ち刷毛目
"Slip patting"; decorative technique executed by using a broad flat brush (*hake*) to create a radial pattern by rhythmically touching a plate covered in wet slip as it revolves on the wheel; typical of Koishiwara and Onta-*yaki* (17, 18).

Uchiharano-yaki 内原野焼
Kiln situated in Kôchi Prefecture (Aki-shi, Uchiharano), currently with four workshops and a small ceramics center (Uchiharano *tôgeikan*); founded by a potter from neighboring Nôsoyama in 1820 (see Odo, 20, on page 97). Domestic ware, large vases, and tea ware are fired, from *yakishime* to glazed stoneware; floral designs on an unglazed background are typical.

Ujô-yaki 烏城焼
Workshop, Misuji Kôbô 三筋工房, situated in Kuroishi (Aomori Prefecture); fires unglazed stoneware in a red-pine-burning *noborigama*. The objects, such as vases and tea bowls, are enhanced with a natural-ash glaze with pronounced glaze flows.

ukibori 浮き彫り
"Floating incision"; relief-carving method that combines linear incisions with deep and broad carvings, varying in depth; often used in combination with celadon glazes.

unkin-de 雲錦手
Cherry blossom (*sakura*) and autumn maple (*momiji*) design in overglaze painting on one object; typical of Kyô-*yaki* (34) and Inuyama-*yaki* (40).

Ushinoto-yaki 牛ノ戸焼
The kiln in what is today Tottori Prefecture (Yazu-gun, Kawahara-chô, Ushinoto); set up by a potter from Iwami in the Tempô period (1830–1844) to produce glazed stoneware. Reopened in 1920; now a folk art kiln producing domestic ware. Transparent, black, or green glazes, with white or iron-brown slip decoration are typical, as are pots glazed half green and half black.

uwa-etsuke 上絵付け
See *etsuke.*

VOC
Vereenigde Oostindische Compagnie; the Dutch East India Company; *Oranda (Rengô) Higashi Indo Kaisha.* Founded in Batavia (Jakarta) in 1602 for trading in textiles, spices, and porcelain; main export was Imari porcelain 1650–ca. 1750 via Dejima, near Nagasaki. Until the opening of Japan, the VOC was present in Dejima.

wabi 侘び
See *sabi.*

Wagner, Gottfried
(1831–1892), also spelled Wagener in Japanese transliteration; born in Hanover, Germany, and studied chemistry in Göttingen. Introduced Western production, glazing, and firing techniques, especially in Nagasaki and Arita; lectured in Tôkyô and Kyôto.

waridakeshiki-noborigama 割竹式登窯
"Split bamboo kiln"; identical to *hebigama* (*hebi*, snake); single-vaulted, multichamber climbing kiln, a narrow precursor of the *renbôshiki-noborigama*, with lateral stoke holes and a honeycomb back wall to allow the smoke to escape. See also *noborigama.*

wax resist
See *rônuki.*

yaki 焼
Ceramics; suffix used in connection with a place or a name; general term for Japanese stoneware (*tôki, sekki*) or porcelain (*jiki*).

yakimono 焼物
General term for ceramics.

yakishime 焼き締め
High-fired, unglazed stoneware. See also **ceramics;** *sekki.*

yakumi-ire 薬味入れ
Spice jar.

yamachawan 山茶碗
Simple, unglazed stoneware bowl (or small plate) for food; mass produced in large areas of Japan from mid-twelfth century on.

yamato-e 大和絵
Traditional painting in Japanese style, with such subjects as the seasons or scenes in Heian-kyô (now Kyôto). Yamato is the old term for Japan—more precisely, the Japanese heartland in the region around Nara.

Yanagi Sôetsu (Muneyoshi) 柳宗悦
(1889–1961), philosopher and leader of the Japanese *mingei* (folk art) movement.

Yayoi ceramics, *yayoi-doki* 弥生土器
Smooth, thin-walled earthenware from the Yayoi period (ca. 300 B.C.–ca. A.D. 300).

Yi dynasty 李朝
Korean Choson, Yi or Ri dynasty (1392–1910), during which *mishima* and *hakeme* techniques evolved in ceramics, as did underglaze painting with cobalt blue and iron brown. *Mishima* and Ido tea bowls were highly esteemed among Japanese tea masters.

yô 窯
See *kama.*

yôhen 窯変
"Kiln change"; also *higawari,* "fire change." The interplay of flames and ash with alternating oxidation and reduction atmospheres during firing produces wide variations of color and surface texture.

yôhen-tenmoku 曜変天目
See *tenmoku.*

yô no bi 用の美
"Beauty in use." Signs of use, such as variations in glaze surface from tea in Hagi-*yaki* (22), for example, and visible repairs using gold lacquer, are valued and can raise the value of a pot. See also *sabi; wabi.*

yubikaki 指描き
Or *shitômon,* finger wipes; decorative technique in which a pattern is combed with the fingers in wet slip to reveal the clay beneath.

yunomi 湯呑み
Teacup.

yûri-kinsai 釉裏金彩
Underglaze gold decoration using gold leaf or gold powder covered by a clear glaze (see photo 144); in contrast to *kinsai,* where gold decoration is applied on the glaze.

yuteki-tenmoku 油滴天目
See *tenmoku.*

yuzamashi 湯冷まし
Water cooler; in preparing tea, vessel for cooling hot water to the optimum temperature (see photo 115). See also **sencha.**

zôgan 象嵌
Slip inlay; decorative technique in which an incised or stamped pattern on the leather-hard pot is filled with slip or clay of a different color; the pot is then covered with celadon or transparent glaze. Dates back to the Korean Yi dynasty (1392–1910).

BIBLIOGRAPHY

When possible, an approximate English translation has been provided in brackets for the titles of Japanese works. When useful to the reader, the language of publication has been added in parentheses.

General Literature

Akanuma, Taka, Ikutarô Itô, and Mabi Katayama. *Chôsen no tôji* [Korean ceramics]. Vol. 5 of *Yakimono meikan* [Ceramics compendium]. Tôkyô: Kôdansha, 2000. (Japanese)

Ayers, John, Oliver Impey, and J. V. G. Mallet. *Porcelain for Palaces: The Fashion for Japan in Europe, 1650–1750.* London: Oriental Ceramic Society, 1990.

Bowes, James Lord. *Japanese Marks and Seals: In Literature and the Arts.* Warren, CT: Floating World Editions, 2003.

Campbell, Alan, and David S. Noble, eds. *Japan: An Illustrated Encyclopedia, 2 vols.* Tôkyô: Kôdansha, 1993.

Choi-Bae, Soontaek, and Kurt Hangst. *Seladon-Keramik der Koryo-Dynastie 918–1392: Bestandskatalog des Museums für Ostasiatische Kunst der Stadt Köln* [Celadon ceramics of the Koryo dynasty 918–1392: Inventory catalog of the museum for East Asian art of the city Cologne]. Translated by Arthur J. Jordan. Cologne: Museum für Ostasiatische Kunst, 1984. (German)

Earle, Joe, Halsey North, and Alice North. *Contemporary Clay: Japanese Ceramics for the New Century.* Boston: MFA Publications, an imprint of the Museum of Fine Arts, Boston, 2005.

Egami, Namio. *The Beginnings of Japanese Art.* Vol. 2 of The Heibonsha Survey of Japanese Art. Translated by John Bester. New York: Weatherhill; Tôkyô: Heibonsha, 1973.

Elisseeff, Danielle. *Histoire du Japon: entre Chine et Pacifique* [History of Japan: between China and the Pacific]. Monaco: Éditions du Rocher, 2001. (French)

Fahr-Becker, Gabriele, ed. *Ostasiatische Kunst.* Cologne: Könemann Verlagsgesellschaft, 1998. (German)

Faulkner, Rupert. *Japanese Studio Crafts: Tradition and the Avant-Garde.* Philadelphia: University of Pennsylvania Press, 1995.

Gorham, Hazel H. *Japanese and Oriental Ceramics.* Tôkyô and Rutland, VT: Charles E. Tuttle, 1971.

Imamura, Keiji. *Prehistoric Japan: New Perspectives on Insular East Asia.* Honolulu: University of Hawai'i Press, 1996.

Impey, Oliver. *Japanese Export Porcelain: Catalogue of the Collection of the Ashmolean Museum, Oxford.* Amsterdam: Hotei Publishing, 2002.

Inoue, Kikuo, and Jûn'ichi Takeuchi. *Yôhen to yakishime tô* [Yohen and Yakishime stoneware]. Vol. 1 of *Yakimono meikan* [Ceramics compendium]. Tôkyô: Kôdansha, 1999. (Japanese)

Inoue, Kiyoshi. *Geschichte Japans* [History of Japan]. Frankfurt, New York: Campus Verlag, 1995. (German)

Jahn, Gisela. *Meiji Ceramics: The Art of Japanese Export Porcelain and Satsuma Ware 1868–1912.* Stuttgart: Arnoldsche, 2004.

Jahn, Gisela, and Anette Petersen-Brandhorst. *Erde und Feuer: Traditionelle japanische Keramik der Gegenwart* [Earth and Fire: Traditional Japanese ceramics of the present]. Edited by Stephan Fitz, Deutsches Museum München. Munich: Hirmer Verlag, 1984. (German)

Jenyns, Soame. *Japanese Porcelain.* London: Faber and Faber, 1965.

———. *Japanese Pottery.* London: Faber and Faber, 1971.

Kaneko, Kenji, et al., eds. *Modern Craft Art Japan: Works from the Crafts Gallery, The National Museum of Modern Art, Tôkyô.* Tôkyô: National Museum of Modern Art, 2002. (Japanese, English)

Kida, Takuya. *Modern Revival of Momoyama Ceramics: Turning Point Toward Modernization of Ceramics.* Exhibition catalog. Tôkyô: National Museum of Modern Art, 2002. (Japanese, English)

Kitaharu, Chiyo, Yukio Suzuta, and Yoshiaki Yabe. *Iro-e jiki* [Porcelain with overglaze painting]. Vol. 4 of *Yakimono meikan* [Ceramics compendium]. Tôkyô: Kôdansha, 1999. (Japanese)

Klein, Adalbert. *Japanische Keramik von der Jômon-Zeit bis zur Gegenwart* [Japanese ceramics from the Jômon Period to the present]. Munich: Hirmer Verlag, 1984. (German)

Kümmel, Otto. *Das Kunstgewerbe in Japan.* 3rd ed. Berlin: R. C. Schmidt & Co., 1922. (German)

Kyûshû Ceramic Museum. *Earth and Fire: The Historical Development of Kyûshû Ceramics.* Permament exhibition guide book. Arita: Kyûshû Ceramic Museum, 1996.

Leach, Bernard. *A Potter's Book.* London: Transatlantic Arts, 1970.

Leach, Bernard. *Hamada: Potter.* New York: Kôdansha International, 1975.

Marra, Michele. *Modern Japanese Aesthetics: A Reader.* Honolulu: University of Hawai'i Press, 1999.

Munsterberg, Hugo. *The Folk Arts of Japan.* Rutland, VT: Charles E. Tuttle, 1958.

———. *The Ceramic Art of Japan: A Handbook for Collectors.* Rutland, VT: Charles E. Tuttle, 1964.

National Museum of Modern Art, Tôkyô. *Japanese Painted Porcelain: Modern Masterpieces in Overglaze Enamel.* New York: Weatherhill; Tôkyô: Tankôsha, 1980.

Noma, Sawako, ed. *Yakimono meikan* [Ceramics compendium]. 6 vols. Tôkyô: Kôdansha, 1999–2000. Inoue, Kikuo, and Jûn'ichi Takeuchi. *Yôhen to yakishime tô* [Yohen and Yakishime stoneware]. Vol. 1, 1999. Yabe, Yoshiaki, Jun'ichi Takeuchi, and Yoshiaki Itô. *Momoyama no chatô* [Momoyama tea ceramics]. Vol. 2, 1999. Akanuma, Taka, and Kazunobu Nakanodô. *Raku to Kyô-yaki* [Raku ware and Kyô ware]. Vol. 3, 1999. Kitaharu, Chiyo, Yukio Suzuta, and Yoshiaki Yabe. *Iro-e jiki* [Porcelain with overglaze painting]. Vol. 4, 1999. Akanuma, Taka, Ikutarô Itô, and Mabi Katayama. *Chôsen no tôji* [Korean ceramics]. Vol. 5, 2000. Yabe, Yoshiaki, and Atsushi Imai. *Chûgoku no tôji* [Chinese ceramics]. Vol. 6, 2000. (Japanese)

Pearson, Richard. *Ancient Japan.* Washington, DC: Arthur M. Sackler Gallery, 1992.

Pitelka, Morgan. *Handmade Culture: Raku Potters, Patrons, and Tea Practitioners in Japan.* Honolulu: University of Hawai'i Press, 2005.

Saint-Gilles, Amaury. *Earth 'n' Fire: A Survey Guide to Contemporary Japanese Ceramics.* 4th ed. Tôkyô: Shufunotomo, 1978.

Sanders, Herbert. *The World of Japanese Ceramics.* Tôkyô: Kôdansha, 1968.

Schiffer, Nancy N., ed. *Japanese Export Ceramics: 1860–1920.* Atglen, PA: Schiffer Publishing, 2000.

Schulenburg, Stephan von der, ed. *The Fascination of Ceramics: Masterpieces of Modern Japanese Pottery from the Gisela Freudenberg Collection.* Cologne: Museum für Angewandte Kunst Frankfurt, Wienand Verlag, 2005. (German, English)

Shimizu, Christine. "La Poterie Jômon: La Plus Ancienne Céramique au Monde." *Revue de la Céramique et du Verre* 102 (1998): 12–17. (French)

Shimizu, Christine. *Le Grès Japonais.* Paris: Éditions Charles Massin, 2001. (French)

———. *La Porcelaine Japonaise.* Paris: Éditions Charles Massin, 2002. (French)

Sôshitsu XV, Sen. *The Japanese Way of Tea: From its Origins in China to Sen Rikyû.* Translated by V. Dixon Morris. Honolulu: University of Hawai'i Press, 1998.

Tagai, Hideo. *Japanese Ceramics.* No. 33 of *Hoikusha's Color Books Series.* Higashi-Ôsaka: Hoikusha Publishing Co., 2002.

Wood, Nigel. *Chinese Glazes: Their Origin, Chemistry and Recreation.* London: A&C Black Publishers; Philadelphia: University of Pennsylvania Press, 1999.

Yabe, Yoshiaki, and Atsushi Imai. *Chûgoku no tôji* [Chinese ceramics]. Vol. 6 of *Yakimono meikan* [Ceramics compendium]. Tôkyô: Kôdansha, 2000. (Japanese)

Yabe, Yoshiaki, et al., eds. *Kadokawa Nihon tôji dai-jiten* [Kadokawa, the Encyclopedia of Japanese Ceramics]. Tôkyô: Kadokawa Shoten Publishing, 2002. (Japanese)

Yabe, Yoshiaki, Jun'ichi Takeuchi, and Yoshiaki Itô. *Momoyama no chatô* [Momoyama tea ceramics]. Vol. 2 of *Yakimono meikan* [Ceramics compendium]. Tôkyô: Kôdansha, 1999. (Japanese)

Yanagi, Sôetsu. *The Unknown Craftsman: A Japanese Insight into Beauty.* Edited by Bernard Leach. Tôkyô: Kôdansha, 1972.

Yellin, Robert. *Ode to Japanese Pottery: Sake Cups and Flasks.* Tôkyô: Coherence, Inc., 2004.

Techniques

Furutani, Michio. *Anagama: Building Kilns and Firing.* Translated by Shiori Noro. Edited by Odin Maxwell and Dick Lehman. Bellingham, WA: Anagama-West, 2006. Originally published as *Anagama* (Tôkyô: Rkogakusha, 1994).

Itabashi, Hiromi, Roppo Tamura, and Naoki Kawabuchi. *Building Your Own Kiln: Three Japanese Potters Give Advice and Instructions.* Translated by Lucy North. Tôkyô: Kôdansha, 2003.

Lancet, Marc, and Masakazu Kusakabe. *Japanese Wood-Fired Ceramics.* Iola, WI: Krause Publications, 2005.

Olsen, Frederick L. *The Kiln Book.* Bassett, CA: Keramos Books, 1973.

Ônishi, Masatarô. *Tôgei no yûyaku* [Ceramic glazes]. Tôkyô: Rikôgakusha, 1981. (Japanese)

———. *Tôgei no dentô gihô* [Traditional ceramics techniques]. Tôkyô: Rikôgakusha, 1982. (Japanese)

———. *Tôgei no tsuchi to kama yaki* [Clay and kiln firing in ceramics]. Tôkyô: Rikôgakusha, 1983. (Japanese)

Sanders, Herbert H., in collaboration with Tomimoto Kenkichi. *Töpfern in Japan: Zeitgenössische japanische Keramik.* Bonn-Röttgen: Hörnemann Verlag, 1977. (German)

Simpson, Penny, et al. *The Japanese Pottery Handbook.* Tôkyô: Kôdansha, 1979.

Tichane, Robert. *Those Celadon Blues.* Painted Post, NY: New York State Glaze Institute, 1983.

———. *Ash Glazes.* Painted Post, NY: New York State Glaze Institute, 1987.

———. *Clay Bodies.* Painted Post, NY: New York State Glaze Institute, 1990.

Wilson, Richard. *Inside Japanese Ceramics: A Primer of Materials, Techniques and Traditions.* New York: Weatherhill, 1995.

Literature on Individual Kilns

AIZU-HONGÔ

Houton, Janel. "Introduction to Tôhoku Ceramics." *Daruma* 29 (2001): 36–46.

Mizuno, Hiroshi. *Famous Ceramics of Japan.* Vol. 3 of *Folk Kilns I.* Tôkyô, New York, San Francisco: Kôdansha, 1981.

AGANO

Môri, Shigeki, ed. *Agano-yaki yonhyaku-nen* [The Agano ware 400 years].

Shôgakukan. *Agano-yaki, Koishiwara-yaki, Onta-yaki.* Vol. 20 of *Yakimono o tanoshimu* [Enjoy Ceramics]. Tôkyô: Shôgakukan, 2003. (Japanese)

ARITA

Doi, Kunio. *Fourteenth Red: Sakaida Kakiemon XIV.* Fukuoka: Kataribe Bunko, 1993.

Impey, Oliver. *The Early Porcelain Kilns of Japan: Arita in the First Half of the Seventeenth Century.* Oxford: Clarendon Press; New York: Oxford University Press, 1996.

Museo Internazionale delle Ceramiche in Faenza [International Museum of Ceramics in Faenza]. *JIKI: Porcellana giapponese tra Oriente e Occidente 1610–1760* [Jiki: Japanese porcelain between East and West 1610–1760]. Exhibition catalog. Milano: Electa, 2004. (Italian, English)

Nagatake, Takeshi. *Classic Japanese Porcelain: Imari and Kakiemon.* Tôkyô, New York, London: Kôdansha, 2003.

Nagatake, Takeshi, and Mutsuo Yamaguchi. *Arita.* No. 2 of *Nihon no yakimono* [Japanese ceramics]. Kyôto: Tankôsha, 1986. (Japanese)

Ôhashi, Kôji. *Kamabetsu gaido: Nihon no yakimono, Arita, Imari* [Kiln site guide: Japanese ceramics, Arita, Imari]. Kyôto: Tankôsha, 2002. (Japanese)

Saga-Shinbunsha. *Saga no kamamoto meguri: Imari, Arita* [Tour of the Saga kilns: Imari, Arita]. Saga: Saga-Shinbunsha, 2002. (Japanese)

Shimizu, Christine. "La Porcelaine d'Arita: Une Tradition Face au III, Millénaire." *Revue de la Céramique et du Verre* 112 (2000): 18–23. (French)

Shôgakukan. *Arita-yaki, Imari-yaki.* Vol. 1 of *Yakimono o tanoshimu* [Enjoy ceramics]. Tôkyô: Shôgakukan, 2003. (Japanese)

Tanigawa, Tetsuzô, and Kôsei Kawabata, eds. *Kakiemon.* No. 9 of *Nihon no tôji* [Japanese ceramics]. Tôkyô: Chûôkôronsha, 1988. (Japanese)

———. *Ko-Imari.* No. 8 of *Nihon no tôji* [Japanese ceramics]. Tôkyô: Chûôkôronsha, 1989. (Japanese)

Ueda, Katsumi, ed. *Imaizumi Imaemon XIII.* Tôkyô: Nihon-Keizai-Shinbunsha, 1998. (Japanese)

ASAHI

Matsubayashi, Mitoko. *Uji Asahi-yaki: dentô o mirai ni takushite—The Asahi pottery in Uji: Tradition in trust for the future.* Kyôto: Asahi Pottery, 1991. (Japanese)

Mitsukoshi. *Asahi-yaki jûgo-sei, Matsubayashi Hôsai satô-ten* [Asahi-yaki 15th generation, Matsubayashi Hôsai's exhibition of tea ceramics]. Kyôto: Mitsukoshi, 1998. (Japanese)

BIZEN

Chang, Beatrice, and Patricia Pelehach. "Bizen: A Living Tradition." *Ceramics: Art and Perception* 38 (1999): 90–92.

Jôsai, Setsuo. *Kamabetsu gaido: Nihon no yakimono, Bizen* [Kiln site guide: Japanese ceramics, Bizen]. Kyôto: Tankôsha, 2002. (Japanese)

Sanyô-Shinbunsha. *Bizen-yaki sakka, kamamoto meikan* [Bizen potters, workshop compendium]. Okayama: Sanyô-Shinbunsha, 2003. (Japanese)

Shimizu, Christine. "Bizen: Cordes de Feu. Mille Ans de Céramique Japonaise." *Revue de la Céramique et du Verre* 96 (1997): 10–15. (French)

Tanigawa, Tetsuzô, and Kôsei Kawabata, eds. *Nihon no tôji* [Japanese ceramics]. No. 6, Bizen. Tôkyô: Chûôkôronsha, 1989. (Japanese)

Yagyû, Takashi. *Bizen yamamoto tôshû* [Traditional Bizen ceramics]. Okayama: Sanyô-Shinbunsha, 1995. (Japanese)

———. Sanyô-Shinbunsha. *Yakimono Bizen* [Bizen ceramics]. Okayama: Sanyô-Shinbunsha, 1999. (Japanese)

Yellin, Robert L. "Bizen okimono." [Bizen: figural ceramics]. *Daruma* 31 (2001): 43–50. (English)

ECHIZEN

Shôgakukan. *Echizen-yaki.* Vol. 15 of *Yakimono o tanoshimu* [Enjoy ceramics]. Tôkyô: Shôgakukan, 2003. (Japanese)

Takahara, Saneyuki. *Echizen yakimono kikô* [Echizen potters]. Fukui-ken: Echizen Yakimono Kikô Henshû-I'inkai, 1993. (Japanese)

Wood, Donald Alan. *Echizen: Eight Hundred Years of Japanese Stoneware.* Exhibition catalog. Birmingham, AL: Birmingham Museum of Art, 1994.

HAGI

Ishizaki, Yasuyuki. *Kamabetsu gaido: Nihon no yakimono, Hagi* [Kiln site guide: Japanese ceramics, Hagi]. Kyôto: Tankôsha, 2002. (Japanese)

Kôno, Ryôsuke. *Hagi-yaki 400-nen-ten: dentô to kakushin* [400 years of Hagi-yaki: tradition and innovation]. Fukuoka: Asahi-Shinbunsha, 2001. (Japanese)

Sakata, Deika. *Hagi.* No. 12 of *Nihon no tôji* [Japanese ceramics]. Color books, no. 459. Ôsaka: Hoikusha, 1994. (Japanese)

Shôgakukan. *Hagi-yaki.* Vol. 10 of *Yakimono o tanoshimu* [Enjoy ceramics]. Tôkyô: Shôgakukan, 2003. (Japanese)

Yoshiga, Taibi, and Noriyuki Kôyama. *Hagi.* No. 4 of *Nihon no yakimono* [Japanese ceramics]. Kyôto: Tankôsha, 1986. (Japanese)

HASAMI

Hasami-*yaki* 400-nen-sai Jikkô-I'inkai. *Hasami-yaki 400-nen no ayumi* [Journey through 400 years of Hasami-*yaki*]. Hasami: Hasami-*yaki* 400-nen-sai Jikkô-I'inkai, 1999. (Japanese)

Kittel, Hubert. *Masahiro Mori: Zeitgenössisches Porzellandesign aus Japan.* Exhibition catalog. Hohenberg/Eger: Deutsches Porzellan Museum, 2000. (German)

Mori, Masahiro, ed. *Yakimono kôen—Ceramics Park.* Hasami: Seibundô, 1997. (Japanese, English)

HIRASHIMIZU

Houton, Janel. "Introduction to Tôhoku Ceramics." *Daruma* 29 (2001): 36–46.

IGA

Ôtsuki, Noriko. *Kamabetsu gaido: Nihon no yakimono, Shigaraki, Iga* [Kiln site guide: Japanese ceramics, Shigaraki, Iga]. Kyôto: Tankôsha, 2003. (Japanese)

Shôgakukan. *Iga-yaki.* No. 14 of *Yakimono o tanoshimu* [Enjoy ceramics]. Tôkyô: Shôgakukan, 2003. (Japanese)

Tanigawa, Tetsuzô, and Kôsei Kawabata, eds. *Iga, Shigaraki, Tanba.* No. 7 of *Nihon no tôji* [Japanese ceramics]. Tôkyô: Chûôkôronsha, 1988. (Japanese)

IMARI

Le Gars, Georges. *Imari: Histoire d'un Style: Faiences et Porcelaine du Japon, de Chine et de l'Europe.* Paris: Massin, 2004. (French)

Ôhashi, Kôji. *Kamabetsu gaido: Nihon no yakimono, Arita, Imari* [Kiln site guide: Japanese ceramics, Arita, Imari]. Kyôto: Tankôsha, 2002. (Japanese)

Rotondo-McCord, Lisa, and Peter James Bufton. *Imari: Japanese Porcelain for European Palaces.* New Orleans: New Orleans Museum of Art, 1997.

Saga-Shinbunsha. *Saga no kamamoto meguri, Imari, Arita* [Tour of Saga kilns, Imari, Arita]. Saga: Saga-Shinbunsha, 2002. (Japanese)

Shimizu, Christine. "La Porcelaine de Nabeshima: Un Art Seigneurial du Japon." *Revue de la Céramique et du Verre* 79 (1994): 12–17. (French)

Tanigawa, Tetsuzô, and Kôsei Kawabata, eds. *Nabeshima.* No. 10 of *Nihon no tôji* [Japanese ceramics]. Tôkyô: Chûôkôronsha, 1988. (Japanese)

INKYÛZAN

Ashizawa, Yoshinori IX. *Tottori-jô oniwa-yaki: Inkyûzan-yaki meihinsen* [Tottori-*oniwa* kilns: Inkyûzan-*yaki* masterpieces]. Kôge: Inkyûzan-*yaki* Kamamoto, 2001. (Japanese)

IZUSHI

Shôgakukan. *Banko-yaki, Izushi-yaki.* No. 10 of *Yakimono o tanoshimu* [Enjoy ceramics]. Tôkyô: Shôgakukan, 2003. (Japanese)

KARATSU

Becker, O. S. B. Johanna. *Karatsu Ware: A Tradition of Diversity*. Tôkyô, New York, San Francisco: Kôdansha, 1986.

Nakazato, Tarouemon XIII. *The Karatsu Ceramics of Japan*. Karatsu: Kyûryûdô, 1979.

——. *Karatsu*. Vol. 9 of *Famous Ceramics of Japan*. Tôkyô: Kôdansha, 1983.

——. *Karatsu*. No. 3 of *Nihon no yakimono* [Japanese ceramics]. Kyôto: Tankôsha, 1986. (Japanese)

Ôhashi, Kôji. *Kamabetsu gaido: Nihon no yakimono, Karatsu* [Kiln site guide: Japanese ceramics, Karatsu]. Kyôto: Tankôsha, 2003. (Japanese)

Shôgakukan. *Karatsu-yaki*. Vol. 3 of *Yakimono o tanoshimu* [Enjoy ceramics]. Tôkyô: Shôgakukan, 2003. (Japanese)

Tanigawa, Tetsuzô, and Kôsei Kawabata, eds. *Karatsu*. No. 5 of *Nihon no tôji* [Japanese ceramics]. Tôkyô: Chûôkôronsha, 1989. (Japanese)

KASAMA

Aoki, Hiroshi. *Kamabetsu gaido: Nihon no yakimono, Mashiko, Kasama* [Kiln site guide: Japanese ceramics, Mashiko, Kasama]. Kyôto: Tankôsha, 2002. (Japanese)

Mizuno, Hiroshi. *Folk Kilns I*. Vol. 3 of *Famous Ceramics of Japan*. Tôkyô, New York, San Francisco: Kôdansha, 1981.

Nodera, Fumio, ed. *Yakimono* [Ceramics]. Tôkyô: Seitôsha, 1998. (Japanese)

Shôgakukan. *Kasama-yaki*. Vol. 11 of *Yakimono o tanoshimu* [Enjoy ceramics]. Tôkyô: Shôgakukan, 2003. (Japanese)

KIRIGOME

Miyazaki-shi Furusato Tôgeikan. *Sai Kirigome: Kirigome-yaki iro-yû no bi* [Sai Kirigome: the beauty of colored glazes]. Exhibition catalog. Miyazaki: Miyazaki-shi Furusato Tôgeikan, 1994. (Japanese)

KOISHIWARA

Koishiwara-mura Kyôiku I'inkai. *Koishiwara yakimono no ayumi* [A journey through Koishiwara ceramics]. Koishiwara: Koishiwara-yaki Tôki Kyôdô-kumiai, 2001. (Japanese)

Shôgakukan. *Agano-yaki, Koishiwara-yaki, Onta-yaki*. Vol. 20 of *Yakimono o tanoshimu* [Enjoy ceramics]. Tôkyô: Shôgakukan, 2003. (Japanese)

KUTANI

Bouvier, Georges. "19th Century Kutani Porcelain." *Daruma* 39 (2003): 35–46.

Ishikawa-ken Kutani Tôjiki Shôkôgyô Kyôdô-kumiai Rengô-kai. *Kutani-yaki: rekidai no sakuhin de tsuzuru Kutani-yaki no rekishi* [History of Kutani-*yaki*: The work of the generation cycle]. Terai: Ishikawa-ken Kutani Tôjiki Shôkôgyô Kyôdô-kumiai Rengô-kai, 1997. (Japanese)

Kitade, Fujio, and Kenzô Yamamoto. *Kutani*. No. 10 of *Nihon no yakimono* [Japanese ceramics]. Kyôto: Tankôsha, 1986. (Japanese)

Shôgakukan. *Kutani-yaki*. Vol. 2 of *Yakimono o tanoshimu* [Enjoy ceramics]. Tôkyô: Shôgakukan, 2003. (Japanese)

Tanigawa, Tetsuzô, and Kôsei Kawabata, eds. *Ko-Kutani*. No. 11 of *Nihon no tôji* [Japanese ceramics]. Tôkyô: Chûôkôronsha, 1989. (Japanese)

Terai-machi Kutani-*yaki* Shiryôkan. *Aka-e kô: 1998 kikaku ten, aka-e saibyô no sekai* [The skill of *Aka-e*: 1998 project exhibition, the world of *aka-e saibyô*]. Terai: Terai-machi Kutani-*yaki* Shiryôkan, 1998. (Japanese)

Terao, Kenichi. *Kamabetsu gaido: Nihon no yakimono, Kutani* [Kiln site guide: Japanese ceramics, Kutani]. Kyôto: Tankôsha, 2003. (Japanese)

KYÔTO WITH KIYOMIZU

Akanuma, Taka, and Kazunobu Nakanodô. *Raku to Kyô-yaki* [Raku ware and Kyô ware]. Vol. 3 of *Yakimono meikan* [Ceramics compendium]. Tôkyô: Kôdansha, 1999. (Japanese)

Hayashiya, Seizo, Taka Akanuma, and Raku Kichizaemon XV. *Raku: Una Dinastia di Ceramisti Giapponesi*. Exhibition catalog. Museo Internazionale delle Ceramiche in Faenza e Raku Museum. Turin, London: Umberto Allemandi, 1997. (Italian)

Kawahara, Masahiro. *The Ceramic Art of Ogata Kenzan*. Tôkyô, New York, San Francisco: Kôdansha, 1985.

Oka, Keiko. *Kamabetsu gaido: Nihon no yakimono, Kyôto* [Kiln site guide: Japanese ceramics, Kyôto]. Kyôto: Tankôsha, 2003. (Japanese)

Shôgakukan. *Kyô-yaki*. Vol. 3 of *Yakimono o tanoshimu* [Enjoy ceramics]. Tôkyô: Shôgakukan, 2003. (Japanese)

Taki, Tôru, ed. *Kyoto Potters I, II*. Vols. 76, 77 of *Tô: The Best Selection of Contemporary Ceramics in Japan*. Kyôto: Kyôto-shoin, 1993. (Japanese, English)

Tanigawa, Tetsuzô, and Kôsei Kawabata, eds. *Ninsei, Kenzan*. No. 12 of *Nihon no tôji* [Japanese ceramics]. Tôkyô: Chûôkôronsha, 1989. (Japanese)

Tanigawa, Tetsuzô, and Kôsei Kawabata, eds. *Kyô-yaki*. No. 13 of *Nihon no tôji* [Japanese ceramics]. Tôkyô: Chûôkôronsha, 1989. (Japanese)

——. *Raku-daidai: Tamamizu-yaki, Ôhi-yaki*. No. 14 of *Nihon no tôji* [Japanese ceramics]. Tôkyô: Chûôkôronsha, 1989. (Japanese)

MASHIKO

Aoki, Hiroshi. *Kamabetsu gaido: Nihon no yakimono, Mashiko, Kasama* [Kiln site guide: Japanese ceramics, Mashiko, Kasama]. Kyôto: Tankôsha, 2002. (Japanese)

Birks, Tony, and Cornelia Wingfield Digby. *Bernard Leach, Hamada and their Circle*. Marston Magna, Yeovil, Somerset: Marston House, 1992.

Jahn, Gisela, and Anette Petersen-Brandhorst. *Shimaoka Tatsuzô*. Exhibition catalog, Städtische Kunsthalle Mannheim. Munich: Verlag Fred Jahn, 1987. (German)

Longenecker, Martha, ed. *Ceramics of Shimaoka Tatsuzô: Living National Treasure of Japan, A Retrospective*. San Diego: Mingei International Museum, 2000.

Patocchi, Luca, ed. *Shimaoka Tatsuzô: Ceramiche, una Collezione Privata—Pottery, a private collection*. Lugano: Fondazione Galleria Gottardo, 1999. (Italian)

Shimono-Shinbunsha. *Dai 40-kai kinen Shimaoka Tatsuzô tôgyô-ten* [40th exhibition: Ceramics by Tatsuzô Shimaoka]. Matsuya ginza exhibition catalog. Tôkyô: Shimono-Shinbunsha, 2003. (Japanese)

Shôgakukan. *Mashiko-yaki*. Vol. 5 of *Yakimono o tanoshimu* [Enjoy ceramics]. Tôkyô: Shôgakukan, 2003. (Japanese)

Yoshida, Kôzô, et al. *The Retrospective Exhibition of Shôji Hamada*. Exhibition catalog. National Museum of Modern Art, Tôkyô. Tôkyô: Nihon-Keizai-Shinbun, 1977.

MIKAWACHI

Commerce, Industry and Labor Division Economic Department. *History and Points of Mikawachi Ceramics: A Tour of Kiln Owners of Mikawachi, Sarayama-zanmai*. Sasebo: Commerce, Industry and Labor Division Economic Department, 1996.

Lawrence, Louis. *Hirado: Prince of Porcelains*. Encyclopedia of Japanese Art Series. Chicago: Art Media Resources, 1997.

Takeguchi, Momoko. "Hirado Porcelain." *Daruma* 14 (1997): 36–42.

MINO

Arakawa, Toyozô, et al. *Mino*. No. 9 of *Nihon no yakimono* [Japanese ceramics]. Kyôto: Tankôsha, 1987. (Japanese)

Barriskill, Janet. *Visiting the Mino Kilns: With a Translation of Arakawa Toyozô's "The Traditions and Techniques of Mino Pottery."* Sydney: Wild Peony, 1995.

Karatsu, Masahiro, and Yoshiaki Itô. *Kamabetsu gaido: Nihon no yakimono, Mino* [Kiln site guide: Japanese ceramics, Mino]. Kyôto: Tankôsha, 2003. (Japanese)

Kuroda, Ryôji. *Shino*. Vol. 12 of *Famous Ceramics of Japan*. Tôkyô, New York, San Francisco: Kôdansha, 1984.

Kuroda, Ryôji, and Takeshi Murayama. *Classic Stoneware of Japan: Shino and Oribe*. Tôkyô: Kôdansha, 2002.

Museum of Fine Arts. *Oribe: Special Exhibition for the 15th Anniversary of the Museum of Fine Arts, Gifu*. Exhibition catalog. Gifu: Museum of Fine Arts, 1997. (Japanese, English)

Shôgakukan. *Mino-yaki*. Vol. 7 of *Yakimono o tanoshimu* [Enjoy ceramics]. Tôkyô: Shôgakukan, 2003. (Japanese)

Tanigawa, Tetsuzô, and Kôsei Kawabata, eds. *Kiseto, Setoguro*. No. 3 of *Nihon no tôji* [Japanese ceramics]. Tôkyô: Chûôkôronsha, 1988. (Japanese)

———. *Oribe*. No. 4 of *Nihon no tôji* [Japanese ceramics]. Tôkyô: Chûôkôronsha, 1988. (Japanese)

———. *Shino*. No. 2 of *Nihon no tôji* [Japanese ceramics]. Tôkyô: Chûôkôronsha, 1988. (Japanese)

MUMYÔI

Mitsukoshi. *Miura Koheiji seiji-ten* [Exhibition of Koheiji Miura's celadons]. Exhibition catalog. Niigata: Mitsukoshi, 1993. (Japanese)

Mitsukoshi. *Watanabe Tôzô ten* [Exhibition of Tôzô Watanabe]. Exhibition catalog. Niigata: Mitsukoshi, 1992. (Japanese)

Niigata-Nippôsha. *Jûyô mukei bunkazai hojisha (ningen kokuhô) nintei tokubetsu kinen-ten-mumyôi godai Itô Sekisui ten* [Exhibition for the designation as a Living National Treasure; Mumyôi Sekisui V Itô]. Exhibition catalog. Niigata: Niigata-Nippôsha, 2003. (Japanese)

ÔBORI SÔMA

See **Aizu-Hongô**

ÔHI

Adachi, Kenji, ed. *Ôhi Toshirô sakuhin-shû* [Work of Toshirô Ôhi]. Tôkyô: Kôdansha, 1985. (Japanese)

Ôhi, Chôzaemon X. *Ôhi Chôzaemon-gama no tôgei* [The ceramic art of the Chôzaemon Ôhi kiln]. Kyôto: Tankôsha, 2001. (Japanese)

Ôhi, Toshio. *Shinseiki-ten*, "New Vessels for the New Century, 2001." Exhibition catalog. Ôsaka Takashimaya / JR Nagoya: Takashimaya, 2001.(Japanese)

ONTA

Nagata, Akihiko. *Onta-yaki: sukoyaka na mintô no bi* [Onta-yaki: the unspoiled beauty of folk art]. Tôkyô: Geisôdô, 1998. (Japanese)

Shôgakukan. *Agano-yaki, Koishiwara-yaki, Onta-yaki*. Vol. 20 of *Yakimono o tanoshimu* [Enjoy ceramics]. Tôkyô: Shôgakukan, 2003. (Japanese)

ÔTANI

Okamura, Kichiemon. *Folk Kilns II*. Vol. 4 of *Famous Ceramics of Japan*. Tôkyô, New York, San Francisco: Kôdansha, 1981.

Shôgakukan. *Tobe-yaki, Ôtani-yaki*. Vol. 18 of *Yakimono o tanoshimu* [Enjoy ceramics]. Tôkyô: Shôgakukan, 2003. (Japanese)

Yano Kan'ichi Kôenkai. *Yano Kan'ichi sakutô-shû* [Collection of the works of Kan'ichi Yano]. Naruto-shi, Ôasa-chô Ôtani: Yano Kan'ichi Kôenkai, 1993. (Japanese)

RYÛMONJI

Minami-Nihon-Shinbun Kaihatsu-sentâ Henshû-bu. *Kagoshima no kamamoto meguri* [Tour of the Kagoshima kilns]. Kagoshima: Minami-Nihon-Shinbunsha, 1998. (Japanese)

SATSUMA

Chin, Jukan XIV. *Rankô senri-Chin Jukan-ke rekidai denseihin shûzôko zuroku* [Catalog of the private museum of Jukan Chin dynasty]. Miyama: Chinjukan-gama, 2002. (Japanese)

Chin, Jukan, and Yashiki Hisamitsu. *Satsuma*. No. 1 of *Nihon no yakimono* [Japanese ceramics]. Kyôto: Tankôsha, 1987. (Japanese)

Minami-Nihon-Shinbun Kaihatsu-sentâ Henshû-bu. *Kagoshima no kamamoto meguri* [Tour of the Kagoshima kilns]. Kagoshima: Minami-Nihon-Shinbunsha, 1998. (Japanese)

Schiffer, Nancy N. *Imari, Satsuma and Other Japanese Export Ceramics*. Atglen, Pennsylvania: Schiffer Publishing, 1997. (Japanese)

Shôgakukan. *Satsuma-yaki*. Vol.16 of *Yakimono o tanoshimu* [Enjoy ceramics]. Tôkyô: Shôgakukan, 2003.

Watanabe, Yoshiro. *Kamabetsu gaido: Nihon no yakimono, Satsuma* [Kiln site guide: Japanese ceramics, Satsuma]. Kyôto: Tankôsha, 2003. (Japanese)

SETO WITH AKAZU

Asada, Kazuyoshi. "Aperçu de la Céramique de Seto à l'Occasion du Colloque au Musée Guimet." *La Revue de la Céramique et du Verre* 85 (1995): 12–15. (French)

Karatsu, Masahiro. *Kamabetsu gaido: Nihon no yakimono, Seto* [Kiln site guide: Japanese ceramics, Seto]. Kyôto: Tankôsha, 2003. (Japanese)

Katô, Tôkurô, and Kiyoshi Fujikawa. *Seto*. No. 8 of *Nihon no yakimono* [Japanese ceramics]. Kyôto: Tankôsha, 1986. (Japanese)

Shôgakukan. *Seto-yaki.* Vol. 9 of *Yakimono o tanoshimu* [Enjoy ceramics]. Tôkyô: Shôgakukan, 2003. (Japanese)

Takatoshi, Misugi. "Origins of Seto Blue and White." *Daruma* 28 (2000): 36–46.

Tanigawa, Tetsuzô, and Kôsei Kawabata, eds. *Seto, Mino.* No. 3 of *Nihon no tôji* [Japanese ceramics]. Tôkyô: Chûôkôronsha, 1989. (Japanese)

Verlag Galerie Fred Jahn. *Mizuno Hanjirô: Keramik.* Exhibition catalog. Munich: Verlag Galerie Fred Jahn, 1986. (German)

SHIGARAKI

Cort, Louise Allison. *Shigaraki, Potter's Valley.* Tôkyô, New York, San Francisco: Kôdansha, 1979.

Hirano, Toshizô, and Kiyonori Konma. *Shigaraki, Iga.* No. 7 of *Nihon no yakimono* [Japanese ceramics]. Kyôto: Tankôsha, 1986. (Japanese)

Shôgakukan. *Shigaraki-yaki.* Vol. 6 of *Yakimono o tanoshimu* [Enjoy ceramics]. Tôkyô: Shôgakukan, 2003. (Japanese)

Tanigawa, Tetsuzô, and Kôsei Kawabata, eds. *Iga, Shigaraki, Tanba.* No. 7 of *Nihon no tôji* [Japanese ceramics]. Tôkyô: Chûôkôronsha, 1988. (Japanese)

SHÔDAI

Fukuda-Chabert, Simon, and Loui Fukuda. *Shôdai Mizuho-gama: Gefäßkunst.* Exhibition catalog. Braunschweig: Städt. Museum, 1998. (German)

SÔMA KOMA

Houton, Janel. "Introduction to Tôhoku Ceramics." *Daruma* 29 (2001): 36–46.

Gendai Kikakushitsu. *Ceramics of the Tôhoku Region since the Edo Period.* Tôhoku Modern Pottery and Porcelain Museum: Gendai Kikakushitsu, 1987.

SUZU

Yoshioka, Koyô, ed. *Suzu no meitô* [Suzu masterpieces]. Suzu-shi: Suzu-yaki Shiryôkan, 1989. (Japanese)

TAKATORI

Maske, Andrew. "The Continental Origins of Takatori Ware: The Introduction of Korean Potters and Technology to Japan through the Invasions of 1592–1598." *Transactions of the Asiatic Society of Japan,* 4th ser., vol. 9 (Yushodo Publishers, 1994): 43–61.

Takatori, Seizan. *Takatori-ke monjo* [Takatori family documents]. Tôkyô: Yûzankaku-Shuppan, 1979. (Japanese)

TAKEO

Saga-Shinbunsha. *Saga no kamamoto meguri: Karatsu, Takeo, Ureshino, Yamauchi.* [Tour of the Saga kilns: Karatsu, Takeo, Ureshino, Yamauchi]. Saga: Saga-Shinbunsha, 2002. (Japanese)

TANBA

Nakanishi, Tôru. *Ko-Tanba meihin-shû* [Old Tanba, collection of masterpieces]. Kawara-machi: Tanba-Kotôkan, 1989. (Japanese)

Narazaki, Shôichi. *Tanba.* No. 11 of *Nihon tôji senshû* [Anthology of Japanese ceramics]. Tôkyô: Chûôkôronsha, 1977. (Japanese)

Rhodes, Daniel. *Tamba Pottery: The Timeless Art of a Japanese Village.* Tôkyô: Kôdansha, 1970.

Shôgakukan. *Tanba-yaki.* Vol. 17 of *Yakimono o tanoshimu* [Enjoy ceramics]. Tôkyô: Shôgakukan, 2003. (Japanese)

Takeguchi, Momoko. "*Tanba Tachikui yaki no nagare.*" [Tanba ware: history of Tanba ware]. Abridged from a publication by Noboru Ôgami. *Daruma* 4 (1994): 31–35.

Tanigawa, Tetsuzô, and Kôsei Kawabata, eds. *Iga, Shigaraki, Tanba.* No. 7 of *Nihon no tôji* [Japanese ceramics]. Tôkyô: Chûôkôronsha, 1988. (Japanese)

TOBE

Shôgakukan. *Tobe-yaki, Ôtani-yaki.* Vol. 18 of *Yakimono o tanoshimu* [Enjoy ceramics]. Tôkyô: Shôgakukan, 2003. (Japanese)

Tobe-chô Kyôiku-l'inkai. *Tobe-yaki no shiori* [Guide to Tobe-yaki]. Tobe-chô: Tobe-chô Kyôiku-l'inkai, 1998. (Japanese)

TOKONAME

Akabane, Ichirô, and Katsuichi Onoda. *Tokoname—Atsumi, Nihon tôji senshû* [Tokoname—Atsumi, anthology of Japanese ceramics]. Vol. 8. Tôkyô: Chûôkôronsha, 1977. (Japanese)

Shôgakukan. *Tokoname-yaki.* Vol. 12 of *Yakimono o tanoshimu* [Enjoy ceramics]. Tôkyô: Shôgakukan, 2003. (Japanese)

Tokoname Shiritsu Tôgei Kenkyûjo. *Ningen kokuhô sandai Yamada Jôzan ten* [Exhibition Jôzan III Yamada, Living National Treasure]. Exhibition catalog. Tokoname: Tokoname Shiritsu Tôgei Kenkyûjo, 1999. (Japanese)

Tokoname-shi Kyôiku-l'inkai. *Tokubetsu-ten: Tokoname-yaki 900-nen no nagare* [900 years of Tokoname-yaki]. Exhibition catalog. Tokoname: Tokoname-shi Kyôiku-l'inkai, 1990. (Japanese)

TSUBOYA

Okamura, Kichiemon. *Folk Kilns II.* Vol. 4 of *Famous Ceramics of Japan.* Tôkyô, New York, San Francisco: Kôdansha, 1981.

Shôgakukan. *Tsuboya-yaki.* Vol. 13 of *Yakimono o tanoshimu* [Enjoy ceramics]. Tôkyô: Shôgakukan, 2003. (Japanese)

Tsuboya Pottery Museum. *Guidebook of the Permanent Exhibitions.* Naha: Naha Municipal Tsuboya Pottery Museum, 2000.

TSUTSUMI

Okamura, Kichiemon. *Folk Kilns II.* Vol. 4 of *Famous Ceramics of Japan.* Tôkyô, New York, San Francisco: Kôdansha, 1981.

UTSUTSUGAWA

Gagyû Tôgei Kabushiki-gaisha. *Magic of Earth and Fire: The Yokoishi Gagyû Collection.* Sasebo: Gagyû Tôgei Kabushiki-gaisha, 1998. (Japanese)

YOKKAICHI BANKO

Banko Tôgei Kyôkai. *Yokkaichi Banko tôgei kyôkai: sakka to sakuhin* [Artists and works of Banko art association]. Yokkaichi: Banko Tôgei Kyôkai, 1998. (Japanese)

Shôgakukan. *Banko-yaki, Izushi-yaki.* Vol. 19 of *Yakimono o tanoshimu* [Enjoy ceramics]. Tôkyô: Shôgakukan, 2003. (Japanese)

POTTERY MUSEUMS

A nearly complete list of pottery museums in Japan that have ceramics in their collections can be found on the internet (in English) at www.e-yakimono.net/html/museums.htm

TÔKYÔ

Idemitsu Museum of Art (*Idemitsu bijutsukan* 出光美術館); 〒 100-0005 Tôkyô-to, Chiyoda-ku, Marunouchi 3-1-1; tel. 03-3272-8600.

Japan Folk Crafts Museum, The (*Nihon mingeikan* 日本民芸館); 〒 153-0041 Tôkyô-to, Meguro-ku, Komaba 4-3-33; tel. 03-3467-4527.

Kikuchi Kanjitsu Memorial Collection, Musée Tomo (*Kikuchi Kanjitsu kinen, Tomo bijutsukan* 掬池寛実記念 智美術館); 〒 105-0001 Tôkyô-to, Minato-ku, Toranomon 4-1-35 Nishikubo Bldg., 4-1-35; tel. 03-5733-5131.

Nezu Institute of Fine Arts (*Nezu bijutsukan* 根津美術館); 〒 107-0062 Tôkyô-to, Minato-ku, Minami-Aoyama 6-5-1; tel. 03-3400-2536.

Tokyo National Museum (*Tôkyô kokuritsu hakubutsukan* 東京国立博物館); 〒 110-8712 Tôkyô-to, Taitô-ku, Ueno-kôen 13-9; tel. 03-3822-1111.

ÔSAKA

Japan Folk Crafts Museum, Ôsaka (*Ôsaka nihon mingeikan* 大阪日本民芸館); 〒 565-0826 Ôsaka-fu, Suita-shi, Senri-Banpaku-Kôen 10-5; tel. 06-6877-1971.

Museum of Oriental Ceramics, Ôsaka (*Ôsaka shiritsu tôyô tôji bijutsukan* 大阪市立東洋陶磁美術館); 〒 530-0005 Ôsaka-fu, Ôsaka-shi, Kita-ku, Nakanoshima 1-1-26; tel. 06-6223-0055.

KYÔTO

See Information on Individual Kilns and Travel Notes.

NARA

Nara Prefectural Museum (*Nara kenritsu bijutsukan* 奈良県立美術館); 〒 630-8213 Nara-ken, Nara-shi, Noboriôji-chô 10-6; tel. 0742-23-3968.

INFORMATION ON INDIVIDUAL KILNS AND TRAVEL NOTES

To make things easier for readers while traveling in Japan, the English terminology used by Japanese tourist offices has been used, along with the Japanese names in Kanji and Rômaji characters.

1 Traveling

Details of departures, which are of course subject to change, refer to JR (Japan Rail) services, which may be used free of charge with the Japan Rail Pass. Where applicable, private railways where fares apply are mentioned.

2 Tourist information offices

Tourist information offices have comprehensive information about workshops, galleries, *mingei* (folk art) shops, and exhibitions in department stores. They also provide information on low-cost local transport facilities.

3 Pottery associations, exhibitions, and salesrooms

Usually, pottery associations have salesrooms and, frequently, exhibitions, with one typical piece from each workshop, along with addresses and telephone numbers. Before visiting a workshop, it is best to call ahead through the pottery association or from your hotel, for example.

4 Literature with short descriptions of active workshops

Literature in the form of brochures, and even substantial booklets and books with local maps are available from the pottery associations and tourist information offices, and less frequently from the workshops themselves.

5 Pottery markets

Dates of pottery markets are liable to change. It is advisable to check these by phone. All workshops give discounts during pottery markets.

6 Museums

The museums listed here focus on local production or cover the respective prefectures. Museums in the large ceramics centers not only organize national and international exhibitions and competitions but also present workshops for amateurs and invited guests.

7 Internet addresses

Agano 上野 (15), near Akaike

1 From Tôkyô 東京 to Fukuoka 福岡, Hakata station 博多, by Tôkaidô-Shinkansen 東海道新幹線 and Sanyô-Shinkansen 山陽新幹線 Hikari (6–6 hours 30 minutes; 12 departures daily, possible change in Shin-Ôsaka 新大阪). From Tôkyô Haneda Airport 東京羽田 to Fukuoka 福岡 Airport (1 hour, 45 minutes; 37 flights daily). From Fukuoka 福岡, Hakata station 博多, to Nôgata 直方 by the Sasaguri Line 篠栗線 (1 hour; 3–4 departures/hour). From there to Akaike 赤池 by the private Heisei-Chikuhô-tetsudô 平成筑豊鉄道 (15 minutes; 2 departures/hour).

2 Akaike Public Office; 〒 822-1193 Fukuoka-ken, Tagawa-gun, Akaike-chô, Ôaza Agano 70-2, Ôaza Akaike 970-2; tel. 0947-28-2004.

3 Agano Pottery Association (*Agano-yaki kyôdô-kumiai* 上野焼協同組合), in the Ceramics Center (*Agano-yaki tôgeikan* 上野焼陶芸館), with salesroom and gallery; 〒 822-1102 Fukuoka-ken, Tagawa-gun, Akaike-chô, Ôaza Agano 2811; tel./fax 0947-28-5864.

4 Môri, Shigeki (ed.), p. 146–176.

5 Last weekend (Friday–Sunday) in April and October; tel. 0947-28-5864.

7 www.kougei.or.jp/english/crafts/0421/f0421.html
www.aganoyaki.com (Japanese)

Aizu-Hongô 会津本郷 (54)

1 From Tôkyô 東京 to Kôriyama 郡山 by Tôhoku-Shinkansen 東北新幹線 (1 hour 30 minutes; 4 departures/hour), then to Aizu-Wakamatsu 会津若松 by Ban'etsu Saisen 磐越西線 (70 minutes; 1–2 departures/hour). Continue to Aizu-Hongô by Tadami Line 只見線 (irregular train departures, 7 departures daily, Aizu-Hongô approximately 1¼ miles/2 km from station) or by taxi.

2 Aizu-Wakamatsu Station Tourist Information Center; 〒 965-0041 Fukushima-ken, Aizu-Wakamatsu-shi, Ekimae-machi 1-1; tel. 0242-32-0688.

3 Aizu-Hongô Pottery Exhibition Hall (*Aizu-Hongô tôjiki-geikan* 会津本郷陶磁器会館), also head office of Aizu-Hongô Ware Association; 〒 969-6152 Fukushima-ken, Ônuma-gun, Aizu-Hongô-machi, Aza Kawahara-chô 1823-1; tel./fax 0242-56-3007.

4 *Ceramic Art Challenge in Aizu-Hongô*, brochure with descriptions of kilns available in the Aizu-Hongô Pottery Exhibition Hall (see 3).

5 First Sunday in August; tel. 0242-56-2113.

6 a. Aizu-Hongô Pottery Museum (*Aizu-Hongô-yaki shiryôkan* 会津本郷焼資料館); 〒 969-6152 Fukushima-ken, Ônuma-gun, Aizu-Hongô-machi, Aza Seto-machi 3208; tel. 0242-56-4637.
b. Aizu-Hongô Kiyosato Museum (*Aizu-Hongô Kiyosato bijutsukan* 会津本郷清郷美術館); 〒 969-6152 Fukushima-ken, Ônuma-gun, Aizu-Hongô-machi, Aza Seto-machi 3131-2; tel./fax 0242-57-1678.
c. In Kami 加美 Tôhoku Ceramic Museum (*Tôhoku tôji bunkakan* 東北陶磁文化館); 〒 981-4261 Miyagi-ken, Kami-gun, Kami-machi, Aza Machi-ura 64; tel. 0229-63-3577, fax 0229-64-1510. Aizu-Hongô, Hirashimizu, Kirigome, Ôbori-Sôma, and Tsutsumi-*yaki* are exhibited.

7 www.kougei.or.jp/english/crafts/0402/f0402.html
www.hongoyaki.or.jp/ (Japanese)

Akahada 赤膚 (32), in Nara and vicinity

1 From Tôkyô 東京 to Kyôto 京都, see Kyôto. From the private Kintetsu Line railway station (next to Kyôto JR station) to Kintetsu-Nara station 近鉄奈良 by Kintetsu Ltd. Express 近鉄特急線 (40 minutes; 2 departures/hour) or from Kyôto JR station to Nara JR station 奈良 by JR Nara Line 奈良線 (approximately 1 hour; 2–6 departures/hour).

2 Nara City Information Center; 〒 630-8215 Nara-ken, Nara-shi, Kami-sanjo-chô 23-4; tel. 0742-22-3900, fax 0742-22-5595. Information also available from Kintetsu Nara Station, tel./fax 0742-24-4858, and JR Nara Station, tel./fax 0742-22-9821.

Arita 有田 (8)

1 From Tôkyô 東京 to Fukuoka 福岡, Hakata station 博多, see Agano. From Hakata to Arita 有田 by Sasebo Line 佐世保線 (1 hour 30 minutes; 1 departure/hour).

2 Commerce, Industry & Tourism; Tourist Section of Arita Town Office; 〒 844-8615 Saga-ken, Nishi-Matsuura-gun, Arita-machi, Iwayagawachi 2-8-1; tel. 0955-43-2101.
Arita Tourist Information Center; in Arita JR station; tel. 0955-42-4052.

3 Saga Prefectural Ceramic Ware Industry Cooperative (Saga-ken tôjiki kôgyô kyôdô-kumiai 佐賀県陶磁器工業協同組合); 〒 844-0026 Saga-ken, Nishi-Matsuura-gun, Arita-machi, Chûbu-Hei 1217; tel. 0955-42-3164. Sales exhibition (see 4).

4 Map of the area with addresses of 198 workshops and dealers: Arita tôki-machi gaido-mappu 有田陶器町ガイドマップ, available from 2.

5 April 29–May 5, and November 19–23; tel. 0955-42-4111.

6 a. The Kyûshû Ceramic Museum (Saga kenritsu Kyûshû tôji bunkakan 佐賀県立九州陶磁文化館); 〒 844-8585 Saga-ken, Nishi-Matsuura-gun, Arita-machi, Chûbu-Otsu 3100-1; tel. 0955-43-3681, fax 0955-43-3324.
b. Arita Porcelain Museum (Arita tôji bijutsukan 有田陶磁美術館); 〒 844-0004 Saga-ken, Nishi-Matsuura-gun, Arita-machi, Ôdaru 1-4-2; tel. 0955-42-3372.
c. Arita Museum of History and Folk Art (Arita-machi rekishi minzoku shiryôkan 有田町歴史民俗資料館); 〒 844-0001 Saga-ken, Nishi-Matsuura-gun, Arita-machi, Izumiyama 1-4-1; tel. 0955-43-2678.
d. Arita Porcelain Park (Arita pôserin pâku 有田ポーセリンパーク); 〒 844-0014 Saga-ken, Nishi-Matsuura-gun, Arita-machi, Chûbu-Otsu 340-28; tel. 0955-41-0030, fax 0955-41-0025.
e. Imaemon Museum of Ceramic Antiques (Imaemon ko-tôjiki bijutsukan 今右衛門古陶磁美術館); 〒 844-0006 Saga-ken, Nishi-Matsuura-gun, Arita-machi, Akae-machi 2-1-11; tel. 0955-42-5550.

7 www.kougei.or.jp/english/crafts/0422/f0422.html
www.arita.or.jp/common/english/make_e.html

Asahi 朝日 (33), in Uji

1 From Tôkyô 東京 to Kyôto 京都, see Kyôto. From Kyôto to Uji 宇治 by Nara Line 奈良線 (15–30 minutes; 6 departures/hour).

2 Uji Tourist Information Center; 〒 611-0021 Kyôto-fu, Uji-shi, Uji-Tônogawa 2; tel. 0774-23-3334.

5 First weekend in April, by the Uji River, Uji; tel. 0774-32-3141.

6 Asahi-yaki Pottery, Museum and Library (Asahi-yaki yôgei shiryôkan 朝日焼窯芸資料館); 〒 611-0021 Kyôto-fu, Uji-shi, Uji-Yamada 11; tel. 0774-23-2511, fax 0774-23-2513.
www.asahiyaki.com (Japanese)

Bihoro 美幌 (66)

1 From Tôkyô 東京 to Sapporo 札幌, see Hokkaidô. From Sapporo 札幌 to Bihoro 美幌 by Ltd. Express Ohôtsuku オホーツク on the Hakodate Line 函館本線 and the Sekihaku Line 石北本線 (approximately 5 hours; 4 departures daily, direct). To the workshop: Bihoro-gama 美幌窯; 〒 092-0018 Hokkaidô, Abashiri-gun, Bihoro-chô, Aza Tanaka 1203-6; tel. 01527-2-1378.

2 Bihoro Tourist Information Center; 〒 092-0015 Hokkaidô, Abashiri-gun, Bihoro-chô, Aza Shin-machi 3, Bihoro Bus Terminal; tel. 01527-3-2211.

5 Third week in September, Bihoro gama tokusetsu kaijô (美幌窯特設会場); Bihoro-gama 美幌窯 (see 1).

Bizen 備前 (29), in Inbe

1 From Tôkyô 東京 to Okayama 岡山 by Tôkaidô-Shinkansen 東海道新幹線 and Sanyô-Shinkansen 山陽新幹線 Hikari (approximately 4 hours; 1 departure/hour), then to Inbe 伊部 by JR Akô Line 赤穂線 (40 minutes; 1 departure/hour).

2 Bizen Tourist Association; 〒 705-8558 Okayama-ken, Bizen-shi, Higashi-Katakami 230; tel. 0869-64-2885.

3 Bizen Pottery Association with sales in Bizen-yaki Traditional Craft Center (Bizen-yaki dentô sangyô-kaikan 備前焼伝統産業会館); 〒 705-0001 Okayama-ken, Bizen-shi, Inbe 1657-7; in Inbe station, second floor; tel. 0869-64-1001.

4 Brochure with town map, addresses, and telephone numbers of potters in Inbe available from 2, 3, and 6. Bizen-yaki sakka • kamamoto meikan (備前焼作家・窯元名鑑), see bibliography (presents all Bizen potters); book available at the museum (see 6).

5 Third weekend in October; tel. 0869-64-1001.

6 Okayama Prefectural Bizen Ceramic Museum (Okayama-ken tôgei bijutsukan 岡山県陶芸美術館), to the right of Inbe station; 〒 705-0001 Okayama-ken, Bizen-shi, Inbe 1659-6; tel. 0869-64-1400, fax 0869-63-8300.

7 www.kougei.or.jp/english/crafts/0418/f0418.html
www.optic.or.jp/bizenyaki/touyuukai/ (Japanese)

Echizen 越前 (44), near Takefu

1 From Tôkyô 東京 to Maibara 米原 by Tôkaidô-Shinkansen 東海道新幹線 Hikari (2 hours 15 minutes; 1 departure/hour), then to Takefu 武生 by Hokuriku Line 北陸本線 (1 hour; 1 departure/hour). From Kyôto 京都 to Takefu 武生 by Kosei Line 湖西線 (1 hour 10 minutes; 1–2 departures/hour). From station forecourt in Takefu to Echizen Pottery Village (Echizen tôgei-mura 越前陶芸村) by Fukutetsu 福鉄 Line bus (for Echizen kaigan 越前海岸), disembark at Tôgei-mura-guchi 陶芸村口 (30 minutes; approximately 3 departures daily), then approximately 550 yards (500 m) on foot.

2 Echizen Town Miyazaki Tourism Association, in Echizen Pottery Village (Echizen tôgei-mura 越前陶芸村); 〒 916-0273 Fukui-ken, Niu-gun, Echizen-chô, Ozowara 7-8; tel. 0778-32-3200, fax 0778-32-3466.

3 Echizen Industrial Pottery Cooperative Association (Echizen kôgyô kyôdô-kumiai 越前工業協同組合), in Echizen Pottery Village (address, see 2); tel. 0778-32-2199; with Echizen-yaki no yakata 越前焼の館, a salesroom overseen by Echizen Industrial Pottery Cooperative Association for Echizen-yaki.

4 Echizen yakimono kikô, see Bibliography. Addresses of the 71 workshops in Miyazaki and Fukui Prefecture, see 7b.

5 Last weekend (Saturday–Monday) in May, Echizen Pottery Village (see 2); tel. 0778-32-3200.

6 Fukui Prefectural Ceramics Hall (Fukui-ken tôgeikan 福井県陶芸館) in Echizen Pottery Village (see 2); tel. 0778-32-2174.

7 a. www.kougei.or.jp/english/crafts/0412/f0412.html
b. www.echizentogeimura.com

Fujina 布志名 (25), near Matsue

1 Travel to Matsue 松江, see Iwami. For Funaki-gama 船木窯 from Matsue station 松江 approximately 15 minutes by taxi to Tamayu-machi 玉湯町, Fujina 布志名 437; tel. 0852-62-0710. For Yumachi-gama 湯町窯 from Matsue station to Tamatsukuri-Onsen 玉造温泉 two stops on the San'in Line 山陰本線 (10 minutes; 2–3 departures/hour), 1 minute from the station; tel. 0852-62-0726.

2 Matsue Tourist Information Center; 〒 690-0003 Shimane-ken, Matsue-shi, Asahi-machi 472-2 (outside the station); tel. 0852-21-4034, fax 0852-27-2598.

3 Shimane Prefectural Products and Tourist Center (Shimane-ken bussan kankôkan 島根県物産観光館); 〒 690-0887

Shimane-ken, Matsue-shi, Tono-machi 191; combined with exhibition of regional products (*Shimane furusato kan nai* 島根ふるさと館内: first floor, sales exhibition of Shimane potters; second floor, exhibition of the most important Shimane kilns); tel. 0852-22-5758, fax 0852-25-6785.

4 Description of the 78 Shimane workshops (*Shimane no yakimono—kamamoto meguri* 島根のやきもの—窯元めぐり); available from *Shimane-ken bussan kankôkan* (see 3).

6 a. Tanabe Museum of Art (*Tanabe bijutsukan* 田部美術館); 〒 690-0888 Shimane-ken, Matsue-shi, Kitahori-chô 310-5; tel. 0852-26-2111.
b. Shimane Prefectural Museum (*Shimane kenritsu bijutsukan* 島根県立美術館); 〒 690-0049 Shimane-ken, Matsue-shi, Sodeshi-chô 1-5; tel. 0852-55-4700. A limited number of local pottery exhibitions in both museums.

7 www.shimane-bussan.or.jp/ (Japanese)

Hagi 萩 (22)

1 From Tôkyô 東京 to Shin-Ôsaka 新大阪 by Tôkaidô-Shinkansen 東海道新幹線 Hikari (3 hours; 2 departures/hour), then to Shin-Yamaguchi 新山口 by Sanyô-Shinkansen 山陽新幹線 (2 hours 15 minutes–3 hours; possible change in Hiroshima 広島, 2 departures/hour). Continue to Hagi 萩, Higashi-Hagi station 東萩, by JR bus (1 hour 30 minutes; 6 departures daily).

2 Hagi City Tourism Section (at Hagi City Office); 〒 758-8555 Yamaguchi-ken, Hagi-shi, Emukai 510; tel. 0838-25-3139. There is also a tourist information booth at Hagi station: Tourist Bureau; 〒 758-0061 Yamaguchi-ken, Hagi-shi, Tsubaki 3537-3; tel. 0838-25-1750, fax 0838-25-2073; and a small one at Higashi-Hagi station (tel./fax 0838-25-3145).

3 Hagi Pottery Association (*Hagi tôgeika kyôkai* 萩陶芸家協会); 〒 758-8555 Yamaguchi-ken, Hagi-shi, Emukai 510; tel. 0838-25-3638. The Hagi Pottery Association has no exhibition or salesroom.

4 List of names and addresses of 101 workshops (*Hagi kamamoto mappu* 萩窯元マップ), available from 2 or 3.

5 May 1–5; Hagi Citizens Gymnasium (*Hagi-shi mintaiikukan* 萩市民体育館); tel. 0838-25-3333.

6 a. Ishii Tea Bowl Museum (*Ishii chawan bijutsukan* 石井茶碗美術館); 〒 758-0077 Yamaguchi-ken, Hagi-shi, Minami-Furuhagi-chô 33-3; tel. 0838-22-1211.
Hagi Pottery Museum (*Hagi-yaki shiryôkan* 萩焼資料館); 〒 758-0057 Yamaguchi-ken, Hagi-shi, Horiuchi; tel. 0838-25-8981.
b. Kumaya Art Museum, Kumaya Family Collection (*Kumaya bijutsukan* 熊谷美術館); 〒 758-0052 Yamaguchi-ken, Hagi-shi, Imauono Tana 47; tel. 0838-22-7547.

7 www.kougei.or.jp/english/crafts/0428/m0428.html
www.e-yakimono.net/guide/html/hagi.html

Hasami 波佐見 (10), near Arita

1 From Tôkyô 東京 to Arita 有田, see Arita. From Arita to Hasami 波佐見 by taxi (approximately 15 minutes, no rail or bus connections).

2 Hasami Tourist Association; 〒 859-3711 Nagasaki-ken, Higashi-Sonogi-gun, Hasami-chô, Isekigô 2255-2; tel./fax 0956-85-2290.

3 a. Hasami Ceramic Industry Association (*Hasami tôjiki kôgyô kyôdô-kumiai* 波佐見陶磁器工業協同組合); 〒 859-3711 Nagasaki-ken, Higashi-Sonogi-gun, Hasami-chô, Isekigô 2239; tel. 0956-85-3003, fax 0956-85-6108.
b. Ceramics Park Hasami (*Hasami-chô tôgei no yakata* 波佐見町陶芸の館); address, see 2; tel. 0956-85-2214, with Ceramics Museum (*tôgei no yakata* 陶芸の館; first floor, salesroom; second floor, exhibition: History of Hasami-*yaki*) and open-air kiln museum (see 6).

4 Area map of 130 workshops/companies (*tôgei no sato-Hasami-yakimono meguri* 陶芸の里-はさみ-やきもの巡り), available from 3b.

5 April 29–May 5; tel. 0956-85-2069.

6 Open-air kiln museum (*sekai no kama hiroba* 世界の窯広場) with 12 kiln types collected worldwide (see 3b). Ceramics Museum (*tôgei no yakata* 陶芸の館), see 3b.

7 www.kougei.or.jp/english/crafts/0425/f0425.html

Hirashimizu 平清水 (58), in Yamagata

1 From Tôkyô 東京 to Yamagata 山形 by Yamagata-Shinkansen 山形新幹線 (2 hours 50 minutes; 1–2 departures/hour); or from Sendai 仙台 (see Kirigome) to Yamagata 山形 by Senzan Line 仙山線 (approximately 1 hour 20 minutes; 1 departure/hour).

2 Yamagata Tourism Information Center (in station building); 〒 990-8580 Yamagata-ken, Yamagata-shi, Jônan-machi 1-16-1, Kajô Central Bldg, first floor; tel. 023-647-2333.

3 Hirashimizu Pottery Association (*Hirashimizu-yaki kyôdô-kumiai* 平清水焼協同組合); 〒 990-8580 Yamagata-ken, Yamagata-shi, Hirashimizu 153; tel. 023-642-7777. 6 workshops in Hirashimizu district, referred to as Hirashimizu Pottery Village (*tôgei no sato Hirashimizu* 陶芸の里平清水).

6 Tôhoku Ceramic Museum, see Aizu-Hongô, 6c.

Hokkaidô 北海道 (62–66)

1 a. Flight: from Tôkyô Haneda Airport 東京羽田 to Sapporo 札幌, Shin-Chitose Airport 新千歳 (90 minutes; 45 flights daily). Shin-Chitose Airport to Sapporo station via any one of several JR lines (50 minutes; 4 departures/hour).
b. Rail: from Tôkyô to Hachinohe 八戸 by Tôhoku-Shinkansen 東北新幹線 Hayate はやて (approximately 3 hours; 2 departures/hour), then to Hakodate 函館 by Hakuchô 白鳥 or Super-Hakuchô スーパー白鳥 (approximately 3 hours 15 minutes; 8 departures daily), from there to Sapporo by Hokuto 北斗 or Super-Hokuto スーパー北斗 (approximately 3 hours; 1 departure/hour).

2 Hokkaidô Tourist Association; Ryokuen Bldg., second floor 〒 060-0001 Hokkaidô, Sapporo-shi, Chûô-ku, N3, W7; tel. 011-231-0941.

3 Hokkaidô Pottery Society (*Hokkaidô tôgeikai* 北海道陶芸会); 〒 004-0012 Hokkaidô, Sapporo-shi, Atsubetsu-ku, Momiji-dai Minami 7-1-9; tel. 011-897-3944, fax 011-897-3954.
a. Otaru 小樽: Exhibition of 18 kilns from Hokkaidô: Hokuren "Fûdokan" (ふうど館); 〒 047-0027 Hokkaidô, Otaru-shi, Sakai-machi 3-18; tel. 0134-27-1111.
b. Ebetsu 江別: Exhibition of 70 kilns from Hokkaidô: Ebetsu Ceramic Art Center (see 6b).

4 Information in Fûdokan (see 3a) and Ebetsu Ceramic Art Center (see 3b).

5 Second weekend in July; Ebetsu; tel. 011-391-2155.

6 a. Otaru City Art Museum (*shiritsu Otaru bijutsukan* 市立小樽美術館); 〒 047-0031 Hokkaidô, Otaru-shi, Ironai 1-9-5; tel. 0134-34-0035.
b. Ebetsu Ceramic Art Center (*Ebetsu-shi seramikku âto-sentâ* 江別市セラミックアートセンター); 〒 069-0832 Hokkaidô, Ebetsu-shi, Nishi-Nopporo 114-5; tel. 011-385-1004.

7 www.hokkaido-tougeikai.gr.jp/
www.city.ebetsu.hokkaido.jp/ceramic/ (Japanese)

Iga 伊賀 (37), in Iga (formerly Ayama) and Ueno

1 From Tôkyô 東京 to Nagoya 名古屋 by Tôkaidô-Shinkansen 東海道新幹線 Hikari (2 hours; 2 departures/hour), then to Kameyama 亀山 by Kansai Line 関西本線 (1 hour 10 minutes; 3–4 departures/hour) and from there to Sanagu 佐那具 or Iga-Ueno 伊賀上野 by Kansai Line (43 and 50

minutes respectively; 1 departure/hour). From Sanagu by taxi to Iga 伊賀 / Ayama 阿山 (approximately 6 minutes).

2 a. Iga: Iga Tourist Association; 〒 518-1395 Mie-ken, Iga-shi, Baba 1128; tel. 0595-43-1544, fax 0595-43-1679.

b. Ueno: Iga-Ueno Tourist Association; 〒 518-0873 Mie-ken, Iga-shi, Ueno, Marunouchi 122-4; tel. 0595-26-7788, fax 0595-26-7799.

3 a. Iga, Marubashira: in *Iga-yaki* Potters' Village *Iga-yaki no sato* 伊賀焼の里: Iga-yaki Pottery Association (*Iga-yaki shinkô kyôdô-kumiai* 伊賀焼振興協同組合) with sales exhibition Iga Ware Traditional Craft Center (*Iga-yaki dentô-sangyô-kaikan* 伊賀焼伝統産業会館) 〒 518-1325 Mie-ken, Iga-shi, Marubashira 169-2; tel./fax 0595-44-1701.

b. Ueno: Iga and Shigaraki Ceramic Hall (*Iga Shigaraki kotôkan* 伊賀信楽古陶館), first floor, sales exhibition; 〒 518-0873 Mie-ken, Iga-shi, Ueno, Marunouchi 57-12; tel. 0595-24-0271.

4 Area map of the 39 workshops in Marubashira district of Iga (*Iga-yaki mappu* 伊賀焼マップ), available from 2a.

5 Last weekend in July (Friday–Sunday); Iga, in the Iga Ware Traditional Craft Center (*Iga-yaki dentô-sangyô-kaikan* 伊賀焼伝統産業会館), see 3a; tel./fax 0595-44-1701.

6 a. Iga Ware Traditional Craft Center (*Iga-yaki dentô-sangyô-kaikan* 伊賀焼伝統産業会館), see 3a.

b. Iga and Shigaraki Ceramic Hall (*Iga Shigaraki kotôkan* 伊賀信楽古陶館), Museum second floor (see 3b).

7 www.kougei.or.jp/english/crafts/0410/f0410.html www.igayaki.or.jp (Japanese)

Imari 伊万里 (Ôkawachi 大川内) (9)

1 From Tôkyô 東京 to Arita 有田 see Arita, then to Imari 伊万里 by Matsuura-tetsudô private railway 松浦鉄道 (25 minutes; 1–2 departures/hour). Or from Tôkyô to Karatsu 唐津, see Karatsu, then to Imari by Chikuhi-Line 筑肥線 (55 minutes; every 1–2 hours). From Imari to Ôkawachi-yama 大川内山 by bus, JR Chikuhi Line 筑肥線 or Matsuura Line 松浦線 (15 minutes; 8 departures daily).

2 Imari City Tourist Association (next to station building); 〒 848-0041 Saga-ken, Imari-shi, Shinten-chô 622-13; tel. 0955-23-3479.

3 Imari Nabeshima Ware Cooperative Society (*Imari Nabeshima-yaki kyôdô- kumiai* 伊万里鍋島焼協同組合), with sales exhibition: Imari Nabeshima Ware Exhibition Hall (*Imari Nabeshima-yaki kaikan* 伊万里鍋島焼会館) 〒 848-0025 Saga-ken, Imari-shi, Ôkawachi-chô, Ôkawachi-yama; tel. 0955-23-7293.

4 *Imari Walking Tour* (*Imari hiyô no sato・Ôkawachi-yama mite aruki* 伊万里秘窯の里・大川内山みて歩き), area map of the workshops; available from 3.

5 April 1–5 and November 1–5; Ôkawachi-yama; tel. 0955-23-7293.

6 a. Imari: Imari Municipal Ceramics Museum (*Imari-shi tôki shôka shiryôkan* 伊万里市陶器商家資料館); 〒 848-0047 Saga-ken, Imari-shi, Imari-chô 555-1; tel. 0955-22-7934.

b. Ôkawachi-yama: Imari-Arita Ware Traditional Crafts Center (*Imari・Arita-yaki dentô-sangyô-kaikan* 伊万里・有田焼伝統産業会館) 〒 848-0026 Saga-ken, Imari-shi, Ôkawachi-chô, Ôkawachi-yama Hei 222; tel. 0955-22-6333, fax 0955-22-6361.

7 www.blueandwhiteamerica.com/imari.html

Inkyûzan 因久山 (28), in Kôge

1 From Tôkyô 東京 to Okayama 岡山, see Bizen, then to Kôge 郡家 (10 minutes before Tottori) by Inbi Line 因美線 on the Inaba Superexpress イナバ (1 hour 30 minutes; 5 departures daily). 15-minute walk to Inkyûzan-*yaki kamamoto* 因久

山焼窯元; 〒 680-0451 Tottori-ken, Yatsu-gun, Kôge-chô, Kunôji 649; tel. 0858-72-0278.

2–6 See Kazuwa.

Inuyama 犬山 (40)

1 From Tôkyô 東京 to Nagoya 名古屋, see Iga, from Shin-Nagoya station 新名古屋 of Meitetsu private railway (next to Nagoya JR station) to Inuyama 犬山 or Inuyama-Yûen 犬山遊園 station by Meitetsu Inuyama Line 名鉄犬山線 (approximately 32 minutes; 3 departures/hour).

2 Inuyama Tourist Information Center; 〒 484-0081 Aichi-ken, Inuyama-shi, Ôaza Inuyama, Aza Fujimi-chô 14 (Meitetsu-Inuyama station, second floor); tel. 0568-61-6000, fax 0568-62-6155.

6 Permanent exhibition of approximately 20 pieces in the Inuyama Cultural History Collection (*Inuyama-shi bunka-shiryôkan* 犬山市文化史料館); 〒 484-0082 Aichi-ken, Inuyama-shi, Ôaza Inuyama, Aza Kita-Koken 8 (to the south of the castle); tel. 0568-62-4802.

7 www.inuyama.gr.jp/ (Japanese)

Isshôchi 一勝地 (4)

1 From Tôkyô 東京 to Fukuoka 福岡, Hakata station 博多, see Agano. From Fukuoka, Hakata station, to Shin-Yatsushiro 新八代 by Kagoshima Line 鹿児島本線 Relay-Tsubame リレーつばめ (1 hour 40 minutes; 1 departure/hour), then by regional rail service to Yatsushiro 八代 (3 minutes), continue to Isshôchi 一勝地 by Hisatsu Line 肥薩線 (45–60 minutes; 1 departure/hour). By taxi 3 miles (5 km) to workshop Isshôchi-*yaki kamamoto* 一勝地焼窯元: Kuma-mura, Isshôchi-Tashiro; tel. 096-632-0457.

2 Kuma Tourist Information Center; 〒 869-6401 Kumamoto-ken, Kuma-gun, Kuma-mura, Ôaza Watari 1730; tel. 096-632-1111, fax 096-632-1230.

3 Sales of local ceramics, e.g. Kôda, Shôdai, Isshôchi, in Kumamoto: Kumamoto Prefectural Crafts Center (*Kumamoto-ken dentô kôgeikan* 熊本県伝統工芸館); 〒 860-0001 Kumamoto-ken, Kumamoto-shi, Chibajô-machi 3-35; tel. 096-324-4930, fax 096-324-4942.

6 Kumamoto: exhibition of local ceramics, e.g. Kôda, Shôdai, Isshôchi: Kumamoto Prefectural Crafts Center, Kumamoto (see 3).

Iwami 石見 (24), in Gôtsu and vicinity

1 From Tôkyô 東京 to Okayama 岡山, see Bizen. Then on to Matsue 松江 by Sanyô Line 山陽線, Hakubi Line 伯備線 and San'in Line 山陰本線 Yakumo やくも Ltd. Express (2 hours 40 minutes; 15 departures daily), then to Gôtsu 江津 by San'in Line 山陰本線 Oki おき Superexpress (approximately 80 minutes; at 1 hour 30 minute–3 hour intervals).

2 Gôtsu Tourist Information Center (in station building); 〒 695-0011 Shimane-ken, Gôtsu-shi, Gôtsu-chô 926-4; tel. 0855-52-0534, fax 0855-52-0644.

3 a. Iwami Ceramic Industry Association (*Iwami tôki kôgyô kyôdô-kumiai* 石見陶器工業協同組合); 〒 699-2841 Shimane-ken, Gôtsu-shi, Ushiroji-chô 1315; tel. 0855-57-0155.

b. Sekiô Traditional Craft Center (*Sekiô chi'iki jiba-sangyô shinkô-sentâ* 石央地域地場産業振興センター); 〒 695-0016 Shimane-ken, Gôtsu-shi, Kakushi-chô I-405; tel. 0855-52-3339; with sales exhibition in *Jibasan-sentâ* じばさんセンター (*Sekiô chi'iki jiba-sangyô-sentâ* 石央地域地場産業センター); tel. 0855-52-0600.

4 List of addresses of the 13 workshops in Gôtsu (*Iwami-yaki kamamoto mappu* 石見焼窯元マップ) from Iwami Ceramic Industry Association (see 3a).

5 a. Third Sunday in March, Sekiō Traditional Craft Center (see 3b); tel. 0855-52-0600.
b. First Saturday in May, *kamadashi* (kiln opening) of the Shimada-*gama* 嶋田窯 with pottery market; 〒 699-2841 Shimane-ken, Gōtsu-shi, Ushiroji-chō 1315; tel. 0855-55-1337.
6 Iwami Adachi Museum of Art (*Iwami Adachi bijutsukan* 石見安達美術館); 〒 697-0004 Shimane-ken, Hamada-shi, Kushiro-chō 1655-28; tel. 0855-28-1920.
7 www.kougei.or.jp/english/crafts/0417/m0417.html
www.gotsu-kanko.jp/10_iwamiyaki/ (Japanese)

Izushi 出石 (30)
1 From Tōkyō 東京 to Kyōto 京都, see Kyōto. From there to Toyo'oka 豊岡 by San'in Line 山陰本線 (2 hours 15 minutes; 4 departures daily). Or from Ōsaka 大阪 (from Shin-Ōsaka 新大阪 5 minutes by any one of several services) to Toyo'oka by Fukuchiyama Line 福知山線 (2 hours 30 minutes–2 hours 50 minutes; 11 departures daily), change in Fukuchiyama 福知山. From Toyo'oka to Izushi 出石 by Zentan bus 全但バス (30–50 minutes; 3 departures/hour).
2 Izushi Tourist Association; 〒 668-0214 Hyōgo-ken, Toyo'oka-shi, Izushi-chō, Uchi-machi 104-7; tel. 0796-52-4806, fax 0796-52-4815.
3 a. Izushi Pottery Association (*Izushi tōkō-kumiai* 出石陶工組合); 〒 668-0246 Hyōgo-ken, Toyo'oka-shi, Izushi-chō, Uchi-machi 53-1; tel./fax 0796-52-3160.
b. Izushi Tourist Center (*Izushi-chō kankō-sentā* 出石町観光センター), with sales exhibition of the seven workshops; 〒 668-0214 Hyōgo-ken, Toyo'oka-shi, Izushi-chō, Uchi-machi 104-7; tel. 0796-52-4806.
7 www.kougei.or.jp/english/crafts/0416/f0416.htm

Karatsu 唐津 (13)
1 From Tōkyō 東京 to Fukuoka 福岡, Hakata station 博多, see Agano. From Fukuoka, Hakata station, to Karatsu 唐津 by Chikuhi Line 筑肥線 (1 hour 20 minutes; 2 departures/hour). Or to Meinohama 姪浜 by underground train (every 3–8 minutes), change there to Chikuhi Line for Karatsu.
2 Tourist Section of Karatsu City Office; 〒 847-8511 Saga-ken, Karatsu-shi, Nishi-Jōnai 1-1; tel. 0955-72-9127.
3 Karatsu Pottery Association (*Karatsu-yaki kyōdō-kumiai* 唐津焼協同組合); 〒 847-0816 Saga-ken, Karatsu-shi, Shinkō-machi 2881-1; tel. 0955-73-4888; with sales and exhibition: Karatsu Alpino Furusato Hall, second floor (*Karatsu-shi arupino furusato kaikan* 唐津市アルピノふるさと会館), next to station.
4 List of 43 workshops (*Karatsu-yaki yume-zukan* 唐津焼夢図鑑), available from 3.
5 September 21–25, Karatsu Alpino Furusato Hall (see 3).
6 Karatsu Castle Donjon (Local History Museum) (*Karatsu-jō tenshukaku* 唐津城天守閣); 〒 847-0016 Saga-ken, Karatsu-shi, Higashi-Jōnai 8-1 (20-minute walk from Karatsu station); tel. 0955-72-5697.
7 www.kougei.or.jp/english/crafts/0423/f0423.html
www.sa-ga.pos.to/karatsuyaki.html (Japanese)

Kasama 笠間 (52)
1 From Tōkyō 東京 Ueno station 上野 to Tomobe 友部 by Jōban Line 常盤線 (70 minutes; 1 departure/hour), then to Kasama 笠間 by Mito Line 水戸線 (9 minutes; 1 departure/hour).
2 Kasama Tourism Association; 〒 309-1626 Ibaraki-ken, Kasama-shi, Shimo-ichige 288-10; tel. 0296-72-9222, fax 0296-72-9211.
3 a. Kasama Pottery Cooperative (*Kasama-yaki kyōdō-kumiai* 笠間焼協同組合); 〒 309-1611 Ibaraki-ken, Kasama-shi,

Kasama 2481-5; tel. 0296-73-0058, fax 0296-73-0708.
b. Ceramic Center: Crafthills Kasama (*Kasama kōgei no oka* 笠間工芸の丘), exhibition and sales; 〒 309-1611 Ibaraki-ken, Kasama-shi, Kasama 2388-1; tel. 0296-70-1313, fax 0296-70-1311 (in Kasama Art Forest Park *Kasama geijutsu no mori kōen* 笠間芸術の森公園; tel. 0296-72-1111).
5 April 29–May 5, mid October, first four days in November, at *Kasama geijutsu no mori kōen* (see 3b); tel. 0296-73-0058.
6 Ibaraki Ceramic Art Museum (*Ibaraki-ken tōgei bijutsukan* 茨城県陶芸美術館); 〒 309-1611 Ibaraki-ken, Kasama-shi, Kasama 2345; tel. 0296-70-0011, fax 0296-70-0012; in *Kasama geijutsu no mori kōen* (see 3b). Kasama Inari Museum (*Kasama Inari bijutsukan* 笠間稲荷美術館); 〒 309-1611 Ibaraki-ken, Kasama-shi, Kasama 1; tel. 0296-73-0001, fax 0296-73-0002.
7 www.kougei.or.jp/english/crafts/0403/f0403.htm
www.kasamayaki.or.jp/ (Japanese)

Kazuwa 上神 (27), near Kurayoshi
1 From Tōkyō 東京 to Shin-Ōsaka 新大阪 by Tōkaidō-Shinkansen 東海道新幹線 Hikari (3 hours; 2 departures/hour). From Ōsaka 大阪 (from Shin-Ōsaka 新大阪 5 minutes by any one of several services) to Tottori 鳥取 by Chizu Kyūkō private line 智頭急行線 Hakuto ハクト Superexpress (2 hours 30 minutes; 7 departures daily). Or from Shin-Ōsaka 新大阪 to Okayama 岡山 by Sanyō-Shinkansen 山陽新幹線 (approximately 50 minutes; 3 departures/hour), then to Tottori 鳥取 by Inbi Line 因美線 Inaba イナバ Superexpress (1 hour 40 minutes; 5 departures daily), then to Kurayoshi 倉吉 by San'in Line 山陰本線 (35–55 minutes; 38 departures daily). From Kurayoshi station by Akasaki-yuki bus 赤碕行バス to Kazuwa, disembark at Teradani-iriguchi 寺谷入口 (approximately 25 minutes; 3–5 departures/hour). Workshop: Kazuwasan-*kamamoto* 上神山窯元; 〒 682-0902 Tottori-ken, Kurayoshi-shi, Kazuwa 326-1; tel. 0858-22-5705.
2 Tottori Prefecture Tourism Association; 〒 680-0011 Tottori-ken, Tottori-shi, Higashi-machi 2-308; tel. 0857-39-2111, fax 0857-39-2100.
3 Sales exhibition of local crafts in *Tottori-ken bussan kankō-sentā* (鳥取県物産観光センター); 〒 680-0833 Tottori-ken, Tottori-shi, Suehiro-Onsen-chō 160, in the Nihon Kōtsū Hondōri building; tel. 0857-29-0021, fax 0857-29-0022.
4 a. *Tottori no kamamoto mappu* 鳥取の窯元マップ, map with addresses of 27 kilns in Tottori Prefecture (available from the Tourist Information Office, see 3).
b. Traditional crafts from Tottori (*Tottori-ken no dentō kōgei-hin* 鳥取県の伝統工芸品), available from *Tottori-ken bussan kankō-sentā* (see 3).
6 Tottori Folk Crafts Museum (*Tottori mingei bijutsukan* 鳥取民芸美術館); 〒 680-0831 Tottori-ken, Tottori-shi, Sakae-machi 651; tel. 0857-26-2367.

Kirigome 切込 (60), near Miyazaki
1 From Tōkyō 東京 to Sendai 仙台 by Tōhoku-Shinkansen 東北新幹線 (1 hour 30 minutes–2 hours 30 minutes; 5 departures/hour), then to Furukawa 古川 by Tōhoku-Shinkansen 東北新幹線 Yamabiko やまびこ (approximately 20 minutes; 1 departure/hour), and by Ōsaki Bus Line 宮交大崎バス to Miyazaki Naka-machi 宮崎仲町 (50 minutes; 6 departures daily), then take a taxi to *Miyazaki tōgei no sato* 宮崎陶芸の里 Ceramic Center (approximately 15 minutes, see 3). Sunday: direct bus line from Furukawa to *Miyazaki tōgei no sato* Ceramic Center by Miyagi-Kōtsū bus 宮城交通バス (50 minutes; 6 departures daily).
2 Kami City Tourist Information Center; 〒 981-4292 Miyagi-ken, Kami-gun, Kami-machi, Aza Nishida 3-5; tel. 0229-63-6000.

3 Miyazaki *tôgei no sato* development fund (*tôgei no sato Miyazaki shinkô kôsha* 陶芸の里宮崎振興公社), and Ceramic Center *Miyazaki tôgei no sato* 宮崎陶芸の里 (museum and sales); 〒 981-4401 Miyagi-ken, Kami-gun, Kami-machi, Miyazaki Aza Kirigome 3-2; tel. 0229-69-5751.

6 a. Kirigome Pottery Remembrance Hall (*Kirigome-yaki kinenkan* 切込焼記念館) in *Miyazaki tôgei no sato* (see 3).
   b. Tôhoku Ceramic Museum, see Aizu-Hongô (6c).

Kôda 高田 (5), near Yatsushiro

1 From Tôkyô 東京 to Fukuoka 福岡, Hakata station 博多, see Agano. From Fukuoka, Hakata station, to Shin-Yatsushiro 新八代 by Kagoshima Line 鹿児島本線 Relay-Tsubame リレーつばめ (1 hour 40 minutes; 1 departure/hour). By taxi to the kilns.

2 a. Kumamoto: Kumamoto City Tourist Information Desk, main exit of Kumamoto station; 〒 860-0047 Kumamoto-ken, Kumamoto-shi, Kasuga 3-15-1; tel./fax 096-352-3743.
   b. Yatsushiro: Tourist Section of Yatsushiro City Office; 〒 866-8601 Kumamoto-ken, Yatsushiro-shi, Matsuejô-machi 1-25; tel. 0965-33-4115.

3 Sales of local ceramics, e.g. Kôda, Shôdai, Isshôchi, in Kumamoto: Kumamoto Prefectural Crafts Center, Kumamoto (see Isshôchi, 3).

6 Exhibition of local ceramics, e.g. Kôda, Shôdai, Isshôchi: Kumamoto Prefectural Crafts Center, Kumamoto (see Isshôchi 3).

Koishiwara 小石原 (17)

1 From Tôkyô 東京 to Fukuoka 福岡, Hakata station 博多, see Agano. From Fukuoka, Hakata station, to Hita 日田 by Kyûdai Line 久大本線 Yufu ゆふ Limited Express or Yufuin no mori ゆふいんの森 (1 hour 20 minutes; 7 departures daily), then to Hikosan 彦山 by Hita Hikosan Line 日田彦山線 (approximately 45 minutes; 10 departures daily); from there, 10 minutes by taxi to Koishiwara (Tôhô 東峰 since 2005).

2 Tôhô Village Society of Commerce and Industry; 〒 838-1692 Fukuoka-ken, Asakura-gun, Tôhô-mura, Ôaza Koishiwara 941-9; tel. 0946-74-2121, fax 0946-74-2284.

3 a. Koishiwara Pottery Association (*Koishiwara-yaki tôki kyôdô-kumiai* 小石原焼陶器協同組合); 〒 838-1601 Fukuoka-ken, Asakura-gun, Tôhô-mura, Ôaza Koishiwara 730-9; tel./fax 0946-74-2266.
   b. Sales exhibition of the Koishiwara-*yaki* cooperative (*Koishiwara-yaki kyôdô tenjijô* 小石原焼協同展示場); 〒 838-1600 Fukuoka-ken, Asakura-gun, Tôhô-mura, Ôaza Tsuzumi 3492-1; tel. 0946-74-2729.
   c. "Michi-no-Eki" Information Terminal (*michi no eki sue no sato* 道の駅陶の里) with ceramics sales hall (*sue no sato kan* 陶の里館); 〒 838-1601 Fukuoka-ken, Asakura-gun, Tôhô-mura, Ôaza Koishiwara 941-3; tel. 0946-74-2300.

4 Description of the 52 workshops in Koishiwara, with map of the area (*Koishiwara yakimono no ayumi* 小石原やきもの歩み), see Bibliography. Available from Koishiwara Traditional Folk Art Center (see 6).

5 May 3–5 and October 8–10; tel. 0946-74-2121.

6 Koishiwara Traditional Folk Art Center (*Koishiwara-yaki dentô-sangyô kaikan* 小石原焼伝統産業会館); Koishiwara Pottery Association, see 3.

7 www.kougei.or.jp/english/crafts/0420/f0420.html www.koishiwarayaki.or.jp/ (Japanese)

Koito 小糸 (48), in Takayama

See **Takayama 高山.**

Kutani 九谷 (45), in Terai and vicinity

1 From Tôkyô 東京 to Maibara 米原 by Tôkaidô-Shinkansen 東海道新幹線 Hikari (2 hours 15 minutes; 1 departure/hour), then to Komatsu 小松 by Hokuriku Line 北陸本線 (1 hour 33 minutes; 1 departure/hour). Or from Shin-Ôsaka 新大阪 to Komatsu by Kosei Line 湖西線 (approximately 2 hours 25 minutes; 1–2 departures/hour). From Komatsu to the *Kutani tôgei-mura* 九谷陶芸村 Ceramic Center in Terai 寺井 (20 minutes by taxi).

2 Ishikawa Prefecture Kanazawa Tourist Information Center; 〒 920-0032 Ishikawa-ken, Kanazawa-shi, Hiro'oka Ro-1, Kanazawa Hyakuban-gai-nai fureaikan (Kanazawa station); tel. 0762-31-6311.

3 Ishikawa Kutani Pottery Center (*Ishikawa-ken Kutani kaikan* 石川県九谷会館), with Kutani Porcelain Association (*Kutani tôjiki shôkôgyô kyôdô-kumiai* 九谷陶磁器商工業協同組合); 〒 923-1121 Ishikawa-ken, Terai-machi, Aza Terai-Yo 25; tel. 0761-57-0125. Sales in *Kutani tôgei-mura* 九谷陶芸村 in: *Terai-machi Kutani-yaki tôgeikan* 寺井町九谷焼陶芸館; tel. 0761-58-6100.

5 May 3–5, Terai Town Hall; tel. 0761-57-3511.

6 a. in Terai: Kutani Reference Museum (*Kutani-yaki shiryôkan* 九谷焼資料館); 〒 923-1111 Ishikawa-ken, Terai-machi, Izumidai-Minami 56; tel. 0761-58-6100, fax 0761-58-6086.
   b. in Kanazawa: Ishikawa Prefectural Art Museum (*Ishikawa kenritsu bijutsukan* 石川県立美術館); 〒 920-0963 Ishikawa-ken, Kanazawa-shi, Dewa-machi 2-1; tel. 0762-31-7580, fax 0762-24-9550.
   c. in Daishôji 大聖寺 (from Kanazawa by Hokuriku Line two stops after Komatsu): Ishikawa Kutani Art Museum (*Ishikawa-ken Kutani-yaki bijutsukan* 石川県九谷焼美術館); 〒 922-0861 Ishikawa-ken, Kaga-shi, Daishôji Jigata-machi 1-10-13; tel. 0761-72-7466.

7 www.kougei.or.jp/english/crafts/0411/f0411.html www.hitwave.or.jp/kutani/index2.htm (Japanese)

Kyôto 京都 with Kiyomizu 清水 (34)

1 From Tôkyô 東京 to Kyôto 京都 by Tôkaidô-Shinkansen 東海道新幹線 Hikari (2 hours 40 minutes; 2 departures/hour).

2 Kyôto Tourist Information Center; 〒 600-8342 Kyôto-fu, Kyôto-shi, Sakyô-ku, Okazaki, Saishôji-chô, Heian-Jingû mae; tel. 075-752-0227. In the station building: Kyôto City Tourist Information Office; JR Kyôto Station Building, second floor; 〒 600-8216 Kyôto-fu, Kyôto-shi, Shimogyô-ku; tel. 075-343-6655.

3 Kyôto Federation of Ceramics Association (*Kyôto tôjiki kyôdô-kumiai rengô-kai* 京都陶磁器協同組合連合会); 〒 605-0865 Kyôto-fu, Kyôto-shi, Higashiyama-ku, Gojô-zaka, Shiraito-chô, 570-3; tel. 075-531-3100; with sales exhibition in the Kyôto Pottery and Porcelain Center (*Kyôto tôjiki kaikan* 京都陶磁器会館); tel. 075-541-1102.

5 July 18–20, in Kiyomizu-*yaki* Danchi (清水焼団地); tel. 075-581-6188. August 7–10, Gojô-zaka Pottery Festival, on Gojô Street near Kiyomizu-dera (temple); tel. 075-525-0210.

6 a. Kyôto Arts and Crafts Museum (*Kyôto kôgeikan* 京都工芸館) in the basement of the Kyôto Museum of Contemporary Arts (*Kyôto gendai bijutsukan* 京都現代美術館); 〒 605-0073 Kyôto-fu, Kyôto-shi, Higashiyama-ku, Gion-machi, Kitagawa 271; tel. 075-525-2811.
   b. Kyôto National Museum (*Kyôto kokuritsu hakubutsukan* 京都国立博物館); 〒 605-0931 Kyôto-fu, Kyôto-shi, Higashiyama-ku, Chaya-chô 527; tel. 075-531-1151.
   c. Fureaikan Kyôto Museum of Traditional Crafts (*Kyôto dentô sangyô fureaikan* 京都伝統産業ふれあい館); 〒 606-8344 Kyôto-fu, Kyôto-shi, Sakyô-ku, Okazaki Enshôji-chô 9-1; tel. 075-762-2670.

d. Kawai Kanjiro's House (*Kawai Kanjirô kinenkan* 河井寛次郎記念館); 〒 605-0875 Kyôto-fu, Kyôto-shi, Higashiyama-ku, Gojô-zaka, Kanei-chô 569; tel. 075-561-3585.

e. Tea Ceremony Research Center (Ura Senke Tea School, *chadô shiryôkan* 茶道資料館); 〒 602-8688 Kyôto-fu, Kyôto-shi, Kamigyô-ku, Horikawa-dôri, Teranouchi Agaru; tel. 075-431-6474, fax 075-431-3060.

f. Raku Museum (*Raku bijutsukan* 楽美術館); 〒 602-0923 Kyôto-fu, Kyôto-shi, Kamigyô-ku, Nakadachiuri Agaru, Aburanokôji; tel. 075-414-0304.

g. Kondô Yûzô Memorial Museum (*Kondô Yûzô kinenkan* 近藤悠三記念館); 〒 605-0862 Kyôto-fu, Kyôto-shi, Higashiyama-ku, Shinmichi, Kiyomizu 1-287; tel. 075-561-2917.

7 www.kougei.or.jp/english/crafts/0414/f0414.html

Mashiko 益子 (53)

1 From Tôkyô 東京 to Utsunomiya 宇都宮 by Tôhoku-Shinkansen 東北新幹線 Yamabiko or Nasuno (50 minutes; 4 departures/hour), from Miya no hashi 宮の橋 bus stop (approximately 110 yards/100 m from station) to Mashiko 益子, either to Uchi-machi 内町 bus stop or Mashiko station 益子駅 by Tôya 東野 bus (1 hour; 1 departure/hour).

2 Mashiko Tourist Information Center (in station building); 〒 321-4217 Tochigi-ken, Haga-gun, Mashiko-machi, Mashiko 1539-2; tel. 0285-70-1120.

3 Mashiko Potters Association (*Mashiko-yaki kyôdô-kumiai* 益子焼協同組合); 〒 321-4217 Tochigi-ken, Haga-gun, Mashiko-machi, Mashiko 4352-2; tel. 0285-72-3107, fax 0285-72-3058. Sales and exhibition:

a. Mashiko Pottery Center (*Mashiko tôgei-sentâ* 益子陶芸センター), Tôgei messe-mae bus stop 陶芸メツセ前; 〒 321-4217 Tochigi-ken, Haga-gun, Mashiko-machi, Mashiko 3021; tel. 0285-72-7555.

b. Mashiko-yaki Kiln Distribution Center (*Mashiko-yaki kamamoto kyôhan kabushiki-gaisha* 益子焼窯元共販株式会社); 〒 321-4317 Tochigi-ken, Haga-gun, Mashiko-machi, Mashiko 706-2; tel. 0285-72-4444.

4 Town map with museums, galleries, and some kilns, available from 2.

5 April 29–May 5; first weekend in November; tel. 0285-70-1120.

6 a. Mashiko Museum of Ceramic Art (*Mashiko tôgei bijutsukan* 益子陶芸美術館) in Ceramic Art Fair Mashiko (*tôgei messe Mashiko* 陶芸メツセ益子); 〒 321-4217 Tochigi-ken, Haga-gun, Mashiko-machi, Mashiko 3021; tel. 0285-72-7555, fax 0285-72-7600.

b. Mashiko Reference Collection Museum (*Mashiko sankôkan* 益子参考館); 〒 321-4217 Tochigi-ken, Haga-gun, Mashiko-machi, Mashiko 3388; tel. 0285-72-5300, fax 0285-72-7533 (work by Hamada Shôji, Bernard Leach, and others).

7 www.kougei.or.jp/english/crafts/0404/f0404.html
www.tochigiji.or.jp/language/English/mashiko.html
www.mta.mshiko.tochigi.jp/mta1/mashikoyaki/p_mashikoyaki/htm (Japanese)

Mikawachi 三川内 (11), near Arita

1 From Tôkyô 東京 to Arita 有田, see Arita, then to Mikawachi 三川内 by Sasebo Line 佐世保線 (8 minutes; 1 departure/hour).

2 Sasebo Tourist Association, Sasebo City Hall, Tourism, Commerce and Industry Department; 〒 857-8585 Nagasaki-ken, Sasebo-shi, Hachiman-chô 1-10; tel. 0956-24-1111.

3 Mikawachi-yaki Traditional Industry Hall (*Mikawachi-yaki dentô sangyô kaikan* 三川内焼伝統産業会館) with:

a. Mikawachi Pottery Industry Cooperative Association (*Mikawachi tôjiki kôgyô kyôdô-kumiai* 三川内陶磁器工業協

同組合); 〒 859-3151 Nagasaki-ken, Sasebo-shi, Mikawachi Hon-machi 343; tel. 0956-30-8311.

b. Exhibition of work by local potters and sales exhibition.

c . Mikawachi-yaki Museum (*Mikawachi-yaki bijutsukan* 三川内焼美術館); tel. 0956-30-8080.

4 Mikawachi Guide Map 三川内ガイドマップ with 36 workshops, available from 3a–c.

5 May 1–5; in all Mikawachi Sarayama kilns.
Five days around October 10th, Mikawachi-yaki Traditional Industry Hall; tel. 0956-30-8311.

6 Mikawachi-yaki Museum (see 3c).

7 www.kougei.or.jp/english/crafts/0424/f0424.html

Mino 美濃 (42), in Tajimi, Toki, and vicinity

1 From Tôkyô 東京 to Nagoya 名古屋, see Iga; from Nagoya to Tajimi 多治見 by Chûô Line 中央本線 (22–45 minutes; 5 departures/hour), or one additional stop by Chûô Line to Toki-shi 土岐市 (5 minutes from Tajimi; 3 departures/hour).

2 a. Tajimi City PR Center; 〒 507-0033 Gifu-ken, Tajimi-shi, Hon-machi 5-9-1; tel. 0572-23-5444.

b. Toki City Tourism Association; 〒 509-5121 Gifu-ken, Toki-shi, Tokitsu-chô, Takayama 6-7; tel. 0572-54-1131.

3 a. Toki Pottery Association (*Toki kamamoto kyôhan kyôdô-kumiai* 土岐窯元共販協同組合); 〒 509-5403 Gifu-ken, Toki-shi, Hida-machi, Hida 286-8; tel. 0572-59-5611.

b. Mino-Ware Traditional Industrial Hall (*Mino-yaki dentô-sangyô-kaikan* 美濃焼伝統産業会館) with exhibition and sales of local pottery; in Mino Ceramic Art Village (*Mino tôgei mura* 美濃陶芸村); 〒 509-5142 Gifu-ken, Toki-shi, Izumi-chô, Kujiri 1429-8; tel. 0572-55-5527, fax 0572-55-7352.

c. Toki Mino-Ware Avenue Donburi Hall (*Michi no eki "Toki Mino-yaki kaidô" donburi kaikan* 道の駅 土岐美濃焼街道 どんぶり会館); 〒 509-5403 Gifu-ken, Toki-shi, Hida-chô, Hida 286-15; tel. 0572-59-5611.

4 *Come and See Tôno* (*Itte miyô Tôno* いってみよう! 東濃), map of the ceramics towns Tajimi 多治見, Toki 土岐, Mizunami 瑞浪, and Kasahara 笠原 with kilns, museums, exhibition and sales spaces; available from 2, 3a, and 3b. Addresses of 96 workshops, published by the Directory of the Mino Ceramic Art Association (*Mino tôgei kyôkai sakka meikan* 美濃陶芸協会作家名鑑): Members' address list (*kai'in jûsho roku* 会員住所録); available from 3b.

5 Toki: third Saturday and Sunday in April, in front of JR Toki station. May 3–5, and fourth Saturday and Sunday in October; Mino-Ware Traditional Industrial Hall (see 3b); tel. 0572-54-1131.
Tajimi: second Saturday and Sunday in April, Hon-machi; tel. 0572-25-5588.

6 a. Gifu Ceramics History Museum (*Gifu-ken tôji shiryôkan* 岐阜県陶磁資料館); 〒 507-0801 Gifu-ken, Tajimi-shi, Higashi-machi 1-9-4; tel. 0572-23-1191.

b. Museum of Modern Ceramic Art, Gifu, Ceramic Park MINO (*seramikku pâku* MINO, *Gifu-ken gendai tôgei bijutsukan* セラミックパーク MINO 岐阜県現代陶芸美術館); 〒 507-0801 Gifu-ken, Tajimi-shi, Higashi-machi 4-2-5; tel. 0572-28-3100, fax 0572-28-3101.

c. Mino Ceramic History Museum (*Toki-shi Mino tôji rekishi kan* 土岐市美濃陶磁歴史館); 〒 509-5142 Gifu-ken, Toki-shi, Izumi-chô, Kajiri 1263; tel. 0572-55-1245.

d. Oribe Park open-air museum (*Oribe no sato kôen* 織部の里公園), with the ruin of the Motoyashiki kiln 元屋敷窯跡; 〒 509-5142 Gifu-ken, Toki-shi, Izumi-chô, Kajiri 1246-1; tel. 0572-54-2710.

7 www.kougei.or.jp/english/crafts/0408/f0408.html
www.minoyaki.gr.jp/ (Japanese)

Miyajima 宮島 (23), off Miyajima Island

1   From Tôkyô 東京 to Hiroshima 広島 by Tôkaidô-Shinkansen 東海道新幹線 and Sanyô-Shinkansen 山陽新幹線 Hikari (4 hours 40 minutes; 1–2 departures/hour; change in Shin-Ôsaka 新大阪 often necessary), then to Miyajima-guchi 宮島口 by Sanyô Line 山陽線 (26 minutes; 2–10 departures/hour); approximately 7-minute walk to pier; to Miyajima Island 宮島 by JR ferry (10 minutes; 4 departures/hour). Kawahara Gen'ei-dô pottery 川原厳栄堂 (tel. 0829-56-0238) is on the way to the ferry, before the pier.

2   Miyajima Tourist Association; 〒 739-0505 Hiroshima-ken, Hatsukaichi-machi, Miyajima-chô 1162-18; tel. 0829-44-2011, fax 0829-44-0066.

3   Miyajima Traditional Crafts Center (*Miyajima dentô-sangyô-kaikan* 宮島伝統産業会館), on Miyajima Island; 〒 739-0505 Hiroshima-ken, Hatsukaichi-machi, Miyajima-chô 1165-9; tel. 0829-44-2017, fax 0829-44-2753.

6   Miyajima Historical and Folklore Materials House (*Miyajima rekishi minzoku shiryôkan* 宮島歴史民俗資料館), on Miyajima Island; 〒 739-0505 Hiroshima-ken, Hatsukaichi-machi, Miyajima-chô 57; tel. 0829-44-2019, fax 0829-44-0631.

Mumyôi 無名異 (51), on Sado Island

1   From Tôkyô 東京 to Niigata 新潟 by Jôetsu-Shinkansen 上越新幹線 (2 hours; 2 departures/hour). From Niigata harbor to Ryôtsu 両津 on Sadogashima Island 佐渡が島 by Sado Kisen Jetfoil (1 hour; depending on season, 3–11 departures daily), then to Aikawa 相川 by Honsen bus 本線 (45 minutes; 2 departures/hour).

2   a. Niigata Kôtsû Information Center, in Ryôtsu at ferry berth; 〒 952-0014 Niigata-ken, Sado-shi, Minato 353-1; tel. 0259-27-5164.
b. Sado Information Center Aikawa; 〒 952-1555 Niigata-ken, Sado-shi, Aikawa, Hama-machi 2; tel. 0259-74-3318.

3   a. Local industrial development agency (*chi'iki sangyô kasseika shinkô shien jigyô* 地域産業活性化振興支援事業); 〒 952-155 Niigata-ken, Sado-shi, Aikawa, Shioya 25; tel. 0259-74-3236, fax 0259-74-3237.
b. The Aikawa Exhibit House of Folk Craft (*Aikawa ginô denshô tenjikan* 相川技能伝承展示館), exhibition of one piece each from Aikawa potters; 〒 952-1555 Niigata-ken, Sado-shi, Aikawa, Sakashita 20; tel. 0259-74-4313.

4   a. Address list and map of the area with 29 workshops on the island (*Kamamoto o tazunete miyô* 窯元を訪ねてみよう), available from Information Center (see 2a).
b. Mumyôi-*yaki*, 12 kilns in Aikawa, local industrial development agency (see 3).

5   Second weekend in August, Aikawa; tel. 0259-74-3318.

6   a. Aikawa Folk Museum (*Aikawa kyôdo hakubutsukan* 相川郷土博物館); 〒 952-1505 Niigata-ken, Sado-shi, Aikawa, Sakashita 20; tel. 0259-74-4312.
b. Museum of the Itô-Family (*Sado mumyôi tôgei, Itô Sekisui sakuhin kan* 佐渡無名異陶芸伊藤赤水作品館); 〒 952-1501 Niigata-ken, Sado-shi, Shimo-Aikawa 808-3; tel. 0259-74-0011.

Nihonmatsu Banko 二本松万古 (55), in Nihonmatsu

1   From Tôkyô 東京 to Kôriyama 郡山 by Tôhoku-Shinkansen 東北新幹線 (1 hour 30 minutes; 4 departures/hour), then to Nihonmatsu 二本松 by Tôhoku Line 東北本線 (25 minutes; 1–2 departures/hour). Workshop: Inoue-*gama* 井上窯; 〒 964-0003 Fukushima-ken, Nihonmatsu-shi, Niidaki 1-456; tel. 0243-23-2195, fax 0243-22-5505.

2   Nihonmatsu Tourist Association; 〒 964-8601 Fukushima-ken, Nihonmatsu-shi, Kanairi 403-1; tel. 0243-23-1111, fax 0243-22-5411.

7   www1.ocn.ne.jp/~inoue456 (Japanese)
www.i-kama.co.jp/ (Japanese)

Ôbori Sôma 大堀相馬 (57), near Namie

1   From Tôkyô 東京 to Sendai 仙台, see Kirigome. From Sendai to Namie 浪江 by Jôban Line 常磐線 (1 hour 15 minutes–2 hours; irregular, 12 departures daily). By taxi approximately 15 minutes to Ôbori Sôma-*yaki bussan kaikan* (see 3).

2   Namie Tourist Association; 〒 979-1521 Fukushima-ken, Futaba-gun, Namie-machi, Ôaza Gongendô, Aza Shimokawahara 9-1; tel. 0240-35-3321, fax 0240-34-3698.

3   Ôbori Sôma Ware Association (*Ôbori Sôma-yaki kyôdô-kumiai* 大堀相馬焼協同組合), with exhibition and sales hall for the workshops (*Ôbori Sôma-yaki bussan kaikan* 大堀相馬焼物産会館); 〒 979-1544 Fukushima-ken, Futaba-gun, Namie-chô, Ôaza Ôbori, Aza Ôbori 37; tel. 0240-35-4917, fax 0240-35-4927.

4   Map with list of addresses of 23 workshops (*Ôbori Sôma-yaki kamamoto mappu* 大堀相馬焼窯元マップ), available from *Ôbori Sôma-yaki bussan kaikan* (see 3).

5   May 1–5, in *Ôbori Sôma-yaki bussan kaikan* (see 3); tel 0240-35-4917.

6   No museum in Namie. Ôbori Sôma-*yaki* is on display at: a Tôhoku Ceramic Museum, see Aizu-Hongô (6c).
b. In Kitakata 喜多方: Kitakata Museum (*Kitakata zôhin bijutsukan* 喜多方蔵品美術館); 〒 966-0821 Fukushima-ken, Kitakata-shi, Aza Umetake 7-294-4; tel. 0241-24-3576.

7   www.kougei.or.jp/english/crafts/0401/f0401.html
www.somayaki.or.jp/ (Japanese)

Odo 尾戸 (20), in Kôchi

1   From Tôkyô 東京 to Okayama 岡山, see Bizen. From Okayama to Kôchi 高知 on Shikokû by Dosan Line 土讃本線 Ltd. Express Nanpû 南風 (2 hours 40 minutes; 1 departure/hour). By taxi to the workshop of the Doi family: Odo-*yaki kamamoto* 尾戸焼窯元; 〒 780-8050 Kôchi-ken, Kôchi-shi, Kamobe 1349-3; tel. 088-844-1095.

2   Kôchi Tourist Information Center (in station building); 〒 780-0056 Kôchi-ken, Kôchi-shi, Kita-Hon-machi 2-7-1; tel. 088-882-4035, fax 088-882-7777.

Ôhi 大樋 (46), in Kanazawa

1   From Tôkyô 東京 to Maibara 米原 by Tôkaidô-Shinkansen 東海道新幹線 Hikari (2 hours 15 minutes; 1 departure/hour), then to Kanazawa 金沢 by Hokuriku Line 北陸本線 (1 hour 50 minutes; 2 departures/hour). From Kyôto 京都 to Kanazawa by Kosei Line 湖西線 (2 hours 20 minutes; 3 departures/hour).

2   See Kutani, 2.

3   a. Studio of Ôhi Chôzaemon X—kiln (*Ôhi-yaki honke-jûdai Chôzaemon—gama* 大樋焼本家十代長左衛門窯); 〒 920-0911 Ishikawa-ken, Kanazawa-shi, Hashiba-chô 2-17; tel. 076-221-2397, fax 076-221-2123.
b. Ôhi Museum Hirosaka Gallery (*Ôhi bijutsukan Hirosaka garari* 大樋美術館広坂 ギャラリ); 〒 920-0911 Ishikawa-ken, Kanazawa-shi, Hirosaka 1-2-34 (Hirosaka-dôri, southern side of Kenroku-en Garden); tel/fax 076-264-2644.

6   Ôhi Museum (*Ôhi bijutsukan* 大樋美術館); address, see 3a.

7   www.hokuriku.ne.jp/ohi/

Onta 小鹿田 (18), near Hita

1   From Tôkyô 東京 to Fukuoka 福岡, Hakata station 博多, see Agano. From Fukuoka, Hakata station, to Hita 日田, see Koishiwara. From Hita to Onta by Hita Bus Onta Line (45 minutes; 2–3 departures daily) to the end of the line. In order to catch the bus, it is necessary to take the 7:45 a.m. train from Hakata; otherwise by taxi from Hita.

2   Department of Commerce and Tourism, Hita City Office; 〒 877-8601 Ôita-ken, Hita-shi, Tashima 2-6-1; tel. 0973-23-3111.
3   Onta-*yaki* Potters Association (*Onta-yaki dôgyô kumiai* 小鹿田焼同業組合); 〒 877-1121 Ôita-ken, Hita-shi, Motoe-machi Sarayama; tel. 0973-29-2440.
Sales exhibition at Hita Industry Promotion Center (*Hita kusu sangyô shinkô-sentâ* 日田玖珠産業振興センター); 〒 877-0016 Ôita-ken, Hita-shi, Sanbonmatsu; tel. 0973-29-2440.
5   Second weekend in October; tel. 0973-29-2440.
6   a. Onta Sarayama: Onta Pottery Hall Hita (*Hita shiritsu Onta-yaki tôgeikan* 日田市立小鹿田焼陶芸館); 〒 877-1121 Ôita-ken, Hita-shi, Motoe-machi Sarayama; tel. 0973-29-2440 (at the bus turn-around, the highest point in village).
b. Hita: Museum for *ko-Onta-yaki* (*Onta kotô kan* 小鹿田古陶館); 〒 877-0014 Ôita-ken, Hita-shi, Hon-machi 7-33; tel. 0973-24-4076.
7   www.yado.co.jp/kankou/ooita/hita/ontayaki/ontayaki.htm (Japanese)

Ôtani 大谷 (21)

1   From Tôkyô 東京 to Okayama 岡山, see Bizen. From Okayama to Takamatsu 高松 on Shikokû by Seto Ohashi Line 瀬戸大橋線 (1 hour; 1–2 departures/hour), on to Ikenotani 池谷 by Kotoku Line 高徳線 (1 hour; 1 departure/hour), then to Awa Ôtani 阿波大谷 by Naruto Line 鳴門線 (3 minutes; 1 departure/hour).
2   Tokushima Prefecture Tourist Association; 〒 770-8055 Tokushima-ken, Tokushima-shi, Yamashiro-chô, Higashi-Hama Bôji 1-1; tel. 088-652-8777.
3   Ôtani Pottery Association (*Ôtani-yaki tôgyô kyôkai* 大谷焼陶業協会); 〒 779-0302 Tokushima-ken, Naruto-shi, Ôaza Ôtani; tel. 088-689-0204.
4   Brochure: *Ôtani-yaki, Ceramics from Awa, 200-Year History* (*Ôtani-yaki awa no yakimono nihyaku-nen no honô no rekishi* 大谷焼阿波の焼物二百年の炎の歴史), available from 2 and 3.
5   Second weekend in November outside Tôrin-in temple; tel. 088-689-0204.
7   www.kougei.or.jp/english/crafts/0429/m0429.html

Otaru 小樽 (62)

1   From Tôkyô 東京 to Sapporo 札幌, see Hokkaidô. From Sapporo to Otaru 小樽 by Hakodate Line 函館線 (31–48 minutes; 5 departures/hour). Workshop: Otaru-*gama* Shirose-tôen 小樽窯白勢陶園; 〒 047-8660 Hokkaidô, Otaru-shi, Irifune 5-1-4; tel. 0134-22-4459.
2   Otaru Enquiries and Tourist Information; 〒 047-8660 Hokkaidô, Otaru-shi, Hanazono 2-12-1; tel. 0134-32-4111.
3–6 see Hokkaidô.

Ryûmonji 龍門司 (3), near Kajiki

1   From Tôkyô 東京 to Fukuoka 福岡, Hakata station 博多, see Agano. From Fukuoka, Hakata station, to Shin-Yatsushiro 新八代 by Kagoshima Line 鹿児島本線 Relay Tsubame リレーつばめ (1 hour 40 minutes; 2 departures/hour), direct to Kagoshima-Chûô 鹿児島中央 by Kyûshû-Shinkansen 九州新幹線 Tsubame つばめ (47 minutes; 2 departures/hour), then to Kajiki 加治木 by Nippô Line 日豊本線 (25–40 minutes; 2–3 departures/hour). By taxi approximately 5 miles (8 km) in the direction of Kurino 栗野 to the Ryûmonji kiln (*Ryûmonji-yaki kamamoto* 龍門司焼窯元); address, see 3.
2   Commerce and Industry Sightseeing Section of General Planning and Policy Division of Kajiki Town Office; 〒 899-5294 Kagoshima-ken, Aira-gun, Kajiki-chô, Moto-machi 253; tel. 099-562-2111.

3   Ryûmonji Syndicate (*Ryûmonji-yaki kigyô-kumiai* 龍門司焼企業組合); 〒 899-5203 Kagoshima-ken, Aira-gun, Kajiki-chô, Koyamada 5940; tel. 099-562-2549.
5   Second weekend in December; at Ryûmonji-*yaki* kiln (see 3).
6   Miyake Museum in Kagoshima; see Satsuma, 6b.

Satsuma 薩摩 (2), in Kagoshima and Higashi-Ichiki Miyama

1   From Tôkyô 東京 to Kagoshima-Chûô 鹿児島中央, see Ryûmonji. To Miyama 美山 (formerly Naeshirogawa 苗代川): from Kagoshima-Chûô to Higashi-Ichiki 東市来 by Kagoshima Line 鹿児島本線 (25 minutes; 2 departures/hour); 3 miles (5 km) by taxi to Miyama.
2   a. Kagoshima: Kagoshima City Tourist Information Center (Kagoshima-Chûô 鹿児島中央 station building); 〒 890-0053 Kagoshima-ken, Kagoshima-shi, Chûô-chô 1-1; tel. 099-253-2500, fax 099-250-8462.
b. Miyama: Higashi-Ichiki Tourist Association; 〒 899-2201 Kagoshima-ken, Hioki-shi, Higashi-Ichiki-chô, Yuda 3299-1; tel. 099-274-5518.
3   a. Miyama Pottery Association (*Miyama Satsuma-yaki shinkô-kai* 美山薩摩焼振興会); 〒 899-2431 Kagoshima-ken, Hioki-shi, Higashi-Ichiki-chô, Miyama 1236-1; tel. 099-274-4404.
b. Miyama Ceramic Hall (*Miyama tôyûkan* 美山陶遊館); 〒 899-2431 Kagoshima-ken, Hioki-gun, Higashi-Ichiki-chô, Miyama; tel. 099-274-5778.
c. Sales of Satsuma and Ryûmonji-*yaki* in Kagoshima in the *tôgeikan* 陶芸館 in the Sengan'en Garden 仙巌園; 〒 892-0871 Kagoshima-ken, Kagoshima-shi, Yohino-chô 9700-1; tel. 099-247-1511.
4   Area map of the Kagoshima kilns with addresses, from 2a. Area map of the Naeshirogawa kilns in Miyama, from 2a and 2b.
5   Around November 3 (4-day fair), in Higashi-Ichiki, Miyama; tel. 099-274-2111.
6   a. Kagoshima: Nagashima Museum (*Nagashima bijutsukan* 長島美術館); 〒 890-0045 Kagoshima-ken, Kagoshima-shi, Take 3-42-18; tel. 099-250-5400, fax 099-250-5478.
b. Kagoshima: Miyake Museum (*Miyake bijutsukan* 三宅美術館); 〒 891-0141 Kagoshima-ken, Kagoshima-shi, Taniyama Chûô 1- 4319; tel. 099-266-0066.
c. Kagoshima: Shôko Shûseikan 尚古集成館, in the Sengan'en Garden (see 3c); tel. 099-247-1511.
d. Higashi-Ichiki Miyama: Naeshirogawa Folk Pottery Museum (*Naeshirogawa mintôkan* 苗代川民陶館); 〒 899-2431 Kagoshima-ken, Hioki-shi, Higashi-Ichiki-chô, Miyama 456; tel. 099-274-2450 (*kuro*-Satsuma).
7   www.kougei.or.jp/english/crafts/0427/m0427.html

Seto 瀬戸 with Akazu 赤津 (41)

1   From Tôkyô 東京 to Nagoya 名古屋, see Iga. Take Higashiyama underground line 東山 in Nagoya to the underground railway station Sakae 栄; from there (Sakae-machi station 栄町) to Seto 瀬戸 (Owari-Seto station 尾張瀬戸) take private Meitetsu Seto Line 名鉄瀬戸線 (30–45 minutes; 2–3 departures/hour).
2   Seto City Tourism Association; 〒 489-0814 Aichi-ken, Seto-shi, Suehiro-chô 1-7-1; tel. 0561-85-2730, fax 0561-85-2570.
3   a. Seto-*yaki* Promotion Association (*Seto-yaki shinkô-kyôkai* 瀬戸焼振興協会) in the Seto City Industry and Tourism Division (*Seto-shi sangyô kankô-ka* 瀬戸市産業観光課), with exhibition and sales; 〒 489-8701 Aichi-ken, Seto-shi, Oiwake-chô 64-1; tel. 0561-82-7111.
b. Seto Underglaze Ware Association (*Seto-sometsuke-yaki kôgyô kyôdô-kumiai* 瀬戸染付焼工業協同組合);

〒 489-0813 Aichi-ken, Seto-shi, Tôgen-chô 1-8; tel. 0561-82-4151; with exhibition and sales at Aichi Prefectural Ceramic Industry Association (*Aichi-ken tôjiki kôgyô kyôdô-kumiai* 愛知県陶磁器工業協同組合); tel. 0561-82-4151.
c. Akazu Ware Ceramic Industry Association (*Akazu-yaki kôgyô kyôdô-kumiai* 赤津焼工業協同組合), with sales exhibition at Akazu-*yaki* Center (*Akazu-yaki kaikan* 赤津焼会館) 〒 489-0022 Aichi-ken, Seto-shi, Akazu-chô 94-4; tel. 0561-21-6508.
Sales:
d. Shinano Ceramic Center (*Shinano tôjiki-sentâ* 品野陶磁器センター); 〒 480-1207 Aichi-ken, Seto-shi, Shinano-chô 1-126-2; tel. 0561-41-1141.
e. Seto-gura Ceramic Plaza (瀬戸蔵セラミックプラザ); tel. 0561-89-5758, fax 0561-82-2122, in Seto-gura (瀬戸蔵) 〒 489-0813 Aichi-ken, Seto-shi, Kurasho-chô 1-1; tel. 0561-97-1555, fax 0561-97-1557.
4 Seto: map of the area with addresses of 45 workshops and dealers (*Seto sansaku ezu* 瀬戸散策絵図); available from 2, 6b, and at Owari-Seto station.
Akazu: brochure with map of the area and addresses of the 41 workshops (*Akazu tokuhon* 赤津読本); available from 2 and 3c.
5 Seto: second Saturday and Sunday in September, from Owari-Seto station along Seto river (Setogawa 瀬戸川); tel. 0561-88-2650.
Akazu: third Saturday and Sunday in April and second weekend in September; tel. 0561-88-2650.
6 a. Aichi Prefectural Ceramic Museum (*Aichi-ken tôji shiryôkan* 愛知県陶磁資料館); 〒 489-0965 Aichi-ken, Seto-shi, Minami-Yamaguchi-chô 234; tel. 0561-84-7474, fax 0561-84-4932.
b. Seto-gura Museum (瀬戸蔵ミユージアム) in Seto-gura (see 3e); tel. 0561-97-1190, fax 0561-97-1557.
c. "*Kamagaki no komichi*" Material Museum (*kamagaki no komichi shiryôkan* 窯垣の小径資料館); 〒 489-0833 Aichi-ken, Seto-shi, Nakabora-chô 39; tel. 0561-82-0714.
d. Seto Ceramics and Glass Art Center (*Seto-shi shin seiki kôgeikan* 瀬戸市新世紀工芸館) of the Seto New Century Art Craft Museum; 〒 489-0815 Aichi-ken, Seto-shi, Minami-Nakabôkiri-chô 81-2; tel. 0561-97-1001, fax 0561-97-1005.
e. Seto City Art Museum (*Seto-shi bijutsukan* 瀬戸市美術館), Seto-shi Bunka Center (瀬戸市文化センタ-); 〒 489-0884 Aichi-ken, Seto-shi, Nishiibara-chô 113-3; tel. 0561-84-1093, fax 0561-85-0415.
7 www.city.seto.aichi.jp/setomono/kankou/
www.city.seto.aichi.jp/organization/sangyo/center/index.html (Japanese/ English)
Seto-*sometsuke*: www.kougei.or.jp/english/crafts//0406/f0406.html
Akazu: www.kougei.or.jp/english/crafts/0405/f0405.html
www.Akazu-kamamawasi.com (Japanese)

Shibukusa 渋草 (47), in Takayama
See Takayama 高山

Shigaraki 信楽 (36)
1 From Tôkyô 東京 to Kyôto 京都, see Kyôto, then to Ishiyama 石山 or Kusatsu 草津 by Biwako Line 琵琶湖線 (14 or 25 minutes respectively; 7 departures/hour). From Ishiyama to Shigaraki 信楽 by Teisan Konan Kôtsû bus 帝産湖南交通 バス to Tôgei no mori mae 陶芸の森前 bus stop (1 hour; 1 departure/hour). Or from Kusatsu to Kibukawa 黄生川 by Kusatsu Line 草津線 (24 minutes; 2 departures/hour) and on to Shigaraki by private Shigaraki Kôgen Line 信楽高原鉄道 (25 minutes; 1 departure/hour).

2 Shigaraki Tourist Association; 〒 529-1851 Shiga-ken, Kôka-shi, Shigaraki-chô, Nagano 1142; tel. 0748-82-2345.
3 a. Shigaraki Pottery Association (*Shigaraki tôki kôgyô kyôdô-kumiai* 信楽陶器工業協同組合); 〒 529-1811 Shigaraki-ken, Kôka-shi, Shigaraki-chô, Ida 985; tel. 0748-82-0831, fax 0748-82-3473.
b. The Shigaraki Ceramic Cultural Park (*Shiga kenritsu tôgei no mori-tôgeikan* 滋賀県立陶芸館の森・陶芸館) with exhibition halls and sales exhibition (*tôgeikan* 陶芸館 and *Shigaraki sangyô tenjikan* 信楽産業展示館); 〒 529-1804 Shiga-ken, Kôka-shi, Shigaraki-chô, Chokushi 2188-7; tel. 0748-83-0909.
4 Shigaraki guide (*Shigaraki michi-shirube* 信楽みちしるべ); town map; available from 2.
5 Fourth weekend (Friday–Sunday) in July; October 8–10; tel. 0748-82-0873.
6 a. Shigaraki Traditional Craft Center (*Kôka-shi Shigaraki dentô sangyô kaikan* 甲賀市信楽伝統産業会館); address, see 2.
b. Shigaraki-*yaki* Museum (*Shigaraki-yaki shiryô bijutsukan* 信楽焼資料美術館); 〒 529-1836 Shiga-ken, Kôka-shi, Shigaraki-chô, Hosohara; tel. 0748-82-1153.
7 www.kougei.or.jp/english/crafts/0413/f0413.html
www.shigarakiyaki.co.jp/ (Japanese)

Shitoro 志戸呂 (43), near Kanaya
1 From Tôkyô 東京 to Kakegawa 掛川 by Tôkaidô-Shinkansen 東海道新幹線 Kodama (1 hour 49 minutes; 2 departures/hour); continue to Kanaya 金谷 by Tôkaidô Line 東海道本線 (15 minutes; 4 departures/hour).
2 Kanaya Tourist Association; 〒 482-0022 Shizuoka-ken, Shimada-shi, Kanaya 14-1; tel./fax 0547-46-2861.
6 Kanaya Green Tea Museum (*Kanaya ocha no sato* 金谷お茶の里); 〒 482-0022 Shizuoka-ken, Shimada-shi, Kanaya 3053-2; tel. 0547-46-5588.

Shôdai 小代 (6), near Arao and in Kumamoto
1 From Tôkyô 東京 to Fukuoka 福岡, Hakata station 博多, see Agano.
a. To Kumamoto 熊本: from Fukuoka, Hakata station, to Kumamoto by Kagoshima Line 鹿児島本線 Relay Tsubame リレーつばめ (1 hour 20 minutes; 2–3 departures/hour).
b. To Arao 荒尾: from Fukuoka, Hakata station 博多, to Ômuta 大牟田 by Kagoshima Line 鹿児島本線 Relay-Tsubame リレーつばめ (50 minutes; 2–3 departures/hour); continue to Arao by local train (4 minutes; 5 departures/hour). By taxi to the kilns.
2 a. Kumamoto: see Kôda, 2a.
b. Arao: Tourist Association of Arao City (in the Town Office); 〒 864-8686 Kumamoto-ken, Arao-shi, Kunaideme 390; tel. 0968-63 -1111.
3 Shôdai Pottery Association (*Arao-shi kankô bussakan Shôdai-yaki kamamoto no kai* 荒尾市物産観光館小代焼窯元の会); 〒 864-0033 Kumamoto-ken, Arao-shi, Midorigaoka 1-1-2; tel. 0968-66-0939.
Sales of local pottery in Kumamoto (see Isshôchi, 3).
6 a. Kumamoto: exhibition of local pottery (see Isshôchi, 3).
b. Arao: small private museum at the Fumoto-*gama* ふもと窯; 〒 864-0166 Kumamoto-ken, Arao-shi, Fumoto 1728-1; tel. 0968-68-0456.
7 www.kougei.or.jp/english/crafts/0430/f0430.html

Sodeshi 袖師 (26), in Matsue
1 For route to Matsue 松江, see Iwami. Workshop: Sodeshi-*gama* 袖師窯; 〒 690-0049 Shimane-ken, Matsue-shi, Sodeshi-chô 3-12; tel. 0852-21-3974.
2–7 See Fujina.

Sôma Koma 相馬駒 (56), in Sôma

1 From Tôkyô (Ueno) 東京(上野) to Sôma 相馬 by Jôban Line 常磐線 (3 hours 30 minutes–4 hours; 4 departures daily). Or from Tôkyô to Sendai 仙台, see Kirigome. From Sendai to Sôma by Jôban Line 常磐線 (1 hour–1 hour 20 minutes; 1–2 departures/hour).
2 Sôma Tourist Association; 〒 976-0042 Fukushima-ken, Sôma-shi, Nakamura, Aza Sakura-ga-oka 71; tel. 0244-36-3171, fax 0244-36-3184.
6 Tôhoku Ceramic Museum (see Aizu-Hongô, 6c).

Suzu 珠洲 (50), in Takojima

1 From Tôkyô 東京 to Kanazawa 金沢, see Ôhi. From Kanazawa to Nanao 七尾 by Nanao Line 七尾線, from there to Takojima terminus 蛸島 by Noto private railway のと鉄道 (total journey time from Kanazawa 4 hours 20 minutes; 3 departures daily). From Takojima station 15 minutes north on foot to Ceramic Center Suzu-yaki no sato 珠洲焼の里. Each day, one bus travels from Kanazawa to the Ceramic Center in under 2 hours 30 minutes, returns less than one hour later.
2 See Kutani, 2.
3 In the Ceramic Center Suzu-yaki no sato 珠洲焼の里: Suzu Ceramic Hall (Suzu-yaki kan 珠洲焼館); 〒 927-1204 Ishikawa-ken, Suzu-shi, Takojima-machi 1-2-480; tel. 0768-82-5073.
6 In the Ceramic Center Suzu-yaki no sato 珠洲焼の里: Municipal Museum of Suzu Ware (Suzu-yaki shiryôkan 珠洲焼資料館); 〒 927-1204 Ishikawa-ken, Suzu-shi, Takojima-machi 1-2-563; tel. 0768-82-6200, fax 0768-82-6045.

Taisetsu 大雪 / Asahikawa 旭川 (65)

1 From Tôkyô 東京 to Sapporo 札幌, see Hokkaidô. From Sapporo to Asahikawa 旭川 by Hakodate Line 函館本線 (1 hour 20 minutes; 1–2 departures/hour).
2 Asahikawa Tourist Information Center (in the station building); 〒 078-0030 Hokkaidô, Asahikawa-shi, Miyashita-dori 8, HBC Hôsôkyoku, first floor; tel. 0166-22-6704.
3 a. Asahikawa Pottery Association (Asahikawa yakimono-kyôkai 旭川やきもの協会); 〒 078-1273 Hokkaidô, Asahikawa-shi, Higashi-Asahikawa-chô, Yonehara 586; tel. 0166-76-2845.
 b. Arashiyama Pottery Village (Arashiyama tôgei no sato 嵐山陶芸の里) with 8 kilns in Asahikawa-shi, Asahigaoka 1–2.
5 Third weekend in September; Asahikawa Jiba Sangyô Sentâ 旭川地場産業センター; tel. 0166-66-1770.

Takatori 高取 (16), in Koishiwara and Fukuoka

1 From Tôkyô 東京 to Fukuoka 福岡, Hakata station 博多, see Agano. To the Takatori kiln Miraku-gama 味楽窯 in Fukuoka by Kûkô underground line 地下鉄空港線 to Fujisaki station 藤崎. To the Takatori kilns in Koishiwara, see that section.
2 Fukuoka Convention and Visitors Bureau, Second Floor, Fukuoka City Hall North Annex; 〒 810-0001 Fukuoka-ken, Fukuoka-shi, Chûô-ku, Tenjin 1-10-1; tel. 092-733-5050.
3–5 See Koishiwara.
7 www.takatoriyaki.jp/ (Japanese)

Takayama 高山 (47–49)

1 From Tôkyô 東京 to Nagoya 名古屋, see Iga. From Nagoya to Takayama 高山 by Takayama Line 高山本線 (2 hours; 2 departures/hour). In Takayama:
 Shibukusa-yaki 渋草焼:
 a. Shibukusa-jiki: Kami-Nino-machi 上二之町, 20-minute walk.
 b. Shibukusa-tôki: Hanakawa-machi 花川町, 7-minute walk.

Koito-yaki 小糸焼: Kami-Okamoto-chô 上岡本町, at Hida Folk Village (Hidaminzoku-mura 飛騨民俗村), 10-minute bus ride from Takayama station toward Hida no sato 飛騨の里, disembark at Hida-Takayama bijutsukan mae 飛騨高山美術館前.
 Yamada-yaki 山田焼: Yamada-chô 山田町, 15 minutes by taxi.
2 Hida Takayama Tourist Information Office (outside station building); 〒 506-0053 Gifu-ken, Takayama-shi, Shôwa-machi 1-1, tel. 0577-32-5328.
3 Local industrial development agency in Hida (Hida-chi'iki jiba-sangyô shinkô-sentâ 飛騨地域地場産業振興センター); 〒 506-0025 Gifu-ken, Takayama-shi, Tenman-chô 5-1-25; tel. 0577-35-0370, fax 0577-33-4325.
6 Matsumoto Heritage House (Matsumoto-ke jûtaku 松本家住宅); 〒 506-0024 Gifu-ken, Takayama-shi, Kami-Kawahara-machi 125; tel. 0577-36-5600.
7 www3.ocn.ne.jp/~wabisuke/index.html (Japanese)
 www.koitoyaki.com/English.htm
 www.shibukusa.co.jp/ (Japanese)

Takeo 武雄 (14)

1 From Tôkyô 東京 to Fukuoka 福岡, Hakata station 博多, see Agano. From Hakata continue to Takeo-Onsen 武雄温泉 by Sasebo Line 佐世保線 (70 minutes; 1 departure/hour); 6¼ miles (10 km) by taxi or approximately 25 minutes by Kotaji bus 小田志バス to Kotaji-guchi bus stop 小田志口, then 550 yards (500 m) to the Tadashi-gama 規窯; 〒 843-0231 Saga-ken, Takeo-shi, Nishikawa-nobori-machi, Kotaji; tel. 0954-28-2138.
2 Takeo Tourist Association (in the station building); 〒 843-0023 Saga-ken, Takeo-shi, Takeo-chô, Ôaza Shôwa 805; tel. 0954-23-7766.
3 Takeo ko-Karatsu Ware Cooperative Society (Takeo ko-Karatsu-yaki kyôdô-kumiai 武雄古唐津焼協同組合); 〒 843-8639 Saga-ken, Takeo-shi, Takeo-chô, Ôaza Shôwa 1-1; tel. 0954-23-9237.
4 Area map of 14 workshops (Kankô to kamamoto no an'nai zu 観光と窯元の安内図); available from 2.
5 Late March, early April, Hiryô kiln; late November, Kuromuta pottery; tel. 0954-23-9237.

Tanba 丹波 (31), in Tachikui

1 From Tôkyô 東京 to Shin-Ôsaka 新大阪, see Hagi. From Shin-Ôsaka 新大阪, 5 minutes, numerous services to Ôsaka station 大阪, then to Aino 相野 by Fukuchiyama Line 福知山線 (50 minutes; 2 departures/hour), continue to Tachikui 立杭 by bus or taxi for 6¼ miles (10 km). To the museum in Sasayama, see 6b: to Sasayama-guchi 篠山口 three stops on the Fukuchiyama Line. From there, 15 minutes to Hon-Sasayama bus stop 本篠山 by Fukuchiyama bus line.
2 Industry Section of Konda Town Office; 〒 669-2397 Hyôgo-ken, Sasayama-shi, Kita-Shin-machi 41; tel. 0795-52-0003.
3 Tanba Tachikui Ware Association (Tanba-Tachikui tôjiki kyôdô-kumiai 丹波立杭陶磁器協同組合); 〒 669-2135 Hyôgo-ken, Sasayama-shi, Konda-chô, Kami-Tachikui 3; tel. 0795-97-2034, fax 0795-97-3232; located in the Tanba Traditional Art Craft Park (Tachikui sue no sato 立杭陶の郷).
4 Exhibition of 57 kilns with addresses and photos on www.tanbayaki.com/t_map_main.html (Japanese).
 In book form: Yakimono no kokyô Tanba-Tachikui II (Tanba-Tachikui-yaki gurûpu-yô やきものの故郷丹波立杭II—丹波立杭焼グループ窯; available from Tachikui sue no sato, see 3).
5 Third weekend in October, Tachikui sue no sato (see 3); tel. 0795-97-2034.

6   a. Tanba Tachikui Traditional Ceramic Center (*Tanba-Tachikui-yaki dentô-sangyô-kaikan* 丹波立杭焼伝統産業会館); *Tachikui sue no sato*, see 3.
    b. Sasayama: Old Tanba Pottery Museum (*Tanba ko-tôkan* 丹波古陶館); 〒 669-2325 Hyôgo-ken, Sasayama-shi, Kawara-machi 185; tel. 0795-52-2524.

7   www.kougei.or.jp/english/crafts/0415/f0415.html
    www.tanbayaki.com (Japanese)

Tobe 砥部 (19), near Matsuyama

1   From Tôkyô 東京 to Okayama 岡山, see Bizen. From Okayama to Matsuyama 松山 by Yosan Line 予讃線 Shiokaze しおかぜ Ltd. Express (2 hours 45 minutes; 1 departure/hour), continue to Tobe 砥部 by Iyotetsu bus 伊予鉄バス disembarking at Tobe-*yaki dentô-sangyô-kaikan mae* 砥部焼伝統産業会館前 (45 minutes; 2 departures/hour).

2   Tobe Tourist Association; 〒 791-2195 Ehime-ken, Iyo-gun, Tobe-chô, Miyauchi 392; tel. 089-962-7288.

3   a. Tobe Ceramics Association (*Tobe-yaki kyôdô-kumiai* 砥部焼協同組合); 〒 791-2132 Ehime-ken, Iyo-gun, Tobe-chô, Ôminami 604; tel. 089-962-2018, fax 089-962-6246.
    b. Tobe-*yaki* Traditional Craft Center (*Tobe-yaki dentô-sangyô-kaikan* 砥部焼伝統産業会館), with exhibition of Tobe potters and sales exhibition; 〒 791-2132 Ehime-ken, Iyo-gun, Tobe-chô, Ôminami 335; tel. 089-962-6600.
    c. Tobe Ceramic Hall (*Tobe-yaki tôgeikan* 砥部焼陶芸館), sales exhibition of 38 workshops; 〒 791-2120 Ehime-ken, Iyo-gun, Tobe-chô, Miyauchi 83; tel. 089-962-3900.
    d. Well-made Tobe-*yaki* can be found in Matsuyama in shops between the tram terminal and Dôgo-Onsen.

4   Map of the area and addresses of the 89 Tobe workshops (*Tobe-yaki monogatari* 砥部焼物語); available from 2 and 6.

5   Third weekend in April; tel. 089-962-7288.

6   Museum in *Tobe-yaki dentô-sangyô-kaikan* (see 3b).
    Umeyama Ancient Pottery Museum (*Umeyama ko-tô shiryôkan* 梅山古陶資料館); 〒 791-2132 Ehime-ken, Iyo-gun, Tobe-chô, Ôminami 1441; tel. 089-962-2311.

7   www.kougei.or.jp/english/crafts/0419/f0419.html

Tokoname 常滑 (39)

1   From Tôkyô 東京 to Nagoya 名古屋, see Iga. From Nagoya Meitetsu station Shin-Nagoya 新名古屋, next to JR Nagoya station, to Tokoname 常滑 by private Meitetsu Tokoname Line 名鉄常滑線 (40 minutes; 2 departures/hour).

2   Tokoname City Office of Commerce, Industry and Tourism Division (in the station building); 〒 479-0838 Aichi-ken, Tokoname-shi, Koie-Hon-machi 5-168-2; tel. 0569-34-8888, fax 0569-34-8880.

3   a. Tokoname-*yaki* Cooperative Society (*Tokoname-yaki kyôdô-kumiai* 常滑焼協同組合) in the Ceramic Hall (*Tokoname-shi tôjiki geikan* 常滑市陶磁器舘); tel. 0569-35-4309, fax 0569-34-8893; with sales exhibition; 〒 479-0836 Aichi-ken, Tokoname-shi, Sakae-machi 3-8; tel. 0569-35-2033.
    b. Ceramall-Tokoname-*yaki* Retail Outlet Cooperative Society (*Seramôru Tokoname-yaki oroshi danchi kyôdô-kumiai* セラモールとこなめ焼卸団地協同組合); 〒 479-0003 Aichi-ken, Tokoname-shi, Kanayama, Aza Kami-Sunahara 99; tel. 0569-43-7111, fax 0569-43-7112.

4   Brochure on some of the workshops (*Tokoname tôgei sakka kyôkai* 常滑陶芸作家協会); available from 2.

5   Last weekend in March and last weekend in August; Tokoname Ceramics Park (see 6c); tel. 0569-34-3200.

6   a. Tokoname City Folk Museum (*Tokoname-shi minzoku shiryôkan* 常滑市民俗資料館); 〒 479-0821 Aichi-ken,

Tokoname-shi, Segi-chô 4-203; tel. 0569-34-5290.
    b. Tokoname Ceramic Art Institute (*Tokoname shiritsu tôgei kenkyûjo* 常滑市立陶芸研究所) 〒 479-0822 Aichi-ken, Tokoname-shi, Okujô 7-22; tel. 0569-35-3970.
    c. Tokoname Ceramics Park (*kama no aru hiroba shiryôkan* 窯のある広場資料館) 〒 479-8586 Aichi-ken, Tokoname-shi, Okuei-chô 1-47; tel. 0569-34-6858.
    d. INAX Tile Museum (*sekai no tairu hakubutsukan* 世界のタイル博物館); 〒 479-8586 Aichi-ken, Tokoname-shi, Okuei-chô 1-130; tel. 0569-34-8282, fax 0569-34-8283.

7   www.kougei.or.jp/english/crafts/0407/f0407.html
    www.tokoname.or.jp/ (Japanese)

Tôraku 北楽 (63), in Naganuma

1   To Sapporo 札幌, see Hokkaidô. From Sapporo to Iwamizawa 岩見沢 by Hakodate Line 函館本線 (25–40 minutes; 6 departures/hour), continue to Yuni 由仁 by Muroran Line 室蘭本線 (30 minutes; irregular, 8 departures daily), from there by local bus to Naganuma 長沼. Workshop: Tôraku-*gama* 北楽窯; 〒 069-1479 Hokkaidô, Yûbari-gun, Naganuma-chô, Nishi-9-sen, Minami-7-gô; tel. 01238-8-3762.

3–6 See Hokkaidô.

Tsuboya 壷屋 (1), in Naha and Yomitan

1   From Tôkyô Haneda airport 東京羽田 to Naha 那覇 on Okinawa (2 hours 45 minutes; 17 flights daily).
    From Naha airport:
    a. to Tsuboya-chô 壷屋町 (district of Naha town), 20–35 minutes by taxi or 25–40 minutes by local bus.
    b. to *Yachimun no sato* 焼物の里 in Yomitan 読谷, 60 minutes by bus, disembarking at Kina 喜名.

2   Okinawa Convention and Visitors Bureau, Okinawa-Sankyôshien-Center, Second Floor; 〒 901-0152 Okinawa-ken, Naha-shi, Oroku 1831-1; tel. 098-859-6123.

3   a. Tsuboya Pottery Cooperative Union (*Tsuboya tôki jigyô kyôdô-kumiai* 壷屋陶器事業協同組合), with sales exhibition: Tsuboya Pottery Hall (*Tsuboya tôki kaikan* 壷屋陶器会館); 〒 902-0065 Okinawa-ken, Naha-shi, Tsuboya 1-21-14; tel. 098-866-3284, fax 098-864-1472.
    b. *Tsuboya tôgei-sentâ* 壷屋陶芸センター (sales); both in Yachimun Street in Naha (*yachimun-dôri* やちむん通り).
    c. Yomitan Village Cooperative Marketing Center (*Yomitan-son kyôdô hanbai-sentâ* 読谷村共同販売センター); 〒 904-0301 Okinawa-ken, Yomitan-son, Aza Zakimi 2723-1; tel. 098-958-1020.

4   Description of work by Yomitan potters in: *Yachimun no. 13* (*Yachimun-kai 30-shûnen kinen;* anniversary edition). Okinawa: Yachimun-kai, 2000.

5   Naha: weekend in mid September, Yogi Park; tel. 098-866-3284.
    Yomitan Village: last weekend in February; tel. 098-958-1020.

6   a. Naha: Naha Municipal Tsuboya Pottery Museum (*Naha shiritsu tsuboya-yakimono hakubutsukan* 那覇市立壷屋焼物博物館), 〒 902-0065 Okinawa-ken, Naha-shi, Tsuboya 1-9-32 (Yachimun Street, *yachimun-dôri* やちむん通り); tel. 098-862-3761, fax 098-862-3762.
    b. Naha: Okinawa Prefectural Museum (*Okinawa kenritsu hakubutsukan* 沖縄県立博物館); 〒 903-0823 Okinawa-ken, Naha-shi, Shurionaka-chô 1-1; tel. 098-884-2243.
    c. Yomitan: Yomitan Museum (*Yomitan sonritsu bijutsukan* 読谷村立美術館); 〒 904-0301 Okinawa-ken, Yomitan-son, Aza Zakimi 708-6; tel. 098-958-2254.

7   www.kougei.or.jp/english/crafts/0426/f0426.html
    www.naha-okn.ed.jp/tsuboya/ (Japanese)
    www.tuboya.com (Japanese)

Tsugaru 津軽 (61), in Hirosaki

1   From Tôkyô 東京 to Hachinohe 八戸 by Tôhoku-Shinkansen 東北新幹線 Hayate はやて (3 hours; 2 departures/hour), continue to Hirosaki 弘前 by Tôhoku Line 東北本線 and Ôu Line 奥羽本線 (1 hour 30 minutes–1 hour 50 minutes; 2 departures/hour; change in Aomori 青森 may be necessary).

2   Hirosaki City Tourist Information Center (in the station building); 〒 036-8096 Aomori-ken, Hirosaki-shi, Omote-machi 1-1; tel. 0172-26-3600, fax 0172-26-3601.

6   Aomori Prefectural Museum (*Aomori kenritsu kyôdokan* 青森県立郷土館), 〒 030-0802 Aomori-ken, Aomori-shi, Hon-chô 2-8-14; tel. 01-7777-1585.

7   www.pref.aomori.jp/dentokougei/t-pottery.htm

Tsutsumi 堤 (59), in Sendai

1   From Tôkyô 東京 to Sendai 仙台, see Kirigome. From Sendai station to Yaotome 八乙女 by Sendai underground railway 仙台地下鉄 (13 minutes), approximately 10 minutes by taxi to the workshop: Kanma-*gama* 乾馬窯; 〒 981-3121 Miyagi-ken, Sendai-shi, Kamiagari, Akasaka 8-4; tel. 022-372-3639.

2   Sendai Tourist Information Center (in the station building); 〒 980-0021 Miyagi-ken, Sendai-shi, Aoba-ku, Chûô 1-1-1; tel. 022-222-4069.

6   Tôhoku Ceramic Museum (see Aizu-Hongô, 6c).

Unzen 雲仙 (7), in Unzen-Onsen

1   From Tôkyô 東京 to Fukuoka 福岡, Hakata station 博多, see Agano.
a. From Fukuoka, Hakata station, to Nagasaki 長崎 by Nagasaki Line 長崎本線 (2 hours 5 minutes; 2 departures/hour), from Nagasaki-ken-ei Bus Terminal (opposite Nagasaki station) continue to Unzen-Onsen 雲仙温泉 by Nagasaki-ken-ei Bus 長崎県営バス (1 hour 45 minutes; 6 departures/daily).
b. From Fukuoka, Hakata station, to Kumamoto 熊本 by Kagoshima Line 鹿児島本線 Relay-Tsubame リレーつばめ (1 hour 20 minutes; 2–3 departures/hour), then by local bus to Kumamoto harbor 熊本港 and to Shimabara 島原 45 minutes by ferry, continue to Unzen-Onsen by Shimabara Line bus 島原鉄道 (36 minutes; 14 departures daily).
Workshop in the center of Unzen: Unzen-*yaki kamamoto* 雲仙焼窯元; 〒 854-0621 Nagasaki-ken, Minami Takaki-gun, Obama-chô, Unzen 304; tel. 050-3424-2485.

2   Unzen Tourist Information Center; 〒 854-0621 Nagasaki-ken, Minami Takaki-gun, Obama-chô, Unzen 320; tel. 095-822-9670.

7   www.fsinet.or.jp/~unzenpot/ (Japanese)

Utsutsugawa 現川 (12), near Arita

1   From Tôkyô 東京 to Arita 有田, see Arita, then 10 minutes by taxi to Gagyû-*gama* 臥牛窯 (*Gagyû tôgei kabushiki-gaisha* 臥牛陶芸株式会社); 〒 859-3166 Nagasaki-ken, Sasebo-shi, Kihara-chô 1897-1; tel. 0956-30-8653, fax 0956-30-8084.

2   See Arita.

6   Nagasaki Prefectural Art Museum (*Nagasaki kenritsu bijutsu hakubutsukan* 長崎県立美術博物館); 〒 850-0007 Nagasaki-ken, Nagasaki-shi, Tateyama 1-1-5; tel. 095-821-6700.

Watasuge 綿スゲ (64), in Kyôgoku

1   From Tôkyô 東京 to Sapporo 札幌, see Hokkaidô. From Sapporo bus station 札幌駅前 (next to JR station) by DONAN bus to Kyôgoku 京極 disembarking at Kyôgoku-Chûô 京極中央 (5 hours 30 minutes; 4 departures daily, change in Kimobetsu 喜茂別). Workshop: Watasuge-*tôbô* 綿スゲ陶房; 〒 044-0112 Hokkaidô, Abuta-gun, Kyôgoku-chô, Aza Kasuga 375; tel. 0136-42-3597.

2   Kyôgoku Tourist Association, Town Hall; 〒 044-0101 Hokkaidô, Abuta-gun, Kyôgoku-chô, Aza Kyôgoku 527; tel. 0136-42-2111.

3–6   See Hokkaidô.

Yamada 山田 (49), in Takayama

See Takayama 高山

Yokkaichi Banko 四日市万古 (38), in Yokkaichi

1   From Tôkyô 東京 to Nagoya 名古屋, see Iga. From Nagoya to JR Yokkaichi 四日市 station by Kansai Line 関西本線 and Kisei Line 紀勢本線 (45 minutes; 4–5 departures/hour), continue from Kintetsu Yokkaichi 近鉄四日市 station (approximately ¾-mile/1-km walk) to Kintetsu Kawara-machi 近鉄川原町 by private Kintetsu Nagoya Line 近鉄名古屋線 (5 minutes; 5 departures/hour).

2   Commerce and Industry Division, City of Yokkaichi; 〒 510-8601 Mie-ken, Yokkaichi-shi, Suwa-chô 1-5; tel. 0593-54-8178, fax 0593-54-8307.

3   a. Banko Ceramic Industry Association (*Banko tôjiki kôgyô kyôdô-kumiai* 萬古陶磁器工業協同組合); 〒 510-0032 Mie-ken, Yokkaichi-shi, Kyô-machi 2-13; tel. 0593-31-7146.
b. Banko China Wholesalers Cooperative Association (*Banko tôjiki oroshi shôgyô kyôdô-kumiai* 萬古陶磁器卸商業協同組合); 〒 510-0035 Mie-ken, Yokkaichi-shi, Tôei-chô 3-18; tel. 0593-31-3496, fax 0593-31-5914.
c. Banko sales and exhibition hall (*Banko no sato kaikan* ばんこの里会館); 〒 510-0035 Mie-ken, Yokkaichi-shi, Tôei-chô 4-8; tel. 0593-30-2020, fax 0593-30-2021.

4   Description of 21 traditional potters (*Yokkaichi Banko-yaki dentô kôgei-shikai* 四日市萬古焼伝統工芸士会); available from 3c.

5   Second weekend in May; tel. 0593-31-3496.

6   a. Yokkaichi Municipal Museum (*Yokkaichi shiritsu hakubutsukan* 四日市市立博物館); 〒 510-0035 Mie-ken, Yokkaichi-shi, Yasujima 1-3-16; tel. 0593-55-2700.
b. Yokkaichi Culture Hall (*Yokkaichi-shi bunka kaikan* 四日市市文化会館); 〒 510-0035 Mie-ken, Yokkaichi-shi, Yasujima 2-5-3; tel. 0593-54-4501, fax 0593-54-4093.

7   www.kougei.or.jp/english/crafts/0409/f0409.html
www.banko.or.jp/index.html (Japanese)

Zeze 膳所 (35)

1   From Tôkyô 東京 to Kyôto 京都, see Kyôto. Continue to Zeze station 膳所 by suburban train of the JR Biwako Line 琵琶湖線 (11 minutes; 5–10 departures/hour), then 1-minute walk to Kyôto-Zeze station 京都膳所. From there to Keihan Kawara-ga-hama station 京阪瓦ケ浜 (5 minutes; 6 departures/hour) by private Keihan-Ishiyama-Sakamoto Line 京阪石山坂本線.

2   Ôtsu City Tourist Information Center (in Ôtsu 大津 station building; one station before Zeze station); 〒 520-0055 Shiga-ken, Ôtsu-shi, Kasuga-chô 1-3; tel. 077-522-3830.

3   Zeze Pottery (*Zeze-yaki kamamoto* 膳所焼窯元); 〒 520-0837 Shiga-ken, Ôtsu-shi, Nakashô 1-22-28; tel. 077-522-6374, fax 077-523-1118.

6   Zeze-*yaki* Museum (*Zeze-yaki bijutsukan* 膳所焼美術館), annex of Zeze Pottery (see 3).

7   www.zezeyaki.jp/ (Japanese)

INDEX

Page numbers for photographs appear in italics.